"Tanya Prewitt-White and Leslee A. Fisher have taken on the ambitious task of illuminating the systemic problem of sexual misconduct in sport contexts, with critical examination of the behaviors of coaches, administrators, athletes, and community members which perpetuate the problem, deter justice for the perpetrators, and hinder healing for survivors. Importantly, the personal accounts of survivors inform and remind readers of the suffering endured and strength realized, evoking both compassion and a call to action to change the problem of sexual misconduct in sports."

Dr. Kendahl M. Shortway, Assistant Professor, Kean University, USA

EXAMINING AND MITIGATING SEXUAL MISCONDUCT IN SPORT

Sexual Misconduct in any environment is a gross abuse of trust and this is no different within the sport world. *Examining and Mitigating Sexual Misconduct in Sport* outlines systemic and sociological explanations for why sport is a site of sexual misconduct. The authors in the text describe cultural realities and considerations sport stakeholders must acknowledge and be informed of to make sport a more equitable and safe space. Personal narratives from a variety of sport stakeholders, which unveil their lived experiences of sexual misconduct and humanize survivor stories in ways often ignored in sport and society, are shared. Authors offer recommendations to all sport stakeholders to mitigate incidents of and harm done by sexual misconduct.

Guidelines and suggestions for sport stakeholder practices that better protect individuals in sport, address sexual misconduct when it occurs, and mitigate the harm and trauma experienced because of incidents of sexual misconduct are also examined and provided. This book is the first text of its kind to invite sport stakeholders to have open, vulnerable, and honest discussions around a timely topic often minimized, denied, and/or ignored in sport.

A ground-breaking new book, *Examining and Mitigating Sexual Misconduct in Sport* is key reading for any sport coach, sport parent, sport psychology professional, or sport administrator.

Tanya Prewitt-White, PhD, is a Certified Mental Performance Consultant and trained Survivor Advocate as well as the owner of Dr. Tanya Raquel, LLC. Dr. Prewitt-White is a consultant to athletic departments and organizations as well as an author and social justice activist in sport and society who currently serves as the Association of Applied Sport Psychology's (AASP's) Advocacy Committee Chair.

Leslee A. Fisher, PhD, is Professor and Director of the Sport Psychology and Motor Behavior Graduate Program at the University of Tennessee, USA. She is a Certified Mental Performance Consultant and has over 117 publications, many related to social justice and cultural sport psychology.

EXAMINING AND MITIGATING SEXUAL MISCONDUCT IN SPORT

Edited by Tanya Prewitt-White and Leslee A. Fisher

NEW YORK AND LONDON

Cover image: Getty Images

First published 2022
by Routledge
605 Third Avenue, New York, NY 10158

and by Routledge
2 Park Square, Milton Park, Abingdon, Oxon, OX14 4RN

Routledge is an imprint of the Taylor & Francis Group, an informa business

© 2022 selection and editorial matter, Tanya Prewitt-White and Leslee A. Fisher; individual chapters, the contributors

The right of Tanya Prewitt-White and Leslee A. Fisher to be identified as the authors of the editorial material, and of the authors for their individual chapters, has been asserted in accordance with sections 77 and 78 of the Copyright, Designs and Patents Act 1988.

All rights reserved. No part of this book may be reprinted or reproduced or utilised in any form or by any electronic, mechanical, or other means, now known or hereafter invented, including photocopying and recording, or in any information storage or retrieval system, without permission in writing from the publishers.

Trademark notice: Product or corporate names may be trademarks or registered trademarks, and are used only for identification and explanation without intent to infringe.

Library of Congress Cataloging-in-Publication Data
Names: Prewitt-White, Tanya, editor. | Fisher, Leslee A, editor.
Title: Examining and mitigating sexual misconduct in sport / edited by Tanya Prewitt-White and Leslee A Fisher.
Description: New York, N.Y. : Routledge, 2022. | Includes bibliographical references and index.
Identifiers: LCCN 2021045884 (print) | LCCN 2021045885 (ebook)
Subjects: LCSH: Sexual harassment in sports. | Sexual harassment in sports—Prevention.
Classification: LCC GV706.7 .E93 2022 (print) | LCC GV706.7 (ebook) | DDC 796.08—dc23/eng/20211023
LC record available at https://lccn.loc.gov/2021045884
LC ebook record available at https://lccn.loc.gov/2021045885

ISBN: 978-0-367-64705-6 (hbk)
ISBN: 978-0-367-64703-2 (pbk)
ISBN: 978-1-003-12588-4 (ebk)

DOI: 10.4324/9781003125884

Typeset in Bembo
by Apex CoVantage, LLC

CONTENTS

About the Contributors — ix
Preface — xvii
Acknowledgments — xxii

SECTION I
Cultural Realities and Considerations — 1

1. Calling All Sport Constituents: Exploring Power *and* Bringing Back Joy Into Sport — 3
   Leslee A. Fisher and Allison D. Anders

2. Stand Up and Stand Tall: Rethinking Sexual Misconduct in Sport — 15
   Robert E. Owens

3. Cisheterosexism and Sexual Misconduct in Sport — 26
   Travis R. Scheadler, Bernie Compton, and Aidan Kraus

4. Grooming and Sport — 37
   Stiliani "Ani" Chroni and Anna Kavoura

5. Sexual Misconduct and Epistemic Injustices in Sport — 51
   Lindsey A. Miossi and Lars Dzikus

SECTION II
Personal Narratives — 67

6. I Was His Litmus Test: Being Groomed as a Child Athlete — 69
   Tanya Prewitt-White

7 Persist: Homophobia in and Survival Through Farm Town High
   School Sports   84
   Lena A. Bequette

8 2/7/2016: The Morning I Was Raped   90
   Eliana (Ellie) Arbetman

9 "You're Not a Good Cultural Fit Here": Being a Woman in Sports   97
   Sara Erdner

10 Experiencing Same-Gender and Trans Violence in Sport   109
   Jordan Forrest Miller

11 I Couldn't Stay Quiet   122
   Shannon Mulcahy

12 Experiencing Sexual Misconduct as a Student-Manager in
   Intercollegiate Athletics   129
   Emily J. Tyler

SECTION III
Recommendations   **139**

13 Athletic Programmatic Prevention: No More, Not Here, Not
   Within These Walls   141
   Tess M. Kilwein, Matt J. Gray, and Taylor A. Stuemky

14 Title IX and Sexual Harassment in Athletics   155
   James H. Bemiller

15 Supporting Survivors of Sexual Violence   168
   Heather Imrie

16 The "Sex Talk" Is a Continual Conversation   187
   Tanya Prewitt-White, Lauren Spirov, and Sarah Malone

17 Moving Forward: No More Sweeping Sexual Misconduct Under the Rug   202
   Tanya Prewitt-White

Index   *215*

ABOUT THE CONTRIBUTORS

Allison D. Anders, PhD, is an associate professor in educational foundations and inquiry, a co-coordinator of the graduate certificate in qualitative research, and a co-director of the Critical Race Theory Summer Institute at the University of South Carolina. She teaches cultural and social foundations of education, critical race theory, sociology of education, and courses on qualitative research methodologies. She studies the everyday experiences of targeted youth, contexts of education, and qualitative methodologies.

Eliana (Ellie) Arbetman was born in Canton, Illinois, on December 9, 1996, and adopted at birth. Her parents took her home to Oak Park, Illinois, where she grew up and attended public school through graduation from Oak Park and River Forest High School in 2015. She has always been an athlete. She started playing soccer when she was four and t-ball at five. She also played basketball and softball. She didn't start playing volleyball until middle school. She made the middle school team and fell in love with the sport. She was a middle blocker. She began high school on both the OPRF volleyball and soccer teams. She hated giving up soccer but chose competitive club volleyball in addition to OPRF volleyball through graduation. This made it possible for her to be a college volleyball player. After high school graduation, she was accepted at Lakeland University near Sheboygan, Wisconsin. She played on Lakeland University's volleyball team for four years. She graduated with a BS in Sports Management focusing on coaching in 2015. Since graduation she has become an ISSA-certified personal fitness trainer with specializations in group fitness and nutrition. She is a workout enthusiast and hype queen for everyone.

James H. Bemiller is an associate professor in the Sport Management program in the Department of Kinesiology, Recreation and Sport Studies at the University of Tennessee. He teaches courses in sport law, governance, and leadership. His primary research interests include risk management, constitutional issues in sport, and elite performance in sport. He earned his B.S. Ed. from Miami University, M.S. Ed. and J.D. from the University of Tennessee. He has published in the *Journal of Sport Management, Journal of Intercollegiate Sport, Scholastic Coach and Athletic Director, The Michigan State University Sport and Entertainment Law Journal*, and *The*

Journal of Physical Education Recreation and Dance. Mr. Bemiller lectures nationally and internationally on elite performance in sport. He coached the 2004 Olympic champion in the pole vault, Timothy Mack, and coached athletes who have broken the Olympic, American, and NCAA records in the vault. He is the author of the chapter on pole vault training and technique in the most recent edition of the USATF Track and Field Coaching Manual, and also serves on the USA Pole Vault Development Staff. He has negotiated endorsement and marketing opportunities for professional athletes, including Olympic and World Champions in Track and Field.

Lena A. Bequette is an Iowa native and a behavior therapist and advocate for children with Autism Spectrum Disorder. She is a former Division-I collegiate athlete in softball and rowing. She is a survivor of homophobia and sexual misconduct within high school sport and she obtained a full-ride scholarship to an East Coast Division-I program; however, she sustained what would ultimately be a career ending injury during her senior season of high school softball. Unable to play her chosen sport, she went through four years of rest and rehabilitation before attempting to join a sport that she had only seen on TV as a child. In 2015, she competed in the NCAA Division I Rowing Championships. After meeting her future spouse in college, she left Ohio and sought out city life in Chicago. She completed a bachelor's degree in Kinesiology with a focus in Movement Science from The University of Illinois at Chicago in 2018. Her education has provided her with the opportunity to work with colleagues and bridge the disconnect of autism and competitive sport. On any given Saturday you can find her tossing a ball around with her wife, Jess, or persuading their two dogs that she is the better mom.

Stiliani "Ani" Chroni, PhD, is Professor of Sport Psychology, Pedagogy, and Sports Coaching at Elverum campus of Inland Norway University of Applied Sciences. Ani possesses extensive, versatile and specialized, high-level international experience with sport, academia, performance consulting, and sport-related action-based organizations. While a native of Greece, today she lives and works in Norway. Through her education, transnational career, work in higher education, as well as mental coach in high-performance sport and business sector, Ani developed a solid multi-cultural know-how. As a researcher, her focus has been on matters of psychological welfare (e.g., sexual harassment of female athletes) and nuances of the mental game for athletes and coaches (e.g., the elite athlete-to-coach transition, elite coach stress, self-talk, cognitive hardiness, competitiveness, and coping), most often through the qualitative research lens. Ani has published her work widely in books and refereed journals, usually not only in English but also in her native Greek language. She built a wide range of skills, experiences, and network via serving in diverse academic and professional development committees, international sport federation committees, professional managing councils, NGO executive board, as well as inter-governmental council roles. Ani comes from the alpine ski family yet as a mental coach has supported performers in more than 20 sports worldwide and still serves as a Technical Delegate official for the FIS at international alpine racing. For the past 20 years she has employed all capacities of her—researching, educating, lobbying, advocating, collaborating, inspiring, leading and following—to support the women and sport movement and advance opportunities for women in and through sport.

Bernie Compton (she/her/hers), MS, MA, is an EdD student in Leadership Studies at Bowling Green State University. She completed her Bachelor of Science in Psychology at the University of Central Arkansas. Bernie then completed her Master of Science in Sport Leadership at Miami University as well as a Master of Arts in American Cultural Studies at Bowling Green State University. Her research interests are focused on social justice activism in sport psychology, burnout and self-care in social justice activism, LGBTQ+ inclusion in sport, and enhancing social justice within higher education.

Bernie developed an LGBTQ+ Inclusion through Sport Psychology program to build inclusive team climates. The program has also been adapted to provide sport psychology professionals practical activities to implement with their teams and coaches. In addition to her sport psychology work, Bernie consults with Athlete Ally in a research and practitioner role to continue to build LGBTQ+ inclusion at all levels of sport. Bernie plans to continue to integrate social justice training, and practices within athletic departments following graduation from Bowling Green State University.

Lars Dzikus, PhD, is Associate Professor (sport studies) in the Department of Kinesiology, Recreation, and Sport Studies at the University of Tennessee, Knoxville. He teaches graduate courses in sport studies and undergraduate courses sport management, with a focus in both sport sociology and sport history. His main research interests are in sport and globalization (e.g., diffusion of American football to Europe), sport and religion (e.g., collegiate sport chaplains), and sport and violence (e.g., sexual abuse in youth sport).

Dzikus earned his master's degree and PhD in socio-cultural studies of sport from The Ohio State University, after having studied chemistry, physical education, and education at the University of Hamburg, Germany. Dzikus is a member of the North American Society for Sport History (NASSH) and the North American Society for the Sociology of Sport (NASSS). He has published in *Sportwissenschaft, Journal of Sport and Social Issues,* and *The Sport Psychologist,* among others. Dzikus serves as the department's Director of Graduate Studies. He has received several teaching awards, including the University of Tennessee's Chancellor's Excellence in Teaching Award (2018). He also received the K. Patricia Cross Future Leaders Award from the American Association for Higher Education (2005). Dzikus has assisted German professional soccer teams visiting the United States as a translator and liaison. The teams included Hamburg SV, Bayer 04 Leverkusen, FC Nürnberg, and the women's national team of Germany.

Sara Erdner, CMPC, PhD, received her PhD in Sport Psychology and Motor Behavior from the University of Tennessee, Knoxville, where she also completed her Master of Science in Communication Studies. She currently works as an Assistant Professor of Coaching and the Coordinator of the Master of Science in Coaching (online) degree at Adams State University. As a Certified Mental Performance Consultant (CMPC®, #712) through the Association of Applied Sport Psychology (AASP), Sara also conducts independent mental performance services for a wide variety of performers, which includes working with college, Olympic, and professional athletes. When she isn't working as either an Assistant Professor or a CMPC, Sara is an author of her book *Dear Coach: What I Wish I Could Have Told You, Letters from Your Athletes.*

As a scholar, Sara has been honored with two national research awards. In 2012, Sara received the top paper award at the 98th Annual National Communication Association Convention. In 2017, she was awarded the Student-Athlete Development Research Award at the National Association of Academic Advisors for Athletics (N4A) Conference. Aside from her scholarly achievements, Sara has presented on the national and international stages, with her most notable appearances at Universität Tübingen in Germany; Jahrestagung der Arbeitsgemeinschaft für Sportpsychologie (German Sport Psychology Conference) at the University of Bern in Switzerland, at the United States Center for Coaching Excellence, and at various annual AASP conferences.

Leslee A. Fisher is Professor and Director of the Sport Psychology and Motor Behavior Graduate Program at the University of Tennessee. She holds a PhD in Sport Psychology (UC Berkeley), an MEd in Counselor Education (University of Virginia), an MS in Education (University of Michigan), and a BS in Education (University of Michigan). Leslee has published over 106 academic and applied articles and has presented at numerous national and international conferences. Her research focuses on feminist cultural sport psychology and caring coaching practices, and can be found in *The Journal of Applied Sport Psychology, The Sport Psychologist, International Journal of Sport and Exercise Psychology, International Journal of Sports Science and Coaching, Women in Sport & Physical Activity*, and *the Journal of Sport and Exercise Psychology*. Leslee is also a Fellow in the Association for Applied Sport Psychology (AASP), served as AASP's Secretary/Treasurer, is a Certified Mental Performance Consultant (CMPC AASP), is a member of the American Psychological Association, and is a Registrant on the United States Olympic Committee's Sport Psychology Registry. In addition, she has served as the Chair of 21 doctoral dissertations, 29 master's theses, and 2 undergraduate honors theses, and has served on an additional 42 doctoral dissertation committees and 14 master's thesis committees. In her spare time, she likes to hang out in her shed in Key West, Florida, and write.

Jordan Forrest Miller, MA, is a doctoral candidate in Sociology at Georgia State University, with concentrations in gender and sexuality. He completed his MA from the Institute for Women's, Gender, and Sexuality Studies at Georgia State University in 2016 and his BSEd in Kinesiology at the University of Tennessee at Knoxville in 2013. His research focuses primarily on the interplay of trans vloggers' narratives on YouTube and the medicalization of trans identity. His dissertation titled "What Makes Trans Lives More Livable?: An Intersectional Content Analysis of #WeHappyTrans* and #TheGenderTag" explores public health implications of digital trans activism for educators, policymakers, healthcare professionals, and community organizers who seek to eliminate trans health disparities.

Matt J. Gray, PhD, is Professor of Psychology at the University of Wyoming. His research interests include sexual assault prevention as well as impacts and treatment of traumatic event exposure. Prior to his appointment at the University of Wyoming, he completed an NIH Postdoctoral Research Fellowship at the National Center for PTSD Behavioral Sciences Division in Boston, MA, and a Clinical Internship at the National Crime Victims Treatment and Research Center in Charleston, SC.

Heather Imrie, MEd, is a PhD student in the Department of Educational Psychology at the University of Illinois at Chicago. Her research interest is how college students reason about sexual violence. She believes that knowledge could help practitioners create more impactful sexual violence prevention education. She has been teaching sexual violence prevention and anti-bias education for over 20 years. For 15 of those years, she ran The Campus Advocacy Network (CAN) at the University of Illinois at Chicago. While at CAN, she worked with and advocated for survivors of interpersonal violence. She has created and presented many educational programs, pieces of training, workshops, and other classes on sexual assault, domestic violence, stalking, sexual harassment, hate crime, systems of oppression, unconscious bias, victim blaming, and bystander intervention to non-profits, corporations, universities, all four branches of the military, and state and federal entities around the United States and the world. She incorporates the latest research, real-life scenarios, and facilitated dialogue to make participants think critically about their world. Lately, she has been thinking about belonging and how to move from scarcity thinking to abundance in her work on creating inclusive living, learning, and working environments. Her goals outside of academia and teaching are to live her values and get more naps. She hopes you are supported, feel like you belong, get plenty of sleep, and will be kind to yourself and others.

Anna Kavoura (PhD in Sport Sciences) is a sport psychology specialist and a postdoctoral fellow at the School of Sport and Service Management at the University of Brighton. Her research interests include gender, sexuality, culture, and identity in sport, martial arts studies, as well as identifying approaches and processes, which contribute toward more inclusive, ethical, and safe sport cultures. Her current research project focusing on gender diversity and transgender inclusion in sport is funded by the Finnish Cultural Foundation for the years 2020–2022. Previously, she has worked in other anti-discrimination projects funded by Erasmus+ and the Ministry of Culture and Education in Finland. While she has positioned most of her work in cultural sport psychology, she is an interdisciplinary scholar drawing on sport sociology, gender studies, cultural praxis, as well as feminist poststructuralist, queer and qualitative perspectives. Her work has been published in edited books and peer-reviewed academic journals and she participates often in scientific conferences and workshops.

Tess M. Kilwein, PhD, is a licensed clinical psychologist at the University of Wyoming in Laramie, Wyoming. Her clinical interests include trauma/PTSD, substance use/addiction, behavioral health consultation, and student athletes. Prior to her appointment at the University of Wyoming, she completed a pre-doctoral psychology internship at Denver Health Medical Center (DHMC) in Denver, Colorado, and a post-doctoral fellowship at Colorado State University Health Network (CSUHN) in Fort Collins, Colorado. During her time at DHMC, Dr. Kilwein provided psychological and consultative services in various settings throughout an integrated healthcare system, including an LGBTQ/HIV primary clinic and psychiatry/addiction consultation-liaison service. While at CSUHN, she provided psychological treatment to college students who use substances and student athletes, as well as behavioral health and sports performance consultation to the CSU's athletic department and the university's primary, urgent, and women/gender medical services. In addition to providing clinical services to undergraduate and graduate students at the University of Wyoming, Dr. Kilwein is active in both clinical research examining risk behaviors (e.g., substance use, risky sexual behaviors, sexual violence) and community activism/organizing. Alongside Dr. Matt J. Gray, she co-chaired the University of Wyoming Sexual Misconduct Taskforce Data Committee, culminating in the campuses first campus climate survey and comprehensive report.

Aidan Kraus (they/them) is a PhD student at Boston University, Wheelock College of Education & Human Development, earning a degree in Counseling Psychology with a Specialization in Sport & Performance Psychology. Aidan earned an Ed.M. in Counseling with a

Specialization in Sport & Performance Psychology at BU Wheelock College in May 2021 and graduated from Smith College in 2019 with a B.A. in American Studies with a Specialization in the Psychology of Sport. Their research interests are focused on the mental health and help-seeking behavior of student-athletes, particularly examining the experiences of transgender and gender-nonconforming individuals within athletic spaces.

Additionally, Aidan is a Student Delegate for the Association for Applied Sport Psychology (AASP) and co-chairs the Student Social Justice Initiative and Pride (LGBTQ+) in Sport Special Interest Group through the organization. Further, they serve the American Psychological Association as a Student Representative of the Division 17 Section for LGBT Issues and are an elected member of the American Psychological Association of Graduate Students' Committee on Sexual Orientation and Gender Diversity (CSOGD). Aidan also holds the Graduate Student Representative position for the Equity, Diversity, and Inclusion Committee through BU Wheelock College and spends their time working with collegiate student-athletes as a mental performance consultant within the Boston area.

Aidan plans to work within a collegiate athletic department as a mental performance consultant and mental health counselor for student-athletes and coaches as well as conducts research as a faculty member. They are especially interested in serving the LGBTQIA+ student-athlete community.

Sarah Malone is a PhD student in the Criminology, Law & Justice Department at University of Illinois at Chicago. Her interests lie at the intersection of disability and criminology, focusing on abolition and disability justice. She is hoping to do participatory action research with the disability community in Chicago where knowledge is developed with, by, and for the benefit of the community. This work is rooted in feminist abolitionist and disability justice perspectives. Additionally, she is the Secretary of the UIC Black Graduate Student Association, where she helped develop and implement a mentorship program for Black undergraduates to receive one-on-one guidance from a graduate student in their field.

Lindsey A. Miossi, PhD, is a lecturer at Arizona State University in the College of Health Solutions. She graduated with her PhD in the Department of Kinesiology, Recreation, and Sport Studies with a specialization in Sport Psychology and Motor Behavior at the University of Tennessee, Knoxville. She holds an MS in Kinesiology with a specialization in Psychology and Promotion of Exercise, Health, and Sport Behavior and a BS in Kinesiology from the University of Illinois at Chicago. She has taught various undergraduate courses, such as Sport Psychology, Motor Behavior, and Health Coaching. Her main research interests are related to sport and social justice including a focus on emotional abuse in sport systems.

To date, Miossi has been invited to write two book chapters, published various articles, and presented at numerous regional and national conferences, including being a keynote panelist for the Midwest Sport and Exercise Psychology Symposium through the Association for Applied Sport Psychology (AASP). Additionally, she co-led a continuing education, pre-conference workshop on antiracism at the AASP conference (2020). Miossi has also won several awards for her research and teaching. Most notably, she won The Sport Psychologist Young Research Award (AASP conference, 2019). She was also awarded the AASP Conference Student Abstract Award (2019) and the A.W. Hobt Memorial Teaching Award UTK (2020). Currently, Miossi is a member of the Association for Applied Sport Psychology, where she served two years as a Diversity Committee student member. Miossi is also a mental performance consultant with various sport teams and individual athletes.

Shannon Mulcahy, MS, is the founder of Mulcahy Performance Consulting—a sport psychology business empowering athletes to drop their unhelpful thoughts to make their wildest dreams a reality. Based in Columbia, Maryland, Shannon holds a Master's degree in Sport and Exercise Psychology and has worked with hundreds of athletes and coaches worldwide in her 5+ years of industry experience. She also has an extensive background as a competitive and masters swim coach. When she's not working with athletes, she can be found on a trail or in a lake training for her own races. Connect with Shannon and explore the current services and resources at mulcahyperformance.com.

Robert E. Owens, PhD, CMPC, is a provisionally licensed therapist in the state of North Carolina and a performance coach. He is a Certified Mental Performance Consultant (CMPC) with the Association for Applied Sport Psychology (AASP) and a Certified Forensic Mental Health Evaluator—Candidate (CFMHE-C) with the National Board of Forensic Evaluators (NBFE). He teaches courses in leadership for the Bryan School of Business and Economics at the University of North Carolina at Greensboro (UNCG) and has conducted workshops on diversity and inclusion, authentic leadership, organizational justice, workplace wellness, and positive organizational psychology practice. His research and professional interests include anti-oppressive consulting practices, and re-conceiving sexual misconduct in high performance settings like sport, the performing arts, and within first responder populations.

Tanya Prewitt-White, (she/her) PhD, CMPC, Survivor Advocate, began her career as a professor of sport psychology and a certified mental performance coach (CMPC). Over time her work with organizations and collegiate athletic departments coupled with her commitment to advocacy and justice unveiled her capacity and gift to hold space for challenging and oftentimes difficult conversations necessary for transformational change. She is a survivor of sexual misconduct, trained Survivor Advocate, and owner of Dr. Tanya Raquel, LLC. In addition to her peak performance applied work, she supports athletes who are sexual abuse survivors and facilitates trainings and co-creates courageous and vulnerable spaces for athletes, parents, coaches, and administrators to talk about healthy sexual relationships, supporting survivors, sexual misconduct prevention, and consent. She has served as a consultant and facilitator to institutions in the United States and Canada. Tanya currently serves as the Association of Applied Sport Psychology's (AASP's) Advocacy Chair.

As a former athlete, Dr. Prewitt-White innately seeks challenge. Though, now believes her most important challenge, as the parent of two sons, is raising socially conscious men and views her life as their model in how to live passionately, contribute to the needs of society, and approach difficult dialogues with grace. Meditating, curating meditations, writing, reading, meeting friends at coffee shops for morning conversations, and spending time with her husband and sons sustain her soul in her life's work.

Travis R. Scheadler (he/him/his) is a MSW and PhD student in Social Work at The Ohio State University and a Junior Associate Editor for the *Journal for Advancing Sport Psychology in Research*. He competed in track and field at Wilmington College, where he earned his

Bachelor of Arts in Psychology. He then completed his Master of Science in Sport & Exercise Psychology at University of Kentucky. While at UK, Travis collaborated with the Center for Sport, Peace, and Society at University of Tennessee and was an ambassador for Ban Conversion Therapy Kentucky. Currently, Travis is an intern with LiFEsports, an organization using sport as a mechanism to teach social skills to underserved youth. He also is the MSW Student Representative for the National Association of Social Workers-Ohio Chapter. He regularly co-leads volunteer advocacy nights with Equality Ohio. His research interests are in athlete activism, sport-based positive youth development, and LGBTQIA+ issues and advocacy. Travis hopes to complete his MSW in 2022 and PhD in 2025.

Lauren Spirov, MS, was born in Chicago, IL, and raised in Minneapolis, MN. She relocated back to Chicago in 2017 to pursue her master's degree in Kinesiology, as well as her 200-hour yoga teacher training. She is currently working in Clinical Research. Lauren serves on the board for the Illinois Caucus for Adolescent Health and considers health equity and youth empowerment to be very important to her. She enjoys exploring Chicago with her dog, reading any autobiography that she can get her hands on, and meeting new people.

Taylor A. Stuemky, MS, currently serves as the Assistant Athletic Director for Internal Operations, overseeing the Excellence at 7220 Student-Athlete Development program, which primarily consists of instructing three courses based on health and wellness, leadership, and skill for life. She also oversees the Athletic Department's policies and procedures for Student-Athlete Sexual Violence Prevention and Student-Athlete Mental Health/Well-being. Stuemky is a trained instructor for both the Green Dot and Step UP! bystander intervention programs. She also collaborates with the Family Consumer Sciences department at UW to implement a "Relationship Smarts" series in her classes for student-athletes. Stuemky works closely with the Dean of Students office and is a member of the UWYO Cares team. Stuemky had previously worked as Director of Student-Athlete Success, Director of Academic Services, and Academic Coordinator with stints directing the support services for football, men's basketball and volleyball, and men's and women's swimming and diving. Stuemky earned her bachelor's degree in Sport and Exercise Science from the University of Northern Colorado in 2010 and her master's degree in Counseling and Student-Development from Kansas State University in 2013.

Emily J. Tyler, MS (she/her), is a Counseling Psychology Psy.D. Candidate at Springfield College in Springfield, Massachusetts. Her research involves studying sexual violence, rape culture, and "locker room talk" in athletic environments. Her various sports roles have included being an athlete, manager, mentor, graduate assistant, mental performance coach, and fan. Though her primary role is now a therapist for college students and student-athletes, she pulls from her own experience in these former roles where she has witnessed and experienced a range of sexual misconduct while working in intercollegiate athletics. Emily hopes that by sharing her stories, it humanizes and brings further attention to the pervasive, problematic, rape culture that exists within college sports.

PREFACE

Our Origin Stories—How We Came to Study Sexual Misconduct in Sport

Leslee A. Fisher, PhD, CMPC, and Tanya Prewitt-White,
PhD, CMPC, Survivor Advocate

In November of 2017, I (Leslee)[1] was glued to the television when Dr. Larry Nassar plead guilty to seven counts of first-degree criminal sexual conduct in connection with female gymnastic survivors who came forward to file a case against him. A week later, Nassar pleaded guilty to an additional (three) charges. Many of his horrific actions against athletes occurred in my hometown and the surrounding counties of East Lansing, Michigan; I had friends of friends who sent their kids to train at Twistars (i.e., the gymnastics facility where anybody who was anybody trained with John Geddert and had Larry Nassar as their physio), and I had taught at Michigan State University (MSU) in the late 1990s.

By the time the trial was completed, over 150 women and teenagers—including Olympic medalists, elite gymnasts, divers, swimmers, runners, and other athletes—made statements at the sentencing hearing in Ingham County, Michigan. In January of 2018, Nassar was sentenced to 40–175 years in federal prison (Hauser & Astor, 2018). Perhaps not shocking, in a separate case brought by the FBI involving more than 37,000 images and videos of child pornography, Nassar was sentenced to 60 years.

However, it turned out that MSU had received reports of the sexual abuse perpetrated by Nassar beginning in the early 1990s. In addition, the National Collegiate Athletic Association (NCAA) did not open a formal investigation into Nassar's actions until January 23, 2018. After MSU's formal investigation began, within days, MSU's president as well as the athletic director resigned; within a week, the entire board of USA Gymnastics had also resigned.

The news of Nassar's crimes against athlete bodies as well as the survivor impact statements (i.e., Denhollander, 2019) hit me like a ton of bricks. How could this happen in my own backyard, the place where I grew up and where I worked in the field of sport psychology? What safeguards were in place to protect these athletes from someone they trusted? The trial also made me think about my own moral and ethical convictions and the kind of culturally reflexive praxis I could engage in to explore the ways that the Nassar case illustrates the oppressive effects of patriarchy, sexism, and sexual exploitation on the bodies and the human spirit of female athletes (Fisher & Anders, 2019). Many questions continued to haunt me, such as: *What is at stake for elite female athletes when they are in subordinate positions in relationships with significant sport others (e.g., coaches, doctors) who devalue and abuse them? How did Nassar's abuse become systemic? What happens to a girl's and young woman's sense of self when a trusted authority figure is also a sexual abuser? To what extent is the field of sport psychology privileging elite athlete performance and performance enhancement above athlete's well-being?* As a social justice advocate in sport psychology, the bottom line for me was: How can I think about and interrogate the ways that specific cultural spaces (i.e., sport) are infused with relational power dynamics that harm athletes, and what can I do to change this?

My writing partner Allison and I also thought about what was at stake if we did not respond (Fisher & Anders, 2019).

Long before this, however, Tanya was actually experiencing being groomed by her high school basketball coach. Long before this, she was speaking out about harm. And, because of her commitment to social justice, she began to conceptualize the book that you are now reading.

Tanya's Story

As a child athlete, I was groomed by my high school basketball coach from 1991 to 1999 (see Chapter 6 for my story). My former coach is in prison as I type these words. I learned from experiences rather than a textbook that people with a responsibility to protect young children and athletes will overlook and dismiss harm as well as side-step personal integrity in the name of reputation, success, championships, and image. I can tell you nothing is worth the harm and hurt; truth and safety have no price tag.

The impetus of this book has been through my advocacy work with survivors and organizations. It has been through this advocacy that I have witnessed the lack of education and the discomfort so many of us hold not only talking about sex (see Chapter 16) but also acknowledging the sexual misconduct that happens in the places and spaces we inhabit. I have wondered if I am the one to co-curate this book. And, I have reckoned with this minimizing and silencing as a weapon, of many, used to keep the status quo.

I have sat with survivors who have shared with me that even after reporting to Title IX, institutions did nothing to protect them. I sat in one-on-one meetings with a chancellor eager to discuss ways to create institutional change whom I later learned knew of sexual violence occurring and did nothing to mitigate it. I began to recognize avoiding a scandal, unpacking what I might know, and keeping me and others silent was the major motivation for our exchanges.

I have held survivors, literally and figuratively, in my arms as a survivor advocate. I shared space with an LGBTQ collegiate athlete as they named the discrimination and pain they experience when institutions attempt to minimize their survivorship. I curated conversations over Zoom calls with parents struggling to best support their daughter athlete after experiencing sexual misconduct within an athletic department. As a facilitator, I witnessed 50+ athletes vulnerably share their survivor stories to move in the direction of individual and community healing.

Perpetrators have disclosed with me they want to make amends and that they live with shame and guilt every day of their lives for the harm they caused. I have shared the journey with a student-athlete struggling with the fact that their perpetrator will not be kicked off the sport team and/or the university immediately. I have publicly advocated for policy change and have done my best to hold institutions accountable. I have co-facilitated conversations and sat in spaces where I have recognized that too many of us lack the tools, knowledge, and sometimes courage, to change the culture. Mostly, I choose not to be silent. Of course, I have been gaslit[2].

I am on an existential healing journey and have a responsibility to continue in community with others. I realize not all are ready to heal; healing is a courageous choice. This book is for any sport stakeholder and sport organization invested in not only examining and mitigating harm but healing from it, too. I also encourage colleagues who are clinically trained to follow up this text with a collaborative project on how clinically trained persons can best respond to sexual misconduct in sport and support survivors.

Purpose of the Book

The purpose of this book is threefold: 1) to describe *cultural realities and considerations* sport stakeholders must acknowledge and be informed of to make sport a more equitable and safe space; 2) to provide *personal narratives* from a variety of sport stakeholders, which unveil their lived experiences of sexual misconduct and humanize survivor stories in ways often ignored in sport and society; and 3) to offer *recommendations* to all sport stakeholders in order to both create a more welcoming and equitable sport environment and mitigate incidents of and harm done by sexual misconduct. It was important to us to outline systemic and sociological explanations for why sport is a site of sexual misconduct and to elevate survivor stories that are often ignored in sport; by bringing them to light, we can address sexual misconduct issues so as to evoke change in sport institutions. Our intention is not to (re)trigger or (re)traumatize but to encourage all sport stakeholders to stop sweeping sexual misconduct under the rug because lives are forever changed because of our negligence and complacency. Guidelines and suggestions for sport stakeholder practices that better protect individuals in sport, address sexual misconduct when it occurs, and mitigate the harm and trauma experienced because of incidents of sexual misconduct are also provided.

We believe that this book is the first text of its kind to invite in sport stakeholders to have open, vulnerable, and honest discussions around a timely topic that is often minimized, denied, and/or ignored in sport. We also provide tangible guidelines and next steps for sport administrators and stakeholders who are floundering to address the needs of their institutions, especially following the #metoo movement.

The book is organized into three sections. First, we introduce the culture of sport as a site of sexual misconduct. Next, humanizing stories of sexual misconduct in sport. Finally, we provide implications and next steps for stakeholders, coaches, parents, survivors, and coaches. At the end of every chapter are 3–5 discussion questions (posed by chapter authors) and a list of keywords to help readers synthesize the material presented. NOTE: Some chapters contain definitions and theoretical and academic information while others focus strictly on survivor stories, told in their own words.

Section 1: In the first section, authors discuss how sexual misconduct is situated in every sport organization and institution due to the power structures, toxic masculinity, cultural norms, and silencing of voices that occur without critique. Also, authors address failed mitigations of sexual misconduct to provide opportunities for critique, improvement, and reflection for readers.

Section 2: In the second section, authors provide case-by-case survivor stories not often elevated in sport. These survivors' lived experiences and voices are central to humanizing the issues and evoking change in sport systems. When discussing sexual misconduct, it is ever important that we are not discussing emotionless statistics but people whose lives have been harmed. Stories from various levels, by both survivors and those who witnessed sexual misconduct in sport, are shared to demonstrate to readers the nuanced and complex experiences, responses, and support provided prior to, during, and following incidents of sexual misconduct. It is important we prepare readers that you may find the content of this section, in particular, triggering.

Section 3: In the last section, authors provide necessary and tangible policy and praxis changes crucial to mitigating sexual misconduct in sport. Furthermore, considerations for athletes, parents, teammates, coaches, practitioners, and administrators who find themselves navigating incidents of sexual misconduct are shared.

As you read, we encourage you to take good care of yourselves (e.g., drink lots of water, take breaks from reading and reflecting on what you've learned, exercise, meditate, talk with others—loved ones, trusted friends and colleagues, your mental health practitioner). If you are a survivor yourself, we especially encourage you to hold your soul with self-compassion and love. Do the things necessary for you to continue your healing journey and we recognize that might mean putting the book down for some time. And, if you are a parent, coach, teammate, or stakeholder struggling with the harm you were unable to prevent, please know you, too, deserve to heal. You also are worthy of care.

We also welcome readers to reckon with what needs to change. For many of us, we may need to move through emotions of fear, guilt, shame, and denial to create caring communities and cultures absent of harm. Thank you, in advance, for having the courage to read and sit with all that will inevitably emerge as you delve into this text.

As editors and authors, we know for sustainable and transformative change to occur it is important for all of us to respond with the convictions of both our intellect and heart. Our intention is for this text to be a living document that calls each of us to be (even) better for future generations, especially as it relates to advocacy and sexual misconduct in sport. Collective healing is necessary, and we hope reading this book is just one step in your journey. Please hold survivor stories with care. Trauma occurs in community and healing does, too (Marte, 2020). It is an honor to heal with you as not only you read this book but also as we take action together to mitigate the harm of sexual misconduct affecting us all.

Notes

1. Most of Leslee's section is modified from Fisher and Anders' (2019) paper related to how cultural sport psychology can be used to shed light on the sexual abuse of athletes.
2. Gaslighting is a means of causing a person, group of people, or community to question their memory, perception, or judgment. To gaslight someone is to also minimize their experience and emotions and to manipulate them by psychological means to question their own sanity or ability to speak about an experience or subject matter.

References

Denhollander, R. (2019). *What is a girl worth? My story of breaking the silence and exposing the truth about Larry Nassar and USA gymnastics*. Tyndale Momentum.

Fisher, L. A., & Anders, A. D. (2019). Engaging with cultural sport psychology to explore systemic sexual exploitation in USA gymnastics: A call to commitments. *Journal of Applied Sport Psychology*. https://doi.org/10.1080/10413200.2018.1564944

Hauser, C., & Astor, M. (Jan. 25, 2018). The Larry Nassar case: What happened and how the fallout is spreading. *The New York Times* (Sports section). https://www.nytimes.com/2018/01/25/sports/larry-nassar-gymnastics-abuse.html

Marte, D. (2020, October 12). *Emotional colonization and labor in the work place*. Association of Applied Sport Psychology, Mid-Career Women's Summit, Online.

ACKNOWLEDGMENTS

This book is a collective, collaborative effort—more than any one person. To every contributor, thank you for your bravery and emotional labor and wisdom. I do not take lightly your commitment to shine light in the darkness. Writing about sexual misconduct (especially for those of us who are survivors), amidst a global pandemic, social and political unrest, and so many uncertainties, was—let's be real—hard. And, to those who began this journey and later recognized you did not have the energy to give or capacity to add another challenge to your responsibilities, I hold you with so much love and honor that you prioritized yourself and loved ones.

To Dr. Leslee A. Fisher, the editing aficionado of this text and my mentor from the University of Tennessee, I could not have done this alone. Your reminders to take space and prioritize my family were a gift I needed. The ways you supported the vision of this book, all the twists and turns we journeyed, and how we navigated roles and experiences we had not previously traveled together taught me so much. You have believed in me since I ventured into your office in 2005 and for that, I am grateful.

To my beloved, Courtney, your love is unwavering, and your support has always allowed me to have the strength to speak my truth, the courage to heal, and the grace to forgive. Thank you for having patience as I sacrificed nights, mornings, and weekends away from you and the boys to see this project to fruition. To my children, Steven Earnest and Devin Justice, may you always know you are loved abundantly and everything about you is beautiful. You are my reason to be better every day I wake and the miracles I did nothing to deserve—thank you for coming to teach me how to love deeper than my heart has ever known. To my mom and dad, Charmaine and Steve, thank you for creating an environment of unconditional love and modeling through your lived example that I can do hard things. I know you have not always known how to hold my pain or my dreams, but your loving presence has meant everything and always been what I needed most. I hope I make you proud.

To every person who opens this text, sits with the emotions that emerge, critiques self, sport, and society, holds a difficult conversation on sexual misconduct, and does something—thank you.

Most of all, to every survivor, I believe you—you are worthy of love, protection, care, and healing.

Tanya Prewitt-White, PhD, CMPC, Survivor Advocate

Co-editing this book was not only more challenging than I anticipated but also one of the most rewarding projects I've ever been a part of. And, none of this was possible without Tanya Prewitt-White, my co-editor, collaborator, peer mentor, former doctoral student, current Sherpa through the complex work of ameliorating sexual misconduct in sport, spiritual beauty, great friend and confidante, and the originator of this book. She conceptualized this book and made it happen, from start to finish. I'm eternally grateful to you, T, for honoring me with an invitation to work with you side by side—virtually and during the COVID pandemic—and asking me to be a part of this amazing labor of love. I truly love you, Tanya Prewitt-White, and I've loved working with you.

I'm also eternally grateful to my partner Dave whose emotional support and love sustained me through this process as well as the pandemic. He fed me, grocery-shopped, cleaned our living space, but most importantly, took emotional care of me as I read these chapters from powerful survivors. I know I would not have gotten through this process without your love, care, and support, hon—I am truly grateful to have you in my life and I love you so very much.

To everyone at Routledge who enabled us to move forward with this project—especially David Varley and Megan Smith—for your endurance and grace. Thank you, David, for sticking with us throughout the entire process, even when it got overwhelming at times. I am truly grateful for your support.

To my immediate family—Cory, Andria, Jordan, Claire, and Calvin—thank you for letting me spend so many months away from you, working on this project as well as my job for over the last 20 years. I am deeply enriched by your presence in my life. And, Claire and Calvin, this book is for you—I couldn't stop thinking about you as I was reading the survivor stories in this book as well as when I was writing the chapter urging parents and other stakeholders to work with us to end violence against children in any form, but especially related to sexual misconduct in sport.

Finally, to all those survivors who were brave enough to share their stories in the pages of this book, I stand with you and support you. I am forever grateful for your courage; this book would not have been possible or meaningful without you. Thank you, thank you, thank you.

Leslee Fisher, PhD, CMPC

SECTION I
Cultural Realities and Considerations

1
CALLING ALL SPORT CONSTITUENTS

Exploring Power *and* Bringing Back Joy Into Sport

Leslee A. Fisher and Allison D. Anders

Introduction

Athletes participate in sport and physical training for a variety of reasons. They love being self-determined and self-directed in the pursuit of meeting their goals. They love being a part of a team, being a "team player,"—and developing relationships with coaches and players. They also love opportunities to display leadership and work toward the best version of themselves.

However, today's athletes face unique challenges. These include mental barriers (i.e., keeping focused, composed, and relaxed under pressure), physical challenges (i.e., always feeling tired, having chronic pain, experiencing injuries, developing burnout), and embedded sport institutional ethics (i.e., a "win-at-all-costs" mentality; a focus on outcome versus process; the desire for celebrity status; overconforming to what the leader wants; accepting no limits in the pursuit of excellence; see Coakley, 2020). Researchers have also seen a rise in the number of athletes who report experiencing emotional abuse (i.e., Stirling & Kerr, 2008), sport-related bullying and hazing (Nery et al., 2020), and sexual abuse and misconduct (see Fisher & Anders, 2019; Johnson et al., 2020).

Sexual misconduct is the focus of this entire book. Sexual misconduct is defined as "engaging in any sexual activity without first obtaining Affirmative Consent to the specific activity" (San Francisco State University, 2021; see also Chapter 18 in this book for a discussion of consent). Sexual misconduct also includes:

- using physical force;
- using violence, threat, or intimidation;
- ignoring the objections of the other person;
- causing the other person's intoxication or incapacitation through the use of drugs or alcohol;
- taking advantage of the other person's incapacitation (including voluntary intoxication) to engage in sexual activity (San Francisco State University, 2021, p. 1).

It is important to point out two additional facts: (a) women as well as men can be survivors of sexual misconduct and (b) [an adult] engaging in sexual activity with a minor "is never consensual when the Complainant is under 18 years old, because the minor is considered incapable of giving legal consent due to age" (San Francisco State University, 2021, p. 1). From the outset, we want to share that addressing both sexual misconduct and power and dominance in sport is challenging. But, it must be done.

Power in sport moves through dangerous binary relations between the dominant (i.e., the powerful) and the dominated (i.e., the vulnerable). These relations are located in institutional and social structures. They move through complex intersections of individual identity, competition, the often-beloved experience of embodying the sport, and, for elite athletes, the pursuit of their zenith.

We must address power in sport if we want our children to experience all the joys that sport has to offer. We must not romanticize our children's participation in sport and turn an ignorant eye to the ways that athletes can be mistreated. A good place to start is to become critical thinkers about our children's welfare before and while they are participating in sport systems. We might ask ourselves questions like: Where's the power in this organization? Who is deploying it and in what ways? How is power getting reproduced? Who is benefiting? And, how does asking these types of questions relate to sexual misconduct (Fisher & Anders, 2019)?

Sport Sexual Misconduct and Power: A Useful Framework

To illustrate the shifts necessary to address power and dominance in athletics, we begin by presenting a framework developed by Nery and colleagues (Nery et al., 2020). While they used this framework to focus on sport-related bullying, it could also be used to explore sport sexual misconduct. In fact, this framework could help sport constituents—like you (i.e., coaches, parents, athletic directors, and sport and exercise psychology professionals or SEPPs)—address sport sexual misconduct and power dynamics moving forward.

Nery et al.'s (2020) framework is very valuable when thinking about power and sexual misconduct in sport spaces because they employed a socio-ecological framework to explore "unsanctioned aggression and violence in amateur sport" (p. 230). They conceptualized violent behaviors as multifaceted and occurring along a continuum ranging from individual to situational to contextual and sociocultural; this framework also aligns with Bronfenbrenner's Ecological Systems Theory (i.e., micro-, meso-, exo-, and macro-levels; Bronfenbrenner, 1977), Stirling and Kerr's (2014) ecological systems approach, and Leahy's (2010) biopsychosocial approach to understanding and preventing sport abuse.

In fact, Nery et al. (2020) summon us to think about the power structures and larger discourses at play when they highlight the different levels where sport misconduct occurs. In this framework, we also see the levels we want sport constituents to use with us as we delve into athletes' lived experiences of sexual misconduct together and remind ourselves that we are all responsible—as parents, coaches, athletic administrators, and SEPPs—for ending it.

As we have written elsewhere (Fisher & Anders, 2019), this begins by asking ourselves new questions centered on the dignity and security of our athletes' bodies in competitive spaces such as: Under what conditions is my athlete training? Are those in power abusing my athlete? Is my athlete training in an environment that includes bullying, hazing, racism, sexism, and homophobia? Is my athlete encouraged and validated for speaking up and speaking out when someone is abused (i.e., physically, psychically, emotionally), or does their inclusion on the team depend on being obedient, submissive, or silent? And, is my athlete (and others in the environment) overlooking misconduct by those in power because they are "celebrities?"

Nery et al.'s (2020) Multi-Level Approach

After exploring these questions together, we find it helpful to now turn to Nery et al.'s (2020) framework and begin to apply it to sexual misconduct in sport. Like Nery et al. (2020), we believe that all sport violence—including sexual misconduct—should first be examined and then eradicated using a multi-level approach like theirs. Additionally, because we want to eradicate abuse in sport, we need to develop more accepting and inclusive sport environments as well as consistent policies surrounding sexual misconduct. As you can imagine, this kind of work takes time; and, in certain cases, a qualified professional to do the work. Like Nery and colleagues, our hope is that by creating inclusive environments, our athletes will develop into their best physical and emotional selves.

Nery et al.'s (2020) four levels include (a) *the individual level* (i.e., one's personal values, the amount of obsessive passion or "the degree to which an athlete identifies with the culture of sport practiced" and the demographic factors of gender and age; (b) *the situational level* (i.e., situational dominance, conflictual interactions, and bystanders); (c) *the contextual level* (i.e., the type and level of sport); and (d) *the sociocultural level* (i.e., masculinity values, social learning, the amount of moral disengagement, and the moral atmosphere within the society; see p. 231).

For our purposes, at the individual level, we are open to hearing athletes' lived experiences of sexual misconduct so that we can better understand what it means to experience abuse from a trusted coach, teammate, or adult. This can also better equip us to identify signs and to prevent future harm. When doing so, we are also mindful that retelling one's survivor story can allow those who have been harmed to reclaim their power. And, too, for others and depending where one is on their healing journey, telling their survivor stories can be a triggering experience; thus, we never pressure any survivor to share their story. Every survivor deserves the right to own their process and healing journey. At the situational level, we are curious about the institutional/political level of disregard and denial of sexual misconduct in some spaces. At the sociocultural level, we also want to know about how the larger discourses of sexism (i.e., discrimination, stereotyping, or prejudice—in general, against women—because of their sex), racism (i.e., antagonism, discrimination, or prejudice based on one's membership in an ethnic or racial group), and cisheteropatriarchy (i.e., in general, a political and social system where those who identify as straight and male have dominance over those people who do not) function together to create conditions of sexual misconduct. We are also interested in why there is a general lack of media coverage about sexual misconduct in sport until long after it has occurred (see also Brackenridge, 2001; Fisher & Anders, 2019; Raj, 2002).

An example might be helpful here. Therefore, we illustrate next how each of these levels contributed to a culture of sexual misconduct in the Larry Nassar case (see also Fisher & Anders, 2019).

The Individual and Contextual Levels

Nery et al. (2020) defined the individual level as made up of an athlete's "personal values, the amount of obsessive passion or the degree to which an athlete identifies with the culture of sport practiced" (p. 231). The demographic factors of gender and age as well as the type and level of sport involved also make a difference in terms of violent or aggressive behaviors occurring in the sport context.

Using the Larry Nassar case and USA Gymnastics (USAG) as an example, we can see that in the sport of elite gymnastics, relatively young and (mostly) female children who are obsessed with being the best they can be were the ones that Nassar targeted. In fact, they knew that he was the one they had to go *to and through* in order to reach their Olympic dreams. Coaches reinforced the directive of getting "treatment" from Nassar and being compliant and obedient with this requirement. Regrettably, that "treatment" included sexual abuse, which was perpetrated onto athletes by Nassar at all the places he was employed (i.e., USAG, Twistars, and Michigan State University).

hooks (2000) believes that we need to critique this kind of everyday deployment of patriarchal power and also critique the knowledge systems that reproduce patriarchal dominance and sexism in those spaces we live in like sport. In fact, she believes that in order to change systems, our work "must be solidly based on a recognition of the need to eradicate the underlying cultural basis and causes of sexism and other forms of group oppression" (p. 33). Paying attention to these types of sport ethics related to power (e.g., the belief that our athletes need to be obedient, submissive, and compliant to get ahead) and that are deployed through and alongside patriarchal dominance allows us to engage and critique ideas and ideologies together as sport stakeholders; in fact, we now know that these kinds of sports ethics create gendered violence and often include notions related to rigid athlete roles and behaviors (Perry, 2005). This is why we believe it is also incredibly important at the individual level to be prepared to hold space for survivors to share their experiences of trauma—the visceral experiences—of sexual misconduct so that we can see, hear, feel, and be educated about what it's like to be violated by the very person who is supposed to have your best interests at heart (see also Fisher & Anders, 2019). We should also be prepared to recommend and refer victims and survivors to licensed clinical professionals to continue their healing process.

The Situational Level

Nery et al. (2020) defined the situational level as including situational dominance, conflictual interactions, and bystanders to violence and aggression in sport. When a USA gymnast decides to participate in sport, she arrives not just in the gymnasium but also in the conditions, rules, and organizational and cultural laws that precede them in the discourse, norms, relationships, and structure (Butler, 1993) of gymnastics. Those conditions, rules, and laws are designed to maintain the status and hierarchical structures of the dominant; this includes those in power like coaches, trainers, athletic directors, organizations/leagues, and governing bodies like USAG.

What we hope is that each athlete plays and competes for themselves. However, what we know is at least at this time in the United States, they play in power-dominated predominantly male and white structures (Jenkins, 2021; NCAA, 2021) driven by commercial and bureaucratic logics that prioritized revenue (Scott, 1998). In other words, sport is set up to serve the interest of dominant groups. Dominant groups are invested in maintaining control and dominance (Stacey & Thorne, 1994); in Olympic sport, this means that athletes are only as good as their earning potential—and, if they aren't competing, they aren't earning.

At the situational level, we are also curious about the institutional/political level of disregard and denial of sexual misconduct in the spaces where Nassar was employed (USAG, Michigan State University, Twistars Gym, etc.) as well as the lack of media coverage related to reports of his abuse. As mentioned in the preface of this book, by the time his trial was over, at least 150 women and teenagers—including Olympic medalists, elite gymnasts, divers, swimmers, runners, and other athletes—provided survivor impact statements at his sentencing hearing in Michigan. There were others who did not speak at the hearing. While Nassar was sentenced to 40–175 years in federal prison (Hauser & Astor, 2018) and another 60 years in a separate case brought by the FBI involving more than 37,000 images and videos of child pornography, it came to light that Michigan State University was aware of reports alleging Nassar's sexual misconduct as early as the 1990s—and did nothing about these allegations. Also shocking is the fact that the National Collegiate Athletic Association (NCAA) did not open a formal investigation of Nassar until January of 2018.

As parents, coaches, ADs, and SEPPs, we need to ask together: What kind of team codes of conduct, moral atmosphere, peer group norms, and attitudes toward sexual misconduct were and should be at play in a situation like this? How were athletes supposed to report sexual misconduct and if they did it correctly—which by all accounts, they did—why didn't anyone *believe* them, at multiple levels? Why were individuals as well as institutions, clubs, and national governing bodies *turning away* when bodies were being ripped apart by sexual abuse? Why was NO ONE acting to protect them from harm? As Rachel Denhollander (2019)—a former gymnast who was also abused by Nassar—asked in her book by the same title, "What is a girl worth?"

The Sociocultural Level

It is at the *sociocultural level* (i.e., masculinity values, social learning, the amount of moral disengagement, and the moral atmosphere within the society; Nery et al., 2020) that we believe we have the most work to do together with other sport constituents. At the sociocultural level, we want to know how the larger discourses of sexism, racism, and cisheteropatriarchy function *together* to create conditions of sexual misconduct. As stated previously, looking at these intersections of identity at the various levels of sexual misconduct is important because it is usually those people who are intentionally ignored that are systematically discriminated against; it seems fairly obvious to us that those who were young children obsessed with becoming the best that they could be were systematically ignored when they were crying for help. And, we need your help to turn this around.

Although we hope the love of sport stays centered in any athlete's experience, we also know the reproduction of a patriarchal and racist structure—as well as other systems of exploitation and domination—are ever-present. Although the discriminatory impact is visible, discourses of sport create tensions by coupling the glorification of sacrifice, specifically winning-at-all-costs, playing through pain and accepting all risks (Coakley, 2020), to the idea of a young athlete's value and worth, and infinitely reproducing labor in the name of future promise. The future promise of a medal (or ring or endorsements or college scholarships) works to control organizational and cultural laws (as well as children's bodies) linked to the generation of capital and to recruit and reinforce children's commitment to labor (Butler, 1993). We want to note here that we are using "medal" both literally and symbolically. And, given the sexual assault, exploitation, and abuse of children in sport, it seems productive to explore the everyday structures of sport that position young athletes as subordinate in multiple ways.

An individual child's dream of reaching the zenith of their sport coexists in a system of capitalism that functions based on the threat of replacement for both athletes and coaches, particularly at the elite level. At the high school and/or club level, too, while social capital as wealth might not be at stake for leaders, their reputation is most definitely required to be invested in children's performance. For example, think of the motivational tactic coaches use when they say, "Don't worry about who you want to beat but who is behind you looking to beat you or take your spot"; leaders are probably feeling that same way about somebody taking their spot. Regardless of any individual child's dream, their labor—as well as their coach's and athletic director's labor—can be replaced in ways that protect people in power's (i.e., the dominant) wealth and capital. And access to placing, ranking, and medaling at the elite level are controlled by policies and rules created by predominately powerful white men and by judges, officials, IOC executive boards, and committees who are predominately white men (Honderick, 2021; NCAA, 2021).[1] In comparison to their male counterparts, access to coaching positions, team ownership, and leadership in the preeminent organizations and governing bodies is disproportionately lower for females and lower yet for females of color; we only need to look at the NCAA's demographic data related to differences based on gender/sex and race for leadership positions to know that this is true (see Lapchick, 2020; NCAA, 2021).

For elite training centers, athletic departments, and other sport structures, the assurance of capital, financial, or social is exactly the promise they seek from young athletes. The promise of medals is the means. The distribution of medals facilitates the commodification of young athletes' labor. Children labor toward the future promise of a medal. The coaches, team, athletic departments, organizations, and governing bodies always win in the commodification of children's dreams; however, the children win only sometimes.

Specific Suggestions for Change for Sport Constituents

We summarize later a few of Nery et al.'s (2020) micro- and meso-level intervention approaches. Our hope is that we can engage with sport constituents to prevent sexual misconduct in sport. Each approach and who the focus is on is presented next. If you are interested in a more complete description of this framework—including the macro- and exo-levels—see our References section for Nery et al.'s work (2020).

The Micro-Level Approach

At this level, the focus is on sport stakeholders, particularly athletes and coaches, and on *developing direct policies and measures* related to violent and aggressive attitudes and behaviors (Nery et al., 2020). This could include sexual misconduct. Training and education about sexual misconduct with a particular focus on developing team policy for preventing sexual misconduct and how to intervene when it does occur is the general intervention. Policy should focus on team codes of conduct, the moral atmosphere, peer group norms, anti-sexual misconduct, and how to report sexual misconduct (Nery et al., 2020); the overall goal is to use an athlete-centered approach and create a change in attitudes regarding sexual misconduct. By doing so, it is hoped that athletes themselves will treat each other with respect, take care of the survivors of sexual misconduct on their team, and know how to report it when it does occur; parents should also be educated and informed about what sexual misconduct is and that it is never okay under any circumstances. There is also a need to put policies in place that describe how parents are supposed to communicate with leaders when sexual misconduct occurs and also how they can best support their children throughout this experience (Nery et al., 2020). Working at the Micro Level: Specific Recommendations

Supporting Athletes Who Have Been Sexually Mistreated

Supporting survivors of sexual misconduct is nuanced (see Chapters 16 and 17 of this book for more information). Our belief is that we need all sport stakeholders to be trained to recognize the signs of sexual misconduct and then to intervene/triage; the next step would be to have clinical professionals further assist and support these survivors. This is because it is usually the academic advisors, coaches, athletic trainers, and strength and conditioning coaches—the people athletes interact with daily—who are the ones (at least at the university level) who are having/needing to have the conversations with athletes rather than clinical professionals who athletes may see once a week/month. Though, we are not minimizing the need for referring to clinical professionals but acknowledging all of us may find ourselves supporting survivors. Thus, we all must be critically reflective of our own limits of training and capacity. We can ask ourselves, "Am I trained to be more than a listener here?" If not, do I know support systems and resources available (see Chapter 17 of this text) near me so I can make a referral?

Working With Witnesses

In terms of *trained professionals* working with those who witness sexual misconduct, it is often the case that bystanders may not understand what they have seen (Nery et al., 2020). The first step is to acknowledge that these behaviors have occurred. Even though witnesses' actions will impact on what happens after an incident occurs, they often don't know that they can make a difference. Abusive behaviors and attitudes are not okay under any circumstances. Therefore, it is crucial that teams, organizations, clubs, etc., develop witness intervention programs to also help witnesses feel empowered to make a difference (Nery et al., 2020).

Working With Teams

For those SEPP professionals working with teams where violence and aggressive behaviors have occurred, three strategies appear helpful (Nery et al., 2020). First, they can help the team develop *injunctive norms*; these norms relate to those behaviors that teammates should expect of each other when they interact together (Nery et al., 2020). Injunctive norms focus on codes of conduct and defining and standardizing what behaviors are expected from all team members; this includes what is okay and what is not okay, especially in terms of de-normalizing behaviors that are abusive. Another strategy is to help the team develop *descriptive norms;* these norms relate to those behaviors that describe best what athletes actually do in training together, and they focus on the social climate on the team. To be sure, every person on the team is influenced by the social climate which is set by the leaders (Nery et al., 2020). This includes how coach-athlete relationships are handled, and how training is organized. Lastly, teaching coaches and team members to be mindful of "hot spots" like the locker room is important because it is more likely that abusive behaviors will occur in less supervised areas (Nery et al., 2020). Monitoring like this can be done indirectly (e.g., players report incidents to the coaches) or directly (e.g., the coach sees misconduct themselves).

Working With Coaches

In addition to parents and team members receiving training, it is vital that coaches be trained in the signs of sport-related abusive behaviors. In fact, it is probably the most important training needed since they are the team leaders. Professionals like SEPPs can provide information in the form of newsletters, booklets, handouts, workshops, or other tools that coaches find useful when learning (Nery et al., 2020). Information about how to help athletes cope with and prevent sport-related abusive behaviors from occurring is also critical. To be sure, it is challenging to help sport constituents discuss sexual misconduct, the harm created by it and other abusive behaviors, how to prevent it, and especially how coaching and parenting styles might relate to it. That is why it is necessary to have a trained professional engage in these conversations with sport constituents. As leaders of their teams, coaches must understand how to define, prevent, and intervene when abusive sport behaviors are occurring to their team members; they also need to thoroughly understand their role in preventing and addressing harm when it occurs (Nery et al., 2020).

Working With Those Who Harm Others

In general, for *trained clinical professionals* working with those who engage in sport-related violent and aggressive behaviors, the obvious overall goal is to reduce the behaviors. One strategy is a *reactive strategy* using motivational interviewing (MI), which allows the perpetrator to explore and potentially resolve why they are engaging in sexual misconduct; the trained clinical professional can explore with the perpetrator why they are engaging in sexual misconduct, how they can change, and then explore next steps to take (Nery et al., 2020). We are not suggesting MI as the only response and it is important to note that for sports played in public schools, legally an MI cannot be the only response. State laws must be followed including contact with child protective services.

Working at the Meso Level: Specific Recommendations

Working With Parents

Improving coach-parent communication is key if we are to combat abusive sport behaviors (Nery et al., 2020). This means that an SEPP could help coaches and parents develop a plan a way of talking, listening, feeling heard, etc., that becomes well-established. In fact, Nery et al. (2020) described developing a "school for parents" that would be:

> managed by a sports psychologist, who is able to inform parents about the importance of the parent—coach relationship, appropriate level of involvement of parents, the nature of sexual misconduct and other forms of abuse and violence, and how to contribute to improve the training process from the parents' perspective.
>
> *(p. 239)*

This step is important because at present, there are very few coach-parent meetings held in sport contexts (Nery et al., 2020). SEPPs could begin by helping coaches communicate to parents their overall coaching philosophies and learning strategies on a regular and consistent basis. By inviting parents in, instead of calling them out, perhaps cooperation and support can be better fostered. A good relationship with parents goes a long way because they are the ones who support their kids, help them with food, travel, training, and support, almost always as volunteers. In addition, if parents know how to spot sport-related abusive behaviors, they can report it to the coach and the administration.

Conclusions and Thoughts About Next Steps

As we explore the effects of sport structure and discourse on our children who are athletes in the everyday discourses and big business of sport, we invite intersectional attention to the need for new "alternative habits of being" (Crenshaw, 1989, 1991; hooks, 2000) in our gyms, on our teams, and in the field of sport psychology (Fisher & Anders, 2019), particularly with regard to sexual misconduct and other sport-related abuses. This includes factors to pay attention to such as the review of our policies, evaluation and research, and at an individual level, systematic reflection on our practice as parents, coaches, SEPPs, ADs, and scholar-practitioners.

Dominance, superiority, and authority function through hierarchal relations in patriarchy, whiteness, and capital. In sport, those with access to capital have directed athletic departments/training centers/organizations, constructed policies, and reproduced discourse in myriad institutions that reinforce the ethics of a "win-at-all-costs" mentality and hierarchical power. In doing so, regardless of who may be in any given leadership position (i.e., as stated previously, not every position is held by someone raced white and gendered male), vertical dichotomous relations of power are entrenched. Those relations of power in sport and media affect athletes' everyday experiences (including sexual misconduct), language about them, and representations of them. The process of objectification materializes in myriad ways. But, there are things we can do as sport parents, coaches, athletic directors, and SEPPs to change this.

Black feminist scholars Davis (1983) and hooks (1990, 1992, 2000) and critical race feminist scholars Crenshaw (1991), Guinier (1990), and Matsuda (1991) have produced incisive theoretical work and intersectional analyses addressing how structures of domination work in our lives. They also focus on systemic intersectional exploitation, discrimination, and disenfranchisement. They help us think about a new way of being; in fact, hooks (2000) drives our engagement with the possibility of new habits of being. As she argued:

> In resistance to exploitation and discrimination that one must not only take up oppositional positions but also to cultivate becoming. Becoming "emerges" as one comes to understand how structures of domination work in one's life, as one develops critical thinking and critical consciousness, as one invents anew, alternative habits of being, and resists from that marginal space of difference inwardly defined.
>
> *(p. 15)*

This includes beginning to ask ourselves critical questions about what is happening to our children in sport, and how we may be contributing to their suffering by not exploring the power dynamics at play.

As we develop new habits of being in sport, we must also pay attention to racial as well as cultural and ethnic diversity in the particularities of support and resources. For example, as Crenshaw (1991) noted:

> Women of color experience racism in ways not always the same as those experienced by men of color, and sexism in ways not always parallel to experiences of white women, antiracism and feminism are limited, even on their own terms.
>
> (p. 1252)

Crenshaw (1991) developed structural, political, and representational intersectionality to mark the qualitative differences that exist between the experiences of Black women and women of Color and white women, and between Black women and women of Color and Black men and men of Color. She invites us to think about ways particular structures and institutions target identities through policies and practice and the intersectional experiences of girls and women located in those spaces. Crenshaw summons attention to the way perspectives of Black women and women of Color have been marginalized and advocates for Black women and women of Color to represent for themselves their own identities in contrast the ways that media and popular culture represent women of Color.

For athletes who identify as girls, women, other intentionally ignored groups and for professionals (i.e., SEPPs who work to support them), for athletic departments, national, and global organizations and leagues committed to health, safety, diversity, and equity in sport, we believe that tactics to revolutionize these entrenched systems of power are needed to keep our children safe. Although some girls, women, gender-nonconforming and intersex people, and allies contest the definitions and the power that maintains them, we need more spaces in sport that center the knowledges girls and women hold. Girls and women—and all athletes who have been harmed—need to be allowed to speak for themselves, speak up, and speak back to structure and policies that harm them and that jeopardize their health and safety.

hooks (1992) encouraged us to challenge the objectification and domination of those who are harmed and disrupt the hierarchy and fictional dichotomy of the dominant and the dominated. When those who have been harmed speak back—in language and decision-making—we challenge the limiting ethics of those in power. Contestation is a skill like others to be learned and practiced. Recently, when Simone Biles—another USAG athlete who experienced sexual abuse at the hands of Nassar—spoke out about her own mental health and the need to pull out of the 2020 Tokyo Olympic competition, she contested the taken-for-granted norms related to what it means to be a champion (i.e., give 110%, don't admit any challenges). We must help cultivate contestation among all athletes and especially those who are dominated in sport, even with the knowledge that its execution is not without consequence, particularly for girls and women of Color who advocate for change (Denyer, 2020; Kilgore, 2021). Creating strategies to manage such backlash is needed as well.

We must also help to hold accountable individuals—including board members like the ones at USAG when Nassar perpetrated his crimes—who jeopardize the safety and mental and physical health of our athlete children. That work includes strategies to censure abusive language, confront and report harassment, and prevent all forms of assault on the body. Concurrently, to disrupt abusive and corrupt power structures, we must learn to identify not only the systemic intersectional experience of sexual misconduct but also the dominance of ablecentrism, classism, and racism as well as cisheteropatriarchy, misogyny, and sexism inside discourses and practices of sport and in recreational and competitive sport leagues, sport organizations, and decision-making bodies.

We must demand that our children's knowledge of themselves and their bodies is valued and heard. We must find new ways to work collectively to cultivate sport as affirming and health-full spaces of belonging for every athlete and for our targeted and marginalized ones in particular. Coming together as sport constituents, we must find ways to secure the safety and mental and physical health of our children who love sport.

Discussion Questions

Explicit commitments to learning about what sexual misconduct is and having policies in place to hold perpetrators of sexual misconduct accountable are needed.

1) How do we identify sexual misconduct? How is it defined?
2) What policies on sexual misconduct are in place in the sports in which you and/or your children are engaged? If policies do not exist, how can they be created?
3) What education and training opportunities are available in your community, organization, institution to learn how to intervene in when abusive language and/or abusive coach-athlete interactions take place? If education and training are not available, how can they be accessed elsewhere?
4) What ways of reporting misconduct are available to you and/or your children?
5) What support and resources are available in your community, organization, institution for survivor of sexual misconduct? If support and resources do not exist, how can they be cultivated?

Note

1. This is not to suggest that ALL people in power in sport are white and male.

References

Brackenridge, C. (2001). *Spoilsports: Understanding and preventing sexual exploitation in sport*. Routledge.
Bronfenbrenner, U. (1977). Toward an experimental ecology of human development. *American Psychologist, 32*(7), 513–531. https://doi.org/10.1037/0003-066X.32.7.513
Butler, J. (1993). Critically queer. *GLQ: A Journal of Gay and Lesbian Studies, 1*(1), 17–32.
Coakley, J. (2020). *Sports in society: Issues and controversies* (13th ed.). McGraw-Hill Education.
Crenshaw, K. (1989). Demarginalizing the intersection of race and sex: Black feminist critique of antidiscrimination doctrine, feminist theory and antiracist politics. *University of Chicago Legal Forum*, 139–168.
Crenshaw, K. (1991). Mapping the margins: Intersectionality, identity politics, and violence against women of color. *Stanford Law Review, 43*, 1241–1299.
Davis, A. Y. (1983). *Women, race, and class*. Vintage.
Denhollander, R. (2019). *What is a girl worth? My story of breaking the silence and exposing the truth about Larry Nassar and USA gymnastics*. Tyndale Momentum.
Denyer, S. (2020, June 8). Japanese tennis player Naomi Osaka speaks out for Black Lives Matter, faces backlash. *The Washington Post*. https://www.washingtonpost.com/world/asia_pacific/japanese-tennis-player-naomi-osaka-speaks-out-for-black-lives-matter-faces-backlash/2020/06/08/f8432ca0-a92f-11ea-a43b-be9f6494a87d_story.html

Fisher, L. A., & Anders, A. D. (2019). Engaging with cultural sport psychology to explore systemic sexual exploitation in USA gymnastics: A call to commitments. *Journal of Applied Sport Psychology*. https://doi.org/10.1080/10413200.2018.1564944

Guinier, L. (1990). Of gentlemen and role models. *Berkeley Women's Law Journal, 936*(1), 93–106.

Hauser, C., & Astor, M. (2018). The Larry Nassar case: What happened and how the fallout is spreading. *The New York Times.* www.nytimes.com/2018/01/25/sports/larry-nassar-gymnastics-abuse.html

Honderick, H. (2021, July 23). Gender disparities still vex Tokyo Olympic games. *BBC News.* www.bbc.com/news/world-us-canada-57937102

hooks, b. (1990). *Yearning: Race, gender, and cultural politics.* South End Press.

hooks, b. (1992). *Black looks: Race and representation.* South End Press.

hooks, b. (2000). *Feminist theory: From margin to center.* South End Press.

Jenkins, S. (2021, July 27). This is what peak performance looks like: Who cares how it's clothed? *The Washington Post.* www.washingtonpost.com/sports/olympics/2021/07/27/olympic-wardrobe-regulations/

Johnson, N., Hanna, K., Novak, & Giardino, A. (2020). U.S. center for SafeSport: Preventing abuse in sports. *Women in Sport and Physical Activity Journal.* https://doi.org/10.1123/wspaj.2019-0049

Kilgore, A. (2021, August 1). As a runner, Allyson Felix didn't want to speak out: As a mom, she felt she had to. *The Washington Post.* www.washingtonpost.com/sports/2019/07/31/runner-allyson-felix-didnt-want-speak-out-mom-she-felt-she-had/

Lapchick, R. (2020). 2020 college racial and gender report card shows "insignificant progress". *ESPN.* www.espn.com/college-sports/story/_/id/30956744/2020-college-racial-gender-report-card-shows-insignificant-progress

Leahy, T. (2010). Sexual abuse in sport: Implications for the sport psychology profession. In T. Ryba, R. Schinke, & G. Tennenbaum (Eds.), *The cultural turn in sport psychology* (pp. 315–334). Fitness Information Technology.

Matsuda, M. (1991). Beside my sister, facing the enemy: Legal theory out of coalition. *Stanford Law Review, 43*(6), 1183–1119.

National Collegiate Athletic Association. (2021). *NCAA demographics database* [Data visualization dashboard]. www.ncaa.org/about/resources/research/ncaa-demographics-database

Nery, M., Neto, C., Rosado, A., & Smith, P. K. (2020). *Bullying in youth sports training: New perspectives and practical strategies.* Routledge.

Perry, B. (2005). *Moving upstream.* Virginia Sexual and Domestic Violence Action Alliance.

Raj, R. (2002). *Women at the intersection: Indivisible rights, identities, and oppressions.* Rutgers, the State University of New Jersey, Center for Women's Global Leadership.

San Francisco State University. (2021). *Title IX terms and definitions.* https://titleix.sfsu.edu/content/terms-definitions

Scott, J. C. (1998). *Seeing like a state: How certain schemes to improve the human condition have failed.* Yale University Press.

Stacey, J., & Thorne, B. (1994). The missing feminist revolution in sociology, 1985. In L. S. Kaufmann (Ed.), *American feminist thought at century's end: A reader* (pp. 167–188). Blackwell.

Stirling, A. E., & Kerr, G. A. (2008). Defining and categorizing emotional abuse in sport. *European Journal of Sport Science, 8*(4), 173–181. https://doi.org/10.1080/17461390802086281

Stirling, A. E., & Kerr, G. A. (2014). Initiating and sustaining emotional abuse in the coach-athlete relationship: An ecological transactional model of vulnerability. *Journal of Aggression Maltreatment & Trauma, 23*(2), 116–125. https://doi.org/10.1080/10926771.2014.872747

2
STAND UP AND STAND TALL

Rethinking Sexual Misconduct in Sport

Robert E. Owens

When Zachary Kaufman published an article in the *Boston Globe* titled, "When sexual abuse is common knowledge—but nobody speaks up," he asked the reader to consider why bystanders keep silent when they know or suspect a sexual crime has occurred (Kaufman, 2018). In asking the question, Kaufman invited us, as casual onlookers, to consider how we go about our daily activities in a democratic society living with the tacit or explicit knowledge of sexual perpetrators and their deeds and do absolutely nothing. In other words, why do some people act when others do not? In answering these questions, it is important to contemplate how the concept of *bystander* has taken on radically new social meanings in the post-Trump era of "stand back and stand by," where a bystander apparently is someone who not only witnesses a violent event but is also someone who stands ready to act on behalf of an unnamed perpetrator.

As bystanders, we are morally divided on what to do about the sexual misconduct of men like Jeffrey Epstein and Harvey Weinstein whose histories of abuse spanned decades (Leopold et al., 2019). In college sport, the sexual misconduct cases of Dr. Larry Nassar (Michigan State University), Dr. Richard Strauss (Ohio State University), and Dr. Robert Anderson (University of Michigan) illustrate how sport is oftentimes a microcosm of society (Coakley, 2016). Sport participation, particularly at the elite level, exemplifies Western cultures penchant for moral relativism and sexual exceptionalism when it comes to performances of white male bodies. This tendency toward moral relativism emboldens white supremacist organizations like the Proud Boys and the Oath Keepers to engage in public displays of hypermasculine vitriol and commit acts of violence against law-abiding citizens while under the gaze of formal institutions like the government or law enforcement (Miller-Idriss, 2020).

Sport is a microcosm of society in that it reflects cultural values and mores (Coakley, 2016). Sport is also a macrocosm of society because it creates its own values that sometimes go against or supersede already established cultural norms (Coakley, 2016). For example, violence in sport is something that is largely tolerated by members of a society who would not tolerate it in other settings (Young, 2019). In other words, sexual misconduct is an accepted part of sport settings and can come in the form of hazing rituals, bullying, and through teammates, coaches, administrators, and medical staff (Stuart, 2013). Sexual misconduct is also interconnected to major sporting events; for example, sex trafficking in Super Bowl host cities increases exponentially just prior to the Super Bowl (Lapchick, 2020). In fact, during the 2020 Super Bowl, 22 women in the Miami-Dade area were rescued from human trafficking operations and 47 individuals were arrested (Robertson, 2020).

Through communicative actions driven by powerful institutional discourses, common knowledge of sexual misconduct brings certain bodies into being, disavowing others, and usually doing so in harmful ways. To disrupt it is to work against the cultural myths that structure it. Just like anti-racist educators who argue that not being a racist is not enough to dismantle racism in sport (e.g., Hylton, 2010), it is crucial for anti-sexist and anti-heterosexist sport stakeholders to embrace practices and confront the gender orthodoxies, which make sexual misconduct in sport so pervasive (e.g., Fisher & Anders, 2020). In this chapter, I argue that in the interests of social justice, we must reject knowledge that blames the victim, does not hold individuals and institutions accountable, and rewards perpetrators. In doing so, I will further argue that we must stand against neoliberal remedies of sexual misconduct by reconsidering what it means to be a bystander, enforcing institutional accountability and advocating for restorative justice.

Theorizing Common Knowledge

To become common knowledge, the *thing* that was previously not shared, a secret, becomes widely known among members of a community. It becomes an open secret. For example, an athlete confides in a fellow teammate that she was sexually assaulted. A coach might have overheard the conversation and reported it to an administrator. Here, a secret becomes a rumor and eventually becomes shared knowledge within the community.

Such was the case of Maggie Nichols, a former elite gymnast and student-athlete at Michigan State University. In 2015, she reported that she had been abused by the team physician, Larry Nassar. One of the coaches, Sarah Jantzi, overheard a conversation between Nichols and another teammate and reported the conversation to USA Gymnastics (Hampel, 2018; Maine, 2020). News of Larry Nassar's deviant sexual behaviors then became public knowledge in September 2016 when Rachel Denhollander, another survivor of Nassar's abuse, told her story to reporters at the *IndyStar* (Evans et al., 2016; Hampel, 2018).

Common knowledge is more than what many or most people know. It can also be thought of as conventional wisdom or "common sense" that is produced and transmitted through powerful institutional discourses and discursive practices (Foucault, 1991). Foucault described discourses as *regimes of truth*: The absolute ideas, thoughts, and knowledge taught to individuals through political, cultural, social, and educational institutions like the government, the media, the family, and schools (Foucault, 1991; Gasparatou, 2017; Snir, 2018, 2020). Through institutions like these, regimes of truth create "common sense" understandings of the human experience that become self-evident and part of an *essential* human condition. By *essential*, I am simply stating these discourses do the concomitant work of creating common sense understandings that make it appear as if they are *normal* and existed prior to the discourses that created them. Said in another way, common knowledge is not located in individual thought; it is socially produced, mutually reinforced, and constantly re-defining itself through institutional discourses—it is the taken for granted ideas we have about the *thing*, whatever that thing may be.

Further, Foucault (1998) argued we should not view the discursive power in binary categories of *dominant* and *subordinate* because discourse, by its very nature, is fragile and constantly contested:

> We must make allowance for the complex and unstable process whereby discourse can be both an instrument and an effect of power, but also a hindrance, a stumbling-block, a point of resistance and a starting point for an opposing strategy. Discourses transmit and produce power; it reinforces it, but also undermines and exposes it, renders it fragile and makes it possible to thwart it. In like manner, silence and secrecy are a shelter, anchoring its prohibitions.
>
> (p. 101)

Discourses that place blame on the victim and holds individuals instead of institutions accountable are not absolute in power. They require enormous resources on the part of an institution to preserve. They also provide space for individual human agency and the possibility for counter-narratives which undermine and expose the lack of institutional accountability.

Lastly, common knowledge is constructed by neoliberal ideologies that privilege certain types of masculinity over others in Western societies (Coakley, 2011). In North American culture, the masculine ideal is embodied as the heterosexual, able-bodied, upper-class white male who is the *big wheel, sturdy as an oak, gives 'em hell*, and is not a *sissy* (Brannon, 1976). These masculine pillars are inextricably coupled to neoliberal ideologies. Coakley (2011) defined neoliberalism as a "web of ideas and beliefs that identifies a combination of free markets, political deregulation and privatization, individual self-interest, and inequality as the foundation for progress" (p. 69). He argued neoliberalism, as a theoretical construct, developed from 19th-century notions of a liberal, a person "who supported individual liberty and opposed the arbitrary and pervasive control of government and religious organizations that supported an exclusive ruling class" (p. 69). Coakley (2011) suggested that as an organizing principle for human relations, neoliberalism emphasizes the individual pursuit of human progress within a free-market system that is not only essential for social progress but also useful for generating solutions to social problems. In other words, common knowledge within a (masculine) neoliberal context is influenced by ideas of individual freedom, autonomy, and accountability where competition and hierarchy are necessary for the maintenance of cultural norms.

In sum, common knowledge is a communicative strategy *and* part of a cultural body project or body pedagogic (Shilling, 2018) that teaches individuals which bodies matter (and subsequently which do not), thus stratifying bodies while simultaneously (de)legitimizing difference. A notable example is the negation of black bodies via legitimizing discourses found in hashtags like #AllLivesMatter; hashtags like these erase histories of disenfranchisement and disempowerment, obscuring white supremacist culture while proclaiming equal opportunity is possible through a strong work ethic. Along these lines (and as I argue next), hegemonic, neoliberal masculine discourses of sexual misconduct work in ways to suture, structure, and limit knowledge about bodies as perpetrators, victims, or bystanders of sexual abuse or sexual violence. Common knowledge and its allusions to human agency as the remedy for sexual misconduct ignore the social structures and institutional barriers which, by design, were created to undermine the agency of certain bodies. In the specific cases of Larry Nassar and Richard Strauss, common knowledge did not stop or hinder abuse or become a safeguard for the athletes; on the contrary, common knowledge led to behaviors that sought to protect the perpetrators.

The Cases of Larry Nassar and Richard Strauss

The sexual misconduct cases of Dr. Larry Nassar and Dr. Richard Strauss are highlighted in this chapter because they represent a pattern of how sexual misconduct in sport can be an *open secret* among athletes, coaches, and administrators, especially when the perpetrator is a well-respected member of a high-performance team (Kaufman, 2018). These cases are unique in that Nassar was the male perpetrator in one case who sexually abused girls and college-aged women, whereas Strauss abused college-aged men. These cases are also significant because they illustrate how common knowledge of sexual conduct in sport operates in ways that make some forms of it more culturally recognizable than others.

Larry Nassar and the USA Gymnastics Case

In January 2018, Ingham County Circuit Court Judge Janice Cunningham sentenced Lawrence G. Nassar up to 175 years in prison for pleading guilty to seven counts of criminal sexual conduct during his tenure as a team physician for Michigan State University (MSU) and USA Gymnastics. Prior to his sentencing, Judge Cunningham allowed more than 150 young women and teenagers to confront Nassar via survivor impact statements (Schonbrum & Hauser, 2018). Nassar also admitted abusing young gymnasts at the Karolyi Ranch Olympic training facility in Texas run by Marta and Bela Karolyi, two pioneers of the sport. In addition, he confessed to abusing athletes at Twistars Gymnastics Club located outside Lansing, Michigan.

Founded by John Geddert in 1996, Twistars was the training ground for some of best gymnasts in the world. Geddert met Nassar in 1996, and eventually coached Aly Raisman, Gabby Douglas, McKayla Maroney, Kyla Ross, and Jordyn Wieber, the members of the *Fierce Five* women's gymnastics team; they earned a gold medal during the 2012 Olympic Games in London. In 2015, Maggie Nichols became the first athlete to report Nassar to USA Gymnastics. Rachael Denhollander brought the case into the public spotlight in September 2016 when she did an interview with the *IndyStar*. In 2017, *Fierce Five* members McKayla Maroney and Aly Raisman also publicly accused Nassar. Maroney tweeted about her abuse under the #MeToo hashtag (Connor, 2017) while Raisman did an interview with CNN and went even further by indicting USA Gymnastics for its toxic culture, which blamed the victims and did little to stop the perpetrator (Fisher & Anders, 2020; Park, 2017).

Richard Strauss and Ohio State University Case

Unlike Larry Nassar, Richard Strauss was never convicted of a sex crime or brought to justice for his alleged crimes as he committed suicide in August 2005. According to a report commissioned by Ohio State University and attained by *The Columbus Dispatch*, Strauss allegedly abused 177 male athletes over the course of his 20-year tenure as a team physician, which included at least 1,429 incidents of fondling and 47 instances of male rape (Smola, 2018; Wertheim, 2020). Strauss began his career at Ohio State in 1978 as an assistant professor in the College of Medicine, and like Nassar who also worked at a Big Ten university volunteered his services with the university's athletics/physical education program before he was hired full-time in 1981 as the associate director of the sports medicine program (Wertheim, 2020). In 1994, he was hired as a part-time doctor in Ohio State's Student Health Center and began providing services to the general student population. Strauss was dismissed from Student Health and the athletics department in 1997 after a university investigation into his misconduct.

Unlike that of Nassar, Strauss's misconduct was not publicly revealed until decades later. His downfall came when male students first notified university officials of Strauss's abuses (Edmondson & Tracy, 2018). One of them, Steve Snyder-Hill, who is currently an advocate for LGBTQ rights having served under the US Army's *Don't Ask, Don't Tell* policy, claimed he was fondled by Strauss in the 1990s during a visit to the Student Health clinic (Edmondson & Tracy, 2018). Strauss was dismissed from his position after additional complaints culminating in a 1996 incident where a student stormed out of the health clinic proclaiming in front of other students that Strauss was a pervert. In an article in *The Columbus Dispatch*, Snyder-Hill, who was student at the time, admitted he was struggling with his sexual identity and Strauss's abuse complicated his ability to come out as it made him feel that he had brought the abuse upon himself (Smola, 2018). Strauss, who was pinned with nicknames like *Dr. Feel Good, Dr. Jelly Fingers*, and *Dr. Drop-Your-Drawers,* was also known to hang out in the wrestlers' shower and locker room (Wertheim, 2020). Strauss allegedly abused several competitive wrestlers, including Mark Coleman, who had been an All-America wrestler at Miami University (Ohio) before transferring to Ohio State; he would later go on to a successful career in mixed martial arts (MMA). While Strauss did not hold an official position in USA Wrestling, Strauss was known for his expertise in performance enhancing drugs (PEDs), publishing articles on the subject in prestigious journals like the *Journal of the American Medical Association* (*JAMA*) (Bresnahan & Desiderio, 2019). In 1998, the Strauss case became part of public knowledge when news accounts surfaced about US Senator Jim Jordan, who was an assistant wrestling coach at Ohio State from 1986 to 1994 during Strauss's tenure; Jordan claimed that at the time he was unaware of Strauss's alleged abuses (Bresnahan & Desiderio, 2019).

Troubling Common Knowledge of Sexual Misconduct in Sport

The Nassar and Strauss incidents illustrate the complexities of sexual misconduct in sport and the ways in which men in power can continue to abuse athletes while under the gaze of administrators, coaches, and other athletes. When the reporters of the IndyStar broke the Nassar case, it took more than public knowledge of the case for other media outlets to pay attention due to gender discrimination and the lack of interest in covering the stories of female athletes (Fisher & Anders, 2020). Likewise, Strauss's conduct was not taken seriously by the Ohio State Buckeye athletics program until Steve Snyder-Hill, a student who was not an athlete, complained about Strauss to university officials.

Both cases also highlight how (communication) networks are instrumental to sustaining sexual misconduct within sport settings. Within these networks, primarily composed of white, powerful men, a definition of what sexual misconduct is and how it should be handled is reinforced through communicative practices. Gentile's (2018) analytic framework, which considers the interconnections among bystanderism, institutional betrayal, and restorative justice, is potentially a useful tool for disrupting or troubling sexual misconduct.

Bystanderism

To contest sexual misconduct, Gentile (2018) asked us to reconsider definitions of what it means to be a bystander. The term *bystander effect* came into prominence after the 1964 Kitty Genovese incident where Genovese was stabbed to death right outside of her apartment complex in the Kew Gardens neighborhood of Queens, New York, while her neighbors looked on and allegedly did nothing (Kaufman, 2018). Although the accuracy of the *New York Times* article has since been refuted and supplemented with accounts that some members of the community did in fact notify authorities (Manning et al., 2007), the concept has become the primary Western cultural understanding of being a bystander and has led to bystander intervention programs that are designed under the false assumption that most individuals will act if they have the necessary knowledge and tools to do so (Gentile, 2018).

Gentile (2018) contended this approach may "disrupt victim-blaming, thereby helping to shift social norms . . . with an understanding of differential positions of cultural power" (p. 655) and may allocate bystander interventions as "communal forms of resistance" (p. 656). Despite its merits, I would argue this understanding of the bystander position has the potential to do harm, particularly in sport settings, because it situates the bystander as a third party who has the victim's best interests in mind. Oftentimes, bystanders in sport settings do not intervene because of fear of a material loss or fear of retaliation.

Steve Penny, John Geddert, and the Karolyis were bystanders and complicit with Larry Nassar's abuse. In many ways, like Nassar, they were co-conspirators or at the very least enablers, as they colluded to socially construct Larry Nassar as a highly competent, ethical, and respected team physician (Cohen & Shenk, 2020). Nassar himself relied on this common knowledge in conversations with law enforcement to deny and negate claims made against him by accusers like Maggie Nichols, asserting these athletes either misinterpreted his intentions or were ignorant of standard medical practices (Cohen & Shenk, 2020). As bystanders, Penny and others were able to "stand back" and let Nassar abuse his victims and were on "stand by" ready to deny and cover up Nassar's abuses.

Following Gentile (2018), I suggest that we re-conceive the bystander as a cultural space that can be jointly occupied by victim and perpetrator:

> The bystander may be the third, the witness, but . . . the bystander position is in close proximity to both victim and perpetrator. After all, a bystander has to know and recognize both the conditions for potential states of victimization and perpetration, and the various ways these co-merge and intermingle. Here the knowledge that we could all be victims or perpetrators is held and used not to fuel blame, disassociation, and shame, but instead to stimulate reflective and realistic action.
>
> *(pp. 665–666)*

To re-think the definition of bystander in sport settings is to consider that all athletes, coaches, officials, and administrators have the potential to be or become sexual perpetrators. An athlete who has been sexually abused by a coach may also have abused one of his teammates during a hazing ritual. A coach who witnessed the sexual abuse of one of her athletes may have at one time been a perpetrator or a victim. Sexual misconduct prevention programs and initiatives that are specifically designed for sport like *Coaching Boys into Men* and *Safe Sport* should consider how language of institutional accountability and responsibility are interwoven into the design, development, and delivery of these programs. *Coaching Boys into Men* specifically states that the program was designed to counter *social norms* (Miller et al., 2016).

Heteronormative discourses inscribe a natural immunity to deviance on white male bodies by upholding upper-class, able-bodied white heterosexual male bodies as the cultural ideal. This goes against Gentile's (2018) claim that most individuals who sexually exploit are white, privileged men in positions of power. In other words, common knowledge, generated by hegemonic discourses, renders the transgressions of normative white male bodies culturally unintelligible—until their transgressions can no longer be denied. Moreover, common knowledge, undisrupted, conceals the intersectional nature (Crenshaw, 1990) of sexual misconduct. Intersectionality refers "various ways in which race and gender interact to shape the multiple dimensions of Black women's . . . experiences" (Crenshaw, 1990, p. 1244). Female athletes of color, for example, may find it even more difficult to confront their abusers due to gender and racial discrimination (Fisher & Anders, 2020). Trans women athletes of color, like former MMA fighter Fallon Fox, can experience even more harm due to multiple, marginalized identities that are systematically ignored or rendered as deviant. Notably, Simone Biles, while one of the most celebrated US gymnasts in history, was one of the last athletes to disclose that she, too, was a victim of Nassar (Connor, 2017).

Strauss may have been protected by the cultural myths that male coaches, athletes, officials, and administrators are heterosexual, that heterosexual men cannot *truly* sexually abuse each other, that men who *are* abused are weak, effeminate, and possibly closeted homosexuals, and that male athletes, especially those who compete in aggressive contact sports like wrestling, fencing, and football are especially immune from abuse. These myths are further complicated by the cultural reality that hazing practices occurring in men's sport—even those of a sexual nature—are oftentimes seen by coaches and other athletes as a valuable component to building team cohesion (Fogel & Quinlan, 2020; Jeckell et al., 2018; Stuart, 2013). While Strauss's fondling of male athletes was not perceived as a hazing ritual to the wrestlers he abused (Edmondson & Tracy, 2018), his conduct was well-known among the coaching staff; nicknames like *Dr. Feel Good* and *Dr. Jelly Fingers* convey that Strauss's alleged abuses were not only part of the common knowledge within the Buckeyes program, but they were also not to be taken seriously.

Institutional Betrayal

Knowledge of sexual misconduct within sport is deeply rooted in institutional betrayal, the "institutional actions or inactions that exacerbate the impact of traumatic experiences" (Smith & Freyd, 2014, p. 577). What is missing from mediated accounts of Nassar and Strauss is a critical analysis of how Olympism and the Olympic sports industry—in addition to the NCAA—allowed these doctors to prey on and victimize athletes. Gentile (2018) noted that institutional bodies—like colleges and universities, the US military, the Boy Scouts of America, and the Roman Catholic Church—adopt similar strategies for dealing with sexual misconduct. These institutions seek to contain "individual bodies of the victim or offender, and one or both are split off and/or silenced for the supposed integrity of the institution" (p. 657). Further, she argued that this behavior allows institutions to protect their reputations and are a kind of boundary work that supports the cultural ideals of male sexual sovereignty, maintains the core values of the institution, and quiets the voices of victims. In sport, these ideals and values are inextricably linked to capitalist, neoliberal ideologies, and the sport ethic (Coakley, 2016).

The sport ethic is a set of guiding, interrelated, and enduring processes in the world of performance sport and promotes ideologies that athletes should strive for distinction, accept risks and play through pain, accept no obstacles in the pursuit of excellence, and be dedicated to the game above all else (Coakley, 2016). The sport ethic has the potential to do at least two things: (a) it encourages victims of sexual abuse to remain silent or be for fear of reprisal, like the loss of an athletic scholarship, and (b) it provides a haven for predators to engage in serial sexual abuse because of the power they have over the athletes. Nassar and Strauss were gatekeepers as athletes needed medical clearance from them to compete; as evidence of this, Strauss's conduct was not taken seriously until it was reported by a student (Steve Snyder-Hill) who was not a competitive athlete.

Less like the military and other well-established institutions, sport is a form of entertainment that generates billions of dollars of revenue each year. In 2017, the year Larry Nassar pleaded guilty to seven counts of criminal sexual misconduct, the sports industry in the United States generated $91 billion (Statista, 2020). In 2018, the Big Ten Conference, which includes universities like Penn State, Ohio State, and Michigan State grossed over $759 million (Berkowitz, 2019). In 2016, the year Nassar was terminated as a team physician, the total revenue for USA Gymnastics was more than $34 million (Pro Publica, 2020). Steve Penny, the president of USA Gymnastics from 2015 until 2017, had a background in sports marketing; concealing the misconduct of a highly respected team physician provided Penny with a competitive advantage in the cutthroat world of international gymnastics.

Institutional betrayal whether systemic or isolated is indicative of an institution's lack of ability or commitment to safeguard its members and is always a traumatic experience for the victim (Gentile, 2018). USA Gymnastics betrayed athletes like Maggie Nichols, who first reported Nassar's abuse to the organization in 2015, and Rachael Denhollander, who went public about her own experiences with Nassar in 2016. Steve Penny admitted he had received complaints about Nassar but initially did not report him to law enforcement, and coaches at Michigan State ignored complaints about Nassar permitting him to continue to treat athletes after he was prohibited to do so by USA Gymnastics (Hampel, 2018). Nichols, Denhollander, and others already traumatized by Nassar's abuses were re-traumatized by a system that would not name or acknowledge Nassar's sexual misconduct. In the Ohio State case, more than 20 coaches acknowledged they were aware of rumors of Nassar's misdeeds, and many of Strauss's male victims reportedly still bear the shame of what happened to them (Wertheim, 2020).

With the increased commercialization of amateur athletics and a sport ethic, which embraces the commodification of athletic bodies, sexual misconduct becomes normalized within the sports industry. Under this system, institutional betrayal becomes the norm, not the exception. Countering this norm requires solutions that not only come from the public good but are also divested from the neoliberal discourses produced within the sports industry.

Restorative Justice: Stand Up and Stand Tall

To remedy sexual misconduct, we must engage in restorative justice by ensuring that the proper procedures are put into place to safeguard victims of all genders and ages and acknowledge that acts committed against the victim are also acts committed against the community

(Gentile, 2018). In sport, coaches and other sport leaders interested in social justice must respond as a community and take responsibility for creating an environment which sanctioned sexual predators to carry out their misdeeds. In essence, we must stand up and stand tall against the oppression of institutional discourses that silence athletes and reject neoliberal ideologies that place burden on victims and ignore institutional responsibility for the acts of perpetrators. We should recognize that when it comes to sexual misconduct, we all have the potential to be victims and perpetrators. We must live with this reality, face it full on, and act as a community of bystanders (Gentile, 2018).

Discussion Questions

1. Contemplate how we define bystander in Western society. How have your notions of bystanderism changed after reading this chapter?
2. After reading this chapter, consider how members of the sporting community can disrupt the communicative practices that marginalize certain bodies in sport, and silences the voices of survivors of sexual misconduct.
3. Consider social/systemic structures of sport (e.g., patriarchy, capitalism, sexism, gender binary, homonegativism, and toxic masculinity), and how these structures align with the cultural norms of our times (e.g., hookup culture, availability of online porn, sexting/nude pic *culture,* and a society that profits from our sexual shame). Are these entities creating a perfect storm for sexual misconduct in sport?

References

Berkowitz, S. (2019, May 15). Big ten conferences had nearly $759 million in revenue in fiscal 2018, new records show. *USA Today.* www.usatoday.com/story/sports/2019/05/15/big-ten-revenue-hit-nearly-759-million-fiscal-2018/3686089002/

Brannon, R. (1976). The male sex role: Our culture's blueprint for manhood, what's it done for us lately. In D. S. David & R. Brannon (Eds.), *The forty-nine percent majority: The male sex role* (pp. 1–45). Addison Wesley Publishing Company.

Bresnahan, J., & Desiderio, A. (2019, May 17). Jim Jordan claims vindication after Ohio state sex abuse report released. *Politico.* www.politico.com/story/2019/05/17/jordan-osu-sexual-abuse-report-1331202

Coakley, J. (2011). Ideology doesn't just happen: Sports and neoliberalism. *Revista da Associación Latinoamericana de Estudios Socioculturales del Deporto, 1*(1), 67–84.

Coakley, J. (2016). *Sports in society: Issues and controversies* (12th ed.). McGraw-Hill Education.

Cohen, B., & Shenk, J. (Dirs.). (2020). *Athlete A* [Video file]. www.netflix.com/search?q=ath&jbv=81034185

Connor, T. (2017, October 18). *McKayla Maroney says Dr. Larry Nassar molested her in #MeToo post.* www.nbcnews.com/news/us-news/olympic-gymnast-mckayla-maroney-says-dr-larry-nassar-molested-her-n811766

Crenshaw, K. (1990). Mapping the margins: Intersectionality, identity politics, and violence against women of color. *Stanford Law Review, 43,* 1241–1446.

Edmondson, C., & Tracy, M. (2018, August 2). "It can happen even to guys": Ohio state wrestlers detail abuse saying #UsToo. *The New York Times.* www.nytimes.com/2018/08/02/us/politics/ohio-state-wrestlers-abuse-me-too.html

Evans, T., Alesia, M., & Kwiatkowski, M. (2016, September 12). Former USA gymnastics doctor accused of abuse. *IndyStar.* www.indystar.com/story/news/2016/09/12/former-usa-gymnastics-doctor-accused-abuse/89995734/

Fisher, L. A., & Anders, A. D. (2020). Engaging with cultural sport psychology to explore systemic sexual exploitation in USA gymnastics: A call to commitments. *Journal of Applied Sport Psychology, 32*(2), 129–145.

Fogel, C., & Quinlan, A. (2020). Sexual assault in the locker room: Sexually violent hazing in Canadian sport. *Journal of Sexual Aggression,* 1–20.

Foucault, M. (1991). *Discipline and punish: The birth of a prison.* Penguin.

Foucault, M. (1998). *The history of sexuality: The will to knowledge.* Penguin.

Gasparatou, R. (2017). On "the temptation to attack common sense". In M. A. Peters (Ed.), *Encyclopedia of educational philosophy and theory.* Springer.

Gentile, K. (2018). Assembling justice: Reviving nonhuman subjectivities to examine institutional betrayal around sexual misconduct. *Journal of the American Psychoanalytic Association, 66*(4), 647–678.

Hampel, K. (2018). Whose fault is it anyway: How sexual abuse has plagued the United States Olympic movement and its athletes. *Marquette Sports Law Review, 29*(2), 547–569.

Hylton, K. (2010). How a turn to critical race theory can contribute to our understanding of "race", racism and anti-racism in sport. *International Review for the Sociology of Sport, 45*(3), 335–354.

Jeckell, A. S., Copenhaver, E. A., & Diamond, A. B. (2018). The spectrum of hazing and peer sexual abuse in sports: A current perspective. *Sports Health, 10*(6), 558–564.

Kaufman, Z. D. (2018). When sexual abuse is common knowledge—but nobody speaks up. *Boston Globe.* https://ssrn.com/abstract=3225992

Lapchick, R. (2020, January 30). *The super bowl remains target for human trafficking.* www.espn.com/nfl/story/_/id/28607449/the-super-bowl-remains-target-human-trafficking

Leopold, J., Lambert, J. R., Ogunyomi, I. O., & Bell, M. P. (2019). The hashtag heard round the world: How# MeToo did what laws did not. *Equality, Diversity and Inclusion: An International Journal.* Advance online publication. https://www.emerald.com/insight/content/doi/10.1108/EDI-04-2019-0129/full/html

Maine, D. (2020, April 16). Oklahoma's Maggie Nichols still the "Jordan of college gymnastics" despite abrupt end to career. *ESPN.com.* www.espn.com/college-sports/story/_/id/29028685/oklahoma-maggie-nichols-jordan-college-gymnastics-abrupt-end-career

Manning, R., Levine, M., & Collins, A. (2007). The Kitty Genovese murder and the social psychology of helping: The parable of the 38 witnesses. *American Psychologist, 62*(6), 555.

Miller, E., Jaime, M. C. D., & McCauley, H. M. (2016). "Coaching boys into men": A social norms change approach to sexual violence prevention. In *Sexual violence* (pp. 227–248). Springer.

Miller-Idriss, C. (2020). *Hate in the homeland: The new global far right.* Princeton University Press.

Park, A. (2017, November 13). Aly Raisman opens up about sexual abuse by USA gymnastics doctor Larry Nassar. *Time.* https://time.com/5020885/aly-raisman-sexual-abuse-usa-gymnastics-doctor-larry-nassar/

Pro Publica. (2020). https://projects.propublica.org/nonprofits/organizations/751847871

Robertson, L. (2020, February 20). Super bowl crackdown on human trafficking yields 47 arrests and rescues of 22 victims. *Miami Herald.* www.miamiherald.com/news/local/crime/article240485101.html

Schonbrum, Z., & Hauser, C. (2018, January 31). Larry Nassar, sentenced in sexual abuse case, is back in court. *New York Times.* www.nytimes.com/2018/01/31/sports/larry-nassar-sentencing.html

Shilling, C. (2018). Embodying culture: Body pedagogics, situated encounters and empirical research. *The Sociological Review, 66*(1), 75–90.

Smith, C. P., & Freyd, J. J. (2014). Institutional betrayal. *American Psychologist, 69*(6), 575–587.

Smola, J. (2018, July 16). Former Ohio state says he filed sexual assault complaint about Strauss in the 90s. *The Columbus Dispatch.* www.google.com/search?q=former+ohio+state+student+says+he+filed+sexual+assault&oq=former+ohio+state+student+says+he+filed+sexual+assault&aqs=chrome.69i57j33i160.19118j0j4&sourceid=chrome&ie=UTF-8

Snir, I. (2018). Making sense in education: Deleuze on thinking against common sense. *Educational Philosophy and Theory, 50*(3), 299–311.

Snir, I. (2020). Gilles Deleuze: Thinking as making sense against common sense. In *Education and thinking in continental philosophy* (pp. 83–113). Springer.

Statista. (2020). www.statista.com/statistics/370560/worldwide-sports-market-revenue/

Stuart, S. P. (2013). Warriors, machismo, and jockstraps: Sexually exploitative athletic hazing and Title IX in the public school locker room. *Western New England: Law Review, 35*(2), 377–424.

Wertheim, J. (2020, October 5). Why aren't more people talking about the Ohio state sex abuse scandal. *Sports Illustrated*. www.si.com/college/2020/10/05/ohio-state-sex-abuse-daily-cover

Young, K. (2019). *Sport, violence and society*. Routledge.

3

CISHETEROSEXISM AND SEXUAL MISCONDUCT IN SPORT

Travis R. Scheadler, Bernie Compton, and Aidan Kraus

Layshia Clarendon, the first openly transgender and non-binary player in the WNBA, spoke publicly in 2018 about being sexually assaulted by an athletic department employee while playing for the University of California at Berkeley in 2009 (Fagan, 2018). Jonathan Vriesema, a gay multisport athlete while growing up, shared his coming out story in 2019 (Vriesema, 2019). While attending Calvin University, Vrisesema was sexually assaulted by one of his close friends. Vriesema discussed not having any LGBTQIA+ role models to look up to while playing youth sports but still found the strength to come out to take back his power and heal from his assault. LGBTQIA+ athletes like Layshia Carendon and Jonathan Vriesema deserve better from those who work and hold leadership positions within sporting institutions.

Sadly, lesbian, gay, bisexual, transgender, queer, intersex, asexual, and other gender and/or sexual minority (LGBTQIA+) students have similar experiences. In some cases, LGBTQIA+ students experience higher rates of sexual violence, assault, and harassment compared to their heterosexual and/or cisgender counterparts (Human Rights Campaign Staff, 2017). The Association of American Universities (AAU) has shown that 23.1% of transgender, genderqueer, gender-nonconforming, and questioning college students have reported being sexually assaulted (Cantor et al., 2015); additionally, this population of young people continues to experience higher rates of nonconsensual sexual contact involving physical force and/or incapacitation (24.4%) compared to male-identified (5.4%) or female-identified students (23.1%). Thus, those who cross normative boundaries of gender, sexual orientation, and/or sexuality challenge such norms by simply existing and are often met with questioning, resistance, hate, discrimination, and violence (Anderson & Hamilton, 2005; Atteberry-Ash et al., 2018).

In addition to the prevalence of sexual misconduct and discrimination LGBTQIA+ people face in educational settings, sport environments are also arenas for homonegativity, heteronormativity, cisheteronormativity, non-cisnegativity, and cisheterosexism. Although individuals in the LGBTQIA+ community can have positive experiences within sport, many are often at risk for mistreatment, harassment, and discrimination (Atteberry-Ash et al., 2018). Further, Gill et al. (2010) presented how athletes who identify within the LGBTQIA+ community might experience disproportionately higher rates of harassment because of

DOI: 10.4324/9781003125884-4

their gender and/or sexual orientation compared to those who identify as heterosexual and/or cisgender. However, reports of sexual assault and abuse targeting athletes who identify as LGBTQIA+ remain extremely limited within the current research (Gill et al., 2010; Kirby et al., 2008; Ohlert et al., 2018).

For example, sexual misconduct within sport has become more widely discussed and publicized in recent years (e.g., Larry Nassar of Team USA Gymnastics sexually abusing young female athletes; Dyer, 2018). However, limited research has been conducted on sexual violence toward LGBTQIA+ athletes despite the pervasive harassment and discrimination challenging them. In this chapter, we explore the unique challenges that threaten the safety of sport for LGBTQIA+ people. First, we discuss the cisheteronormative nature of sport and then examine several macro-factors contributing to this problem. We conclude with a call to action and offer ways to address these issues to make sport safe for LGBTQIA+ people.

Cisheteronormativity in Sport

Sport culture is steeped in cisheteronormativity which traditionally privileges individuals with identities that are cisgender, heterosexual, and White yet negatively impacts everyone in sport, especially LGBTQIA+ people (Linghede & Larsson, 2017). Historically, this has been a cause of concern for LGBTQIA+ individuals as they have experienced heightened prejudices and exclusion. Many in sport have not only ignored the existence of LGBTQIA+ participants but at times even been openly hostile toward the LGBTQIA+ community. For example, by June 2021, seven states had passed laws that prohibit participation of transgender girls and women in sport (Feliciano, 2021). Fans of the Mexican National Soccer Team have also been known to consistently use anti-gay slurs during matches. Fédération Internationale de Football Association (FIFA) penalized Mexico in June 2021 requiring two home games to be played without spectators; however, the two games were not specified, and the next home games are 2022 World Cup qualifiers (Goff, 2021).

Although some research suggests that instances of homonegativity in sport are decreasing (e.g., Anderson et al., 2016), other researchers highlight the persistence of sexual prejudice in sport (e.g., Denison & Kitchen, 2016; Sartore-Baldwin, 2013). While the United States Women's National Soccer Team (USWNT), for example, has openly embraced LGBTQIA+ athletes, other organizations and governments have openly expressed anti-LGBTQIA+ perspectives or have no protections for LGBTQIA+ people. For example, the Fellowship of Christian Athletes (FCA) has been known to have discriminatory beliefs toward the LGBTQIA+ community (Nye, 2019).

Melton (2013) utilizes systems theory to explain how lesbian stigma can marginalize women. Specifically, the lesbian stigma assumes that all sport women are lesbian; this limits women's opportunities and experiences in sport due to the fear of being outed (Melton, 2013). This same approach can be used to understand how LGBTQIA+ people are marginalized and can be abused in sport. For example, according to systems theory, three factors influence LGBTQIA+ stigma: Societal, organizational, and individual (Melton, 2013). Societal factors include those external to sport but that may still affect the individuals; this includes how cultural norms for gender may impact how a female athlete behaves or expresses their gender. Organizational factors operate at a group level and often include family members, peers, coaches, and athletic department culture (Melton, 2013). Athlete Ally publishes the Athletic Equality Index (AEI), which measures LGBTQ+ inclusion in collegiate athletics policies and practices (see *https://aei.athleteally.org*) which collegiate coaches, administrators, and athletes can utilize when looking at programs. Finally, individual factors include direct relationships with a coach, administrator, teammate, religious beliefs, and mental health (Greim, 2016; Melton, 2013). LGBTQIA+ people may have internalized homophobia/transphobia or the stress of being outed, impacting their mental health and performance. Thus, it is critical to understand these three systemic factors and how they operate together to reinforce the cisgender and heterosexual nature of sport.

In addition, conventionally, sport has been a space where traditional gender roles are embraced and often celebrated, especially for male athletes (Messner, 2002). Male athletes are expected to be strong, lack certain emotions, show aggression, and be both able-bodied and heterosexual. On the other hand, female athletes are encouraged to be petite, graceful, and be both able-bodied and heterosexual. Individuals who push against these roles/standards of femininity and masculinity prescribed to them are more likely to experience harassment and discrimination (e.g., Griffin, 1998; Krane & Barber, 2003). Sport also may be used as a tool to socialize and reinforce gender roles in young children (Chalabaev et al., 2013). People learn at an early age that any crossing or challenging of gender or sexuality boundaries is met with resistance, such as exclusion from peer groups (Anderson, 2005). These challenges and subsequent consequences are then reinforced throughout one's time in sport through various policies and practices. For example, in athletic handbooks, dress code policies often enforce the traditional gender norms for masculinity and femininity by limiting what athletes are to wear to certain clothing such as skirts or dresses for women (Larsen et al., 2020). These policies are often rooted in sexual stereotypes and prejudices targeting the LGBTQIA+ community.

For example, sexual prejudice refers to the negative attitudes one holds toward LGBTQIA+ individuals (Herek, 2000). These negative attitudes result from stigmas learned through personal interactions and general attitudes in our lives (Link & Phelan, 2001). Sexual stigmas are not only accepted but also sanctioned within sport; it is not unheard of for coaches to call players "soft" or "weak" or claim they "play like a girl" as a motivational tool. However, statements such as these reinforce male superiority in sport and work to develop a climate where male athletes are discouraged from displaying any feminine qualities. Therefore, the heteronormative climate created in sport favors heterosexual, cisgender individuals over LGBTQIA+ people. These power differences from sexual prejudice often result in a select few people controlling narratives about sport participation. In 2021, for instance, legislators across the United States introduced a variety of transnegative bills in attempts to limit transgender individuals' access to healthcare and ban them from participating in sport (Ronan, 2021b).

In addition, Satore and Cunningham (2010) argued that individuals have some awareness of the stigmas and expectations within sport. In fact, the stress of facing sexual misconduct—by just being one's authentic self—can impact one's overall mental and physical well-being as well as their performance (Herek, 2009). The psychological and physical toll of having to conceal one's identity is a form of abuse that often goes unnoticed within sport. Also, LGBTQIA+ individuals may blame themselves for the negative treatment they receive in sport, even though it is the responsibility of those with power in the sport system who do not always provide a safe and supportive environment. For instance, one web-based survey of 564 LGB individuals found that participants often blamed themselves for being discriminated against, resulting in feelings of rejection and internalized homonegativity (Denton et al., 2014). Self-blame for perceived or real discrimination then worsened their mental health.

Herek (1991) explained that the LGBTQIA+ population in general has been vulnerable to sexual harassment and abuse. LGBTQIA+ people in sport may also be vulnerable to such experiences within the sport environment. The bottom line is that power and power relationships are at the center of sexual abuse and harassment discussions (Kirby et al., 2008). This is because the power relationships within sport may help to set the stage for the sexual misconduct of LGBTQIA+ people.

Most sport cultures include power relationships between athletes and coaches, younger and more experienced athletes, and athletes and athletic trainers, to name a few. These imbalanced power relationships inherently put individuals with less power in vulnerable positions of experiencing sexual misconduct that may go unnoticed within sport.

For example, a coach may overhear that one of their athletes is gay. The coach may take this as an opportunity to exert their power over the athlete by explaining they will keep their secret and provide them with athletic benefits (e.g., a starting position, not getting cut from the team) in exchange for sexual favors. The LGBTQIA+ athlete is then placed in a no-win situation. Seeking help may entail identity self-disclosure (i.e., coming out), disbelief from authorities and teammates, and maltreatment from the perpetrator (e.g., verbal harassment, threats, being kicked off the team). The athlete may not even know who to seek help from, as their most trusted confidant may be their abuser. As an illustration of this, Layshia Clarendon's abuser was in a position of power as the athletic director for student services (Fagan, 2018).

A coach's or team doctor's power over an athlete also puts the athlete in a vulnerable position where they are more likely to be abused (Ohlert et al., 2018). This may especially be true for those already vulnerable to wider prejudice and discrimination such as LGBTQIA+ individuals. This power dynamic contributes to a cycle of violence and silence. In other words, the power a perpetrator has over victims often forces them into silence and prevents the victim from seeking help (Armstrong et al., 2018).

In sum, even though little research exists documenting LGBTQIA+ athletes' experience of sexual misconduct, survivor insights (e.g., Layshia Clarendon, Jonathan Vriesema) inform us that such a problem exists in sport. Results from research on the impacts of discrimination and violence suggests LGBTQIA+ athletes may be at risk of experiencing sexual misconduct as they are vulnerable—both as an athlete and as a gender or sexual minority—to compounded discrimination and violence. Policies and practices within institutions often uphold the cisheteronormative expectations that deny the LGBTQIA+ community from benefiting from sport participation. As leaders in sport, we must critically analyze how sports culture can put LGBTQIA+ people at risk of experiencing sexual misconduct.

Cisheterosexist Policies Affecting LGBTQIA+ People in Sport

The cisheterosexist culture ingrained in sport and society results in a less affirming and unsupportive environment for LGBTQIA+ people in sport, especially for those who experience sexual assault or harassment. The values of cisheterosexist culture have informed policies in governments and other institutions (e.g., sport organization, college, or university). Subsequently, various policies act as barriers for LGBTQIA+ athletes who experience sexual violence.

Baylor University in Texas, for example, has clearly stated their disdain for non-heterosexual relationships of any kind (see Baylor University, n.d.). Athletes such as Brittney Griner, a lesbian basketball player who formerly competed for Baylor University, have been and continue to be asked not to disclose their identity as LGBTQIA+. Indeed, Baylor University arguably commodified Griner's talent while simultaneously dehumanizing her by disapproving of her authentic self. Athletes at other schools or organizations may also be expected to comply with cisheteronormativity or remain silent. Asbury University, a private Christian school in Kentucky, recently allegedly dismissed two faculty members for being affirming of LGBTQIA+ students (Blackford, 2020). Even in the NFL, prospects have been questioned about their sexual orientation as if being LGBTQIA+ would be detrimental to their athletic potential (see Ziegler, 2018).

This sends a clear message to LGBTQIA+ athletes and allies that they are devalued and unwelcome. If an athlete is told to remain silent about who they are, what are the chances they will seek help if they experience any type of trauma such as sexual violence? Effective treatment would involve discussing one's sexual orientation and/or gender identity. However, coming out within such an organization may not be safe. Seeking help for sexual violence within a non-affirming organization may require an athlete to face ridicule from the services meant to support them during such a challenging time. Nonetheless, help-seeking is a critical step to address traumatic experiences (e.g., Dworkin, 2018; Dworkin et al., 2018).

Transgender individuals may face additional barriers which discourage help-seeking and limit support services. Legislators in North Carolina, for example, have previously pushed for legislation preventing transgender individuals from utilizing bathrooms which match their gender identity. Proponents of these laws suggest this would protect women and girls from sexual violence from men who enter women's and girls' restrooms (see Davis, 2018 for a review). Davis (2018) addressed this concern, contending that such an argument inappropriately assumes a perpetrator is not going to be of the same sex or gender and that a sexual perpetrator, who already is breaking a law by sexually violating someone, will not break any other laws. Indeed, these assertions inappropriately sexualize and demonize transgender individuals, and such policies create unique barriers for transgender athletes.

Additionally, transgender athletes may be provided with fewer opportunities and resources that accept and affirm their identity. However, no reputable evidence corroborates these claims. Hasenbush and colleagues (2019), for example, found that gender-inclusive non-discrimination public accommodation laws did not increase crimes in public restrooms, locker rooms, or changing rooms; instead, the authors provided evidence that such laws may decrease crimes, although at an insignificant level. Level and Levy (2017) also found that pro-equality policies decrease hate crime incidents based on sexual orientation. Inclusive, non-discriminatory policies, therefore, are important to protect LGBTQIA+ athletes and boost their well-being.

Despite the lack of evidence to support a need for proposed legislation against transgender individuals, attacks continue. At the time of this writing (July, 2021), 20 states in the United States have proposed bills to legally discriminate against transgender athletes, especially transgender girls and women. In fact, a group of Ohio Republican State Representatives introduced a bill to ban transgender athletes from participating in sport; they were even emboldened to title the bill "Save Women's Sports Act" as if transgender girls and women are not girls and women (Detwiler, 2020; Goldberg, 2021). Yet, transgender girls and women are girls and women, and gender and sex are not binaries. Concurrently, an Arkansas legislator has proposed a new amendment to their state constitution that would ban transgender people from participating in sport; the amendment, if enacted, would even subject girls to a genital examination and hormone and chromosome tests if they are questioned about their gender (Ronan, 2021a).

Gender verification is harmful and extremely invasive for cisgender and transgender girls who are questioned about their gender. Wiesemann (2011), for example, weighed the ethics of gender verification in sports and highlighted evidence of how the practice leads to all harm and no good. Specifically, the author shared that gender verification has led to unjustified disqualification from sport as well as gender and sex identity crises, social isolation, and mental health crises, including suicide. Moreover, gender verification is a form of gender-based sexual harassment and puts athletes at risk of sexual abuse (e.g., Lager & Lundberg, 2011). The process forces someone to undress, be touched, and get tested against their will. Not only is this a form of sexual harassment and assault, but it also makes athletes vulnerable to those in power—those in power can easily take advantage of their vulnerability and assault them. Transgender athletes, however, may remain silent so that they can continue participating in sport, putting them at risk for continued abuse and worsened mental health.

To be clear, these policies send a message that many politicians believe gender and sexual minority lives are not as valuable as cisheterosexual ones. The policies may also limit the resources available to an LGBTQIA+ athlete. However, it is possible, and likely, that a trans woman or gay man in sport experiences sexual violence. Not only would these athletes be struggling with sexual violence, but they must also do so with fewer resources and less justice while simultaneously managing society's belief that they are subhuman.

Instead, LGBTQIA+ athletes should be affirmed and provided with supportive resources when they experience sexual violence. Anti-LGBTQIA+ policies deny LGBTQIA+ athletes the resources required for them to move forward in their identity development to reach identity acceptance (i.e., when one validates and approves of oneself as LGBTQIA+), identity pride (i.e., when one positively reacts to and embraces oneself as LGBTQIA+), and identity synthesis (i.e., when one's identity as LGBTQIA+ is integrated with their other identities), and for them to cope with their trauma (Cass, 1979; Grossman et al., 2011; McFadden et al., 2013; Singh et al., 2011; Singh & McKleroy, 2011).

Moreover, it must be noted that this is not a comprehensive list of policies that disproportionately harm LGBTQIA+ people. Unfortunately, this only represents a brief overview of anti-LGBTQIA+ legislation within the United States. Nonetheless, these policies and many others—both within and outside US borders—need to be updated and challenged to protect LGBTQIA+ people.

Other aspects of intersectionality should also be considered when evaluating the experience LGBTQIA+ athletes have with sexual violence and the related policies that affect LGBTQIA+ people. For example, LGBTQIA+ racial minorities experience anti-LGBTQIA+ discrimination at higher rates than White LGBTQIA+ people (Whitfield et al., 2014). Cyrus (2017) also explained that LGBTQIA+ racial minorities experience discrimination from each of their minority identities, which adversely impacts their mental health. Many LGBTQIA+ athletes may also struggle with incongruence between their identity as a gender and/or sexual minority and their (or someone else's) religious beliefs. Lefevor et al. (2021), for example, argued conservative religious environments put LGBTQIA+ people at risk of rejection, remaining closeted, internalized spiritonegativity, and other forms of discrimination that negatively impact one's mental health.

However, those in sport can play a unique role in combating sexual violence and providing a safe space for LGBTQIA+ people. Leaders in sport can set an example by explicitly denouncing sexual violence, affirming LGBTQIA+ people in sport, and addressing barriers for LGBTQIA+ survivors of sexual violence. Stakeholders should also advocate for athletes, vote for legislators who support social justice causes, urge their legislators to reject these attacks, and consider testifying against these bills. Moreover, it is important to implement policies that will support LGBTQIA+ survivors of sexual violence and protect them from further perpetration by strengthening attitudes of acceptance and affirmation toward gender and/or sexual minorities.

Call to Action

For change, we urge sport leaders to take a greater interest in critically analyzing the factors affecting LGBTQIA+ people from fully and safely participating in sport. As described throughout this chapter, the cisheteronormative nature of many sport cultures creates several barriers preventing LGBTQIA+ athletes from enjoying and benefiting from sport. In fact, these cultural norms create a toxic environment detrimental to the well-being of LGBTQIA+ people. Such norms put LGBTQIA+ athletes at risk of prejudice, discrimination, and sexual misconduct (e.g., Gill et al., 2010; Melton, 2013; Osborne, 2007).

We charge sport leaders with the responsibility of taking swift action to protect LGBTQIA+ athletes. Scholars have previously suggested that teams and organizations should host pride nights or tournaments, an in-season event to promote gender and/or sexual diversity, usually during a home game (Denison & Toole, 2020; Jeanes et al., 2020). The authors found that pride events decrease homophobic language among teammates, especially when accompanied by relevant training and when team captains discourage teammates from using homophobic language (Denison & Toole, 2020; Jeanes et al., 2020). In addition, sport leaders have an obligation to inspect the manuals and other training resources they rely on to ensure they are inclusive and based in science. They should also enforce policies banning homophobic and transphobic language (i.e., discouraging such language and holding others accountable for their actions); this is an imperative action for all sport stakeholders.

Moreover, sport leaders have power, and we strongly challenge them to wield their power by challenging existing and proposed organizational and legal policies that contribute to the cisheteronormativity of sport which put LGBTQIA+ athletes at risk for experiencing prejudice, discrimination, and sexual misconduct. Freedom For All Americans (*https://freedomforallamericans.org/legislative-tracker/*) provides a useful tool that sport leaders may consider using to track legislation. However, this tool does not track organizational policies; sport leaders must do that on their own.

For sport leaders to be true allies, they must use their platforms to denounce the endless attacks against LGBTQIA+ athletes. For example, they can vote in elections, write letters to the editor, contact their legislators, and submit testimonies in support of LGBTQIA+ athletes. They can also propose policy changes within their organizations and provide affirmative care and confidential trauma-informed support for LGBTQIA+ athletes.

Conclusion

Ultimately, sport leaders have many opportunities to spark positive change to decrease the risk for prejudice, discrimination, and sexual misconduct within sport. Moreover, they have an ethical responsibility to protect the human rights and humanity of all athletes, especially athletes intentionally ignored or marginalized. Indeed, LGBTQIA+ athletes deserve to be in sport. Further, LGBTQIA+ athletes deserve to *thrive* in sport. It is long past time for sport to be a positive and inclusive space for all.

Discussion Questions

1. What does it mean for sport to have a cisheteronormative culture?
2. How do cisheteronormative culture and policies put LGBTQIA+ athletes at risk of experiencing prejudice, discrimination, and sexual misconduct?
3. What are some strategies you can use to protect LGBTQIA+ athletes?

References

Anderson, D. A., & Hamilton, M. (2005). Gender role stereotyping of parents in children's picture books: The invisible father. *Sex Roles*, *52*, 145–151. https://doi.org/10.1007/s11199-005-1290-8

Anderson, E. (2005). *In the game: Gay athletes and the cult of masculinity*. SUNY Press.

Anderson, E., Magrath, R., & Bullingham, R. (2016). *Out in sport: The experiences of openly gay and lesbian athletes in competitive sport*. Routledge.

Armstrong, E. A., Gleckman-Krut, M., & Johnson, L. (2018). Silence, power, and inequality: An intersectional approach to sexual violence. *Annual Review of Sociology*, *44*, 99–122. https://doi.org/10.1146/annurev-soc-073117-041410

Atteberry-Ash, B., Woodford, M. R., & Spectrum Center. (2018). Support for policy protecting LGBT student athletes among heterosexual students participating in club and intercollegiate sports. *Sexuality Research and Social Policy*, *15*, 151–162. https://doi.org/10.1007/s13178-017-0283-z

Baylor University. (n.d.). *Human sexuality at Baylor university*. www.baylor.edu/diversity/index.php?id=963497

Blackford, L. (2020, March 4). Asbury university confronts student anger, pain over dismissal of LGBTQ-affirming professors. *Lexington Herald Leader*. www.kentucky.com/opinion/linda-blackford/article240810706.html

Cantor, D., Fisher, B., Chinbnall, S., Townsend, R., Lee, H., Bruce, C., & Thomas, G. (2015). *Report on the AAU campus climate survey on sexual assault and misconduct*. The Association of American Universities. www.aau.edu/sites/default/files/%40%20Files/Climate%20Survey/AAU_Campus_Climate_Survey_12_14_15.pdf

Cass, V. C. (1979). Homosexual identity formation: A theoretical model. *Journal of Homosexuality*, *4*(3), 219–235. https://doi.org/10.1300/J082v04n03_01

Chalabaev, A., Sarrazin, P., Fontayne, P., Boiché, J., & Clément-Guillotin, C. (2013). The influence of sex stereotypes and gender roles on participation and performance in sport and exercise: Review and future directions. *Psychology of Sport and Exercise*, *14*(2), 136–144. https://doi.org/10.1016/j.psychsport.2012.10.005

Cyrus, K. (2017). Multiple minorities as multiply marginalized: Applying the minority stress theory to LGBTQ people of color. *Journal of Gay & Lesbian Mental Health*, *21*(3), 194–202. https://doi.org/10.1080/19359705.2017.1320739

Davis, H. F. (2018). Why the "transgender" bathroom controversy should make us rethink sex-segregated public bathrooms. *Politics, Groups, and Identities*, *6*(2), 199–216. https://doi.org/10.1080/21565503.2017.1338971

Denison, E., & Kitchen, A. (2016). *Out on the fields: The first international study on homophobia in sport*. Nielsen, Birmingham Cup Sydney 2014, Australian Sports Commission, Federation of Gay Games. www.outonthefields.com/

Denison, E., & Toole, D. (2020). Do LGBT pride games stop homophobic language in sport? In L. Walzak & J. Recupero (Eds.), *Sport media vectors: Digitization, expanding audiences, and the globalization of live sport* (pp. 129–146). Common Ground Research Network.

Denton, F. N., Rostosky, S. S., & Danner, F. (2014). Stigma-related stressors, coping self-efficacy, and physical health in lesbian, gay, and bisexual individuals. *Journal of Counseling Psychology, 61*(3), 383–391. https://doi.org/10.1037/a0036707

Detwiler, D. (2020, March 11). So-called "save women's sports act" flies in the face of NCAA guidelines on transgender athletes. *Equality Ohio.* https://equalityohio.org/so-called-save-womens-sports-act-flies-in-the-face-of-ncaa-guidelines-on-transgender-athletes/

Dworkin, E. R. (2018). Risk for mental disorders associated with sexual assault: A meta-analysis. *Trauma, Violence, & Abuse, 21*(5), 1011–1028. https://doi.org/10.1177/1524838018813198

Dworkin, E. R., Ojalehto, H., Bedard-Gilligan, M. A., Cadigan, J. M., & Kaysen, D. (2018). Social support predicts reductions in PTSD symptoms when substances are not used to cope: A longitudinal study of sexual assault survivors. *Journal of Affective Disorders, 229,* 135–140. https://doi.org/10.1016/j.jad.2017.12.042

Dyer, O. (2018). Former USA gymnastics team doctor sentenced for abusing hundreds of girl athletes. *BMJ, 360,* 1–2. https://doi.org/10.1136/bmj.k429

Fagan, K. (2018, January 17). Layshia Clarendon says in suit she was sexually assaulted while attending Cal. *ESPN.* www.espn.com/wnba/story/_/id/22136438/layshia-clarendon-alleges-sexual-assault-lawsuit-cal-employee

Feliciano, I. (2021, June 6). Pride: 2021 has set a record in anti-trans bills in America. *PBS.* www.pbs.org/newshour/show/pride-2021-has-set-a-record-in-anti-trans-bills-in-america

Gill, D. L., Morrow, R. G., Collins, K. E., Lucey, A. B., & Schultz, A. M. (2010). Perceived climate in physical activity settings. *Journal of Homosexuality, 57*(7), 895–913. https://doi.org/10.1080/00918369.2010.493431

Goff, S. (2021, June 18). FIFA punishes Mexico for fans' repeated use of homophobic slur. *The Washington Post.* www.washingtonpost.com/sports/2021/06/18/fifa-mexico-sanctions-slur/

Goldberg, S. K. (2021, February 8). *Fair play: The importance of sports participation for transgender youth.* Center for American Progress. www.americanprogress.org/issues/lgbtq-rights/reports/2021/02/08/495502/fair-play/

Greim, R. D. (2016). *You can play, but can you be yourself?: How LGBT and non-LGBT student-athletes perceive the climate of NCAA division I athletic departments* [Doctoral dissertation, University of Missouri-Kansas City]. ProQuest. https://search.proquest.com/openview/ed06f444ac4ee0e0206332a7bb52b3ab/1?pq-origsite=gscholar&cbl=18750&diss=y

Griffin, P. (1998). *Strong women, deep closets: Lesbians and homophobia in sport.* Human Kinetics.

Grossman, A. H., D'augelli, A. R., & Frank, J. A. (2011). Aspects of psychological resilience among transgender youth. *Journal of LGBT Youth, 8*(2), 103–115. http://doi.org/10.1080/19361653.2011.541347

Hasenbush, A., Flores, A. R., & Herman, J. L. (2019). Gender identity nondiscrimination laws in public accommodations: A review of evidence regarding safety and privacy in public restrooms, locker rooms, and changing rooms. *Sexuality Research and Social Policy, 16,* 70–83. https://doi.org/10.1007/s13178-018-0335-z

Herek, G. M. (1991). Stigma, prejudice, and violence against lesbians and gay men. In J. C. Gonsiorek & J. D. Weinrich (Eds.), *Homosexuality: Research implications for public policy* (pp. 60–80). Sage Publications. https://doi.org/10.4135/9781483325422.n5

Herek, G. M. (2000). The psychology of sexual prejudice. *Current Directions in Psychological Services, 9,* 19–22. https://doi.org/10.1111/1467-8721.00051

Herek, G. M. (2009). Sexual stigma and sexual prejudice in the United States: A conceptual framework. In D. A. Hope (Ed.), *Contemporary perspectives on lesbian, gay, and bisexual identities: The 54th Nebraska symposium on motivation* (pp. 65–111). Springer.

Human Rights Campaign Staff. (2017, June 23). Queer sexual assault survivors need department of education to enforce Title IX. *Human Rights Campaign.* www.hrc.org/news/queer-sexual-assault-survivors-need-department-of-education-to-enforce-titl

Jeanes, R., Lambert, K., O'Connor, J., Bevan, N., & Denison, E. (2020). *Evaluating LGBTI+ inclusion within sport and the pride cup initiative: Final report.* Monash University.

Kirby, S. L., Demers, G., & Parent, S. (2008). Vulnerability/prevention: Considering the needs of disabled and gay athletes in the context of sexual harassment and abuse. *International Journal of Sport and Exercise Psychology, 6*(4), 407–426. https://doi.org/10.1080/1612197X.2008.9671882

Krane, V., & Barber, H. (2003). Lesbian experience in sport: A social identity perspective, *Quest, 55,* 328–346. https://doi.org/10.1080/00336297.2003.10491808

Lager, G., & Lundberg, L. (2011). *Doping's nemesis: Arne Ljungqvist.* Sports Books Limited.

Larsen, L. K., Fisher, L. A., Shigeno, T. C., Bejar, M. P., & Madeson, M. N. (2020). "Do not question authority": Examining team rules in national collegiate athletic association division I women's basketball. *International Sport Coaching Journal, 7,* 317–325. https://doi.org/10.1123/iscj.2019-0077

Lefevor, G. T., Huffman, C. E., & Blaber, I. P. (2021). Navigating potentially traumatic conservative religious environments as a sexual/gender minority. In E. M. Lund, C. Burgess, & A. J. Johnson (Eds.), *Violence against LGBTQ+ persons* (pp. 317–329). Springer. https://doi.org/10.1007/978-3-030-52612-2_25

Level, B. L., & Levy, D. L. (2017). When love meets hate: The relationship between state policies on gay and lesbian rights and hate crime incidence. *Social Science Research, 61,* 142–159. https://doi.org/10.1016/j.ssresearch.2016.06.008

Linghede, E., & Larsson, H. (2017). Figuring more livable elsewheres: Queering acts, moments, and spaces in sport (studies). *Journal of Sport and Social Issues, 41*(4), 290–306. https://doi.org/10.1177/0193723517707700

Link, B. G., & Phelan, J. C. (2001). Conceptualizing stigma. *An Annual Review of Sociology, 27,* 363–385. https://doi.org/10.1146/annurev.soc.27.1.363

McFadden, S. H., Frankowski, S., Flick, H., & Witten, T. M. (2013). Resilience and multiple stigmatized identities: Lessons from transgender persons' reflections on aging. In J. D. Sinnott (Ed.), *Positive psychology: Advances in understanding adult motivation* (pp. 247–267). Springer Science+Business Media, LLC. http://doi.org/10.1007/978-1-4614-7282-7_16

Melton, N. E. (2013). Women and the lesbian stigma. In M. L. Sartore-Baldwin (Ed.), *Sexual minorities in sports: Prejudice at play* (pp. 11–30). Lynne Rienner Publishers.

Messner, M. A. (2002). *Taking the field: Women, men, and sports.* University of Minnesota Press.

Nye, E. (2019, January 7). Fellowship of Christian athletes targets LGBTQ community with statement of faith. *Outsports.* www.outsports.com/2019/1/7/18173087/fellowship-of-christian-athletes-gay-lgbt

Ohlert, J., Seidler, C., Rau, T., Rulofs, B., & Allroggen, M. (2018). Sexual violence in organized sport in Germany. *German Journal of Exercise and Sport Research, 48,* 59–68. https://doi.org/10.1007/s12662-017-0485-9

Osborne, B. (2007). "No drinking, no drugs, no lesbians": Sexual orientation discrimination in intercollegiate athletics. *Marquette Sports Law Review, 17*(2), 481–501. https://scholarship.law.marquette.edu/sportslaw/vol17/iss2/3/

Rankin, S., & Merson, D. (2012). LGBTQ national college report. *Campus Pride.* www.campuspride.org/wp-content/uploads/CampusPride-Athlete-Report-Exec-Summary.pdf

Ronan, W. (2021a, March 25). Breaking: Arkansas Gov. Asa Hutchinson signs anti-trans sports bill. *Human Rights Campaign.* www.hrc.org/press-releases/breaking-arkansas-gov-asa-hutchinson-signs-anti-trans-sports-bill

Ronan, W. (2021b, May 7). 2021 officially becomes the worst year in recent history for LGBTQ state legislative attacks as an unprecedented number of states enact record-shattering number of anti-LGBTQ measures into law. *Human Rights Campaign.* www.hrc.org/press-releases/2021-officially-becomes-worst-year-in-recent-history-for-lgbtq-state-legislative-attacks-as-unprecedented-number-of-states-enact-record-shattering-number-of-anti-lgbtq-measures-into-law

Sartore-Baldwin, M. L. (2013). Gender, sexuality, and prejudice in sport. In M. L. Sartore-Baldwin (Ed.), *Sexual minorities in sports: Prejudice at play* (pp. 1–10). Lynne Rienner Publishers.

Satore, M. L., & Cunningham, G. B. (2010). The lesbian label as a component of women's stigmatization in sport organizations: An exploration of two health and kinesiology departments. *Journal of Sport Management, 24,* 481–501. https://doi.org/10.1123/jsm.24.5.481

Singh, A. A., Hays, D. G., & Watson, L. S. (2011). Strength in the face of adversity: Resilience strategies of transgender individuals. *Journal of Counseling and Development, 89*(1), 20–27. http://doi.org/10.1002/j.1556-6678.2011.tb00057.x

Singh, A. A., & McKleroy, V. S. (2011). "Just getting out of bed is a revolutionary act": The resilience of transgender people of color who have survived traumatic life events. *Traumatology, 17*(2), 34–44. http://doi.org/10.1177/1534765610369261

Vriesema, J. (2019, September 26). A shattering sexual assault led gay athlete to confront his identity and seize control of this life. *Outsports*. www.outsports.com/2019/9/26/20861926/jonathan-vriesema-gay-sports-coming-out

Whitfield, D. L., Walls, N. E., Langenderfer-Magruder, L., & Clark, B. (2014). Queer is the new Black? Not so much: Racial disparities in anti-LGBTQ discrimination. *Journal of Gay & Lesbian Social Services, 26*(4), 426–440. https://doi.org/10.1080/10538720.2014.955556

Wiesemann, C. (2011). Is there a right not to know one's sex? The ethics of "gender verification" in women's sports competition. *Journal of Medical Ethics, 37*(4), 216–220. http://doi.org/10.1136/jme.2010.039081

Ziegler, C. (2018, March 8). NFL team that asked player about being gay should lose a draft pick. *Outsports*. www.outsports.com/2018/3/8/17095278/nfl-draft-gay-pick-derrius-guice-punishment

4
GROOMING AND SPORT

Stiliani "Ani" Chroni and Anna Kavoura

Who doesn't like and want to receive one-to-one attention, to be enchanted, to feel special? Athlete development is contingent upon individualized attention, training, feedback and care from the coach, and athlete entourage, yet upon listening to the many stories of athlete abuse, we have come to understand that individualized attention is not always genuine. Hanne's experience with attention received from her coach—as she retold her story—(Fasting & Sand, 2015) is a perplexing one:

> She lived far from where they practised and it all started when the coach started driving her home. Since they both lived in a different direction from the rest of her team it was natural. She had the coach for one or two years before the relationship started to change
>
> But then he started asking if we could go for a ride. He wanted to talk to me. And I thought that there was nothing wrong with that. Of course we can. And then he told me that he was getting divorced from his wife and that he liked me really a lot. . . . He told me that he had a hard time, and that his wife wasn't nice to him. He played on my feelings, on me as caring, and you know, I then felt sorry for him. I remember he touched my hair and said, 'She's not like you.' And he charmed me, you know. And there I was, a victim in his world, I believe.
>
> (Hanne's story, as cited in Fasting & Sand, 2015, p. 579)

Alas, the attention, charm, and affection provided to Hanne by her coach bore no resemblance to that of a caring coach (see Cronin & Armour, 2018; Fisher et al., 2019; Purdy et al., 2016). Instead of being attentive to, or caring about and for Hanne, the coach tried to control, manipulate her feelings with amplified attention, charm her, and show care as a way to prime her to be seduced. Soon enough, his attention became disagreeable and offensive to Hanne—it became unwanted attention.

In the past 50 years, law enforcement specialists, lawyers, and scholars have placed particular attention on clarifying, understanding, and locating the process of priming a person

DOI: 10.4324/9781003125884-5

(particularly children) for being sexually exploited (Lanning, 2018). According to Lanning (2018), who worked with children's cases of sexual victimization for more than four decades, perpetrators nurture control over their victims mainly through the seduction or grooming process.

Grooming: An Act of Preparation

In looking at how the term evolved, it appears that "the concept and use of the term *grooming* gradually emerged during the 1980s with the growing recognition of cases perpetrated by extrafamilial acquaintance offenders (i.e., *sexual exploitation of children*)" (Lanning, 2018, p. 7). As Lanning (2018) noted, what was of importance in the 1980s was understanding the technique and process of gaining access to and control over child victims. Among law enforcement experts, the term *seduction* was initially used to describe well-planned nonviolent ways to lure child victims by providing attention, affection, kindness, privileges, games, gifts, trips, alcohol, drugs, and money. The technique appeared to be simple:

> These offenders essentially seduced children much the same way as adults seduce one another. Between two adults or two teenagers, it might be considered part of dating. Use of these nonviolent techniques increased the likelihood of cooperation of and continued access to the victim and, very important to the offender, decreased the likelihood of disclosure even of a nonfamily offender whose identity is well known to the victim. Use of violence would increase the likelihood of early discovery and disclosure of such acquaintance offenders.
>
> *(Lanning, 2018, pp. 8–9)*

According to Lanning (2018), Conte (1984) was the first to label this repulsive process as grooming in a written document. Yet, in the description he offered for it—"the perpetrator involves children in sexual abuse through a grooming process in which a combination of kindness, attention, material enticement, special privilege, and coercion are expertly applied" (p. 558)—he referenced the work of Groth and Birnbaum (1979).

A number of definitions and terms for grooming are in place today. These include *seducing, priming, conditioning, and training* (i.e., Lanning, 2018; Sinnamon, 2017).

Some scholars delineate grooming as a concept and others as a process (e.g., Brackenridge, 2001; Gillespie, 2002; Lanning, 2018; Sinnamon, 2017). However, the lack of a universally accepted definition makes it difficult to pinpoint grooming as it occurs (Bennett & O'Donohue, 2014; Craven et al., 2006).

Grooming as a Process

Lanning (2018) defines grooming as a concept which "generally refers to specific techniques used by some child molesters to gain access to and control of their child victims" (p. 6) and points out how a perpetrator's practices are influenced by the relationship between the perpetrator and the target. He and others who describe grooming as a process also comment on how difficult it is to pinpoint when it starts and ends or the length of it; it can last from weeks to years as the perpetrator progresses slowly and carefully to avoid exposure (Gillespie, 2002; Lanning, 2018). They attempt to avoid discovery by testing the victim to see whether they will disclose the coercion or exploitation of power (Brackenridge & Fasting, 2005). Gillespie (2002) also defined grooming as a process by which a child is befriended by a would-be abuser in an attempt to gain the child's confidence and trust, enabling them to get the child to acquiesce to abusive activity. It is frequently a pre-requisite for an abuser to gain access to a child (p. 411).

Sinnamon's (2017) definition is somewhat shorter, outlining grooming as a "process of deliberately establishing a connection in order to prepare a person for sexual exploitation and/or abuse" (p. 462).

In general, therefore, grooming refers to the activities that prepare a person for abuse which might not be aggressive, violent, abusive, or illegal in and of themselves. For instance, a coach driving an athlete home after practice is a harmless act; yet, for Hanne in Fasting and Sand's (2015) study, the drive home was the way for her coach to charm, prime, seduce, and groom her. Looking at grooming from a forensic perspective (and what could and could not be admissible in forensic settings), Bennett and O'Donohue (2014) critically evaluated grooming definitions. They found commonalities in the criterion for preparing one for abuse, in the ways of gaining one's trust, the accounting of particular tactics used to groom, etc. They also found essential differences, with some definitions being concrete examples, some vague and brief, and others being long and detailed on what grooming looks like. Furthermore, they placed attention on complications apparent in existing definitions such as some definitions employing terms that require further definitions and others proposing stages of grooming.

On the basis of the commonalities, differences, and complexities identified, Bennett and O'Donohue (2014) proposed a definition which they thought was more operational than ones previously reviewed. They defined grooming as an "antecedent inappropriate behavior that functions to increase the likelihood of future sexual abuse" (p. 969) and proposed that two individual criteria ought to be met for a behavior to be considered as grooming:

> (a) the behavior being evaluated must in and of itself be inappropriate and a case for this inappropriateness must be made, and (b) a sound argument must be presented that the behavior or behaviors increases the likelihood of future sexual abuse.
>
> (p. 969)

Bennett and O'Donohue (2014) further clarified their definition through a number of grooming exemplars such as inappropriate touching (e.g., excessive hugging, tickling), inappropriate isolation of the child (e.g., trips alone with the athlete-target), inappropriate nonsexual communication (e.g., saying that only the victim understands the perpetrator), and asking one to keep secrets. In Fasting and Sand's (2015) case of Hanne, the coach driving her home from practice satisfies the second criterion of Bennett and O'Donohue (2014) with the sound argumentation that the drive home was an act of inappropriate isolation of the athlete combined with inappropriate nonsexual communication.

Grooming in the Sport Realm

Leberg (1997) looked beyond defining grooming as a behavior toward a particular person and acknowledged grooming as a wider social process. Leberg categorized grooming into three domains: Physical, psychological, and grooming of social environments. According to Dietz (2018), perpetrators "groom children and the parents of those children, the organizations through which they work or volunteer with children, and the communities in which they function" (p. 30). Perpetrators enter an environment and can get very good at reading the community, understanding and fulfilling its needs (Hare & Hart, 1993), even making themselves indispensable (Leberg, 1997). This is a groomer's pathway to gaining the trust from others in the environment.

Tanner and Brake (2013) discussed the different purposes that environmental grooming can serve: "To find victims, reduce the probability of being reported, and if reported, reduce the probability of victims being believed" (p. 2). Once a perpetrator successfully grooms a social environment, any association with a targeted victim can be viewed as legitimate, even positive and valued, which subsequently reduces the probabilities of the victim reporting him/her/them out of fear of losing this association's value but also of not being heard and believed when reporting a behavior opposite to the collective view (Craven et al., 2006; Tanner & Brake, 2013).

In the realm of sport, Brackenridge (2001) was the first to define grooming, which she captured as a process "by which a perpetrator isolates and prepares an intended victim" (p. 35). As Prewitt-White (2019) outlined on the basis of Lanning's (2010, 2018) work, the perpetrator picks a target, collects information about the target's goals, dreams, interests, and weaknesses, gains access to the target in order to spend time alone, weakens the target's reservations, and through bonding activities secures and maintains control over the target. Whether inside or outside sport, the process of grooming does not appear to be different; yet, inside sport—besides the nonviolent and calculated practices—the perpetrator also tenders the athlete-target with "intangible feelings of being special, high self-esteem, confidence, superiority and security" (Brackenridge & Fasting, 2005, p. 36).

In addition, the process of grooming is not affected much by the gender of the athlete-target (Hartill, 2009, 2014) and does not appear to be different between children and adult victims (Sinnamon, 2017). Because early grooming behaviors appear to be innocent and harmless—and if they occur between adults could easily be part of dating (Lanning, 2018)—it is challenging to establish the occurrence of these as grooming (Bennett & O'Donohue, 2014) and the perpetrators may continue and assess carefully and strategically the response(s) of the athlete-target and persons close to them (e.g., parents, guardians, siblings, teammates) before deciding to step back if they meet resistance from the athlete-target or those in their environment (Brackenridge & Fasting, 2005).

Grooming in Sport: Priming an Athlete to Hurt: The process of grooming in the context of sport has been the focus of scholarly attention since the mid-1990s, when critical and feminist scholars revealed the occurrence of sexual harassment and abuse in our sporting cultures (e.g., Brackenridge, 1997; Lenskyj, 1992; Volkwein et al., 1997). Since then, several studies have explored the different elements that are associated with the grooming process in sport (Bisgaard & Støckel, 2020; Brackenridge & Fasting, 2005; Fasting & Sand, 2015; Hartill, 2014; McElvaney, 2019; Owton & Sparkes, 2017; Prewitt-White, 2019). Grounded in athletes' narratives of sexual abuse (Bisgaard & Støckel, 2020; Hartill, 2014), these studies have generated knowledge about the risk factors in coach-athlete relationships (Brackenridge & Fasting, 2005; Fasting & Sand, 2015) as well as theoretical frameworks and models of abuse in sport (Brackenridge, 2001; Cense & Brackenridge, 2001; Stirling & Kerr, 2014). A few rare studies have also drawn on the narratives of coaches, generating knowledge and conceptual models of their perceptions on the topic (e.g., Bringer et al., 2006).

Grooming has become a great concern for sport stakeholders, sport administrators, and parents, as athletes who experience grooming feel completely entrapped in the process and unable to resist the perpetrator's advances (Brackenridge & Fasting, 2005). In addition, the context of sport appears to offer an ideal scene for such advances to occur (Prewitt-White, 2019). Scholars have pointed out that certain elements in the sport context provide favorable conditions for sexual grooming (Mountjoy et al., 2016); one of these elements is the physicality of sport that requires close bodily proximity (Brackenridge, 2001). Sport coaching often involves touch and physical support or correction, giving opportunities for invasions of privacy (Bjørnseth & Szabo, 2018; Brackenridge & Fasting, 2005; Fisher & Anders, 2020). In fact, with regard to closeness, coach-athlete relationships in many sport subcultures resemble relationships between family members; it is perfectly normal for the coach to touch the athlete as part of their work, with the parents' trust and consent (Chroni, 2015). As such, sport has been criticized as an environment ideal for sexual abuse (Bjørnseth & Szabo, 2018).

While some sport organizations have adopted codes of contact and athlete protection guidelines to mitigate this risk, research shows that some coaches are reluctant to change their coaching behavior and often experience role conflict and ambiguity (Bringer et al., 2006). Furthermore, not all coaches view coach-athlete sexual relationships as problematic when the athlete is above the age of consent (Bringer et al., 2006). The unclear boundaries and the absence of sport-specific laws on this topic create further ambiguities.

Another favorable condition for sexual grooming in sport is the normalization of emotional abuse in our sporting cultures and especially in the coach-athlete relationship (Stirling & Kerr, 2014; Stirling et al., 2020). In fact, researchers suggest that emotional abuse (such as belittling, humiliating, shouting, scapegoating, rejecting, isolating, threatening, and ignoring) might be the most frequent form of abuse in sport (e.g., Gervis & Dunn, 2004; Kavanagh et al., 2017); sadly, it is closely tied to practices and philosophies of athlete development (Stirling & Kerr, 2014). Stirling and Kerr (2014) further noted that parents are often present when these harmful behaviors occur and athletes might be reluctant to report such abusive practices. The normalization of emotionally abusive practices in sport and the culture of acceptance and silence that surrounds them have been identified as risk factors for sexual grooming and abuse in sport (Brackenridge, 2001; Stirling et al., 2020).

Furthermore, in reading the existing literature on this topic (e.g., Brackenridge, 2001; Brackenridge & Fasting, 2005; Hartill, 2014; Owton & Sparkes, 2017), it is evident that any effort to understand the process of grooming in sport should incorporate understandings of the power dynamics and gender relations aspects of the coach-athlete relationship. As explained by Stirling and Kerr (2009), the coach-athlete relationship is often one of the most significant and influential relationships experienced by athletes. Athletes (especially those who enter the elite level at a young age) often develop a dependent relationship with their coaches—who definitely have power over them—on the basis of their knowledge and access to resources, their past sport successes, their authority to make decisions and to reward or punish, as well as their age and gender (Stirling & Kerr, 2009). Therefore, the power dynamics of the coach-athlete relationship undoubtedly contribute to an athlete's vulnerability to grooming (Brackenridge, 2001).

The gender/power hierarchies and the masculinist discourses that continue to dominate our sporting cultures also serve as a risk factor for grooming (Hartill, 2014). Critical scholars of sport have long been arguing that gender stereotypes and prejudices, man-making narratives, and the overt celebration of male hypersexuality and aggressive versions of masculinity are the antecedents of many forms of abuse in sport (Brackenridge, 2001; Lenskyj, 1992). According to Hartill (2014), these masculinist forces in sport have served to silence athletes and to protect the (usually male) perpetrators of grooming and sexual abuse in sport. The heteronormative and often homophobic scripts of sport make it even harder for male victims of grooming to speak up (Hartill, 2014), which is also the case for women who have been groomed by women (see Johansson, 2018).

However, while women can also be perpetrators of grooming (Johansson, 2018), in the vast majority of the sport-related recorded cases, the perpetrators are males in a position of power (Bjørnseth & Szabo, 2018). In fact, incidents in which male coaches have abused their positions of power to facilitate sexual relationships with much younger (often minor) athletes seem to make up most of the known cases of grooming in sport (Bjørnseth & Szabo, 2018). One explanation for this might be that up to now, women are not afforded equal power with men in sport—they are constructed as the weaker and inferior sex, and their participation in sport is often sexualized (Matthews & Channon, 2019). Yet, some studies are challenging the "male-perpetrator-female-victim" paradigm, shedding light on the perspective of the sexually abused male in sport (Hartill, 2009, 2014) as well as on cases with female perpetrators (Johansson, 2018; Sand et al., 2011). Therefore, it appears extremely important to explore how sexual abuse is situated within the power dynamics that are inherent in our sporting systems (i.e., coach-athlete relationships) versus locating sexual abuse based on a person's gender identity.

Regarding the profile of the people targeted for grooming, some studies reveal that female, children, elite, and lesbian, gay, bisexual, and transgender (LGBT) athletes, as well as athletes with disabilities might be more at risk (Bjørnseth & Szabo, 2018; Brackenridge, 2001; Parent & Vaillancourt-Morel, 2020; Vertommen et al., 2016). Young athletes at the elite level are at greater risk as they spend a great deal of time with their coaches, and, as a consequence, often consider their coach as a parental figure (Stirling & Kerr, 2014). However, more research is needed.

Grooming in Models: The Stages of Hurt: While a number of models have been developed which outline the process of grooming, retrospective identification of grooming is easier than prospective identification (Craven et al., 2006). However, understanding the process of grooming and grasping how sexual exploitation occurs are both critical for prevention and protection (Parent & Demers, 2011). We discuss next one sport-specific and one non-sport-specific model to shed light on grooming; furthermore, we use the case of one athlete to help the reader understand how a sexual abuse experience unfolds through the stages of the two models (see Table 1).

Brackenridge's Model

The most frequently cited model of grooming in sport is the one suggested by Brackenridge (2001). While she placed focus on the grooming of children, adult athletes appear to be going through the same process (Brackenridge & Fasting, 2005). Brackenridge's (2001) model has the following four stages: (1) targeting a potential victim, (2) building trust and friendship, (3) developing isolation and control, building loyalty, and (4) initiating sexual abuse and securing secrecy. According to this model, the process of grooming in sport starts by identifying a potentially vulnerable athlete-target and striking up a friendship by being nice to them, building up a parent-like relationship, or by helping the athlete-target achieve their goals, making them feel special, offering gifts, rewards, and gradually gaining their trust. The perpetrator is also checking the athlete-target out for secrecy and commitment through small tests. The initiation of sexual abuse is then facilitated by gradually tearing down the athlete-target's sexual boundaries, invoking cooperation and guilt, and threatening the victim (Brackenridge, 2001).

With regard to the victim's age, while the process of grooming may not be different for children, adolescent, and adult athletes, the societal view appears to be different on how the acts of perpetrators are perceived. In the case of children and youths, sexually coercive and manipulative tactics which gain the target's trust, break down interpersonal boundaries, and invade one's personal space are easily and clearly viewed as immoral, unethical, and, of course, illegal. In adult victims, such tactics are met with skepticism by others who doubt the legitimacy of victims' claims when occurring between two adults (Sinnamon, 2017).

Sinnamon's Model

Sinnamon (2017) developed a seven-stage model to explain the targeting of adults, their engagement in the preparatory processes for abuse, and how sexually exploitative and abusive relationships with adult victims start and continue. He characterized grooming as "an effective tool for a sexual predator as it creates a space in which the grooming process and often the abuse itself, at least initially, may be identified by the victim as a positive experience" (p. 462). In addition, confusion, guilt, fear, or a threat (overt or covert) by the abuser prevents victims from reporting the lived experience. Sinnamon (2017) defined adult sexual grooming as "any situation in which an adult is primed to permit themselves to be abused and/or exploited for sexual gratification of another . . . focusing on emotional and psychological manipulation tactics" (p. 462). Grooming progresses through a series of stages that involve the groomer masking their intentions and priming the target.

With regard to the targeting of adults, Petherick and Sinnamon (2013) found that maintaining or rebuilding sex offenders' self-esteem is what typically motivates them and they reap satisfaction for this desire via manipulating and controlling others. In addition, exhibiting power, dominance, and superiority over others equally excites and motivates them. Exerting power over a victim and one's environment is contingent upon personal characteristics of the predator like "notoriety, charisma, social status, personal standing, and the predator's willingness and ability to translate the potential power they have from these factors into action" (p. 465).

With regard to the targeted victim, they often have psycho-emotional (e.g., desire, avoidance, self-value), physical (e.g., age, physical size, disability, cultural factors), or financial vulnerabilities that make them susceptible to exploitation. Grooming is effective in the early stages because the predator provides the victim with strong elements of reward for his/her/their needs and wants. Sinnamon (2017) argued further that in preparation for grooming, perpetrators will first groom the adult victim's space; in this process, they have three objectives: To insert themselves in the target's milieu, to build credibility in the eyes of those in the target's milieu, and to deflect attention, perspective, and suspicion to remain protected by the target's social milieu.

Sinnamon's (2017) description of the stages of the grooming process describes a gradual and well-planned progression where the predator manages to entrap adults in inappropriate, exploitative, and abusive sexual relationships. Stage 1 entails *selecting the victim*; predators are very skilled in identifying potentially vulnerable adults within an environment. Stage 2 entails *gathering information*; getting to know the person well will allow the predator to exploit the target by helping them to fulfill their wants and needs. Stage 3 is about *gaining personal connection*; the aim is to strengthen the personal connection, deepen the friendship, and gain the necessary trust. Stage 4 entails *meeting the need of the target and building credentials*; here, the predator secures credibility, trust, and secrecy with the target. Stage 5 is about *priming the target*; the predator uses the previously gained trust to increase the target's psycho-emotional dependence and isolate them further from others they are close to, aiming at "lowering inhibitions, and desensitizing and habituating the target to increased sexualized intimacy" via interactions that "break down the final barriers of resistance held by the target" (p. 479). Stage 5 is the last stage of priming before a predator tries full sexual contact with the target where some nonsexual touching, dirty jokes, and intimate conversations are employed by the predator to escalate over time the sexualization of the interactions. Stage 6 entails *creating the victim* as sexual contact is instigated; once the predator assesses that the target is aptly primed, "increasingly overt sexualized interactions are introduced" (p. 480). This subtle move from priming to exploitation may make the target—now victim—feel like there was a spontaneous escalation of "an otherwise 'innocuous' interaction" (p. 481). Lastly, stage 7 is about *controlling the victim*; the predator uses guilt, secrecy, threat, bribery, and promises of reward to control the victim, and, of course, the victim's environment to sustain the exploitative relationship.

As research on grooming, abuse, abusive relationships, offenders, and victims grew in the past 40 years, Sinnamon's (2017) work delivered a far more detailed model than others on grooming. In his view, the grooming of adults is more common than generally believed. In the Table 4.1, we share the story of Sofia—a gold and bronze Olympic medalist in sailing from Greece—and situate it within the stages of Brackenridge and Sinnamon's models. Sofia broke her 23-year silence at the age of 44 following 11 years of therapy, and succeeded in firing up the #metoo movement in Greece, four years after it went viral in 2017. In Sofia's case, the perpetrator gained the athlete-target's trust by helping her (and her crew) with their federation-related problems. The text we scrutinize is the verbatim transcription of a television interview of hers (Mavridis, 2021) provided to us by Sofia as the most complete public account of her experience (S. Bekatorou, personal communication, February 10, 2021).

While one model has seven stages and the other four, the unfolding of Sofia's story helped us adjoin the stages. In other words, we found that by placing Sofia's raw story and the two models side by side, it was easier to understand how the absurd could happen. It is valuable both for researchers and safeguarding practitioners to notice how the details of Sinnamon's model can help us navigate with more clarity through the stages that Brackenridge (2001) identified almost two decades earlier.

Further, while the grooming of children and adults is not very different, Sinnamon (2017) suggested that breaking free from it appears to be a more viable option for adults. When it comes to children, their voices appear to be more marginalized in our adult-centered sporting cultures (Walters et al., 2012) and it is more difficult for them to speak up. According to Sinnamon (2017), "As adults generally have a greater potential to identify and halt the predator from progressing through the grooming process, a sexual predator who engages with adult victims will likely have their plans fractured regularly" (p. 486). However, with regard to sport and its nuances, it appears that exiting an exploitative relationship or stopping an abusive behavior may still be challenging for the adult athlete, considering what is at stake for the victim (Chroni, 2015); in Sofia's case, the scale tilted heavily toward safeguarding her participation at the Olympic Games versus saving herself from the predator.

TABLE 4.1 How does it happen: An Olympic athlete's story and the stages of grooming by Brackenridge (2001) and Sinnamon (2017).

Brackenridge (2001)	Sinnamon (2017)	The account of Sofia's experience of sexual abuse and the stages of grooming
Stage 1 Targeting a potential victim	Stage 1 Selecting the victim Stage 2 Gathering information	We were at war with the federation. Some of the federation board members had intimidated us [Sofia and crew]; at various meetings I was personally attacked, I was told I am nothing, that I won't manage to bring medals and that they didn't expect a thing from me. . . . Every time we visited the federation we had to negotiate for things we were entitled to, like going to certain trips, representing our country, having money for traveling, and of course for equipment as sailing is a technical sport.
Stage 2 Building trust and friendship	Stage 3 Gaining personal connection	One person from the federation board was actually more friendlier so we had turned all our hopes to him thinking he could defend our rights; he was the only one who didn't seem to be ill-intentioned. Gradually a friendlier relationship developed with him
	Stage 4 Meeting the target's need and building credentials	[W]hen we had problems, my crew and I mainly talked with him, and he would then represent us to the president of the federation . . . through his representation our issues somehow were being resolved.
Stage 3 Developing isolation and control; building loyalty	Stage 5 Priming the target	we thought this man was on our side . . . and when we heard he would be with us on that trip we were relieved. We were travelling with the men's team and our coach . . . I was the youngest on the team and for me it would be my first participation at the Olympics [in that trip Sofia qualified for the OG]. The last day we went out to celebrate all together . . . and returning to the hotel we walked in pairs. The federation board member and I left last and were talking; I was excited waiting to share my experiences and talk about the Olympics, I was going to Sydney! As we were walking, suddenly he turned and kissed me. I froze, I was surprised. I couldn't understand where this came from. I didn't know what to do . . . we were walking uphill . . . I walked away from him . . . and then [walking on different sidewalks] we continued towards our hotel.
Stage 4 Initiating sexual abuse and securing secrecy	Stage 6 Creating the victim	We got into the elevator and when it stopped at his [floor], he asked, will you come to my room? I replied, there is no reason and [said] good night. He went on saying, Come [for] two minutes, [I want] to talk to you. I was scared from his previous move, so I was very hesitant. He said, come on, are you scared? Of course not, I'm not afraid, I replied. I wasn't a little girl who didn't have a personality; I thought I could handle any difficulty, I will go [I decided] . . . When I entered at first we were talking about the regatta, then he started getting closer to me. I started defending myself. Then he started trying to persuade me saying, come here for a while, let me talk to you. Eventually, he started to touch me

(Continued)

TABLE 4.1 (Continued)

Brackenridge (2001)	Sinnamon (2017)	The account of Sofia's experience of sexual abuse and the stages of grooming
		more, kiss me, threw me on the bed . . . I told him, I do not want. Come on, it's nothing [he mumbled] . . . I do not want [I said again]. I tried in my way to show him that there's no mutual desire, there's no consent. He was ignoring what I was saying, acting as if I was crazy. At moments he was getting rough, he saw I was moving away, he would stop. He waited a bit [and] the same thing again. I got up to leave, come on, where are you going now, he would say. At one point he was on top of me, [I remember] I told him, I can't believe you don't understand I am telling you I don't want [this]. He continued. I was frozen. The first thing I thought at that time was to react, to beat the shit out of him, but I knew he had a very vital position with the federation and there was no one to witness, no one knew what was going on, and everyone would say, why did you go back with him, and why didn't you walk back with the others? But [earlier] I wasn't afraid, didn't have a reason to be afraid to go back alone [with him]. Besides, I was always independent. When it was over . . . I realized that he had raped me.
	Stage 7 Controlling the victim	. . . since they had so much power over us, and despite our [sailing] abilities we needed to have a good relationship with them [the federation] so that our preparation could continue. I felt helpless, I felt like a . . . pawn that doesn't play the game but others play with it . . . I felt trapped.

Conclusions

The truth of the matter is that if we cannot see grooming for what it is, we cannot stop it when it occurs, or better still, prevent it from happening. As Gillespie (2004) noted, grooming is "a transient feature that is difficult to capture and virtually impossible to decide when it begins and ends" (p. 586). The critical element is identifying grooming before the abuse takes place to prevent the harm. To do so, two things need to be in place: One, seeing things clearly; and, two, speaking up and saying no to the groomer.

The world of sport has become rather myopic, almost blinded, by the glorification of the elite sport narrative (Carless & Douglas, 2013) as a singular pathway to sport achievements, medals, and international success. In contrast, for Brackenridge (2012), "A performance rationale for prevention [would be] our holy grail"—where care will be equally provided to the person (human being) and not only to the performer (human doing) and where care for athlete welfare will become an amplifier for performance success. One element that prevents us from preventing grooming is by and large the culture of sport which is coach-centered—hence power-centered—and where abuse has been normalized as the price to pay for succeeding (Brackenridge, 1997; Cense, 1997; Chroni, 2015). Accordingly, it is next to impossible for athletes to speak up against grooming in progress when their sport dream is at stake if/when they disclose the experience (Brackenridge et al., 2012; Fasting et al., 2010). Most athletes are also hesitant to speak up because they know that they will not be believed. Starr (2013), an abuse survivor herself, talked about coach-perpetrators who—once exposed—continued to receive sympathy and support from those who admire and respect their *work* (read *winning*).

The belief that sport is a source of all good and a *sacred* part of our culture (Bjørnseth & Szabo, 2018, p. 366) is another major barrier in recognizing and addressing the problem of grooming in sport. As critical scholars of sport have argued (e.g., Brackenridge, 2001; Fisher & Anders, 2020), this narrative serves to hide social processes intrinsic to sport itself that contribute to the occurrence of grooming and require the awareness of and preventive actions from all involved in sports. In addition, the belief that sport teams are like families and "whatever happens in the family, stays in the family" (Stirling et al., 2020) further work to conceal grooming and make it difficult for athletes to speak up.

How could we then overcome these persisting barriers? As our knowledge base on grooming from inside and outside sport has grown, the timing might be right for Brackenridge's (2001) four-stage model to be further enriched with a cultural praxis approach (Chroni & Kavoura, 2020; Fisher & Anders, 2020; Ryba & Wright, 2010). With this focus, scholars could take into consideration gender identity, level, sexual orientation, and any sport factor that makes the experience of grooming unique in addition to exploring the power flows within the institution of sport, sub-culturally situated. We hope that such an advancement will help all involved in sport to see grooming more clearly.

In tackling the problem of grooming in sport more effectively, future action plans could also incorporate the four commitments suggested by Fisher and Anders (2020). These include, namely, (1) taking into account the particular circumstances of each case and avoiding generalized claims that might assist in perpetuating existing power relations; (2) drawing attention to the interrelationships among multiple dimensions of targeted identities in order to identify the most vulnerable groups of athletes and develop action plans in response; (3) mobilizing every source that we can in order to better understand what makes our sporting cultures ideal grounds for grooming to occur; and (4) engaging respectfully with the testimonies of survivors as a way of learning about grooming and how to tackle it, even if this requires working against our own status, authority, and prejudices. While these commitments were originally developed for sport psychology researchers and practitioners, we believe that they could inform future safeguarding interventions and education programs for all those involved in sport as well.

Considering the knowledge accumulated through years over the subtle acts of grooming and how grooming unfolds in the world of sports and hurts children and adult athletes of all genders, levels, abilities, and cultures, one would think that sport stakeholders and adults in positions of authority would (and could) do better to proactively safeguard athletes and sport milieus from sexual exploitation. However, the number of victimized athletes throughout the world shows that this is not the case. What appears to be the case is that the barrier of remaining forever silent is slowly conquered and more and more survivor-athletes speak up in retrospect. While we are heading to the right direction of breaking the silence of abuse, preventive mechanisms need to be enhanced for athletes and those in their environment; sport stakeholders need to learn to recognize the process of grooming and to feel safe to speak up and halt the process before harm occurs.

Discussion Questions

1. Of the different definitions presented in this chapter, which one(s) fits with your culture(s); your national culture, sport culture, club culture? In what way(s) do these help you understand grooming, as a concept, process, or both?
2. Based on these definitions, what could we do on a daily basis to prevent and/or halt acts of grooming? What kind of protective mechanisms or interventions would be appropriate for your sporting context?
3. What kind of responses/interventions would be appropriate for the different stages of grooming?
4. Could the models and scholarship presented in this chapter be useful in reflecting on your personal or observed experiences in sport and identifying potentially harmful acts or situations?

References

Bennett, N., & O'Donohue, W. (2014). The construct of grooming in child sexual abuse: Conceptual and measurement issues. *Journal of Child Sexual Abuse, 23*(8), 957–976. https://doi.org/10.1080/10538712.2014.960632

Bisgaard, K., & Støckel, J. (2020). Athlete narratives of sexual harassment and abuse in the field of sport. *Journal of Clinical Sport Psychology, 13*(2), 226–242. https://doi.org/10.1123/jcsp.2018-0036

Bjørnseth, I., & Szabo, A. (2018). Sexual violence against children in sports and exercise: A systematic literature review. *Journal of Child Sexual Abuse, 27*, 365–385. https://doi.org/10.1080/10538712.2018.1477222

Brackenridge, C. (1997). "He owned me basically...": Women's experience of sexual abuse in sport. *International Review for the Sociology of Sport, 32*, 115–130. https://doi.org/10.1177/101269097032002001

Brackenridge, C. (2001). *Spoilsports: Understanding and preventing sexual exploitation in sport*. Routledge.

Brackenridge, C. (2012, November). *What we know about sexual harassment and abuse in sports*. Keynote presentation at the EU Conference, Better, Safe and Stronger! Prevention of Sexual Harassment and Abuse in Sport.

Brackenridge, C., & Fasting, K. (2005). The grooming process in sport: Narratives of sexual harassment and abuse. *Auto/Biography, 13*, 1–20. https://doi.org/10.1191/0967550705ab016oa

Brackenridge, C., Kay, T., & Rhind, D. (2012). *Sport, children's rights and violence prevention: A sourcebook on global issues and local programmes*. Brunel University.

Bringer, J. D., Brackenridge, C. H., & Johnston, L. H. (2006). Swimming coaches' perceptions of sexual exploitation in sport: A preliminary model of role conflict and role ambiguity. *The Sport Psychologist, 20*(4), 465–479.

Carless, D., & Douglas, K. (2013). Living, resisting, and playing the part of the athlete: Narrative tensions in elite sport. *Psychology of Sport and Exercise, 14*, 701–708.

Cense, M. (1997). *Red card or carte Blanche: Risk factors for sexual harassment and sexual abuse in sport: Summary, conclusions and recommendations*. NOC & NSF.

Cense, M., & Brackenridge, C. (2001). Temporal and developmental risk factors for sexual harassment and abuse in sport. *European Physical Education Review, 7*, 61–79. https://doi.org/10.1177/1356336X010071006

Chroni, S. (2015). Sexual exploitation in women's sport: Can female athletes respond to it? In R. Bailey & M. Talbot (Eds.), *Elite sport and sport-for-all: Bridging the two cultures?* (pp. 119–133). Routledge.

Chroni, S., & Kavoura, A. (2020). Cultural praxis. In D. Hackfort & R. J. Schinke (Eds.), *The Routledge international encyclopedia of sport and exercise psychology. Vol. 2: Applied and practical measures* (1st ed., pp. 227–238). Routledge.

Conte, J. R. (1984). The justice system and sexual abuse of children. *Social Service Review, 58*, 556–568.

Craven, S., Brown, S., & Gilchrist, E. (2006). Sexual grooming of children: Review of literature and theoretical considerations. *Journal of Sexual Aggression*, *12*(3), 287–299. https://doi.org/10.1080/13552600601069414

Cronin, C., & Armour, K. (2018). *Care in sport coaching: Pedagogical cases*. Routledge.

Dietz, P. (2018). Grooming and seduction. *Journal of Interpersonal Violence*, *33*(1), 28–36. https://doi.org/10.1177/0886260517742060

Fasting, K., Brackenridge, C., & Knorre, N. (2010). Performance level and sexual harassment prevalence among female athletes in the Czech Republic. *Women in Sport & Physical Activity Journal*, *19*, 26–32.

Fasting, K., & Sand, T. S. (2015). Narratives of sexual harassment experiences in sport. *Qualitative Research in Sport, Exercise and Health*, *7*(5), 573–588. https://doi.org/10.1080/2159676x.2015.1008028

Fisher, L. A., & Anders, A. D. (2020). Engaging with cultural sport psychology to explore systemic sexual exploitation in USA gymnastics: A call to commitments. *Journal of Applied Sport Psychology*, *32*(2), 129–145. https://doi.org/10.1080/10413200.2018.1564944

Fisher, L. A., Larsen, L. K., Bejar, M. P., & Shigeno, T. C. (2019). A heuristic for the relationship between caring coaching and elite athlete performance. *International Journal of Sports Science & Coaching*, *14*(2), 126–137. https://doi.org/10.1177/1747954119827192

Gervis, M., & Dunn, N. (2004). The emotional abuse of elite child athletes by their coaches. *Child Abuse Review*, *13*, 215–223. https://doi.org/10.1002/car.843

Gillespie, A. (2002). Child protection on the internet—challenges for criminal law. *Child and Family Law Quarterly*, *14*, 411–425.

Gillespie, A. (2004). "Grooming": Definitions and the law. *New Law Journal*, *154*(7124), 586–587.

Groth, A. N., & Birnbaum, H. J. (1979). *Men who rape: The psychology of the offender*. Plenum Press.

Hare, R. D., & Hart, S. D. (1993). Psychopathy, mental disorder, and crime. In S. Hodgins (Ed.), *Mental disorder and crime* (pp. 104–115). Sage Publications.

Hartill, M. (2009). The sexual abuse of boys in organized male sports. *Men and Masculinities*, *12*(2), 225–249. https://doi.org/10.1177/1097184X07313361

Hartill, M. (2014). Exploring narratives of boyhood sexual subjection in male-sport. *Sociology of Sport Journal*, *31*(1), 23–43. https://doi.org/10.1123/ssj.2012-0216

Johansson, S. (2018). "Am I sexually abused?" Consent in a coach-athlete lesbian relationship. *Sport, Education, & Society*, *23*, 311–323. https://doi.org/10.1080/13573322.2016.1202819

Kavanagh, E., Brown, L., & Jones, I. (2017). Elite athletes' experience of coping with emotional abuse in the coach—athlete relationship. *Journal of Applied Sport Psychology*, *29*(4), 402–417. https://doi.org/10.1080/10413200.2017.1298165

Lanning, K. (2010). *Child molesters: A behavioral analysis* (5th ed.). National Center for Missing and Exploited Children.

Lanning, K. (2018). The evolution of grooming: Concept and term. *Journal of Interpersonal Violence*, *33*(1), 5–16. https://doi.org/10.1177/0886260517742046

Leberg, E. (1997). *Understanding child molesters: Taking charge*. Sage Publications.

Lenskyj, H. (1992). Unsafe at home base: Women's experiences of sexual harassment in university sport and physical education. *Women in Sport and Physical Activity Journal*, *1*, 19–33. https://doi.org/10.1123/wspaj.1.1.19

Matthews, C. R., & Channon, A. (2019). The "male preserve" thesis, sporting culture, and men's power. In L. Gottzén, U. Mellström, & T. Shefer (Eds.), *The Routledge handbook of masculinity studies* (pp. 373–383). Routledge.

Mavridis, G. (Producer). (2021, January 21). *Live news* [Television broadcast]. Mega TV, Greece. www.youtube.com/watch?v=aZmOpF0CAqQ

McElvaney, R. (2019). Grooming: A case study. *Journal of Child Sexual Abuse*, *28*(5), 608–627. https://doi.org/10.1080/10538712.2018.1554612

Mountjoy, M., Brackenridge, C., Arrington, M., Blauwet, C., Carska-Sheppard, A., Fasting, K., Kirby, S., Leahy, T., Marks, S., Martin, K., Starr, K., Tiivas, A., & Budgett, R. (2016). International Olympic committee consensus statement: Harassment and abuse (non-accidental violence) in sport. *British Journal of Sports Medicine*, *50*(17), 1019–1029. https://doi.org/10.1136/bjsports-2016-096121

Owton, H., & Sparkes, A. C. (2017). Sexual abuse and the grooming process in sport: Learning from Bella's story. *Sport, Education and Society, 22*(6), 732–743. https://doi.org/10.1080/13573322.2015.1063484

Parent, S., & Demers, G. (2011). Sexual abuse in sport: A model to prevent and protect athletes. *Child Abuse Review, 20*(2), 120–133. https://doi.org/10.1002/car.1135

Parent, S., & Vaillancourt-Morel, M. P. (2020). Magnitude and risk factors for interpersonal violence experienced by Canadian teenagers in the sport context. *Journal of Sport and Social Issues*. https://doi.org/10.1177/0193723520973571

Petherick, W., & Sinnamon, G. (2013). Motivations: Offender and victim perspectives. In W. Patherick (Ed.), *Profiling and serial crime: Theoretical and practical issues* (3rd ed., pp. 393–430). Academic Press.

Prewitt-White, T. R. (2019). I was his litmus test: An autoethnographic account of being groomed in sport. *Journal of Clinical Sport Psychology, 13*(2), 180–195.

Purdy, L., Potrac, P., & Paulauskas, R. (2016). Nel Noddings, caring, moral learning and coaching. In L. Nelson, R. Groom, & P. Potrac (Eds.), *Learning in sport coaching* (pp. 215–226). Routledge.

Ryba, T. V., & Wright, H. K. (2010). Sport psychology and the cultural turn: Notes toward cultural praxis. In T. V. Ryba, R. J. Schinke, & G. Tenenbaum (Eds.), *The cultural turn in sport psychology* (pp. 3–27). Fitness Information Technology.

Sand, T. S., Fasting, K., Chroni, S., & Knorre, N. (2011). Coaching behavior: Any consequences for the prevalence of sexual harassment? *International Journal of Sports Science & Coaching, 6*(2), 229–241.

Sinnamon, G. (2017). The psychology of adult sexual grooming: Sinnamon's seven-stage model of adult sexual grooming. In W. Petherick & G. Sinnamon (Eds.), *The psychology of criminal and antisocial behavior* (pp. 459–487). Academic Press.

Starr, K. (2013). *When did the system fail Kelley Davies Currin and the rest of us?* www.huffingtonpost.com/katherine-starr/when-did-the-system- fail_b_3328817.html

Stirling, A. E., & Kerr, G. A. (2009). Abused athletes' perceptions of the coach-athlete relationship. *Sport in Society, 12*(2), 227–239. https://doi.org/10.1080/17430430802591019

Stirling, A. E., & Kerr, G. A. (2014). Initiating and sustaining emotional abuse in the coach—athlete relationship: An ecological transactional model of vulnerability. *Journal of Aggression, Maltreatment & Trauma, 23*(2), 116–135. https://doi.org/10.1080/10926771.2014.872747

Stirling, A. E., Tam, A., Milne, A., & Kerr, G. (2020). Media narratives of gymnasts' abusive experiences: Keep smiling and point your toes. In R. Kerr, N. Barker-Ruchti, C. Stewart, & G. Kerr (Eds.), *Women's artistic gymnastics: Socio-cultural perspectives* (pp. 81–98). Routledge.

Tanner, J., & Brake, S. (2013). *Exploring sex offender grooming.* www.kbsolutions.com/Grooming.pdf

Vertommen, T., Schipper-van Veldhoven, N., Wouters, K., Kampen, J. K., Brackenridge, C. H., Rhind, D, J. A., Neels, K., & Van Den Eede, F. (2016). Interpersonal violence against children in sport in the Netherlands and Belgium. *Child Abuse & Neglect, 51*, 223–236. https://doi.org/10.1016/j.chiabu.2015.10.006

Volkwein, K. A. E., Schnell, F. I., Sherwood, D., & Livezey, A. (1997). Sexual harassment in sport: Perceptions and experiences of American female student-athletes. *International Review for the Sociology of Sport, 32*, 283–295. https://doi.org/10.1177/1012690297032003005

Walters, S. R., Payne, D., Schluter, P. J., & Thomson, R. W. (2012). "It just makes you feel invincible": A Foucauldian analysis of children's experiences of organised team sports. *Sport, Education and Society, 20*(2), 241–257. https://doi.org/10.1080/13573322.2012.745844

5
SEXUAL MISCONDUCT AND EPISTEMIC INJUSTICES IN SPORT

Lindsey A. Miossi and Lars Dzikus

The harms a survivor of sexual misconduct experiences are varied and grave. Not only can a survivor experience an assault on their physical body, mind, and psychological well-being from the direct perpetrator, but they may also suffer consequences from those around them (e.g., institutions, administrators, family members) directly and indirectly as they disclose (or not) their testimony (Fricker, 2007; Kidd et al., 2017; Stewart, 2019). That is, they may experience harm not only from the assaulter but also from everyone, including themselves, as a result of epistemic injustice (Stewart, 2019). Throughout this chapter, a variety of forms of epistemic injustices including testimonial injustice, gaslighting, testimonial smothering, and institutional betrayal, and their associated epistemic harms will be discussed in relation to survivors of sexual misconduct. Understanding the role of sport institutions and individual stakeholders, including family and administrators, in enacting and avoiding epistemic harm is of the utmost importance to protecting athletes who have been sexually assaulted.

Epistemic Injustice

When someone experiences a wrong such as sexual violence, they become a knower—meaning they have a testimony of their experience they can share. Epistemic injustice is the wrongs one faces in their capacity as a knower (Stewart, 2019). Kidd et al. (2017) stated, "Epistemic injustice refers to those forms of unfair treatment that relate to issues of knowledge, understanding, and participation in communicative practices" (p. 1). Testimony, which is a critical foundation for knowledge and information, is often restricted to those who are seen as reliable, trusted, competent, and sincere, for example (Stewart, 2019). Although seemingly that makes sense, this can be problematic when someone's testimony is negatively assessed due to "stereotypes, prejudices, and/or biases" (Stewart, 2019, p. 70), which can be a result of social inequalities (Fricker, 2007).

Unfortunately, when there is a news headline regarding sexual violence, typically the case has a large number of survivors. Consider, for example, Jerry Sandusky, the Penn State football coach who abused 10 boys over a 15-year period (CNN Editorial Research, 2020); Larry Nassar, USA gymnastics and Michigan State University (MSU) team doctor who abused over

DOI: 10.4324/9781003125884-6

300 women and girls for more than 20 years (Eggert & White, 2018); Richard Strauss, the Ohio State University (OSU) team doctor who abused 177 male students during an 18-year period (Perret, 2020); and Greg Stephens, a youth basketball coach in Iowa who exploited over 400 boys over several years (Spoerre, 2019). Those are only a few examples within sport alone. The number of examples that could be provided are seemingly infinite, and unfortunately, as Stewart (2019) discussed, the survivors of these cases are often met with, "Why didn't you say something sooner?" (p. 68).

Epistemic injustice is present in both the meaning-making and knowledge-producing processes, contributing to one's decision if, when, and how they will share their experience (Kidd et al., 2017). Thus, epistemic injustice is present before one even discloses their experience. The knower likely heavily weighs the potential situations that could occur if they decide to share their testimony (e.g., lose their starting spot on the team, decreased playing time, public ridicule). After a decision is made, whether they share or not, they are likely to experience epistemic injustice harms (Stewart, 2019). They may even begin to question themselves and their experience and perception of the events that occurred.

For example, think back to a time when you experienced something where you felt wronged, and when you told someone about the situation, instead of listening, they discredited you, attempted to convince you that it didn't actually happen, and/or completely ignored you. Subsequently, you may have felt confused, belittled, and unimportant among an array of other emotions. This is what one may experience as they disclose their sexual misconduct experiences.

This pervasive doubting of the survivor, which is omnipresent in sexual misconduct cases and all the more visible with the rise of the #MeToo movement (Stewart, 2019), can lead to epistemic harm (Fricker, 2007; Stewart, 2019). Specifically, it is experienced when a survivor's speech goes unheard, they are viewed as unintelligible, and/or the assault is thought of as impossible; thus, their speech is ineffective, and no action is taken. Epistemic harm undermines one's knowledge and capacity as a knower causing an array of primary, secondary, and practical consequences (Kidd et al., 2017; Stewart, 2019). Although there are a variety of ways epistemic injustice may play out, Stewart (2019) identified three main methods enacted against a knower: (a) testimonial injustice, (b) gaslighting, and (c) silencing and testimonial smothering. A fourth main method of epistemic injustice—institutional betrayal—may be particularly pertinent to sport.

Epistemic injustice—through testimonial discrediting, gaslighting, silencing and testimonial smothering, and institutional betrayal—engenders a distinct set of consequences, epistemic harms (Stewart, 2019). These harms are in addition to the many other injuries suffered from the sexual violation act itself (Stewart, 2019; Sweet, 2019). Subsequently, it is of the utmost importance that these additional harms are mitigated. Each of the epistemic injustices results in similar but distinct consequences. These four epistemic injustice methods and their associated harms are explored next.

Testimonial Injustice

Testimonial injustice is not giving someone's testament appropriate credibility. McKinnon (2016) explained that credibility is based on who the person is and what they are saying, establishing a *credibility economy* in which people are attributed differing amounts of credibility based on their identities and other aspects (e.g., emotions; Fricker, 2007). Resultantly, "regardless of how qualified the speaker is with respect to the subject of their testimony, they are *already* discounted or disbelieved in advance" (Stewart, 2019, p. 71). One example of this is the common notion that, in Western societies, emotionality and rationality are at odds, and, subsequently, women's testimonies are often discounted through the argument that they are too emotional to be logical (McKinnon, 2017; Stewart, 2019). Unfortunately, this can become a vicious cycle. If one experiences sexual violation, they are likely to be emotional (and understandably so). However, if they suffer testimonial injustice because of their display of that emotion as they share their testimony, they may become angry, frustrated, etc., and thus, more emotional. This additional emotion can be turned into more reason to discredit the testimony further (McKinnon, 2017) and the cycle continues. It is important to consider how credibility and prejudicial stereotypes can be decreased with each compounding marginalized identity one has (e.g., BIPOC, woman, disability, social class).

In contrast, some individuals have credibility excess (Medina, 2013). While credibility deficits and excesses can be accredited in many ways, one example in sport is the credibility excess of a coach (e.g., be knowledgeable about the sport and have inherent power in the structure of sport). This may become all the more apparent the more a coach wins. For example, in Prewitt-White's (2019) autoethnography on being groomed by her high school basketball coach, she discussed many of the coach's achievements including multiple state appearances and said, "He was charming, successful, and seemingly unstoppable. I was challenged to find an audience who wanted to hear my truth" (p. 183). Prewitt-White shed light on peoples' decision to turn their heads instead of listening to her and other players' indications of a sexually abusive coach, potentially due to his many successes and winning titles. It was not until 14 years after her experience and many "conquests" later that the coach was imprisoned for sexual misconduct with minors (Prewitt-White, 2019). In other examples, the team doctors from USA gymnastics (Correa & Louttit, 2018) and Ohio State University (Perret, 2020) were given a large credibility excess due to their perceived medical expertise while a number of survivors who came forward were neither listened to nor taken seriously. For example, when Amanda Thomashow—an MSU student and survivor of Nassar—reported the sexual assault she experienced, the university told her that she "did not understand the difference between sexual assault and a medical procedure" (Correa & Louttit, 2018, para 19).

Evidently, if an athlete decides to make a report against a powerful coach, they are likely to have to go to great lengths to be heard and taken seriously. When someone has to go to such extremes to *prove* their experience, this can compound the stereotype, for example, that women and girls are over-dramatic, hysterical, and too emotional (Stewart, 2019). This could be a reason why some cases do not become publicized (or are not taken seriously) until there are a large number of survivors who come forward. Again, the vicious cycle is consistently and continually perpetuated, and additional harm results.

Testimonial injustice results in multiple harms. The first harm, *primary harm*, disregards the knower as a knower which "is central to human dignity and value" (Fricker, 2007; Stewart, 2019, p. 77). Therefore, primary harm is also a moral harm as it violates the survivor's humanity (Fricker, 2007). To know, to make sense of, and to testify one's own experience and then be undermined in that capacity is an attack on one's subjective self (e.g., identity, agency), stifling their humanity (Pohlhaus, 2014). The practical *secondary harm* is when there is a negative practical consequence (Fricker, 2007), such as if the perpetrator is not convicted or removed from the institution and the survivor has to continue to be in that same space with the very person that harmed them in the first place (Stewart, 2019). Remaining in the same space could be physically, mentally, and/or emotionally dangerous. Lastly, an *epistemic secondary harm* is when the knower internalizes the doubt of the hearer and begins questioning their own knowledge and self (Stewart, 2019). This harm results in one questioning if they remembered or interpreted the situation properly, thus doubting their own agency and losing trust in their own judgment. In this light, self-trust is relational and developed through our interactions with others. Jones (2012) stated, "we come to have trust in our cognitive abilities as their reliability is confirmed by their results being seconded by trusted figures, whether parents, teachers, or peers" (p. 245). Consequently, unjust social relations undermine self-trust in marginalized individuals which perpetuates epistemic injustice and leads to a continuous cycle (Jones, 2012).

In sum, testimonial injustice in sexual misconduct cases is likely to be present, especially for athletes. Athletes, who typically have little perceived power and agency, are going to be given less testimony credibility compared to a coach, physician, or powerful other (e.g., prized athlete, administrator), especially if the powerful other has a successful reputation or has been in the program a long time. As already stated, this can be exacerbated if the survivor has multiple vulnerable identities (e.g., minor, woman, transgender, single-parent home). Moore (2012) discussed structural inequalities as being evident in Sandusky's case stating, "One would conclude . . . that Sandusky chose them out of a certain risk calculation: They were targeted because of their perceived lack of voice and power" (p. 362). Unfortunately, these very individuals who may be more likely to experience abuse are also less likely to be listened to and taken seriously if they decide to disclose their testimony.

Gaslighting

Gaslighting is emotional manipulation (Abramson, 2014) through "attempts to create a 'surreal' (Ferraro, 2006) social environment by making the other in an intimate relationship seem or feel 'crazy'" (Sweet, 2019, p. 852). Gaslighting occurs specifically in intimate relationships due to the use of strategies involving trust and coercion (Sweet, 2019), which includes undermining reality, confidence, and mental well-being (Ahern, 2018). Essentially, gaslighting involves altering one's reality of an experience or situation which results in cognitive dissonance, confusion (Ahern, 2018), and an inability to disagree or create a logical argument (Abramson, 2014). It is also the refusal to validate one's experience (Abramson, 2014). Abramson (2014) argued that gaslighters "induce in someone the sense that her reactions, perceptions, memories, and/or beliefs are not just mistaken, but utterly without grounds—paradigmatically, so unfounded as to qualify as crazy" (p. 2). The claim "crazy" or "over sensitive" is important here as it not only implies the individual is wrong but that they are also not rational enough to even judge or debate the situation (Abramson, 2014). Ultimately, then, the aim of gaslighting is not to just dismiss someone, but instead to make that individual question themselves and not take themselves seriously, essentially destroying independent thought while simultaneously destroying credibility through claims of "crazy" (Abramson, 2014).

Additionally, gaslighting involves multiple incidents over a period of time and typically includes several gaslighters for the same situation (Abramson, 2014). For example, *direct gaslighters* are conscious and intentional on what they are doing. Direct gaslighters can include third-party actors as was the case for Jamie Dantzscher, gymnast and Olympic medalist and survivor of Nassar. After going public about her experience, she stated

> I was attacked on social media. . . . People didn't believe me, even people I thought were my friends. They called me a liar, a whore, and even accused me of making all of this up just to get attention.
>
> (Correa & Louttit, 2018, para 17)

Indirect gaslighters, on the other hand, commit the act unconsciously, unintentionally, and may actually be well-intended (Abramson, 2014; Stewart, 2019). Indirect gaslighting occurs when people comment on someone's sexual assault case publicly, in-person or via online sources (e.g., social media, webpages, news stories), and dismiss the importance of it, victim-blame the knower, etc. (Stewart, 2019). When survivors hear those comments, they are likely to internalize them and come to realize that those individuals who commented may think the same about the survivor's own personal experiences. For example, if a case goes public such as the Nassar case, and an athlete overhears her parents discussing the case and denying the seriousness of it, this is indirect gaslighting. That same survivor may also read comments that others who have come forward have received, like Jamie Dantzscher did from peers and acquaintances on social media, and then be indirectly gaslit. If that athlete has not disclosed to her parents yet, she may now perceive that her parents and others will think the same thing about her experience. Thus, she may opt to remain silent and not share her testimony to avoid the potential consequences. Unfortunately, indirect gaslighting can be just as harmful as direct gaslighting, especially when it is coming from people the individual is close to (Stewart, 2019).

Similar to testimonial injustice, gaslighting has additional and distinct harms (McKinnon, 2014; Stewart, 2019). As Sweet (2019) explained, gaslighting yokes "together physical and verbal incidents of abuse into an overall sense of lost reality and confusion" (p. 865). Of the epistemic harms, gaslighting is considerably different in that it is done within an intimate relationship, and therefore, occurs between trusted individuals. Considering, then, that the confusion is stimulated by a trusted partner, betrayal is a distinct harm from gaslighting and may subsequently lead to isolation (Stewart, 2019).

With a newfound distrust of others, the survivor may feel alone and confused. Moreover, distrust of self can have implications on self-esteem, self-concept, and confidence (Abramson, 2014; Ahern, 2018). Further, as the aim of gaslighting is to undermine one's agency, additional harms may include a loss of independence, moral standing, and ability to engage in deliberations (Abramson, 2014). Thus, it is important to consider what this does to one's ability to begin or continue seeking action against a perpetrator when one is unable to form one's own arguments or articulate their experiences through no fault of their own. This makes it incredibly important for third-party actors to beware of their indirect gaslighting. If a survivor is being gaslit by their perpetrator but third-party actors avoid additional indirect gaslighting and instead listen, support, and credit what the knower experienced, then the resulting action may be more successful.

In conclusion, gaslighting is when others deny a survivor's experiences altogether, discrediting the seriousness of the situation, and/or claiming a survivor is overreacting, oversensitive, or misinterpreting the events (Abramson, 2014; McKinnon, 2017). Unfortunately, when one's experience is denied or distorted, they may end up smothering their own testimony and opt to remain silent.

Silencing and Testimonial Smothering

Silencing, the prevention of or inability to use one's voice, can occur in active and passive ways and can be enacted by both others and self (i.e., testimonial smothering; Dotson, 2011). Silencing by others can occur from individuals, organizations, and third-party actors and is mediated by power which, according to Wang and Hsieh (2013), can be defined as one's position within a hierarchy. Silencing by organizations can occur through passive, "non-coercive, discursive means" (Fernando & Prasad, 2019, p. 1568). For example, an organization may have a lack of resources or spaces for survivors to voice concerns within an organization (Donaghey et al., 2011). Moreover, if there are resources in place for survivors, there may be discouragement, explicitly or otherwise, to actually utilize those resources (Pinder & Harlos, 2001). Silencing by third-party actors also plays a large role in mediating silence of survivors (Fernando & Prasad, 2019). Similar to gaslighting, individuals can indirectly silence someone even if they are well-intentioned. They can convince survivors to not share a testimony, believing they have a good intention in what they are saying to the survivor; however, in reality they are silencing them. For example, athletes may share testimonies with their parents or teammates of a situation involving their coach, and the parents then may caution them that they will lose their starting position or spot on the Olympic team if they opt to go to the administration. This is indeed a silencing tactic employed, even if well-intentioned. This silencing could cause an array of harms far greater than the loss of a starting position.

If we continue with that example and the athlete opts to not tell anyone, this would be considered *testimonial smothering,* which refers to the survivor knowing that people will not give much thought or credit to their testimony while also considering the consequences they will face by sharing their testament, and thus, they self-silence (Dotson, 2011). *Self-silencing*, also called *coerced silence*, is a result of the influences from the context and conditions of the situation or organization (Dotson, 2011; Stewart, 2019). Self-silencing can be further categorized as *quiescence* and *acquiescence* (Harlos, 2016; Pinder & Harlos, 2001). Quiescence silence is the active withholding of one's testimony out of anger and fear of the consequences. For example, this can include fear of isolation from the group (Bowen & Blackmon, 2003), anticipation of and shame in being labeled a "troublemaker," or the fear of suffering career consequences (Fernando & Prasad, 2019). In contrast, acquiescence silence is the less conscious, unintentional withholding of voice due to the acceptance of others' worldview instead of challenging it and giving up hope for improvement (Harlos, 2016). Fernando and Prasad (2019) discussed a subcategory of these, *reluctant acquiescence*, which is when someone starts to voice their concern but becomes conflicted through third-party actors and reluctantly self-silences as was demonstrated in the aforementioned example.

Testimonial smothering and silencing harms individuals in similar ways to testimonial injustice and gaslighting while adding an additional barrier to getting help. When someone is coerced into silence, they are unable to get help, protect themselves, and seek justice as few, if anyone, may even know about the incident (Stewart, 2019). Additionally, individuals with less social, financial, or organizational power are more likely to experience silencing (Wang & Hsieh, 2013). More specifically, marginalized individuals may self-silence to a greater degree due to testimonial smothering and the belief (and lived reality) that their testimony will not be given the appropriate amount of credibility (Armstrong et al., 2018; Stewart, 2019).

Institutional Betrayal

> *I reported it. Michigan State University, the school I loved and trusted, had the audacity to tell me that I did not understand the difference between sexual assault and a medical procedure.*
> —Amanda Thomashow (as quoted in Correa & Louttit, 2018, para 19), first woman to file an official Title IX Larry Nassar (Casarez et al., 2018)

Similar to gaslighting and betrayal in interpersonal relationships, individuals can experience institutional betrayal when trusted institutions fail to prevent sexual assault and/or do not react supportively (Rosenthal et al., 2017; Smith & Freyd, 2013). Thus, institutional betrayal includes acts of commission (e.g., cover-ups, retaliation) and omission (e.g., negligence; Smidt & Freyd, 2018). Examples of this are creating an environment that makes sexual assault more common and creating barriers for survivors to report crimes, inadequate responses, and penalizing survivors and whistleblowers (Smith & Freyd, 2014).

Institutional betrayal can lead to additional injury beyond that experienced as a result of the initial harm. Smith and Freyd (2013), for example, found female undergraduate students who had experienced unwanted sexual experiences *and* institutional betrayal reported higher levels of anxiety, trauma-specific sexual symptoms, and problematic sexual functioning. Similar findings have been reported, for example, in childhood sexual and physical abuse, where negative psychological outcomes were greater when the abuse took place in institutionalized childcare (Carr et al., 2010).

Studying institutional betrayal requires attention beyond individual dynamics to systematic factors. Such a change in perspective can be challenging in a traditional psychological paradigm (Fisher & Anders, 2020). According to Smith and Freyd (2014), "to examine institutional betrayal, it is necessary to extend focus outward from individual to systemic factors in a way that often challenges the status quo of research in psychology" (p. 579). Smith and Freyd (2014) considered several institutional characteristics that can make betrayal more likely, including "institutional-level policies, practices, and cultures that can serve to condone, hide, or normalize trauma" (p. 580). Among these institutional policies were (a) membership requirements (e.g., strict membership definitions where conformity is valued and deviance corrected), (b) prestige (e.g., the higher the status of the leader, the more potential for abuse), (c) priorities (e.g., performance prioritized over well-being), and (d) denial (e.g., "othering" the individual making the claim against the institution).

Sport organizations and teams often have several formal and informal norms that help to define who belongs and who doesn't (Coakley, 2017). Such membership requirements create group cohesion and conformity. Strict requirements for membership and a strong sense of community, however, can also foreshadow institutional betrayal (Smith & Freyd, 2014). Smith and Freyd (2014) pointed out, "the key feature appears not to be the form of these membership features but rather the institutional or societal value placed on their importance" (p. 579).

Sport organizations and their representatives can have tremendous prestige, which can result in being seen as trustworthy and elicit desire among individuals to be associated with the institution (Smith & Freyd, 2014). Athletes can be particularly dependent on the acceptance and support of their coaches who yield various forms of power (e.g., the ability to grant or withhold scholarships, playing time, attention; Anderson, 2010). Along with the social standing enjoyed by institutions and their representatives comes the potential to betray trust placed in them (Smith & Freyd, 2014). Further, prestige and power can also be used to punish whistleblowers (Ahern, 2018). Thus, institutions have a particular responsibility to live up to their prestige and power. Ahern (2018) referenced the Jerry Sandusky case in Penn State University's football program as a case when an institution seemingly valued its own reputation over the well-being of those who trusted the institution to protect them. For many years, Penn State allegedly had buried allegations of child sexual abuse. In Ahern's (2018) assessment, "the University's leaders had made a series of decisions that prioritized Penn State's good name over all else" (p. 62).

A case in point is the 2020 news story which broke regarding Louisiana State University's "mishandling sexual misconduct complaints"—the story was referencing a number of reports with various perpetrators and survivors, including multiple female athletes who reported Derrius Guice, a star running back at the time, as a perpetrator (Jacoby et al., 2020). In response to the mishandling, Taylor, a Temple University professor shared:

> I think they're (coaches) making decisions that are best for the success of the program, and they're making the decision to put the safety and well-being of other students behind a player's ability to play on a Saturday afternoon.
> *(Jacoby et al., 2020, para 34)*

As one survivor of a non-athlete perpetrator stated about the University, "I just think that honestly they don't care, the whole system is on the side of the accused" (Jacoby et al., 2020, para 11). By placing reputation over well-being of those in their care, institutions exhibit their true priorities, making institutional betrayal more likely (Smith & Freyd, 2014). Specific aspects of institutional betrayal and related concepts can further be illustrated in three sport-related case studies.

Case Studies of Institutional Betrayal in Sport

Case Study 1. Smith and Freyd (2014) discussed institutional betrayal and the 2010 case of Elizabeth "Lizzy" Seeberg, who committed suicide after reporting sexual assault by a Notre Dame football player. After Seeberg had made a report to campus police, it reportedly took the university two weeks to interview the alleged perpetrator while they repeatedly interviewed Seeberg and other witnesses (Lombardi, 2013; Smith, & Freyd, 2014). In the meantime, after receiving a threatening text message cautioning her about "messing with" Notre Dame football, Seeberg had committed suicide (St. Clair & Lighty, 2010, para. 2). After three months and a closed-door campus disciplinary hearing, Notre Dame found the athlete not responsible. Lizzy's father, Tom Seeberg, later accused the university of delaying the initial investigation to prepare its legal defense and avoid interference with the ongoing football season (Pinto et al., 2010). Reportedly, Notre Dame's president declined to speak with the Seebergs, and the family was denied access to records of their daughter's complaint and the disciplinary hearing (St. Clair & Lighty, 2010).

As discussed by Smith and Freyd (2014), the Seeberg case illustrates the concept of institutional betrayal. Tom Seeberg expressed:

> Ultimately, there's a sense of betrayal. There's a sense of the university not living its values. . . . It is not our intention to take down this great institution. But it has disappointed us. That hurts, and it hurts our family.
>
> *(as quoted in St. Clair & Lighty, 2010, para. 7)*

The sense of institutional betrayal was especially intense for the Seeberg parents, and possibly Lizzy, as the family had several Notre Dame alumni and were long-standing fans of the Fighting Irish (Smith, & Freyd, 2014). The Seeberg case can be understood to involve two dimensions of institutional betrayal. The first is "omission of protective, preventative, or responsive institutional actions," in the form of the university's police department failing to interview the accused party for two weeks (Smith, & Freyd, 2014, p. 579). The second is the intuition's active commission to deny the family access to records relevant to the investigation (Smith, & Freyd, 2014).

As seen in the Seeberg case, *institutional denial* is another factor that increases the likelihood of betrayal (Smith & Freyd, 2014). Those with institutional power must take great care not to "other" those who make allegations or raise critical questions. Smith and Freyd (2014) noted it is important to avoid an "us versus them" mindset which "may represent an additional level of betrayal when divided loyalty within an organization leads to further isolation" (p. 581). Sport settings are particularly sensitive in this regard, as individual and collective identities can be closely tied to each other (Coakley, 2017). When reporting abuse and filing lawsuits, team members and fans might have their allegiance questioned. Going against their own team or university might cause conflicting feelings for survivors.

Case Study 2. The case of Ohio State and team physician Dr. Richard Strauss (Perret, 2020) illustrates the concepts of *institutional denial* and *betrayal blindness*. Former student-athletes who have sued the university might wonder if they should still cheer on the university's teams. Given that the accused Strauss could not stand trial, since he had committed suicide in 2005 (Perret, 2020), survivors expected the university to live up to its responsibilities. Wertheim (2020) reported:

> The scandal has imbued the former athletes with ambiguous feelings toward the school. This terror had happened at *the* Ohio State, a school many had supported since they were kids, a school that conferred on them a scholarship. DiSabato [one of the plaintiffs], for instance, has worn his scarlet-and-gray letterman's jacket to hearings, a symbolic gesture that he still considered himself part of the tribe.

This case also highlights that it can often take survivors several years and possibly decades to fully comprehend they were abused (Perret, 2020). *Betrayal blindness*—"the state of being consciously unaware of interpersonal abuse committed by a trusted or depended upon other" (Smith & Freyd, 2013, p. 119)—can lead to survivors not realizing the abuse they are experiencing and having few or no memories of it. As an adult, Dzikus (2012), for example, reported having only "shreds of memory" of the sexual abuse he suffered from his youth swimming coach (p. 155). Though leaving the target open for continued abuse, betrayal blindness and traumatic amnesia can be understood as coping mechanisms or adaptive responses whereby survivors manage to maintain necessary relationships with abusers on whom they depend (Freyd, 1994; Smith & Freyd, 2014).

Case Study 3. American colleges and universities commonly regard varsity sports, especially football, as a way to develop attachment to the institutions among students, donors, and fans (Baade & Sundberg, 1996; Eggers et al., 2019; Pope & Pope, 2009). Athletic malfeasance resulting in negative media coverage (e.g., academic fraud resulting in a postseason ban) can adversely affect the quantity and quality of newly admitted students (Eggers et al., 2019). Therefore, the ethical conduct of academic institutions can greatly influence stakeholder perceptions and trust.

Rosenthal et al. (2017) examined university employees regarding their experiences of institutional betrayal following a case of a sexual assault committed by three student-athletes. Subsequent media coverage included the revelation that the athletic department knew that one of the athletes had been accused of sexual assault at another college as well as an alleged cover-up and mishandling of the investigation (Kingkade, 2014a, 2014b). The researchers surveyed university employees regarding their perceptions of the case. They found the vast majority of participants (83.3%) reported at least one type of institutional betrayal and that experience resulted in a decreased attachment to the institution. Those with an already tenuous relationship to the university were especially negatively impacted by the school's failure to prevent and respond to the assault, whereas employees with previously strong attachments were more forgiving (Rosenthal et al., 2017). The findings underscore the need for institutions to demonstrate ethical behavior and effective crime prevention and responses.

The case studies we highlighted demonstrate that how sincere organizations and their stakeholders are in preventing and mitigating sexual misconduct can make a major difference in the healing process of survivors (Freyd, 1994, 1996; Freyd et al., 2007; Smith & Freyd, 2013). Athletes who often proudly represent their sport organizations trust those entities to support and protect them. When that is not the case, survivors can experience institutional betrayal and additional harm (Freyd, 1994, 1996; Freyd et al., 2007; Smith & Freyd, 2013).

Recommendations

Ultimately, if organizations and institutions are responsible for protecting athletes, as is often outlined in organizational mission statements, then they have a critical responsibility to mitigate any and all potential for epistemic harms before (e.g., avoiding negative stereotypes and biases) and after sexual violence occurs. For example, on the front page of the NCAA's webpage, they outline three main priorities, including "well-being" which states, "We were founded to keep college sports safe. Today, we work hard to promote safety, excellence, and physical and mental well-being for student-athletes" (NCAA, n.d.). If the NCAA wishes to uphold this priority, then it is critical it not only works to prevent sexual violence, but also prioritizes protecting survivors when they share their testimony. Succinctly, the harms one suffers from sexual violence are already grave and institutions need to have proper resources, systems, and support in place and enacted to protect athletes from further harm. Many of the following recommendations apply to both the prevention and mitigation of sexual misconduct. Though it is an obvious point, the first recommendation regarding mitigating sexual misconduct in sport must be prevention.

Prevention. In protecting their members from epistemic injustice, sport organizations and their representatives must pay attention to both proactive and reactive measures. In their study of female undergraduate students, Smith and Freyd (2013) emphasized the need for universities to strengthen their efforts to prevent sexual assaults. Participants in this study reported institutional betrayal more often in relation to factors leading up to the assault (e.g., creating an environment that makes abuse more likely) than in relation to the institution's reaction (e.g., the reporting process).

Smith and Freyd (2014) offered a number of ways to prevent institutional betrayal which can also be applied to other forms of epistemic injustice. They emphasized the need for institutions to improve transparency and stress institutional values that protect and support their members. Stewart (2019) stated:

> We—as individuals, as institutions—can no longer feign ignorance, and no longer fail to hear victims/survivors when they speak, and no longer fail to respond empathetically and responsibly to the force of their demands. A real movement for social change must be guided by the voices of victims/survivors, and demands for those around them with power to act on their testimonies to listen better.
>
> *(p. 89)*

It is imperative that individuals and institutions take responsibility for protecting survivors by listening and empathetically responding instead of immediately dismissing the experience.

Protection. In regard to protecting athletes who report abuse, there are a number of measures that individuals and organizations can take. To address discrepancies in testimonial credibility and rates of epistemic harm for individuals of intersecting marginalized identities, it is crucial to change prejudicial stereotypes and biases (Epstein, 2020). Doing so, however, is not easy. As Epstein acknowledged, it requires "motivation, awareness and effort. Each of us in our capacity as listeners, must take responsibility to intentionally and consciously shift our assumptions" (p. 39). That is, listeners should question their assumptions and biases before distrusting the survivor. However, this does not mean listeners should:

> Go to the other extreme and automatically credit all survivor stories. Instead they need only resist the reflexive presumption *against* crediting women's stories, make an effort to overcome hermeneutic gaps and open their minds to accepting a broader range of stories and storytellers.
>
> *(Epstein, 2020, p. 39)*

Further, if officials were to notice gaps in survivor testimonies, they should gather information about how witnesses have been impacted by the trauma rather than immediately discount the account (Epstein, 2020). Understanding the effects of betrayal blindness and traumatic amnesia could change how others perceive survivors and react to them (Freyd, 1994; Smith & Freyd, 2014). Similarly, if gatekeepers notice either a lack of or extensive amount of emotion, they should reflect on this through their questions with the survivor as both are trauma responses. This systematic reorientation of beliefs has the possibility to reverse automatic and biased presuppositions resulting in the discredit of one's testimony. Lastly, another potential option is to promote the use of technology for reporting via smartphone applications like

Callisto (2021) and JDoe (2017). These apps allow survivors to report through encrypted, time-stamped reports that mitigate the potential for credibility deficits. Although Epstein's (2020) recommendations were made specifically in the context of women survivors in the workplace, these recommendations can and should certainly be considered within broader sport organizations.

Institutional Courage

Smidt and Freyd (2018) noted that the antidote to institutional betrayal is institutional courage, "it is accountability, transparency, actively seeking justice, and making reparations where needed" (p. 494). As part of betrayal reparations, institutions should undertake "careful self-study of past abuse, risk factors, and protective factors within its environment" (Smith & Freyd, 2014, p. 584). One example of this is the Strauss case at Ohio State. After failing to respond adequately to initial reports of the abuse, the university finally commissioned an investigation by an independent law firm in 2018. The resulting report is published on the site of the Office of University Compliance and Integrity (Ohio State University, n.d.).

Institutions, however, must also be transparent about limitations of such reports. In Ohio State's case, the law firm

> only interviewed survivors who proactively came forward to share their story, meaning the actual number of survivors reaches into the many hundreds, and possibly even a thousand or more.
>
> *(O'Shea, 2020, p. 2)*

Further, the law firm's report

> did not assess or otherwise provide recommendations to the University regarding its current or historical policies, procedures, or practices related to sexual abuse or sexual misconduct.
>
> *(Trombino & Funk, 2019, p. 7)*

Sport organizations should make preventing, recognizing, reporting, and prosecuting abuse part of their core values (Smith & Freyd, 2014). Ahern (2018) suggested that the importance of reviewing codes of conduct is critical as some codes of conduct are only present to meet legal or social standards. Ahern stated:

> clues include the use of 'should' or 'shall' (instead of 'must') and 'guidelines' rather than 'procedures.' Words such as 'should' mean that policies can be interpreted as suggestions rather than requirements.
>
> *(p. 63)*

Therefore, it is important that sport organizations review their codes of conduct and update them accordingly to be held accountable in the event that an athlete or someone else is sexually violated.

Further, institutions should "honor the courage of whistle blowers [sic] who speak up about their own or others' abuse" (Smith & Freyd, 2014, p. 584). As such, it is especially important for survivors and their associated support system (e.g., parents, teammates) to understand the reality of their experience (Nicholson & Lutz, 2017). Then, as Miller (2013) suggested, they could reframe themselves as "truth tellers" as opposed to "whistleblowers."

Policies

When crafting treatment-related policies for survivors, stakeholders must be aware of the particular dynamics of betrayal trauma (Smith & Freyd, 2014). Individuals who were harmed by an institution might not trust that organization to offer support. To access services, limiting the need to be in contact with the institution can be very meaningful for survivors. When Ohio State offered to cover the cost of counseling services for survivors in the Strauss case, it partnered with an independent third party "experienced in providing confidential and sensitive support services" to connect survivors with service providers (Ohio State University, n.d.). On its Compliance and Integrity site, the university noted:

> No contact with the university is required, and Praesidium will not share information with Ohio State. Affected individuals can engage in counseling for as long as needed. For those who have received counseling as a result of Strauss' actions, the university will reimburse those costs.
>
> (Ohio State University, n.d.)

At a basic level, to mitigate epistemic injustice related to sexual misconduct, sport organizations must implement and uphold effective organizational policies and procedures as well as local and national laws. More fundamentally, significant change will require education, consciousness raising, and institutional courage. In many sport settings, no less is needed than a paradigm shift in culture that values the well-being of people over winning and financial gain.

Discussion Questions

1. Consider instances of reported sexual misconduct in your organizations. How have experiences or reports of the institution's response made you feel? How does betrayal trauma theory help you understand your feelings?
2. Research whistleblower policies in your organizations. How encouraged and protected would you feel to report sexual misconduct?
3. The authors stated, "Understanding the effects of betrayal blindness and traumatic amnesia could change how others perceive survivors and react to them." How could learning about these concepts prepare you to listen to a report of sexual misconduct with an open mind?

References

Abramson, K. (2014). Turning off the lights on gaslighting. *Philosophical Perspectives, 28*(1), 1–30.
Ahern, K. (2018). Institutional betrayal and gaslighting: Why whistle-blowers are so traumatized. *Continuing Education, 32*(1), 59–65.
Anderson, E. (2010). *Sport, theory, and social problems: A critical introduction.* Routledge.

Armstrong, E. A., Gleckman-Krut, M., & Johnson, L. (2018). Silence, power, and inequality: An intersectional approach to sexual violence. *Annual Review of Sociology*, *44*(1), 99–122.

Baade, R. A., & Sundberg, J. O. (1996). Fourth down and gold to go? Assessing the link between athletics and alumni giving. *Social Science Quarterly*, *77*(4), 789–803.

Bowen, F., & Blackmon, K. (2003). Spirals of silence: The dynamic effects of diversity on organizational voice. *Journal of Management Studies*, *40*(6), 1393–1417.

Callisto. (2021). *A new way to take action against sexual assault*. www.mycallisto.org

Carr, A., Dooley, B., Fitzpatrick, M., Flanagan, E., Flanagan-Howard, R., Tierney, K., . . . Egan, J. (2010). Adult adjustment of survivors of institutional child abuse in Ireland. *Child Abuse & Neglect*, *34*(7), 477–489. https://doi.org/10.1016/j.chiabu.2009.11.003

Casarez, J., Grinberg, E., Moghe, S., & Tran, L. (2018, February 1). She filed a complaint against Larry Nassar in 2014: Nothing happened. *CNN*. www.cnn.com/2018/02/01/us/msu-amanda-thomashow-complaint-larry-nassar/index.html

CNN Editorial Research. (2020, July 1). Penn state scandal fast facts. *CNN*. www.cnn.com/2013/10/28/us/penn-state-scandal-fast-facts/index.html

Coakley, J. (2017). *Sports in society: Issues and controversies* (12th ed.). McGraw-Hill.

Correa, C., & Louttit, M. (2018, January 24). More than 160 women say Larry Nassar sexually abused them: Here are his accusers in their own words. *New York Times*. www.nytimes.com/interactive/2018/01/24/sports/larry-nassar-victims.html

Donaghey, J., Cullinane, N., Dundon, T., & Wilkinson, A. (2011). Reconceptualising employee silence: Problems and prognosis. *Work, Employment, and Society*, *25*(1), 51–67.

Dotson, K. (2011). Tracking epistemic violence, tracking practices of silencing. *Hypatia*, *26*(2), 236–257.

Dzikus, L. (2012). Shreds of memory: A first-person narrative of sexual acquaintance-exploitation in a youth sports experience. *Athletic Insight*, *14*(2), 155–169.

Eggers, A. F., Groothuis, P. A., Redding, P., Rotthoff, K. W., & Solimini, M. (2019). Universities behaving badly: The impact of athletic malfeasance on student quality and enrollment. *Journal of Sports Economics*, *21*(1), 87–100. https://doi.org/10.1177/1527002519859416

Eggert, D., & White, E. (2018). Michigan state reaches $500M settlement for 332 victims of Larry Nassar. *Chicago Tribune*. www.chicagotribune.com/sports/college/ct-spt-michigan-state-larry-nassar-settlement-20180516-story.html

Epstein, D. (2020). Discounting credibility: Doubting the stories of women survivors of sexual harassment. *Seton Hall Law Review*, *51*(2), 289–329.

Fernando, D., & Prasad, A. (2019). Sex-based harassment and organizational silencing: How women are led to reluctant acquiescence in academia. *Human Relations*, *72*(10), 1565–1594.

Ferraro, K. J. (2006). *Neither angels nor demons: Women, crime, and victimization*. Northeastern University Press.

Fisher, L. A., & Anders, A. D. (2020). Engaging with cultural sport psychology to explore systemic sexual exploitation in USA Gymnastics: A call to commitments. *Journal of Applied Sport Psychology*, *32*(2), 129–145. https://doi.org/10.1080/10413200.2018.1564944

Freyd, J. J. (1994). Betrayal trauma: Traumatic amnesia as an adaptive response to childhood abuse. *Ethics & Behavior*, *4*(4), 307–329. https://doi.org/10.1207/s15327019eb0404_1

Freyd, J. J. (1996). *Betrayal trauma: The logic of forgetting childhood abuse*. Harvard University Press.

Freyd, J. J., DePrince, A. P., & Gleaves, D. (2007). The state of betrayal trauma theory: Reply to McNally (2007)—Conceptual issues and future Directions. *Memory*, *15*(3), 295–311. https://doi.org/10.1080/09658210701256514

Fricker, M. (2007). *Epistemic injustice: Power and the ethics of knowing*. Oxford University Press. https://doi.org/10.1093/acprof:oso/9780198237907.001.0001

Harlos, K. (2016). Employee silence in the context of xunethical behavior at work: A commentary. *German Journal of Human Resource Management*, *30*(3–4), 345–355.

Jacoby, K., Armour, N., & Luther J. (2020, November 16). LSU mishandled sexual misconduct complaints against students, including top athletes. *USA Today*. https://www.usatoday.com/in-depth/

sports/ncaaf/2020/11/16/lsu-ignored-campus-sexual-assault-allegations-against-derrius-guice-drake-davis-other-students/6056388002/

JDoe. (2017). *Together we are loud*. https://jdoe.io

Jones, K. (2012). The politics of intellectual self-trust. *Social Epistemology*, *26*(2), 237–251. https://doi.org/10.1080/02691728.2011.652215

Kidd, I. J., Medina, J., & Pohlhaus, G. (2017). Introduction to the Routledge handbook of epistemic injustice. In I. J. Kidd, J. Medina, & G. Pohlhaus (Eds.), *The Routledge handbook of epistemic injustice* (pp. 1–12). Taylor & Francis.

Kingkade, T. (2014a). University of Oregon allowed 3 basketball players accused of gang rape to play march madness. *The Huffington Post*. www.huffingtonpost.com/2014/05/09/university-of-oregon-rape_n_5297928.html

Kingkade, T. (2014b). Oregon finds 3 basketball players guilty of sexual assault, will remove them from campus. *The Huffington Post*. www.huffingtonpost.com/2014/06/23/oregon-sexual-assault-basketball-players_n_5522915.html

Lombardi, K. (2013, January 7). Accusation, suicide cast shadow over Fighting Irish's return to glory. *NBC News*. www.nbcnews.com/news/investigations/accusation-suicide-cast-shadow-over-fighting-irishs-return-glory-flna1B7864306

McKinnon, R. (2016). Epistemic injustice. *Philosophy Compass*, *11*(8), 437–446. https://doi.org/10.1111/phc3.12336

McKinnon, R. (2017). Allies behaving badly: Gaslighting as epistemic injustice. In G. Pohlhaus, I. J. Kidd, & J. Medina (Eds.), *The Routledge handbook of epistemic injustice* (pp. 167–174). Taylor & Francis.

Medina, J. (2013). *The epistemology of ignorance: Gender and racial oppression, epistemic injustice, and resistant imaginations*. Oxford University Press.

Miller, L. A. (2013). What you should know before you "blow": Nurses and whistle-blowing in healthcare. *Journal of Perinatal Neonatal Nursing*, *27*(3), 201–202. https://doi.org/10.1097/JPN.0b013e31829c8a90

Moore, E. E. (2012). "Sexual hyenas" and programs for at-risk youth: Structural opportunities for abuse. *Cultural Studies ↔ Critical Methodologies*, *12*(4), 361–364.

NCAA. (n.d.). *Creating a pathway to lifelong success*. Retrieved January 14, 2021, from www.ncaa.org/

Nicholson, S. B., & Lutz, D. J. (2017). The importance of cognitive dissonance in understanding and treating victims of intimate partner violence. *Journal of Aggression Maltreatment & Trauma*, *26*(5), 475–492. https://doi.org/10.1080/10926771.2017.1314989

Ohio State University. (n.d.). *Strauss investigation*. https://compliance.osu.edu/strauss-investigation.html

O'Shea, A. (2020). Survivors of Strauss abuse decry OSU's attempt to dismiss claims on statute of limitations grounds as yet another betrayal. *Public Justice*. www.publicjustice.net/wp-content/uploads/2020/08/OSU-MTD-Press-Release-0805.pdf

Perret, C. (2020, May 9). Ohio state university will pay out $41 million to 162 men who say they were sexually abused by a longtime team doctor. *Business Insider*. www.businessinsider.com/ohio-state-41-million-richard-strauss-sexual-assault-2020-5

Pinder, C. C., & Harlos, K. P. (2001). Employee silence: Quiescence and acquiescence as responses to perceived injustice. *Research in Personnel and Human Resources Management*, *20*, 331–369. https://doi.org/10.1016/S0742-7301(01)20007-3

Pinto, B., Weaver, J., & Hopper, J. (2010, December 21). Notre Dame scandal: Family of Lizzy Seeberg speaks out. *ABC News*. https://abcnews.go.com/US/family-lizzy-seeberg-college-freshman-accused-notre-dame/story?id=12448195

Pohlhaus, G. (2014). Discerning the primary epistemic harm in cases of testimonial injustice. *Social Epistemology*, *28*(2), 99–114.

Pope, D. G., & Pope, J. C. (2009). The impact of college sports success on the quantity and quality of student applications. *Southern Economic Journal*, *75*(3), 750–780.

Prewitt-White, T. R. (2019). I was his litmus test proof: An autoethnographic account of being groomed in sport. *Journal of Clinical Sport Psychology*, *13*(2), 180–195.

Rosenthal, M., Smith, C. P., & Freyd, J. J. (2017). Behind closed doors: University employees as stakeholders in campus sexual violence. *Journal of Aggression, Conflict and Peace Research, 9*(4), 290–304. https://doi.org/10.1108/jacpr-02-2017-0272

Smidt, A. M., & Freyd, J. J. (2018). Government-mandated institutional betrayal. *Journal of Trauma & Dissociation, 19*(5), 491–499. https://doi.org/10.1080/15299732.2018.1502029

Smith, C. P., & Freyd, J. J. (2013). Dangerous safe havens: Institutional betrayal exacerbates sexual trauma. *Journal of Traumatic Stress, 26*(1), 119–124. https://doi.org/10.1002/jts.21778

Smith, C. P., & Freyd, J. J. (2014). Institutional betrayal. *American Psychologist, 69*(5), 575–587. https://doi.org/10.1037/a0037564

Spoerre, A. (2019, May 2). Ex-youth coach accused of sexually exploiting more than 400 boys gets 180-year sentence. *USA Today*. www.usatoday.com/story/sports/2019/05/02/greg-stephen-youth-coach-180-years-sexual-exploitation/3656830002/

St. Clair, S., & Lighty, T. (2010, December 16). It feels like a betrayal. *Chicago Tribune*. www.chicagotribune.com/news/ct-xpm-2010-12-16-chi-20101216-nd-story-story.html

Stewart, H. (2019). "Why didn't she say something sooner?": Doubt, denial, silencing, and the epistemic harms of the #MeToo movement. *South Central Review, 36*(2), 68–94.

Sweet, P. L. (2019). The sociology of gaslighting. *American Sociological Review, 84*(5), 851–875.

Trombino, C., & Funk, M. (2019). *Report of the independent investigation: Sexual abuse committed by Dr. Richard Strauss at the Ohio state university*. https://compliance.osu.edu/assets/site/pdf/Revised_report.pdf

Wang, Y., & Hsieh, H. (2013). Organizational ethical climate, perceived organizational support, and employee silence: A cross-level investigation. *Human Relations, 66*(6), 783–802.

Wertheim, J. (2020, October 5). Why aren't more people talking about the Ohio state sex abuse scandal? *Sports Illustrated*. www.si.com/college/2020/10/05/ohio-state-sex-abuse-daily-cover

SECTION II
Personal Narratives*

---

* A gentle reminder to readers that this section includes personal narratives from individuals who have experienced or witnessed sexual misconduct. We encourage you to take good care of your emotional wellbeing and to seek out survivor advocates and/or clinical professionals for support if/when necessary.

6

I WAS HIS LITMUS TEST

Being Groomed as a Child Athlete

Tanya Prewitt-White

Grooming refers to practices used by adult acquaintances to gain sexual access to and control over children (Brackenridge & Fasting, 2005; Dietz, 2018; Lanning, 2018; Lanning & Dietz, 2014). The purpose of grooming on the behalf of a child sex offender is often, but is not always, to eventually engage in sexual acts with a child (Lanning, 2018). It involves the child sex offender slowly gaining trust before systematically breaking down relational barriers between the perpetrator and the child prior to committing sexual exploitation. This process may take anywhere from weeks to several years with the perpetrator usually progressing slowly to maintain secrecy (Lanning, 2018).

To avoid discovery, child sex offenders manipulate the child and test her[1] to see if she will disclose the coercion or exploitation of power. It is because the initial grooming behavior equates to seemingly innocent and harmless conduct that the perpetrator is able to carefully and strategically assess the response(s) of his[2] target child as well as others connected to such children (e.g., parents, grandparents, guardians, siblings, teammates) and to retreat or withdraw without consequence should he be faced with resistance (Brackenridge & Fasting, 2005).

Nonaggressive and calculated grooming practices generally entail the perpetrator in (1) identifying his preferred child target; (2) gathering information about her goals, dreams, and interests as well as her vulnerabilities; (3) gaining access to spend one-on-one time with her; (4) lessening her inhibitions; and (5) securing and maintaining control over her through bonding activities (Lanning, 2010, 2018). The perpetrator combines outwardly benevolent, helpful, and caring comportment with attention, gifts, and presents as well as individual privileges to gradually coerce, seduce, and gain control of the child (Dietz, 2018; Groth & Birnbaum, 1979). In the sport setting, grooming also involves providing "intangible feelings of being special, high self-esteem, confidence, superiority and security" (Brackenridge & Fasting, 2005, p. 36) for the child target on the athletic team. Moreover, sport grooming is facilitated by the gradual building of the athlete's trust in the coach as he scaffolds her performance or presents the possibility of achieving her athletic dreams such as winning championships or earning an athletic scholarship (see Brackenridge & Fasting, 2005).

DOI: 10.4324/9781003125884-8

Leberg (1997) suggested three categories of grooming: (1) *physically* grooming the target child (e.g., inappropriately putting a hand—which could be perceived or claimed to be inadvertent—on the athlete's thigh as he demonstrates how to properly block out an opponent in basketball); (2) *psychologically* grooming both the child and her family (e.g., a coach telling an athlete and her parents she needs to go to a summer camp to improve her skills and he happens to be one of the overnight camp counselors); and (3) *grooming of the social environment* or the community (e.g., a coach building a winning program to ensure no one challenges his practices and, thus, his reputation serves as his alibi).

As the perpetrator employs these three forms of grooming concurrently, the gradual and systematic erosion of boundaries escalates and goes unnoticed, unrecognized, and/or unreported by the community, parents, fellow athletes, and coaches as well as the athlete herself. The child is usually unsuspecting and unaware of the measured destruction of the interpersonal boundary between her and her coach. Once, and if the athlete recognizes the lack of personal boundaries between her and her coach, she already feels and is entrapped (Brackenridge, 2001; Brackenridge & Fasting, 2005).

If the grooming practices work (i.e., sexual abuse occurs), the resulting compliance of the child is often improperly interpreted as a lack of victimization or consent (Lanning, 2005). Grooming brings about the appearance of cooperation from the child, making the sexual abuse seem consensual. Unfortunately, the results of this vindictive, deliberate process are often easier to identify as grooming than the progression of techniques utilized by the perpetrator. Consequently, there is grey area that must be acknowledged and understood though certain grooming behaviors (e.g., affection, touching, hugging, massaging may provide sexual gratification for the offender and constitute sex offenses by themselves; Lanning, 2018). Thus, not surprisingly, ambiguity is one of the skills the successful perpetrator has in his selection of vindictive grooming practices (Brackenridge, 1997, 2001; Cense, 1997; Lanning, 2018).

This brings me to sharing my experience of recalling countless incidents of manipulative emotional and psychological exploitation I experienced at the hands of a former basketball coach.[3] I did not realize and hence admit until I was 31 years of age that I had been violated by Coach. The more memories I painstakingly ruminated on, the more memories surfaced. As a young girl the only thing I ever wanted was to be a great basketball player. I was convinced Coach could help me do this. He swayed the community, the basketball program and its parents, my parents—namely my father, a man who at one point was his friend and fellow coach, the school system and most importantly, me. But, he did not end his conquest there. His conquests continued for 14 more years before being imprisoned. He was sentenced in 2013 for thousands of phone calls and text messages over a six-month span to a 15-year-old girl who he groomed, coerced into a romantic relationship, and later sexually assaulted. Though the court could not prove without a reasonable doubt the sexual assault occurred, the fact that he had used a cell phone to solicit and commit a sex crime with a minor was undeniable. From the moment I learned of the allegations, I believed with certainty Coach was capable of molesting a young girl. Unbeknownst to my adult psyche, he had fine-tuned his grooming skills and worked on perfecting his sexual dishonor on my younger self.

I recognize the narrative is seldom solely the author's own (Morse & Richards, 2002). I do not own the entirety of this story, yet I do own how I share my truth. As a former child and female athlete, who was groomed for sexual advances, I do not believe in keeping secrets and thus, choose to tell and reveal my story (see Ellis, 2007). The ensuing narrative inevitably involves individuals from my hometown (e.g., former teammates, family members, and parents of teammates as well as the perpetrating coach, his family members and defenders who all may be further roused by the accounts); thus, names and identities are used only when necessary to minimize continued harm.

I hope my narrative allows for moments of clarity, connection, transformation, and examination; the self, others, and culture positioned not in equilibrium but in flux throughout an autoethnographic narrative (Jones, 2005)—a space sexual misconduct in sport necessitates. The piece "does not simply look at [the] social phenomena, [it] situates [me] in a personal story walking the readers through a journey" (Prewitt, 2010, p. 73). As Goodall (1997) states, "we are never detached neutral observers" (p. 127); thus, I am not a neutral onlooker in my own experience nor are you, as the reader, a neutral observer of yours or others. Thus, I expose feelings, biases, and assumptions in order for them to be analyzed and reflected upon (see Ellis, 1999). If nothing else, this work may assist in revealing the complexity of being groomed as a child in sport and not realizing it until over a decade later. The story began long before I wrote it and will remain long after it is read. Together, readers and I can process experiences of sexual misconduct through sharing parts of our lives rather than isolating ourselves from the world in and outside of sport. Ellis (1997, 2004) claims that both reading and writing will simultaneously be therapeutic, theoretical, emotional, and cognitive; this is my aspiration.

Most importantly, I do not seek to take claim over work in sexual misconduct that has been collectively journeyed by others (e.g., the research and advocacy work of Celia Brackenridge, Kari Fasting, Gretchen Kerr, and Ashley Sterling). I rely and lean on the work, expertise, and support of others and do not claim myself as knowing all, though I am a vocal advocate and community activist in sexual misconduct work both in and out of sport. Unashamed, I now disclose my #metoo story of being groomed by a former coach.

I Was His Litmus Test

Sometimes I have had to stand still in silence to process my experience. I am no longer standing still, and I am no longer silent. This narrative is a panorama of my reckoning with the reality of being groomed by a coach whom I at one time revered and later grew to despise. I am beyond believing it is mere coincidence that my former coach is in prison for sexual assault of a minor—I was being primed as a sexual conquest of his from 1991 to 1999. Countless memories casted far away in my subconsciousness had not become existent until the summer of 2013 when I talked over the phone and met with his child target and survivor.

As a former athlete under Coach, a woman who believed the survivor, an advocate for girls in sport and someone who had made a career in sport, I felt it my responsibility to support her. She would soon be providing her testimony, sitting in a court room to relive her dreadful experience in front of a jury, judge, spiteful family, and friends of Coach, and of course Coach himself. I had given my accounts to the detective working for the District Attorney and was subpoenaed but never called to the stand in the case. I sat rows behind the survivor in the courtroom at the final sentencing to physically display my allegiance and was only further horrified for all she endured. I listened to her experiences and empathized with her pain. Though, I was not only empathizing with her; I realized I was a survivor, too, regardless if the courts, or a lawyer, or even Coach would name me as such. Her strength and bravery amidst injustice stirred me in person, over the phone and when I observed her presence in the courtroom.

I always knew there was something tasteless and unsuitable about Coach; and, following my high school playing years I had strong opinions that he was ill-equipped to coach females. Others silenced me and forbade me to speak my convictions. I found it unacceptable that he told sexual jokes to high school girls, that he enjoyed playing mind games with the female athletes he coached and that his strategy was to pit girls against one another. Moreover, a renowned womanizer should not have the opportunity to influence impressionable young girls. I felt guilty that I could not stop him from negatively influencing young female athletes from my hometown. I could not prove he was unfit to coach girls' basketball especially since he had produced so many conference, regional, and sectional championship teams as well as made numerous state appearances as a coach. He was charming, successful, and seemingly unstoppable. I was challenged to find an audience who wanted to hear my truth. The truth can be a shifting target when it comes to grooming behavior and I was his litmus test before anyone, even I, recognized. I started practicing with his teams when I was only a fourth grader. At the time, he was my idol and someone who I wanted to play for if I earned the chance. Years later that could not be farther from my hopes.

I soon learned of similarities between the survivor's experience and my own; and, each time she gave name to her experience, my body clenched. I could not help but question why he had never *crossed the line* with me. Yet, when the survivor described how *icky* she felt when Coach held her hand and how he caressed the base of her wrist with his middle finger— I froze. Time stood still. I thought, *"How do I know exactly what she is describing?" "Did he hold my hand, too?" "Did I put it so far out of my conscious memory to forget it?"* He did hold my hand—tears escaped my eyelids like a runaway fugitive. My body remembered it; I felt as if he was touching me that very moment as the hair on my arms stood perked. I knew the caress she described. I could not deny or escape it. Viscerally distraught I could not breathe enough air into my lungs. I felt suffocated as the shock paused the beating of my heart. I took deep breaths to keep my own emotions in check. What started off as me attempting to support the survivor transpired into my recognition I was surviving my own past. But, then she shared what this universal sign communicated—*I want to have sex with you*. This time slow, solitary traveling tears traversed my cheekbone and chin until I wiped them with my bare forearm.

Equally weakening to my physical and spiritual body, the survivor described being in Coach's house alone recalling the first time he put his hand on her thigh. Again, my body tensed, a chill quivered the length of my spine and tears regathered glossing my gaze. I knew this happened to me—at least once. As she described his living room and him closing his front curtains, I knew it in my body—I had sat in that same space. She was naming my experience, too. I listened and attempted to support her as countless summer afternoons besieged my memory. Memories where I sat on his family's couch or at their counter as he made me a meal—just the two of us, curtains closed. And, I cannot tell you how many more additional times I felt awkward when his daughters or wife would come home to Coach and me playing cards or him making a meal as the two of us sang to oldies, Coach's favorite music genre, playing on the radio. I never put together that the majority of time I spent alone with Coach never revolved around playing or practicing basketball.

That evening I wept rushes of salty tears I could taste on my cotton pillowcase as I lay in my childhood home unable to sleep as a 31-year-old woman. I had no choice but to acknowledge and admit to myself more than anyone that I had been violated, though not sexually penetrated, by my high school basketball coach. I wracked my brain—*Did anything more happen? Can I recount anything else? Did he kiss me on the lips? What else had I forgotten?*

Was my memory failing me—protecting me from the possibilities? Yet, when I heard the stories, my body knew.

I conceded that this was only the beginning of my journey of recognizing I had been groomed by Coach. I had been oblivious to this fact and even when giving a statement to the detective investigating the case, I had not recognized the reality of my experience. Sadness, anger, shame, and disappointment overwhelmed my limp spirit, soul, and body. *How did I never put it all together until I spoke with the survivor?* I began to wonder what was real, what was imagined, and what had I forgotten? I learned to become accustomed to my new lived reality—I was not only a vocal advocate but a survivor.

I do know after all of my reflection, Coach had always taken a liking to me but not for the reasons I had thought as an adolescent. I was one of his favorites and when asking former teammates, parents, and fans they all knew it, too. In my naivety, I thought it was because I was a hard worker not because he was attracted to me. I was motivated to be the best I could be. I was a leader, the kid who wanted to do the right thing and that you did not have to push me because I had even higher expectations for my comportment and performance than anyone else could.

Coach told my parents they were "lucky to have a kid who loved basketball as much as Tonner, (my childhood nickname he had given me)." My parents recalled countless times Coach told them, "I love Tonner like a daughter." My parents beamed and were led to believe that Coach's special taking to me was for my love of the game and because I was "such a great kid."

As a 12-year-old pubescent girl, I sat in the living room of my childhood home innumerable times looking out into the street through the large bay window as I chatted with Coach on our family portable telephone—short chats no longer than five minutes. He often called to tell me I was *special* and was going to be the best point guard to ever come out of my high school. At the end of every conversation, he consistently chimed, "don't tell your dad we had this talk." As a young girl, I thought it was because he did not want my father to think he was telling me I could be better than the current point guard on the varsity team. I felt awkward about those phone calls even as a child. Although, I could not put my finger on it—I could never put my finger on it until, that is, it was too late.

Coach and I spent time together during summer months when I would be at home while my parents worked to provide opportunities for my sister and me. He often took me raspberry or strawberry picking, to breakfast in a nearby rural community or invited me to his home to play bridge. He would always tell me, "I think you're going to be the best guard to ever come out of this town, but don't tell your dad I told you that;" and "Don't tell your dad I called;" and, "Don't tell your dad I came to visit." Often people assume that sexual predators lure on children from broken homes or on kids with uninvolved parents. My family, parents, and home were a strong and solid foundation and unselfishly involved in the community, faith, and philanthropic organizations. My older sister and I were latch key kids; but, it was a time when two working parents often left their children home alone checking in with them via phone and always having neighbors on the lookout. I was a book smart rule follower, a high achiever and was taught to respect authority. Regrettably, I now understand all of those times he was advising not to tell my dad he was only testing and waiting to see if I would snitch.

One afternoon Coach phoned me to see what I was up to and what was going on at my house. My sister, and feisty protector, was away at softball practice and my parents were working. Coach asked if he could stop by and I obliged. Minutes later, his six-foot-plus frame, wide shoulders, and athletic build shadowed any sun light as I opened the double door to the entryway of our bi-level family home. In his large hands laid a leather Lakers jacket and he said, "This is for you, Tonner. You can be a great point guard like Magic." I was only a kid. The head high school basketball coach bought me a leather jacket. I was astonished. I gave him a hug as a sign of my gratitude and he whispered in my ear, "Now, don't tell your parents who you got it from. Love you, Tonner."

This was strange to me; it did not feel right in my body. I felt torn between feeling special and awkward. *How could I get away with not telling my parents where I got the Lakers leather jacket?* I was not one for hiding things from people. *Why didn't my sister get a leather jacket—she was special? Was I more special than my teammates? Could I tell anyone that Coach got me this?* Confusion and isolation consumed me. I hid the jacket, never wore it while it was in my possession and I desperately hoped that Coach would not bring up that fact. After giving it to me, Coach and I never spoke of the leather Lakers jacket again.

Years later in 1998, the summer between my sophomore and junior year of high school, I spent abundant one-on-one time with Coach. Monday, Wednesday, and Friday mornings before the heat and humidity became too strong, I would drive to Coach's house and we would go for a three to four-mile jog. According to Coach, as a point guard I needed to be the most fit player on the court and I took his word as commandment. His cologne pungent, running shirtless through town with my 16-year-old self. Once he asked if I thought he looked good with his shirt off. *How was I to respond?* I did not find him attractive, but I did not want to disappoint him. I remember, again, feeling this was strange but he was my coach. Mostly I wondered, "*What if my teammates saw me running with him? How should I react if they saw us?*" I dreaded my teammates seeing us because I did not want them to think Coach favored me. Looking back, he did.

Following our runs, Coach would go and shower quickly or make me something to eat as I sat at his kitchen island. Sometimes it would be just the two of us and other times his wife or one of his three daughters would be home. Ironically, I felt relief when his wife or daughters were not in the space because the attention Coach gave me in their presence caused unease one could not see but I felt in my stirred body.

Coach and I would often play a game of bridge. He would give me something he had prepared for me—soup, venison, pickled vegetables—to take home before my parents returned from a day's work. He shared with me that summer that his three daughters claimed he loved and spent more time with me than he did them. I did not want him to be fonder of me than his own daughters. I had a Dad and a great one.

That same summer Coach gifted me a session with a masseuse in town. I do not know if I ever told a soul I received that massage as a 16-year-old—a secret between Coach, the masseuse, and me. He asked me if I enjoyed it. I kept it simple with a "yes, thanks Coach." Though, in truth, I felt uneasy about it and did not want another massage gifted to me. As a kid, I must have realized the expectation of reciprocation and knew I had no gifts or favors to give in return.

Coach maneuvered his way in when my parents might be working or pre-occupied during busy holidays for their floral business. As a proclaimed friend of my father, he offered to drive me to and from my sixth-grade basketball game on Valentine's Day, the busiest day of the year for my parents' flower shop. It is the first time he told me, on Valentine's Day nonetheless, that he "loved me like a daughter." A year later I received Valentine's Day flowers from Coach as a seventh grader. I came across the handwritten card when I was frantically cleaning out my childhood closet at my parents' home looking for any evidence to prove I had been groomed and it read, "*Thanks for coming to the game. Love, Coach.*" Looking back, I received numerous Valentine's gifts from Coach—incremental nudges to see how I and others would respond. I did not love him like a father and I never told him so. *Was that what he was waiting for?*

I was gifted balloons in eighth grade after going to the first varsity basketball game of the season. The handwritten card read, "*It won't be long before you're playing varsity. Keep working hard. Love, Coach.*" I could recognize his handwriting anywhere. The irony—he bought the cards, balloons, and other gifts at one of my parents' floral shops. Though, he always handwrote the card. His scheme playing out in front of my parents, me, and others in the community to see (e.g., secretaries, school teachers and fellow athletes and parents of the athletes). He did not have to follow the rules. He was like Teflon—he thought nothing would stick, no rules applied to him. It was all a game to him—the one-on-one time, the gifts; I was a game to him.

Frankly, everyone knew that Coach gave gifts to athletes and he disguised it by claiming he gave all of the athletes who played for him presents. My father, who coached with him, even thought it strange he gave the entire basketball team jewelry for Christmas one year. Some teammates' parents complained to the athletic director though nothing came of it besides advising Coach to stop giving gifts to female athletes. He simply selectively and secretly gave gifts after that. Though I cannot remember every gift I ever received from Coach I can unquestionably share that I received more gifts from Coach than any other man, aside from my husband.

In this light, Coach never wanted me to have a boyfriend and would make comments that I would not focus on basketball if I had a boy in my life. *Was Coach the reason I neglected to and often feared dating in high school?* This is a hard realization to reflect upon and admit as a grown woman—to realize Coach did not take a liking to me only because I was a good basketball player, but mostly because he had sexual intentions for the two of us.

When I was a freshman in high school, during the week of sectional finals, I made the juvenile choice to go to a boys' hockey playoff game rather than go to basketball practice. My parents knew I had decided to go to the hockey game and said it was my choice to make as long as I was prepared for any consequences. The next day before practice, Coach pulled my freshman petite frame aside, hovered over me and spewed with resentment, "You're special, Tonner. You've disappointed me. I love you like a daughter and you're putting me in a hard position." He shared he was still going to allow me to dress for the game, but I should never do something like that again—especially for a boys' hockey game. Before finishing his forewarning, he once more reminded me he loved me like a daughter and that I need to stay away from boys, especially a hockey player, because they and he would distract me. My focus should be on my academic success and playing basketball. With further reflection, I admitted to myself he consistently asked who I had a crush on, who my dates to dances were or would be—my dating life, or lack thereof, was always his concern.

There was a plethora of pretty girls on my team, I could not fathom Coach would like me in a way that I now know he undeniably did. As a grown woman, my mind went in circles to attempt to discover the reasons Coach had disciplined me as one of his chosen ones. It took time to convince myself it had more to do with my characteristics, personality, and looks than anything else. They say 20/20 vision makes all things clear, and in this light, Coach had a history of choosing the girl who wanted to win, to be the best she could, was a hard worker and respected authority. Most importantly, she must be attractive (from my opinion of the girls he targeted). He told me ceaselessly I was "pretty" and "cute." My sister was known for being the pretty Prewitt girl growing up and I was simply her sweet little sister, so I never took to heart what he said.

Moreover, I suspected he was more attracted by other women since he openly made comments about high school girls who were "lookers," especially those who had voluptuous chests or bouncy backsides, or which girls had pretty moms and would become the same. I never put together that my mother was attractive, often being adored for her beautiful skin and gorgeous face, and he may have seen some future possibility in me.

Simply, talking about the female body was commonplace for Coach even while coaching adolescent girls in his immediate presence. I am saddened that I never had *hard* evidence to prove he was the last man who should be coaching young girls. Somehow, to others it seemed, his comments were not enough—locker room talk with no intent. Intuitions, gut feelings, and impressions only seemed to get me so far in proving anything. Plus, how could I ever prove that his comments were not in jest but that he had intention behind them? Unfortunately, the evidence was right in front of my very eyes—my lived experience—the space and place where he displayed his plethora of grooming behaviors. Indeed, I was his litmus test.

My teammates and I knew he was having an affair my junior year of high school. We were ranked #1 in the state all season long, we remained undefeated, and it was during the thick of the season. The last thing Coach wanted was his personal drama negatively influencing the team; though it already had. As teenage girls, my teammates joked about his marital transgressions and public affair when preparing for a game in the locker room. I told my father that my teammates did neither respect Coach nor did they want to play for him. Later that week my father told Coach he needed to address the team about the situation because we all knew and were talking about it.

The next day, Coach decided to take care of it by attempting to employ me to do his dirty work. Prior to practice, as athletes were having their ankles taped and nonchalantly tossing basketballs at the hoop, Coach moved toward me as I came out of the locker room and told me to come with him to get the weighted basketball out of storage. *Why me and not the team manager who always gets the equipment?* I questioned myself silently. Once we reached the dark, suffocating closet, he told me to come inside and then shut and locked the door behind me. I inhaled the smell of his cologne that permeated the stale air. His taller, broader, and stronger presence intimidated me. He pressed his body close to mine in the crowded closet and looked down at me with his exhalation clouding my forehead. His words spattered with saliva on my bare forehead as he shared he loved me like one of his own kids and I was *special*. He proceeded to tell me he loves his wife and family and would never cheat on her and pleaded for me to believe him. He further defended he loved me like a daughter, too. He asked, "Do you believe me? You must believe I didn't have an affair?" I stood in disbelief at what was transpiring. *Did I have a choice but to mutter "yes?"*

Once he felt vindicated, Coach commanded I go into the locker room after practice and tell my teammates that it was a rumor, he was not having an affair; and, it was my job as the captain of the team to make it right. He questioned me to confirm I understood his directive. I complied, "yes, Coach." Before leaving the closet again he told me he loved me like one of his own and reached out for a smothering hug. I felt the entirety of his body clammed up against mine and the bulge of his manhood around my belly button. Confusion and embarrassment poured through my veins as he held the embrace for what felt like minutes. Then, he unlocked the closet door and motioned for me to leave the storage space.

I never went into the locker room and claimed that his affair was simply a small-town rumor as he had instructed me to do nor did I tell my teammates Coach locked me in a closet. I said nothing. I felt awkward, violated, and perplexed. While I could not name it, I knew something was not right. I never shared with a soul that Coach locked me in a closet until I was 31 years old. In fact, I had forgotten about it. To this day I do not know why I did not say something at the time. And, at 31, I questioned former teammates if Coach ever said he loved them like a daughter and they told me "no." I was disheartened because I was fully conscious of the reality of my lived truth—I was his litmus test and my body knew it first.

I wanted to quit basketball after that season. We had lost in the state semi-final, our only loss of the season. It was my father who I first told that I intended to hang up my shoes. I shared that I never wanted to play basketball again even though our team remained was ranked #1 in the state for my senior year and four of us starters were returning. Coach made it miserable for me and I had lost my love for the game. *Maybe it was the pressure?* I was unsure and unable to name it.

My father, a basketball junky, assured me I should not play unless I had a passion for the game. *Did he see a change in me?* I know he saw that I was no longer having fun. As a kid, I never went more than a day without a ball in my hand but did not touch a basketball for two months that spring. In May, I asked my father if we could go to the Indiana basketball camp we had gone to when I was a sixth grader. He signed me up and took me to the camp. I was a camper and Dad was a camp counselor for another age group. It was the most memorable week I ever shared with my father while he was living. I won the free-throw and three-point contest and earned second place amidst 300 campers in the one-on-one tournament. I beamed not because of my success in the camp but because my passion was back.

I had and have always been very close to my father, but after that I have no recollection of inappropriate behavior from Coach occurring. Coach could not get to me because of a wall my father built to protect me. He could not get in—there was no room for him. Years later, after Coach was being convicted of sexual abuse of a minor, my father shared with me that he confronted Coach that summer and told him to stay away from his daughter. Though my father was attempting to protect me from having to get in the middle of Coach's family drama—his affairs with his wife and its impact on his ability and effectiveness to coach. Dad had told Coach to keep me out of his dirty work and to stop using me as a decoy in his play-boy ways. He had not been consciously aware that I had been the target of Coach's grooming behavior; nevertheless, Dad intervened. I was Coach's unsuccessful litmus test and from there on out, he would treat me as though he had no use for me unless it was on the basketball court. My teammates and I went undefeated my senior year and won a state championship despite Coach's antics and drama; sadly, our success provided him a better alibi and he was onto his next child conquest.

Reflections

Some stories people do not want me to tell. Remaining in my timidity and silence serve the fragility and comfort for those who were involved in or observing the story unfold over the years. It is easier to turn away, neglect, or avoid—pretending such violations to young girls did not occur as the community watched, cheered on, and revered him, his teams, and the athletes who played for him. Further, I recognize it is easier to name me as the distasteful messenger of the vicious truth. Possibly, sitting with and speaking my truth causes others to reflect on their co-creation and negligence of misconduct against children. Thus, some have attempted to convince me that my truth is only self-serving and indulgent navel gazing (Mykalovskiy, 1997)—my experience not severe enough to classify as abuse. I have learned not to give my experiential, psychological, emotional, and intellectual labor to those who have not asked for it or those not ready to receive it (Jerkins, 2018). If they do not want to believe it, then they cannot see or envision it. If anyone can understand this, it is me. I did not want to believe that I had been groomed. In fact, that was the last reality I wanted to envision. Recognizing all of those times alone with Coach were not what I had thought they were, caused me to question my own ability to recall and make sense of my past.

I never cooperated with his advances, yet I never fully turned him away either. I was in no way physically attracted to Coach and did not need him for emotional support; though, when I look back he often tried to pit me against my father whom I love(d) dearly. My conscious and sub-conscious discomfort aligned with recognizing that most of my experiences with Coach were unwanted and, undoubtedly, classify as harassment. Sexual harassment is unwanted and, to the novice bystander, sexual abuse that occurs following a process of grooming may seem desired and even consented to when a child has been groomed by a perpetrator (Brackenridge & Fasting, 2005). Since I did not experience "coerced collaboration in genital acts. . . . [I]t could be argued that [I] had not been abused but merely harassed" (Brackenridge & Fasting, 2005, p. 35). Whatever it is named, I was his failed attempt to generate intimate sexual contact.

I have grappled with the guilt that I did not recognize his behavior, but he had groomed me (and others connected to me) to see it as normal. I have asked myself why he did not sexually violate me? I know that he held my hand, placed his hand on my exposed thigh, caressed my wrist, gave me hugs—his presence unsettling my equilibrium. It is a terrible thing to wish that someone would have violated you so you might have been able to stop the pain of others. I spent countless nights wishing for this.

But, would I have stood up, then and there, and spoken out? Would others have believed me? Or, would they have silenced me further? They silenced me when I was in college and openly shared that I was appalled he was allowed to coach female athletes. After Coach's court hearing I read in the comment section of the local online newspaper that adults in my hometown knew of his behavior for decades. Then, why didn't they stop it? Did they try? Did they tell the school board? And, did the school board turn away? Members of administration and leadership attended games and joined the bandwagon. No one stood up and stopped the hurt, the cycle. I wrestled with being angry that adults did not do more—adults who I love and adore. I have been angry that people did not believe me and that I allowed people to silence me. But, mostly I felt sadness and isolation. I have healed and am healing by coming to terms with the fact that it was never my fault. Coach was a master manipulator who not only groomed me but also bullied and groomed an entire community. My resultant strength is my counterstory to the pain he inflicted.

Recommendations for Adult Readers Who May Be Triggered

It is possible someone reading this autoethnography has been triggered by subconscious childhood memories of your own. You may be questioning an experience(s) or a relationship with an adult and grappling with your past. You might be wondering if you had been groomed or sexually violated and are second-guessing the memoirs you had believed were your childhood. Possibly, you are grieving what you thought you lived and the new realized reality is heartbreakingly painful. I believe you and irrespective of the end result, the length of time you endured your experience or how many years or decades have passed, reliving it is grave and feels awful. I am here with you. You are not alone. I believe you.

I also recognize denial feels safe and you do not want to analyze or re-imagine or relive. Take the time you need—it certainly is a lot to process. Journal, exercise, cry—cry a lot, do something you love, spend time alone, and please find someone who can provide the emotional, psychological, and physical space for you to share and heal. For some, this is seeking a licensed counselor or psychologist, a trusted faith leader, a parent, a relative, or a friend. Through survivor advocacy organizations we can also join support groups if we feel comfortable doing so. Please know, too, our parents, family members, friends, and partners may have their own ways to cope with learning of our experience. It is neither our job to protect them from our truth nor may we be able to hold their pain while sitting in our own. We must also recognize that sometimes our anguish is too much for those who love us to bear and if we experience this, we might need to seek a licensed professional for both our own and for the well-being of our loved ones.

Wherever you are in the process, whatever you feel, however is the best way for you to healthily cope, survive, function, and manage, give yourself the permission to be in that space. I know it hurts. We all survive and thrive differently. We can and do heal. We do not control what happened to us; we own how our story ends.

Call to Action for Grooming Prevention and Boundary Education Training in Sport

It is challenging to foresee how seemingly harmless behaviors lead to sexual abuse in sport (Brackenridge & Fasting, 2005; Wurtele, 2012). These exploitations are often overlooked since perpetrators "groom children and the parents of those children, the organizations through which they work or volunteer with children, and the communities in which they function" (Dietz, 2018, p. 30). Unfortunately, coupled with the trust bestowed to the coach, the permission to be around the child on a regular basis and the power in his position of authority provides a camouflage for grooming (Brackenridge, 2001; Brackenridge & Fasting, 2005). High-profile cases have brought attention to sexual misconduct in sport (e.g., Jerry Sandusky at Penn State, Larry Nassar with Michigan State and USA Gymnastics, Rick Curl with USA Swimming, and the former Amateur Athletic Union President, Robert Dodd) and sport stakeholders are aware much work needs to be done though they are unsure of what direction to take in education and training. Since millions of children are playing sport, it is imperative that organizations implement, among other things, grooming prevention and boundary education training targeting athletes, parents, coaches, staff members, and administrators alike (Stirling & Kerr, 2009; Wurtele, 2012).

Grooming Prevention and Boundary Education for Coaches

The success a perpetrator has in masking his grooming for mentoring or coaching can make it challenging to overcome the false belief that such a *nice guy* could have an intent to harm or be harming children (Lanning & Dietz, 2014). To further complicate the issue, many coaches fear their well-intentioned and non-manipulative actions could be wrongly mistaken for grooming due to the grey area between mentoring and grooming (Brackenridge & Fasting, 2005; Lanning & Dietz, 2014). Thus, and rightly so, coaches express concern of being falsely accused of harassment or abuse when they express care or affection for the athletes they coach (Brackenridge, 2001; Brackenridge & Fasting, 2005). These are concerns that must be addressed and validated while also highlighting the risk factors they may face as coaches. For example, the personal contact coaches have with athletes and "given the right combination of personal and professional circumstances, [every coach] is at risk for sexual misconduct" (Fibkins, 2006, p. 19). In this light, Celenza (2007) reminds us that "we are all vulnerable to this type of transgression" (p. xxiii) and this is a possibility every coach and sport stakeholder must wrestle with.

Moreover, rather than transgress with intention and premeditation, some who sexually exploit children appear to make bad judgments and fall into a slippery slope of boundary violations (Simon, 1995). Toftegaard Nielsen (2001) shared that coaches' motivation to engage in a sexual relationship may not have existed when their grooming process began. Thus, more reason for grooming in sport, which begins with boundary crossing and violating, to be openly discussed and explored in boundary education training with coaches. Such training should also include: (1) how to avoid boundary violating relationships with athletes as well as how to steer clear of behaviors that may be misinterpreted as sexual misconduct; (2) how to develop close connections with youth while avoiding sexual misconduct; (3) how to recognize when they or other coaches are becoming too emotionally involved with or sexually attracted to an athlete; and (4) how to intervene should it appear boundaries are being crossed (Wurtele, 2012).

Grooming Prevention and Boundary Education for Athletic Administrators

Athletic administrators need to be "vigilant with respect to the behavior of coaches" (Cense & Brackenridge, 2001, p. 27) as they have opportunities to observe athletes for warning signs of grooming and abuse and can prevent serious transgressions (Brackenridge, 2001; Cense & Brackenridge, 2001). Through surveys, Noble and Vermillion (2014) found that youth sport administrators believed child abuse is a serious problem, though they did not view it as an issue at their respective institutions or organizations. Moreover, one-third of respondents did not feel confident in their ability to detect sexual abuse. Thus, sport administrators need increased training in sexual misconduct, in particular the ability to identify not only the behavioral responses of potential victims but also the warning behaviors of perpetrators (Noble & Vermillion, 2014). Unquestionably, athletic administrators play a key role in ensuring the training, monitoring, and supervision of coaches; thus, by assisting coaches in maintaining appropriate professional boundaries, athletic administrators can protect the integrity of the organization and might also help prevent sexual exploitation (Cense & Brackenridge, 2001; Wurtele, 2012).

Additionally, in terms of education for athletic administrators, having awareness that a power imbalance between men and women is regarded as a predisposing risk factor for sexual misconduct is paramount. Sexual misconduct is a common issue in spaces where men hold positions of power (such as in the majority of sport organizations; Cense & Brackenridge,

2001; McCabe & Hardman, 2005; Willness et al., 2007). Whether they involve athletes, coaches, or administrators, the masculine domain of sport creates an organizational culture that may become tolerant of unethical behavior such as sexual misconduct (Taylor & Hardin, 2017). If the sexual exploitation of athletes is to be contested, it behooves all athletic administrators to examine the problem seriously (Fasting et al., 2007). Therefore, athletic administrators must engage in critical reflection and conversations to transform the culture. Even more so, they should commit to create and maintain a zero-tolerance culture for any sexual misconduct (Cense & Brackenridge, 2001).

Grooming Prevention and Boundary Education for All Parties Involved in Sport

While boundary education is important for coaches and athletic administrators, history demonstrates that individuals holding these positions may be perpetrators and/or complicit to the behavior of perpetrators. In this light, boundary education should be delivered to not only coaches and athletic administrators but also staff members involved with sport teams, athletes, and parents. The said training for all parties in sport should be comprised of discussions unpacking: (1) the imbalance of power between coaches and athletes; (2) the difference between personal and professional boundaries; (3) the warning signs of potential boundary violations; (4) the need for all parties to avoid boundary violations; (5) the harm caused by sexual boundary violations; and, (6) acknowledging barriers to intervening when boundaries are violated (Wurtele, 2012).

Additionally, since much of the training and education will only inform those coaches who do not want to harm athletes or cross barriers, to minimize coaches' ability to violate athletes, it is important to reduce the omnipotence of coaches. To do this, sport organizations should assign multiple coaches to each team and when able, coaches should represent a diversity of gender identities (e.g., man, woman, non-conforming on the gender continuum) and incorporate parents in appropriate aspects of coaching their children (see Cense & Brackenridge, 2001). Last but not least, sport organizations will need trained individuals to facilitate grooming prevention and boundary education and should seek out experts qualified, prepared, and committed to doing this work (e.g., contact the Association of Applied Sport Psychology for recommendations or a local rape survivor advocacy organization; www.appliedsportpsych.org).

Sexual Misconduct Training for Sport Psychology Professionals

Without question, sport psychology professionals may have opportunities to identify and ameliorate grooming behaviors due to the one-on-one and team settings we often work in and thus may be very familiar with athletes' emotional states and personality traits (Fasting et al., 2007). Further, Fasting et al. (2007) suggest sport psychology professionals be trained to equip athletes with skills and coping responses to avert or confront perpetrators. In this light, all sport psychology professionals, even those not clinically trained, should acquire training in how to intervene and support (with trauma-informed understanding and practice) a survivor when sexual misconduct has been shared with the practitioner (e.g., how to emotionally support the survivor in the acute moment and what steps to take to assist the survivor in getting the medical and psychological care the situation may warrant).

Furthermore, all involved in sport, especially sport psychology professionals, need to be educated on the warning signs athletes may display if they are abused. This applies to athletes who:

> lose enthusiasm for their sport, are reluctant to go to particular practices, start giving worse performances than usual, turn things around or lie about their whereabouts, become ill or develop an (eating or sport) addiction or whose behavior changes (becoming very withdrawn or, on the contrary, very noisy.
>
> *(Cense & Brackenridge, 2001, p. 72)*

More than anything else, if any warning sign behaviors are observed or an athlete shares being violated, regardless of the severity, it is paramount that the sport psychology professional (and others) tell her that she is believed, and it is not her fault. Lastly, do not silence her voice and though she may not be able to name specificities of inappropriate behavior(s), believe her when she tells you that she *feels it in her body*.

Discussion Questions

1. Trauma occurs in community. In what ways did the Coach in this narrative groom an entire community? What family, community, and sport stakeholders may have had opportunities to intervene in Coach's grooming of child female athletes?
2. How will you actively teach others about grooming behaviors and how to not only identify but mitigate grooming?
3. What actions will you take if you believe a colleague, subordinate, or fellow coach may be grooming an athlete or child?
4. How might you support a survivor who has repressed memories of trauma they experienced in childhood?

Notes

1. As the author, I have chosen to use feminine gender pronouns; however, children of all gender identities are potential targets and survivors of sexual exploitation and abuse.
2. Though masculine gender pronouns are applied throughout the article, men, women and non-gender conforming adults are capable of being perpetrators of sexual violence and abuse.
3. My former high school basketball coach will be referred to as Coach throughout the remainder of the article.

References

Brackenridge, C. (1997). He owned me basically: Women's Experiences of sexual abuse in sport. *International Review for the Sociology of Sport*, 32, 115–130.

Brackenridge, C. (2001). *Spoilsports: Understanding and preventing sexual exploitation in sport*. Routledge.

Brackenridge, C., & Fasting, K. (2005). The grooming process in sport: Narratives of sexual harassment and abuse. *Autobiography Journal*, 13, 33–52.

Celenza, A. (2007). *Sexual boundary violations: Therapeutic, supervisory, and academic contexts*. Rowman & Littlefield Publishing.

Cense, M. (1997). *Red card or carte blanche: Risk factors for sexual harassment and sexual abuse in sport: Summary, conclusions and recommendations*. National Olympic Committee and National Sports Federation.

Cense, M., & Brackenridge, C. H. (2001). Temporal and developmental risk factors for sexual harassment and abuse in sport. *European Physical Education Review*, 7(1), 61–79.

Dietz, P. (2018). Grooming and seduction. *Journal of Interpersonal Violence, 33*(1), 28–36.

Ellis, C. (1997). Evocative autoethnography: Writing emotionally about our lives. In *Representation and the text: Re-framing the narrative voice* (W. Tierney & Y. Lincoln, Eds., pp. 116–139). SUNY Press.

Ellis, C. (1999). He(art)ful autoethnography. *Qualitative Health Research, 9*, 653–667.

Ellis, C. (2004). *The ethnographic I: A methodological novel about autoethnography*. Rowman & Littlefield Publishers.

Ellis, C. (2007). Telling secrets, revealing lives: Relational ethics in research with intimate others. *Qualitative Inquiry, 13*(1), 3–29.

Fasting, K., Brackenridge, C., & Walseth, K. (2007). Women athletes' personal responses to sexual harassment in sport. *Journal of Applied Sport Psychology, 19*, 419–433.

Fibkins, W. L. (2006). *Innocence denied: A guide to preventing sexual misconduct by teachers and coaches*. Rowman & Littlefield Education.

Goodall, H. (1997). Transforming communication studies through ethnography. In J. Trent (Ed.), *Communication for the 21st century*. Allyn & Bacon.

Groth, A., & Birnbaum, H. (1979). *Men who rape: The psychology of the offender*. Plenum Press.

Jerkins, M. (2018). *This will be my own undoing: Living at the intersection of black, female and feminist in (white) America*. Harper Perennial.

Jones, S. (2005). Autoethnography: Making the personal political. In N. Denzin & Y. Lincoln (Eds.), *The Sage handbook of qualitative research* (3rd ed., pp. 763–791). Sage Publications.

Lanning, K. (2005). Compliant child victim: Confronting an uncomfortable reality. In E. Quayle & M. Taylor (Eds.), *Viewing child pornography on the internet* (pp. 49–60). Russell House.

Lanning, K. (2010). *Child molesters: A behavioral analysis* (5th ed.). National Center for Missing and Exploited Children.

Lanning, K. (2018). The evolution of grooming: Concept and term. *Journal of Interpersonal Violence, 33*(1), 5–16.

Lanning, K., & Dietz, P. (2014). Acquaintance child molesters and youth serving organizations. *Journal of Interpersonal Violence, 29*, 1–24.

Leberg, E. (1997). *Understanding child molesters: Taking charge*. Sage Publications.

McCabe, M., & Hardman, L. (2005). Attitudes and perceptions of workers to sexual harassment. *Journal of Social Psychology, 145*, 719–740.

Morse, J., & Richards, L. (2002). *Read me first for a user's guide to qualitative methods*. Sage Publications.

Mykalovskiy, E. (1997). Reconsidering table talk: Critical thoughts on the relationship between sociology, autobiography and self-indulgence. In R. Hertz (Ed.), *Reflexivity and voice* (pp. 229–251). Sage Publications.

Noble, J., & Vermillion, M. (2014). Youth sport administrators' perceptions and knowledge of organizational policies on child maltreatment. *Children and Youth Services Review, 38*, 52–57.

Prewitt, T. (2010). *More than pretty faces and miniskirts: An autoethnographic story of female sport hostess experience* [Unpublished doctoral dissertation, University of Tennessee].

Simon, R. (1995). The natural history of therapist sexual misconduct: Identification and prevention. *Psychiatric Annals, 25*(2), 90–94.

Stirling, A., & Kerr, G. (2009). Abused athletes' perceptions of the coach-athlete relationship. *Sport in Society, 12*(2), 227–239.

Taylor, E., & Hardin, R. (2017). A gap in the sport management curriculum: An analysis of sexual harassment and sexual assault education in the United States. *Journal of Hospitality, Leisure, Sport & Tourism Education, 20*, 65–75.

Toftegaard Nielsen, J. (2001). The forbidden zone: Intimacy, sexual relations and misconduct in the relationship between coaches and athletes. *International Review for the Sociology of Sport, 36*(2), 65–183.

Willness, C., Steel, P., & Lee, K. (2007). A meta-analysis of the antecedents and consequences of workplace sexual harassment. *Personal Psychology, 60*, 127–162.

Wurtele, S. (2012). Preventing the sexual exploitation of minors in youth-serving organizations. *Children and Youth Services Review, 34*, 2442–2453.

7

PERSIST

Homophobia in and Survival Through Farm Town High School Sports

Lena A. Bequette

Uninterrupted glares and camera flashes drew upon me as I lowered my black ballpoint pen to the document. This was the moment I felt like I worked my entire adolescent and teenage life for—Signing Day. I could feel a heat erupt throughout my body and butterflies flutter within my core, I actually made it. I was signing the next four years of my life over to a game I loved and a coach that I had only met three times prior. This piece of paper was my ticket out of a farm town in Iowa, nicknamed The Black Hole, that unapologetically swallowed its female residents whole. Women do not leave, women are not awarded Division I scholarships, women are made to be mothers, beauticians, and cook dinner for their husbands as they trickle home from a long day of harvest. The population of my farm town was 298 residents and I was determined to make it 297 upon graduation.

Slowly, I etched my autograph on the line of commitment presented in front of me. If I could imagine the moments before death, this is what it must feel like. My life flashed before my eyes as I was surrounded by loved ones and strangers while passing on to another world. The excitement and pain of the past played through my mind like a movie. In chronological fashion, my best and worst moments in sports filtered through like the slideshow presentation I had given in my American History class just the week before.

I come from a large family, much like the family from the movie *Yours, Mine, & Ours*. We were seven children who were brought together by marriage when I was three years old. We were the only friends each other had and I was the only girl in a boys' world. My closest sister was eight years older than I and a cheerleader who drove all of the football boys' pubescent minds crazy. I never much cared to be like her. I wanted to be the athlete playing the sports and driving cheerleaders crazy.

I looked up to my youngest stepbrother who was only a few months older than I. He introduced me to t-ball when I was five. That was the moment that changed my life. My mom bought me my first baseball glove, and the rest was history. It was green and yellow with a picture of Donatello, from the Teenage Mutant Ninja Turtles, on the inside. I was a girl who was about to destroy the boys' world mentality of my small town at the ripe age of five.

It was at five years old that I realized my home life was not that of a typical five-year-old. I was petrified and crying, bent over the knee of my stepfather. My pants were down, and

DOI: 10.4324/9781003125884-9

my bottom was bare as I was being spanked with a grill fork. My mother was at work and my stepfather just arrived home from work to find me without a shirt on. It made him angry that I, as a five-year-old girl, would walk around without a shirt on. He told me it was inappropriate for me to show my chest. He never asked why I had no shirt and why I could not find my shirt. He just beat me. My shirt was missing because my much older stepbrother took it off of me while we were playing "doctor" and threw it somewhere. After school, my older stepbrother would want to play doctor with me often. He would make me touch him and he would touch me, because this is how he told me the game was played and the game needed to be our secret. If I told anyone about his game, he told me he would make all of my siblings hate me and that I would have no friends anymore. His mother was a police officer, so if I told anyone, he would make sure his mother put my mother away in jail. My mother was my hero and that threat scared me to my core.

Donatello may have been a mythical hero to the world, but he was a real hero to me. He was with me for my introduction to organized team sport. My youngest stepbrother was excited that I got a glove and that we were going to play t-ball together. For the next year, we would be outside playing ball every day after school until our parents would get home. Playing ball became my safe space and reduced the amount of alone time that I had to spend with the "doctor." Donatello would protect me for as long as he could, until the game was over and the lights went out.

Fast forward two years, I was seven years old and going into the second grade. I dressed in baggy jeans, boxers, and an Atlanta Braves jersey. I was never made fun of because my youngest stepbrother would have beaten anyone up who said anything bad about me. It wasn't that I wanted to be a boy, I just wanted to be one of the boys. At recess, I was not a fan of playing on the swings with the other girls. I was always down on the flat field roughing it with my male classmates in a game of soccer or kickball. Through my head flashed the time I crossed up Kirk, a freckle-faced redheaded boy, and scored a goal. He was the best athlete and the boy that all of the girls had a crush on and I just embarrassed him. It wasn't that I wanted to emasculate him, I just wanted to show the boys that I was one of them. After I scored that goal, I anxiously watched the clock for the rest of the day until the final bell rang. After an hour and a half bus ride, I finally made it home to the object that I had been thinking about since I made that goal, my diary. I feverishly wrote down my accomplishment of beating Kirk and how it made me feel on the same level as him. I wasn't that typical little girl who wrote about crushes on boys in her diary but about my defeats over boys.

My thoughts flashforward to the summers of sixth- and seventh-grade softball. By this time, I was already recruited to play baseball with the boys during elementary school, but my parents chose for me to stay with softball so I didn't have to readjust once I reached middle school. It was those two summers when I made a real name for myself in softball and as an athlete in general. I was an all-star on my team and we won championships each of those two years. College attention started to arrive. At the age of 12, I was flattered when a recruiter from a small Division II school approached me after our championship game. From that day on, I knew that softball was going to be my free ride out of The Black Hole.

At 13 years of age—when I was the youngest in my class—I was asked to try out for the high school varsity softball team. Knowing what I know now, I would have waited a year. I ended up being the eighth grader who took the junior centerfielder's starting position. This was not the best way to make friends on the team; yes, I had the talent to make me appreciated, but I wanted to be liked by the other girls. I wanted to make friends. Some liked me, the ones closer to my age, but most of the upper-class athletes ignored me. I took their friend's position.

During the next couple of years, I was busy six days a week with sports (Sunday was God's day). On God's day, my mother would take my youngest stepbrother and me to the United Church of Christ, a congregation of around 50 worshipers, for a youth group which was followed by a grueling two-hour sermon. Going to church made me nauseous and full of fear. When I was six years old, the preacher's son lured me into a dark and musty room in the basement on the premise to play hide and seek. We were hiding for minutes when I realized there was no seeker. He wanted to see what animated character was on my underwear and what my parts looked like. Church was never a safe space. *God, our Heavenly Father*, did nothing to save me in his own house. I drowned myself in athletics, as I knew this would keep me away from the places I feared most—home and church. I played softball, volleyball, basketball, golf, and track and field. The typical life of a teenager might involve hanging out with friends, going to the movies, having sleepovers, shopping, and talking about crushes. As most of the girls did this after school and in the summer, I found myself getting lessons in softball. My head coach thought I could benefit from batting lessons with a former Major League Baseball (MLB) player who took up residency in our town. I was young and believed my coach was my ally who had my athletic development in mind; so, I followed his every demand.

Sophomore year and I dig my cleats into the dirt at third base. I can feel the metal rectangles scrape against the fine pebbles beneath my feet as I coil my body and leap into the air to snag a line drive hit over my head. Out. Game over. I get to the end of the line to shake hands and I feel a calloused hand tightly grip my shoulder with a gravelly voice preceding it, "Not only does she look good, but she plays good too!" It was the head coach of the opposing team, the Panthers. I wanted to shake him off like I would to a spider crawling up my arm, but this spider bit too hard. His venom was the chill that went through my body. When we played his team the year prior, I heard the comments dripping with sexual innuendo that he made at his players. "They are going to bury him under home plate when he dies so he can keep an eye on all of the girls" was the type of rumor that circulated between teams. He was a 65-year-old man who was beloved by his small town and coached the team for 30 years. I was thankful that I had a coach who cared and treated me with respect. Never would my coach do something so sick.

During my junior year of high school, we played the Panthers again. Except this time their coach was not in attendance. He had unexpectedly retired after last season. I looked up at the scoreboard and noticed that they had named the field after him as an ode to his dedication. What I also noticed was one of their role players left the team that year.

> A player caught him in the concession stand pushing her against a counter with his pants around his knees. They don't want us talking about it and we'll get in trouble if they hear us.

It had felt like my life had left my body as my friend, who was the pitcher for the Panthers, told me that the coach believed the player was gay and he was setting her right by sexually "freeing" her. This was all on the premise that the girl had never had a boyfriend, played sports, and only spent time with her teammates so that inherently made her a lesbian. I thought if a rapist is celebrated for attempting to fix a girl's sexuality and claiming *God's will*,

I was in danger. God wants women to be obedient and women were made to sexually serve men. Of course, no person in my town would outwardly say that, but it was implied by how women were treated in our own households. Men decided what women should and should not do by putting it under the umbrella of God's word.

Back to signing day . . . numb in my cold, rusted chair I sat at a fold-out table in front of the entire junior and senior high school packed into the gymnasium. I could see someone in the corner of my eye with a scornful look on their face. I turned to see my softball coach standing there with his arms crossed acting uninterested. I feel anger and pain as I think about all of the low things he put me through at the start of my junior season. I believed he was on my side but over the course of a year, everything changed. He and I developed a toxic relationship, and he refused to help me get recruited. We butted heads a lot during my last two seasons playing for him.

A bouncing grounder was hit in my direction while I was playing third base during my junior season. As I fielded the ball and went to make the play at first base, I felt a horrible pain shoot down my arm. The throw that I made was less than impressive and did not have the normal zip I usually was able to put on the ball. It was as if everything around me was happening in real time but the ball was traveling in slow motion. The runner was safe and my coach proceeded to call "timeout" and stomp onto the field and scold me for making a throw that seemed lackadaisical in effort. I had to hide my pain because to him *pain was a state of mind* and *girls were too emotional*. In that moment I realized he didn't care the slightest about me or what I sacrificed for this team. He would intentionally embarrass me and treat me differently than the other players. I was a pawn who he used to reach his goal for *Coach of the Year*.

I had a feeling that my coach knew my biggest secret—I am gay. It was my senior year and my mother decided to *let* my 17-year-old self live in an apartment to get used to being away from home, in preparation for dorm life in college. I had one of my friends over who I had a suspicion was gay, too, though we never came out to each other. We were best friends and inseparable which made my coach suspicious. The day after she spent the night at my place, along with another teammate, my coach decided to bench us. His excuse was that he had reason to believe we were drinking and committing *unholy acts*; therefore, his response was to bench not only me but also the entire varsity team.

In The Black Hole, if you are gay, you're committing unholy acts. If you are gay, you don't play. If you are gay, you are less than human. What he did not know is that I knew the Superintendent at our school on a personal basis. He had nominated me for national academic awards honors, chaperoned my National Honor Society trips, and helped me get a job at a local bank by writing me a reference. Halfway through the game, with junior varsity athletes playing and losing by eight, the Superintendent refused to allow my coach to throw baseless allegations against us anymore. He knew my coach was lying because his wife did my makeup for prom. I got the lecture about teenage drinking and I told him I was scared to drink because alcoholism runs in my family. My coach was exposed as a liar, and I won my right to play.

This wasn't the first time he had tried to turn my teammates and friends against me. My grandmother passed away a few weeks before and I had to miss a game for her funeral. He belittled me at the next practice claiming I abandoned the team and that was why we lost. He blamed a loss on my grandmother's death. I was ostracized and thought, "Maybe if I act more feminine and hide in the shadows, then I will be treated like the other players?" The only problem was that I did not know how to be the type of feminine that was desired in The Black Hole. I always felt awkward giving any girl a hug when greeting them, I had no desire to gossip about boys, and I could not figure out how to wear eyeliner without looking like I tried to apply it with my feet. So, I left that thought in the trash along with my empty Gatorade bottle.

CRACK! Two games left in my high school career and a screaming line drive is hit right up the middle, past my second base position. There is a runner at second, so I know I am the cut-off person and need to throw the ball home as quickly as I can. With my cleats caught in the dirt of a poorly maintained field, I turn and throw the ball as hard as I can to home plate. I never heard the out being called. I never heard praise from my teammates for a good play. All I could feel was a razor-sharp pain cut through my spine and my own cry.

"What's wrong with you?" was the response from my coach at the inning switch. At that point, I could not twist my upper back and he prescribed me with 1000 mg of Tylenol and some BioFreeze pain gel while proceeding to tell me I'm on deck to bat. I already felt like I was walking on eggshells with him, so I swallowed my pain and a handful of Tylenol. Meanwhile, our pitcher had a cut on her non-throwing hand and was directed to run over to the baseball field to get the trainer to take a look at it. *Why am I treated like I am disposable, yet not replaceable?* My coach wanted my talent, but he did not want me, my full self, and my identity along for the season.

Back to signing day . . . I could hear the applause as I put my pen down next to the contract. There was this feeling of a walnut-sized lump in my throat as I slowly looked up at the crowd. *Who are these people?* I had dedicated my entire being to this sport and was now realizing that I had missed out on so much more. I was the star athlete in their eyes and I could only pick out a handful of people who actually knew me from the crowd. I was unsure what I had just done. I gave up being open about my sexuality, never knowing if a crush liked me back, and missing out on authentic friendships.

Is playing in the ACC really worth giving all of that up for this? It was then that I realized I had been in love with a sport that never loved me back.

With my letter of intent signed, I woke up the morning before the final game of my senior season. I could not move without excruciating back pain. My mother drove me to the doctor and we had x-rays taken of my spine. "I've never seen anything like it," said my doctor. My trapezius was tearing away from my spine and my spine was starting to twist in a spiral. I called my coach to let him know about the injury. His response, "You deserve everything that has and will come your way for the lifestyle you chose to live." His words felt like acid being poured into my heart, as my heart pumped it through to every limb on my body. I was burning alive, and I needed to get out before The Black Hole sentenced me to life. I had thought about how naive this man must be to think his words could hurt me after how challenging my childhood was. The acid was the gas to my car and I was going to drive that car to greener pastures and never turn back.

I was denied proper care and concern from my coach for every injury I had because of his homophobia. I left for college soon after, but was never able to rehabilitate and return to competitive playing form. In the past 12 years, I have never stepped up to the plate to lead off a game, waited for a pitch to leave a hand before stealing a base, dove in the dirt for a ground ball, or celebrated a win with teammates again.

I participated in sports because I longed to feel connected to others outside of my family. I wanted friends, other than my siblings, and to be valuable to those people. I was always competitive but when I look back, I was searching for a place where I could belong. Half of me feels that sport has really done great things for my character and the other half feels that sport has harmed me and denied me different opportunities. The lack of leadership is what tainted the sport of softball for me. Softball is where some of my best and worst memories reside.

I always hoped to play the guitar or drums in the high school band, but with my sports schedule that was impossible. I missed being creative with arts and music, which was a true enjoyment of mine. My social skills were stunted. Sport conversation is scripted. Unless socialized by coaches to do so, athletes do not inherently share personal aspects of themselves while on the field or in the dugout; they discuss how to execute plays and win rather than getting to genuinely know one another. Softball often left me feeling used by my coach and school. I put on a jersey and competed to be a part of a family, but from all of the different teams I've been on, I only speak to two former teammates.

My identity was formed as a softball player, not Lena—a young woman who was goofy, loved classical music, to draw, and would have to be nearly pulled into the house each night because she all but lived outdoors; she just happened to like girls, too. Sports closeted me; I did not want to be ostracized or be the stereotypical lesbian who plays softball. It closeted me because homophobia is so rampant in sport that there is a risk of being sexually assaulted for not identifying as heterosexual. Being on a team made me care more about what my teammates thought about me than what I thought about myself. I molded myself to be who they wanted me to be. I never allowed myself to be who I really was and I now realize that through the winning and all of the congratulations, I had no identity.

Through all of the bad I listed, sports have given me great opportunities as well. Softball gave me a guaranteed ride to a big city once I signed that contract. It was there that I realized I needed to be myself and felt free to do so. Softball made it easier for me to have an excuse to leave my small town, The Black Hole, behind. My coach was an awful person, but being put in the position to stand up to him unveiled how strong I really am. My leadership and persistence was developed through sport.

However, I can still feel that calloused hand on my shoulder. I still shudder and cower if someone asks me if I need to see a doctor when I feel ill. I still cannot watch Disney's *Pocahontas* because of character images on underwear. However, I still feel that acid running through my veins and the need to persist. I can feel the gravel beneath my feet and the soft leather of a glove. I can feel the soft cushion of the batting helmet as it hugs my head and protects me from harm, a helmet that protected me from more harm than anyone knew about. Because of sport—and writing—I can feel.

Discussion Questions

1. What role does religion play in homophobia and sexual misconduct?
2. What resources or methods could we use to challenge homophobia in sport and make it a true microcosm of society?
3. Do you believe homophobia in sport has improved or diminished in the last five years? If so, why and if not, what are your reasons?
4. Compare and contrast your coaching experience with the athlete's coaching experience? What makes for an effective coach in youth sport especially as it pertains to creating an inclusive environment where all athletes feel embraced?

8
2/7/2016

The Morning I Was Raped

Eliana (Ellie) Arbetman

In the winter of 2016, I was a freshman at Lakeland University and an outside hitter on the Lakeland Volleyball team. My second semester had just started and my roommate from the fall semester had decided to transfer. I found myself living alone in a third-floor dorm room in a female-only residence hall on the small Lakeland University campus near Sheboygan, Wisconsin.

Looking back, I was simply trying to figure college life out in my second semester of college. I was just learning how to live alone, manage academics and athletics, and understand how social connections worked on the small campus.

February 6 was a cold, wintery Saturday night. I went out with some friends and we had fun hanging out. I did not drink alcohol that night. I was completely sober the entire evening. It shouldn't matter anyways, but I feel I need to make it clear when I share my story. I was sober when I was raped on the morning of February 7, 2016.

I had been texting this guy named Tom (pseudonym) who was a 6'7" star player on Lakeland's basketball team. Tom and I were more like acquaintances, just getting to know each other, but I thought maybe we could be friends. I have a big heart—I will always be there for anyone at any time. So, even though I was just getting to know Tom, I listened to him and tried to be friends with him.

He sent me some texts that made me think he was really upset about something. He didn't want to text me about it, he wanted to talk in person. He just kept telling me he wanted to see me in person that night. The text messages began around 1:00 am. Tom kept saying he wanted to come and see me. I texted back to him that he could come to my room to talk, but I told him that nothing else would happen between us. The messages went back and forth for about an hour. I knew Tom had been drinking, but I trusted that he heard and believed me. I told him I didn't want to hook up or have a one-night stand with him. He told me he wanted to talk to me. I believed him.

I told him "no" before he even asked for consent. Actually, he never did ask for consent anyways. In our text messages that night I had repeatedly told him that no, nothing would happen between us; and, I told him that I didn't want anything sexual to happen between us. I told him I am someone who doesn't do one-night stands. I sent him several text messages that repeated my "no" to him. I was clear and firm and believed I would be heard and respected.

Yes, I did know he was wasted drunk. But, I'm also a strong independent woman. I believed that I was in a safe situation. So, I met him in in the campus center Sunday, February 7 around 2:30 am and we walked back to my room. We sat on my bed which is commonplace in college dorm rooms; he talked, and I tried to listen to him. I was confident that he had gotten my clear message earlier when I told him before he came to my room that NOTHING would happen between us. But once we were in my room, I began to feel nervous—his energy unsettled me. I tried to listen to him and figure out what he was upset about. But he wasn't making sense.

Then, he started trying to kiss me. I was absolutely not interested. I told him to stop but I knew he was not hearing me at all. He pushed me back on my bed and he was on top of me, and I couldn't get him off me. I knew that Tom was going to do what he wanted, and the strength of his physical force stopped me from fighting him off. I couldn't move. Suddenly, I was terrified. I said "no," but he didn't seem to hear me. He pulled my pants off and locked me in place. He pushed himself into me and it hurt so much. I was saying "NO NO NO" repeatedly, and he wouldn't get off me until he finished. As soon as he let go a little, I was able to push him off me and kick him out. Before he left me crying in my doorway, he told me to take a shower and wash off. He saw that I had some vaginal bleeding from this violent act, and I think he was proud of that. After he left, I was in unbearable pain, crying, and not knowing what to do. I took a shower because I felt disgusting. Slowly, it was sinking in. I had just been raped by a guy I know who I thought was my friend.

There was blood on my sheets, underwear, and I was lost. After the shower, I didn't know what to do next. I was embarrassed to tell anyone what had just happened to me. I was sure it was my fault. I let this drunken 6'7" man into my room and it was all my fault. I was sure everyone would judge me for being this stupid.

I didn't even have the strength to tell my own mom what had happened. First, I called my older sister, Laura, who was a senior at a small college in Florida at that time. I knew she would be awake, and she would listen to me and know what to do next. I was crying over the phone to her with absolutely no clue on how to tell her what had just happened to me. She asked me yes and no questions because I really couldn't get a full sentence out of my mouth. Laura was able to figure out what happened to me pretty quickly. She told me that it was not my fault Tom raped me. I hated hearing the word "rape." I hated accepting that I had been raped. I was embarrassed this had happened to me. I actually felt a lot of shame right after it happened.

I called my mom to tell her what happened. But, when I heard her voice, I just couldn't bring myself to tell her that I had been raped. I hated having to tell her this terrible thing happened to me. I told my mom to call my sister Laura. My sister Laura was the one who told my mom that I was raped. I felt so much shame. It was easier to ask my sister to tell my mom I was raped, even though I am very close with my mom.

At this point, it was about 3:30 am. I stayed in my room after that because I didn't want to show my face to anyone. My sister forced me to get one of my teammates who lived down the hall to come to my room. I told her what happened, and I was so scared that she would be mad at me. She wasn't mad at all. She stayed with me until my mom got to campus.

That early Sunday morning, the only people on campus who knew what had happened were two of my teammates in my residence hall and two other friends of mine. I personally told each of these people what happened to me. Rumors were not going around campus yet. At that point, I just wanted to go home and never go back to Lakeland University.

My Small Campus Suddenly Was Much, Much Smaller

My mom arrived on campus and wanted me to report what had happened. I didn't want to—I just wanted to go home and deal with it later. We packed up my stuff and I got in the car with her. While we were driving toward the interstate, one of my friends called me to come back to campus. My friend was a sophomore and she wanted me to report the rape. She told me that she had been stalked by a male athlete the previous year. This one security guard, everyone called him "Big Mo," had helped her. My friend told me that Big Mo was waiting to meet with me and take down my story. My mom turned the car around and we went back to campus. I was nervous, but I also knew this was the right thing to do.

When I was sitting in the security office meeting with Big Mo, the real nastiness against me started. People saw me chatting with Big Mo and the rumors started flying. Mostly the hate and chatter I received were text messages, but also on an iPhone app that was popular at the time, *Yik Yak*. In the meantime, Tom had been texting me all day apologizing. He admitted that he did something wrong, but he told me that he never heard me say "no." He did remember that I told him I didn't want to have sex with him earlier in the evening. I thought he was worried about me and wanted to make sure I was alright. Later on, I learned that he was just trying to keep himself out of trouble. All of our conversations were through text messages. I was able to print out these text messages and give them to the Title IX Administrator later that week.

I told Big Mo the story, showed him the text messages, and we looked at my room. Big Mo encouraged me to report the rape to the Sheboygan Detective. He was able to explain the importance of this to me with kindness, which motivated me to agree to the meeting. He explained to me that I did not have to press charges, but I really did have to file a police report for the incident. He provided me easy steps to move forward—I followed his directions.

I agreed to make a report with the police and a detective from Sheboygan came to campus to get my story. More people were walking around outside the security building trying to figure out what I was doing in there. The added presence of the Sheboygan police car really got people talking on campus. Somehow, it felt like everyone on campus seemed to immediately know that I was accusing Tom, the star basketball player, of rape.

I then told my story for a second time to the Sheboygan detective. It was a little easier the second time through. When I explained how Tom locked me in position, the detective told me it was likely he had done this before. She stopped writing and put her pencil down when she told me that. The detectives went to my dorm room and took my shorts, underwear, and sheets for evidence. I had showered so I did not do a rape kit. The detective also told me that Tom might have advised me to shower to make a rape kit useless.

Finally, around 9:00 pm Sunday night, I started the two-hour drive home with my mom. The school gave me two weeks off for a *Title IX issue*, but none of my instructors were told what the issue was. I was told I would have to meet with the Title IX Administrator at Lakeland later in the week. In the meantime, the Title IX Administrator was investigating the incident.

At home, the last thing I wanted was to go back to school. I visited my doctor first thing Monday morning and was tested for STDs and pregnancy, both fortunately negative. My doctor had me take another medication to prevent other infections from even beginning. Like all the important people in my life, my physician also let me know that this was not my fault, I didn't make it happen, and this was about power and violence, not love or sex.

A few days later, my mom and I made the trek back to Lakeland so I could meet with the Title IX Administrator and gather assignments for my classes. We met with my volleyball coach and told him what happened. He told us that Tom had been removed from the team and temporarily from the school while the Title IX investigation was underway. My coach cried right in front of me; he told me that he feels protective of the athletes on his team. He also said the basketball coach would most likely never put Tom back on the team.

Challenges, Struggles, and Title IX

Lakeland is a small campus, and everyone was talking about whether or not I was telling the truth. Most upsetting was a text message I received from a female athlete on the softball team. This athlete was one of my rapist's girlfriend's best friends. Tom's girlfriend lived right down the hall from me. This text told me I was destroying Tom's life and there are better ways for me to get attention. I couldn't believe this girl chose to attack me instead of helping her friend who was dating a rapist. I sent all text messages like that to Big Mo, and he subsequently contacted the senders and gave them no-contact orders regarding me and the situation.

At the time, there was a cell phone app popular on college campuses called *Yik Yak*. This was an anonymous social media platform for students at Lakeland University. My rape was the hottest topic on Lakeland's *Yik Yak* in February of 2016. It was called *Team Tom* against *Team Ellie* or *Team Psycho Bitch*. Let me be clear—I am neither *psycho* nor a *bitch*. People began to keep score of points for and against me. And, someone posted that I had a history of making fake rape accusations (I don't). I shared every *Yik Yak* post with the Title IX Administrator, but, unfortunately, he could not take the app down or identify the anonymous posters. He agreed that the chatter was offensive. All of the chatter was anonymous and cruel.

Tom was told he could have no contact with me. He could not call or text me. If I entered the student center or athletic center while Tom was in attendance, Tom had to leave the facility, pending the result of the investigation. However, the situation on campus had gotten so out of control, especially due to the anonymous and hateful *Yik Yak* chatter, that Lakeland's administration removed Tom from campus during the investigation. Tom was also temporarily suspended from the basketball team. People on campus were furious with me because Tom was suspended from the basketball team and removed from campus. They told me things like:

> *I should have known better with him.*
> *Everyone knows Tom goes crazy when he is drunk.*
> *Why would Tom have to rape anyone anyways?*

I was also accused of making up this story because I am just *crazy*. In fact, I was called all kinds of terrible names. I felt a lot of pressure to give up, but I didn't give in to it. I'm not crazy, I didn't make it up and I don't want to quit anything because of fear.

My parents were also coming to meet with the Title IX Investigator after my interview. I am grateful that Tom was off campus that week because I don't think I would have handled that well. Big Mo had kept me informed about the investigation and he did a great job of making me feel a little safer on campus. Mostly, he just kept the haters away from me.

The morning of my Title IX Administrator meeting, I was about to walk over to the administrative building when a friend stopped me. She told me there was another female athlete, a basketball player, who wanted to talk to me. I didn't know her at all. She told me she would walk me to the administrative building and stay with me during the interview. As we walked, she suddenly burst into tears and told me that it was her fault this had happened to me. Tom had done the same thing to her, yet she never reported it. In fact, I learned there were actually three other female athletes on campus, that is four including me, who were raped or sexually assaulted by Tom. I learned this as I walked into the Title IX Administrator's office for my interview.

I sat down with the Title IX Administrator and told my story. I was hopeful that this interview would not be too difficult for me. He had printouts of all the text messages between Tom and me, and in those messages, I clearly did NOT give Tom consent for sex. I finished my story and he thanked me, told me that he would let me know their final decision. My heart sank, thinking Tom would be back on campus. Then, the female basketball player whom I never met before that day—who was sitting next to me for support—spoke up.

The Title IX Administrator had no idea she was also there to report. He thought she had just joined me to provide moral support. She told him she was also there to report Tom for rape and shared with the administrator about the other two females who he allegedly raped. His face turned the brightest red I have ever seen on human skin. He picked up his phone, called the dean of students, and said Tom had to be expelled from campus as of that day.

My parents arrived at campus later that day and met with the administrator and me. He told us that Tom had been expelled and if he returns to Lakeland, he will be arrested for trespassing. I returned home again that day with my parents to spend a few days away from campus. However, beginning that moment, I knew I would go back to Lakeland at minimum to finish my freshman year. Tom being removed from campus made this possible. If he had not been expelled, I might not have returned to campus that semester. However, although I returned to school, I struggled to get my grades up.

I had missed a few weeks of classes and felt distracted. After Tom was expelled, things also changed for me socially at Lakeland. I lost friends; some people completely stopped talking to me. The entire men's basketball team hated me. I was judged wrongly and unfairly. People made fun of me, disregarded me completely, and blamed me for the rape. It was either all my fault or I was making it all up. Either way I was seen as the liar. It felt like people held me accountable for the crime, even though I was the victim. I felt like I was being blamed for the basketball team losing a star player. Tom had been removed from campus after an investigation; there were four women accusing him of rape, but no one seemed to think he had done anything wrong. I felt socially alienated and lonely. My coach said he felt bad when he met with me and my mom, but he never brought the team together to talk about what happened. I wish my team and coach had been more of a support system for me. My teammates knew what happened, but no one ever really talked to me about it except for the two friends who were there for me the night it happened. The silence was difficult for me because I always felt judged by the people looking at me. Did my teammates doubt me too? I hope not. I never felt safe sharing these feelings with most of my teammates. I wish my coach had encouraged me to talk with teammates about what I was going through. Truth is I didn't trust most of them at the time because the campus became so toxic for me. I saw Tom's girlfriend all the time. Part of me actually felt bad for her. I knew he was using her to make him look "normal." We never spoke to each other. I felt like people were always whispering around me. Even though it was clear that Tom had raped four women on campus, I was still seen as the problem.

Somehow, I made it to the end of the semester and earned a C average, which kept me eligible to continue as a student-athlete at Lakeland. But that C average became my motivation and inspiration.

I realized how strong I could be, that I can survive and live and go on and be stronger again. I got over the first hurdle, I survived and did not quit school.

Even still, I was so relieved to go home at the end of the school year. I was working with a fitness trainer at my local gym and shared with him what had happened to me. My experience left him without words. Through my work with him I began to learn that there are men I can trust to be friends. Then, he helped me be as physically strong as possible and he always encouraged my spirit, too. That relationship with a male fitness trainer really helped me begin to trust people, especially men, again. He listened to me, helped me feel better physically and emotionally, and was a true friend—a friend Tom never intended to be to me.

I spent the summer of 2016 learning to feel strong again. I learned how to tell my story so I could own it but not let it disable me. I also learned that when I tell my story it helps others who are afraid to tell their stories.

I started hearing from other women at Lakeland who were assaulted by Tom and did not come forward to report it. They were afraid, too. I listened to and heard their stories; and I told them I was *there* for them, without judgment, and that it was 110% not their fault and that they should come forward only if they were ready and comfortable.

When summer ended, I headed back to Lakeland for my sophomore year because I felt very strong and confident that I am a survivor and not a victim. I put a wall up on the people judging me for something that wasn't my fault. I shared a single room suite with some of my teammates and had a blast my sophomore year.

There were still times when people made rape jokes in front of me and on purpose. And, there were times I called home crying about it. But, I made it.

Justice in the End

I never followed through on pressing charges with the police against Tom. I felt there was justice for me, and for the other female students at Lakeland, when Tom was expelled. A lawyer advising me on this explained that in court anything can happen. Although the Title IX Investigation had ruled in my favor, there was no guarantee the same would happen in a State of Wisconsin court room. I was advised that in court sometimes evidence is not accepted, and outcomes are not always fair or just. I struggled with the idea of pressing charges against Tom in June of 2016 as I watched Stanford rapist Brock Allen Turner literally walk out of court with a slap on the wrist punishment after committing violent and public rape. He was found guilty in court for raping an unconscious woman next to a garbage dumpster—in public—and sparred any real consequence by a judge who didn't want to ruin the life of the young rapist.

I did not want to risk feeling like a victim again. I decided that as a survivor who already felt some justice from the Title IX decision, I could move on without pressing further charges. I am grateful that Big Mo helped me so much at Lakeland. I am grateful the Title

IX investigation gave me and other survivors some peace of mind. I graduated from Lakeland University in 2019 with a degree in Sports Management and Coaching and was an athlete on Lakeland's volleyball team for four years. I am so much more than what happened to me on 2/7/2016, the morning I was raped. I believe that I will get more out of life with a positive mindset, and that is how I live each day. I still like to play volleyball; I am still an athlete and today I also celebrate being a survivor. I tell my story and encourage others to do so too.

Discussion Questions

1. What were the reasons Ellie felt shame immediately after the rape?
2. Why was it hard for her to tell her mom directly that she was raped?
3. How did Big Mo help shape Ellie's story at Lakeland?
4. Ellie learned about other victims of the same rapist because she reported. What might have stopped those victims from reporting this rapist?
5. What role did social media play in this story and what role does it play broadly in cases of sexual misconduct?
6. How and why did the school community actively victim blame the survivor in this story?

9
"YOU'RE NOT A GOOD CULTURAL FIT HERE"

Being a Woman in Sports

Sara Erdner

The nitty gritty of my story doesn't start the moment the first physical encounter happened. It began when they reminded me that I was a woman, day after day, which warrants some backstory. I was granted access into spaces that most women never have the chance to experience: All-male sport teams. They hired me because they felt I "could add value." When I arrived, though, I realized there was a discrepancy between how we both viewed my *value*. I thought I was going to be useful via offering novel mental strength approaches to each sport. On the second day of each job, I understood what they actually meant, which, in one way or another, was verbally communicated to me in the following way: "Well, I have to say. We figured it out. They realized we need to hire more women if we want to keep any of the guys engaged." These sexist comments are how it always started. The remainder of this chapter is how it unfortunately escalated.

What you are about to read is a composite letter (Ellis, 2004) I wrote to my sexual harassers. I chose this method to reinforce confidentiality by infusing multiple narratives into one storyline with one composite character. After the letter, I offer an intimate dialogue—in the form of a question-and-answer forum—I engaged in with the editors as a way to best situate you, the reader, to my story. Following, I provide my final thoughts along with reflection questions I believe all sport stakeholders should consider to provide a safer environment for all.

A Composite Letter to [You],

It was in that chair. The one that swiveled. The chair that everyone fought for among the other boring, stationary chairs. I was in the physical training room by myself at the time. The physical therapy staff were out [in the field] with the rest of the team, which is where I thought you were, too. With my back turned to the door, I didn't see you walk in; so, I was startled when you placed your hands on my shoulders. I tensed up, which happened after getting that gut-cringing feeling when I registered it was *your* hands on my neck.

You noticed my tension, which you used as your cue to lean in a little further. You stated: "Wow. You're tense. Let me help you out with that." And, just like that, without asking for my consent, you started to give me a neck massage. I was paralyzed in that moment. I knew I didn't want you to touch me, but you were also the person giving me the physical relief I needed from the internal chaos I was feeling in this moment. That is, as your fingers pressed into my knotted muscles, I felt those tingly goosebumps that brought release. It felt confusingly good. That's often what you did to me. You made me feel disgusted, which physically manifested as tension throughout my body. You were the cause of my pain, something I think you knew, while also knowing how to be the antidote, something you prided yourself in.

You knew I was stressed. When we first met, you acted in such a way as to make me feel like you were one of the safe ones: Someone I could talk to about anything. I visited your office regularly to chit-chat about anything from the everyday average concerns of my life to the larger frustrations I experienced both within and outside of sport. Over a three-month timespan, we created a trusting relationship that was founded upon laughter. You were like a second Dad to me. You were aware of this, but, as time passed, you started using this information to your own advantage.

The neck massage in that swivel chair wasn't our first encounter. Our relationship started innocently—us joking about the finicky nature of the weather, laughing because you spilled coffee all over yourself, and arguing about whether dogs or cats were the superior animal. Then came the first instance when you made a strange joke about my underwear, which you saw as I bent over to pick up my bag off the floor. "Tie-dye thongs, huh? Are you the groovy, sensual type?" you said as you chuckled in your usual, joking manner. I remember chuckling, too, while simultaneously feeling confused. It wasn't until later that night I thought, *Did you really say that? Insinuating that I am sensual. Am I sensual?* It was the first time I thought about myself in that way.

You see, that morning, I got dressed with practicality in mind. I was running late. I threw on a basic set of clothes—a team t-shirt with sweatpants—and hurried to brush my teeth and throw my hair in a bun as I frantically checked my watch to assess whether I was going to be late. What didn't happen that morning was this: I never thought about the sensual nature of my clothes, or, more specifically, if they would arouse another person on a Tuesday. I didn't think I needed to double-check my attire in such a way. So, when you made that comment, I was perplexed. After reflecting upon what you said, I made the subconscious, sequential connections in my brain: *Am I sensual? Am I supposed to be sensual? What is the relationship between being sensual and my job performance? Is this how you see me? Is this how you are supposed to see me? Is my identity as a woman the only way to achieve a higher, optimal level of job performance?*

I wanted to address your comment but struggled with how to go about it. Like a broken record playing over and over in my head, *Should I say anything? If I do, would there be repercussions? Gosh. There would probably be repercussions. I'm already an outsider. I don't want to reinforce that anymore than it already is. But, I should say something. I have to say something. Maybe that's not actually what he said? I'm blowing this out of proportion; that's probably what they are going to say.* My stomach was in knots; my brain was spinning out of control. I finally decided not to say anything because the consequences far outweighed the positives in my exhausted mind.

I started losing sleep, which, at the time, I simply chalked up to being stressed about everything else in my life. As days passed and I fell into deeper sleep debt, my ability to emotionally stabilize myself lessened. I was exhausted by 11:00 am every day; so, by the time I encountered you at 2:00 pm, my emotional and rational brain were checked out. It started with your comment about my thong and was perpetuated by a series of verbal and nonverbal remarks you made in the months that followed:

> "I heard you and your boyfriend broke up. I'm sorry. Is it because he wasn't good in bed? Maybe [as you chuckled, looking over to your coaching buddies] because you weren't good in bed?" As I'm squatting in the weight room, "I'm sure most women wish they had your ass. I know most men wish they could be with it. Am I right?" [nudging your colleague's arm].
>
> "You're not allowed to be in the training room during these times because you'd be a distraction to the guys."
>
> The uncomfortable moments when you realized I caught you looking at my ass.
>
> The time I walked past your lunch table to hear you joking among your other male colleagues about "the body your wife used to have."
>
> After I finished lifting weights when you said, "Your arms are more jacked than most guys. Lesbians must love you." After leading a presentation, you told me, "You should let me take you out to dinner sometime."

As the months progressed, I subconsciously started to wear baggier clothes, which I now realize was my way to hide and protect my body from you. I stopped visiting your office and became more silent around the team. When the team noticed my subdued personality, I simply wrote it off as exhaustion from life. I stressed this so much that I started to believe it myself.

The final straw happened when I received that text from you at 2:00 am asking, "You up?" This is a text that most people would interpret as a booty call. I never responded. That same morning, when I showed up to practice at 8:00 am, you initially ignored me until you couldn't anymore. We accidently ran into each other as we both turned the corner at the same time.

Bam! There I was, smack in your face. Jolted, you stuttered as you asked, "Um, how's it going?" For a few moments, I silently looked at the floor and then quickly moved past you to continue walking. You grabbed my arm, pulled me close, and whispered in my ear, "Can we go somewhere and talk?" I aggressively pulled my arm away and exclaimed, "Absolutely not," which made the veins in your neck pop out. You quickly fired back, red-faced, "You'll regret this."

The next day, I was called into the administrators' offices. Before I fully sat down, I was asked why I was being so disrespectful. That's when I knew. I had to share, to finally talk about the sexual harassment I experienced from you. I mentioned the neck massage, the comments, the texts, and, as tears streamed down my face, how you forcefully grabbed my arm. When I finished, I sat there with my head down, sobbing. When I looked up, I was greeted with skeptical looks. There was no remorse, no apology, no concern for my well-being. The administration simply stated: "Well, that's one side of the story. We need to ask [your sexual harasser] what [they] have to say about it."

I was stunned. My story, my tears, my pain. They meant nothing. It was clear my experiences were only going to be considered valid if you validated them for me. After an awkward moment of silence, they finished our meeting with what they believed was a lesson I needed to learn:

> I just finished reading a book about Abraham Lincoln's life. In one of the chapters, it talked about how he dealt with conflict. He often would write a letter to those who

rubbed him the wrong way, and, instead of sending the letter, he would just lock it away in a drawer and never send it. Maybe you would benefit from taking Abe's advice.

The days that followed were brutal. You stopped associating with me. The entire organization, one by one, started treating me differently. I was no longer "Sara," but treated as the person who, as one coach put it, "had all the power and knew it." Thus, I was no longer treated as a human; I was now only considered a threat. I was just a woman, an inferior woman, which meant I wasn't cut out for the job responsibilities originally assigned to me. I went from leading discussions in a room full of men to only be allowed to staple and organize papers in the back closet.

I had to clear the air. I wanted, nay, I needed to clear the air because the tension was too much to bear. So, I told you I needed to talk. You didn't let me finish, and you interrupted me to say:

> Sara, don't. It's just best that we go our separate ways. You're not a good cultural fit here. You don't have any *feel* for this game, so it's probably best if you look for work elsewhere.

My entire career flashed before my eyes. I remembered receiving the call when I got offered the job. I was so excited that the organization wanted to "have me as a part of the team" and was confident that my "expertise would add value to the organization." I felt all of this, too; thus, I never imagined this is how it would end: Being released for "not being a good cultural fit" and years later, sitting here writing a chapter about my personal experience with sexual misconduct because of you. I was devastated. All my big hopes and dreams were shattered.

If you wouldn't have rudely interrupted me, this is what I would have said:

> Yes, I am a woman. There's nothing inherently wrong with that. Yet, you and the rest of the organization only regarded me as such. What I needed from you was to not be so unidimensional in your approach. I needed you to see that, yes, I am a woman and an intelligent, caring, hard-working, no nonsense, creative worker. My vagina doesn't negate any of the aforementioned qualities, similar to how your penis doesn't enhance any of those qualities in you. So, no, I am not, and will never be, "proud to wear [the team's] logo on my chest," something you always liked to remind me of after I complained to administration about you. Quite frankly, that logo, the one you said you owed your life to, represents trauma to me.

An Intimate Dialogue

Reacquainting myself with my story was difficult, especially doing so in such an intimate fashion—via a letter. For me, I've come to learn that this is where the depths of healing reside. To mentally come into that space, to envision writing a letter to my sexual harassers in such a way that I can see and feel them reading those words, whether they actually read it or not, brings me emotional release.

It also brings me peace knowing my story might help one of you reading my letter. I hope you know that I see, hear, and believe you; that what happened to me isn't just something that happened to me. It happened to many of us. To continue our healing journey, I want to transition into an intimate dialogue—in the form of a question-and-answer forum—between the editors and myself as a way to continue situating you, the reader, into my story. The editors asked me to reflect on these questions as a potential way into writing about my experience. Following, I provide my final thoughts along with reflection questions to consider if we want to move sport forward in a more diverse and equitable direction.

Questions & Answers

Editors: What have you learned about yourself by immersing yourself in your story?
Erdner:

Who I was then and who I am now are two completely different people. Up to that point, when I began working in all-male environments, I felt I was privileged to be a part of social and professional circles which included men who interacted with me in such a way as to empower my mind and champion my soul. When I walked into these all-male sport spaces, I assumed similar interactions would surface. Namely, I expected to be treated as the intellectual, emotional, and spiritual being that I am. As time progressed, I began to realize that such attributes were a threat to their fragile male identity.

What I ultimately learned by immersing myself in my story was this: On paper, women are welcome in sport. Sport organizations love to hire women so they can publicize their *inclusive* behaviors, which probably happens on a subconscious level. Many people will forward articles related to women being hired in sport settings to me, usually saying something as follows: "This is cool to see, women starting to gain traction in male-dominated spaces." On the surface, such articles seem hopeful. Once I read the article, though, I usually find that it never reaches beyond the simple celebration of a woman—or other marginalized groups such as LGBTQIA, BIPOC, or disabled folx—being hired into a coaching gig with an all-male sport team.

Beyond just speaking about my experience as a female in male-dominated sport, it is necessary to highlight similar oppressions for other marginalized groups—we must keep in mind the intersectional nature of people's demographics. Namely, if you do not fully identify as a White, male, middle- to upper-class, cisgender, heterosexual, Christian, non-disabled, strong, 25 to 55 years old, and an educated person, you are not overtly or covertly promised to be treated with the assured respect that such privileged social identities are offered (Samuels, 2014). Thus, when I received those articles or others similar, which celebrated other marginalized groups shattering the glass ceiling in privileged spaces, I always cringed. Why? Because we need to look beyond the red ticker tape headlines and begin thinking critically about the potential ramifications of such a hire without proper care.

For instance, when reading those articles, my mind immediately goes to the well-being of the female in those spaces. How is that particular organization treating her behind closed doors? Have they asked her how she would like to be treated, or are they simply subjugating her body into the patriarchal—men being privileged relative to women (Coakley, 2007c)—norms also being forced upon the men in the organization? Have they brought up the elephant in the room and discussed how she would like to navigate hard situations such as sexism when, not if, it arises?

What I learned most, not just about myself but our society, is this: We love the optics of diversity, equity, and inclusion. In immersing myself in my own story, I've learned that I am exhausted, frustrated, and struggling to keep my hope afloat. Because I, in all-male spaces, was and still am considered the token female (e.g., Kampoff et al., 2010; Taylor & Hardin, 2016), nothing more or less. To even type that statement makes me feel extremely uncomfortable, queasy, and worthless. How can I love myself when the foundation from which sport was built deems me, a female, lesser than?

Editors: How does your identity relate to your sexual misconduct story? For example, how do your demographics shape how you understand your story?
Erdner:

To properly address this question, I need to provide some context from which my answer can best be situated. Men created sport to act as a masculinity-validating experience (Dubbert, 1979); thus, sport became a place that reinforced the *assumed* natural superiority of men over women (Messner, 1988). Understanding this, I now realize how they treated me was directly correlated with the threat I posed. So, in order to survive, I had to police my own body to ensure men didn't fall into temptation and consequently act out of line. That is, I had to use a large majority of my daily energy to surveil my femaleness with the intention of upholding and validating the goodness of men, an energy I could have dispersed to my job responsibilities.

Foucault's (2003) work on relational power suggests that those in authority (i.e., men) exercise their power "through permanent mechanisms of surveillance and control" (p. 87). Thus, when these various men that I worked with would overtly and covertly remind me of my femaleness via their comments about and other nonverbal actions toward my body (e.g., sickening stares at my body, glances away when I spoke intellectually), they were exercising their privileged power by forcing me to surveil myself in such a way that it diverted my attention away from my job responsibilities. This reinforced the stereotype that I/women were not as adept as men in the workplace. In terms of my body, this reduced me to nothing but a vagina. All of these things caused me to work twice as hard to overcome the exhaustion of such a diversion and re-focus my attention on the tasks for the day.

I wish I could say I was successful at overcoming these sexist obstacles every day. I often felt ashamed that I let it "get the best of me," as most male colleagues cautioned me against. They said things like "Don't let 'em get under your skin, Sara. Just laugh it off;" they constantly reminded me of this. *I wish I was strong enough. Why am I not strong enough? Something must be wrong with me because they are telling me I need to be stronger.* These were thoughts that often crossed my mind on several occasions, which has caused me a lot of shame in the years following—a shame that I finally began to unpack in counseling.

During my time working in all-male spaces, I also wrote a great deal in my journal. On most days, I wrote about the philosophical manner of humanity. On other days, I wrote letters to and from my emotions to process my feelings. On the day I received the neck massage in that swivel chair, I couldn't find the words. When I put pen to paper, like a record stuck on a loop, I wrote: "I just wish I was a f****** man," over and over again. When I read it back to myself, I sobbed. The reality was that I learned to disregard myself, to hate myself. There I was, finally seeing the root of it all. My subconscious was brought to conscious awareness, which left me wondering: *What did I do to deserve this? Were the chosen ones the people who were born men? Did I do something wrong in my past life to be brought into this world as the inferior sex and gender? If so, maybe I should start analyzing what I did wrong, so I can then ask for forgiveness.* All these thoughts rampaged through my mind like a wild stallion in suffocated quarters.

Considering the question, "What does my identity have to do with my sexual misconduct story?" I believe my gender moderated it. That is, no matter my intellectual abilities, because of the sociocultural narrative created around sex and gender, my identity as a cis woman sabotaged it. Intersected with my youthful age, my gender influenced the strength from which my personal and professional abilities were perceived.

Editors: How is power revealed and concealed in your story?

Erdner:

As I stated earlier, sport was created by white, middle-class, able-bodied men to produce "*better*" white, middle-class, able-bodied men (Coakley, 2007a). Women were asked to politely chassé into a man's world and subsequently asked to fit our beautiful *square* bodies into the round hole of male sport. The expectation that anyone other than a cis-gendered *masculine* man must fit our bodies into that mold reveals one way that power is exercised in sport. The following is another story from my own experience working in all-male sport to help illustrate both the explicit and implicit ways this occurs.

I often attended regular developmental meetings that were aimed at teaching *boys* (e.g., the athletes) how to become *men* (e.g., the coaches and other authority figures). Settling into the back row, I proceeded to observe a coach approach the whiteboard and write the word "boy." After he underlined it, he asked, "What attributes characterize a boy?" One athlete piped up, "Emotional." Another chimed in, "Weak." From way in the back, "A pussy." The coach listed their responses without challenge. Once there was a fairly long list of *boy* attributes, the coach then wrote "man" on the whiteboard. After he underlined it, he asked, "What does it mean to be a man?" In rapid succession, the athletes shouted: "Brave, aggressive, a leader, strong, responsible, provider, alpha."

I sat in horror. The coach went on to emphasize that the "man" list consisted of the qualities needed to make it in sport. At the conclusion of the meeting, he asked if there was anything else anyone in the room would like to share. I raised my hand while simultaneously asking, "What's the subtext we are writing here?" Confused, the coach asked me to elaborate. "The subtext," I reiterated. "If I asked, 'What is the opposite of a man, what would you say?'" Already knowing where this message was headed, one brave soul chimed in, "A woman."

The room was now awkwardly quiet. Thus, I proceeded.

> By making this a "boys to men" session, you are implicitly perpetuating a bigger problem here. Considering the fact that I actually have a pussy yet you listed "pussy" as a "boy" characteristic, how do you feel about me or other women? If being a "boy" is what you are preaching against, then the subtext you are campaigning is against me as well. With that in mind, I encourage all of us to consider these meetings "child to adult" developmental sessions. That way, we are providing all humans a place at the table even if they are not represented in the room because people other than just cis-gendered men can be brave, aggressive, a leader, strong, responsible, provider, alpha.

It probably goes without saying that my response was not well-received. I, as a woman, just revealed the nasty, sexist, patriarchal narrative that acts as the underbelly of these organizations. Thus, in the days that followed, they revved up their power by ostracizing me and then concealed such power by shutting me down when I brought my sexual harassment story to their desk. These developmental meetings were one example of how we—both men and women—are indoctrinated into patriarchal thinking, which Real (2002) calls the "normal traumatization" of boys:

> The way we turn "boys into men" is through injury: We sever them from their mothers, research tells us, far too early. We pull them away from their own expressiveness, from their feelings, from sensitivity to others. The very phrase "Be a man" means suck it up and keep going. Disconnection is not fallout from traditional masculinity. Disconnection is masculinity.
>
> (p. 60)

Editors: What truths seem to be missing from the account of your story—upon reflection—that you think could be explored further and that you think others could benefit from?

Erdner:

I believe it is easier for us to see how a patriarchal narrative negatively influences women. However, we've failed to directly discuss how such a narrative hurts men. Rereading my letter, I can't help but read between the lines and subsequently empathize with my harassers, which might sound odd but hear me out. At some point, boys *and girls* learned that domination over girls was behaviorally okay and even championed in some masculine-validating circles. For example, I grew up being taught that when a boy bullied me on the playground, it meant he *liked* me and vice versa; thus, from a young age, both girls and boys are taught that patriarchy is *the Way*, with a capital W. In this narrative, we often only place the magnifying glass upon boys harming girls; we hardly ever stop to question the injustices happening to boys. Was it their parents, friends, and/or teammates who dominated them when they were younger, thereby causing anger and thus leading to them releasing such anger in domineering ways now?

In her book, *The Will to Change: Men, Masculinity, and Love*, hooks (2004) mentions that "anger can be, and usually is, the hiding place for fear and pain" (p. 44). She goes on to mention that men, especially, are imprisoned by a patriarchal system that stifles their ability to access their full emotional well-being, which undermines their overall mental health. Within such a narrative, men are forced into

> blind obedience—the foundation upon which patriarchy stands; the repression of all emotions except fear; the destruction of individual willpower; and the repression of thinking whenever it departs from the authority figure's way of thinking.
>
> (p. 23)

This same blind obedience is inherent in sports. What does it mean to be a *good* athlete? In my dissertation research (Erdner, 2021), each athlete at their respective level of play voiced the deleterious effects of having to blindly obey the commands of the coach. Such a trait—blind obedience—is a foundational characteristic glorified in sport. If an athlete does not possess it, then a coach likely will deem the athlete defective (Erdner, 2021), which leads the athlete to experiencing emotional abuse from the coach via denial of attention and support (Stirling & Kerr, 2008). Further, sociological and developmental scholars also discovered that this coaching approach, often found in power and performance sports, can hinder the creative and innovative components needed to properly develop individuals starting at the youth level (Bowers & Green, 2013; Bowers et al., 2014; Coakley, 2007b). Related to my sexual misconduct story, as a woman in all-male sport spaces, male authority figures often expect me to be silent when sexism rears its nasty head, to politely ignore—turn a blind eye—when such occurrences arise. This expectation hindered the creative and innovative energy I needed to do my job properly.

While it would be easy, and, quite frankly, warranted, to stay angry at my harassers, with hooks' (2004) words in mind, directing hate toward another individual would perpetuate the same problem. Rather, we need to engage love. Such love, Freire (2005) suggests, acts to transform domination:

> Dialogue cannot exist, however, in the absence of profound love for the world and for people. The naming of the world, which is an act of creation and re-creation, is not possible if it is not infused with love. Love is at the same time the foundation of dialogue and dialogue itself. It is thus necessarily the task of responsible Subjects and cannot exist in a relation of domination. Domination reveals the pathology of love: sadism is the dominator and masochism in the dominated. Because love is an act of courage, not of fear, love is commitment to others. No matter where the oppressed are found, the act of love is commitment to their cause—the cause of liberation. And this commitment, because it is loving, is dialogical.
>
> (p. 89)

As I continue to honor my sexual misconduct story while also leaning into the injustices placed upon boys and men in our society, I daydream about a world in which men are fully allowed to access their emotional selves. What would our world would be like if we could see their hurt, show them we care via loving dialogue, and provide them the support necessary to overcome such pains? Thus, I don't think it would be fair to *only* paint my sexual harassers as monsters. What I needed most was to be seen and heard when I shared my sexual misconduct story with the administrators. I wanted them to empathize with and believe me. In good conscience, I cannot write this chapter in such a way as to *not* give the same care to those who harmed me, the care that I so desperately needed to receive in their offices that day.

I think the answer resides in showing up for boys and men in such a way as to nurture their emotional selves. We need to provide them space to process through the pains they suffer from being forced into a patriarchal narrative that defines being a *man* by way of athletic ability, sexual conquest, and economic success (Ehrmann & Jordan, 2011). Such glorified masculine-validating attributes robs men of the chance to choose the kind of man they want to be (Plank, 2019; Sexton, 2019), which hurts us all.

Afterword

While I believe my story speaks for itself, I also believe hooks' (2000) words highlight a necessary conviction we need to adopt in sport:

> Leaders are needed, and should be individuals who acknowledge their relationship to the group and who are accountable to it. They should have the ability to show

> love and compassion, show this love through their actions, and be able to engage in successful dialogue.
>
> *(p. 692)*

Within such a system of domination—as sport currently stands—love cannot exist, which is precisely what we need. As Freire (2005) states:

> Only by abolishing the situation of oppression [via domination] is it possible to restore the love which that situation made impossible. If I do not love the world—if I do not love life—if I do not love people—[we] cannot enter into [healing] dialogue.
>
> *(p. 90)*

If I was sitting at that table with various sport leaders, entering that healing dialogue the following is what I would say.

From a systemic level, how much safer might marginalized individuals *and men* feel if we didn't just allocate most organizational funds to athlete mental health initiatives but also cared about all sport stakeholders? They matter as well, and not just as a means to an end—getting the win—but in and of themselves. As I mentioned in my book, *Dear Coach: What I Wish I Could Have Told You, Letters from Your Athletes* (Erdner, 2021), sport has done a fairly good job at financially funding programs that offer athletes—the glorified money-makers—with resources that will help them tap into and unpack the various abuses they've endured within and outside of sport. Yet, what about the coach, the sport administrator, the support staff? What about the marginalized trying to navigate work in a sea of the privileged majority? Where are the mental health initiatives for us?

When I mentioned this much needed shift in a room full of sport authority figures, demanding care because we matter, too, I watched tears fill the eyes of some. As stated in my book:

> The idea that [coaches, administrators, support staff] sacrifice their own mental health resonated. They are drowning, losing precious time with family, and sacrificing time to nurture a genuine connection with [others]. Their giving, helping role makes them stressed out and exhausted, with no one to turn to for support. When their world gets chaotic, where is their encourager, their cheerleader? When the pressure to win gets so unbearable, who do they have to talk to? I think the honorable thing to do here is to support them, and I am not just talking about turning to their significant others or chatting with fellow coaches. I am talking about actual, financially funded access to mental performance *and* clinical counseling services.
>
> *(Erdner, 2021, p. 168)*

By providing all sport authority figures with both mental performance *and* clinical counseling services, this will allow those in power the opportunity to model healthier behaviors, which will create a contagious environment where their enhanced self-actualization will positively influence all other sport stakeholders. How much more then, when we have mentally healthier authority people in sport, would that caring energy trickle down and enhance the overall environment for all? Water doesn't flow up stream.

Another avenue to consider is the hiring, retention, and firing process of those in authority. How much safer might marginalized members *and men* feel if we infused diversity, equity, and inclusion (DEI) measures into these processes? Enacting such measures would uphold a new, necessary level of accountability which would provide more security for those who report a sexually harassing or abusive occurrence to feel more reassured that their humanity means more than a win-loss record. As sport currently stands, power figures in sport are often only hired, retained, and/or subsequently fired based whether they can produce wins. What we need are employment procedures that

> align with scientifically supported, inclusive, best practices that will hold sport accountable to a higher standard than just being able to make employment decisions vaguely based on a "good cultural fit".
>
> (Erdner, 2021, p. 179)

Such actions—sponsoring mental health initiatives for all and enhancing the hiring, retention, and firing process to include DEI measures—would promote the very love needed to transform sport for the better. And, in sport spaces where we champion *tough love*, how much more emotionally, mentally, and physically safer of an environment would we create for all if we finally decided to drop the *tough* and just lead with love?

Discussion Questions

1. What kind of stories did you hear growing up related to what it meant to be a *man* and *woman*?
2. How do such narratives for both men and women hurt those who do not fit neatly into how we traditionally define being a *man* or *woman*?
3. In what ways are *you* seeing, hearing, and championing all women and those who do not identify as *masculine* cis-gendered men in your life? What are you doing well? What could you do better? How?
4. In what ways is your *organization* seeing, hearing, and championing all women and those who do not identify as *masculine* cis-gendered men in your sport environment? What are you doing well? What could you do better? How?
5. How are you making sure that *all* individual's—including men's—mental, emotional, and spiritual health are nurtured as they navigate their work and life environments? What are you doing well? What could you do better? How?

References

Bowers, M. T., & Green, B. C. (2013). Reconstructing the community-based youth sport experience: How children derive meaning from unstructured and organized settings. *Journal of Sport Management*, 27(6), 422–438.

Bowers, M. T., & Green, B. C., Hemme, F., & Chalip, L. (2014). Assessing the relationship between youth sport participation settings and creativity in adulthood. *Creativity Research Journal*, 26(3), 314–327.

Coakley, J. (2007a). Studying the past. In *Sports in society: Issues and controversies* (pp. 54–85). McGraw-Hill.

Coakley, J. (2007b). Sports and children: Are organized programs worth the effort? In *Sports in society: Issues and controversies* (pp. 120–148). McGraw-Hill.

Coakley, J. (2007c). Sport and religions: Is it a promising combination? In *Sports in society: Issues and controversies* (pp. 528–561). McGraw-Hill.

Dubbert, J. L. (1979). *A man's place: Masculinity in transition* (p. 164). Prentice Hall.

Ehrmann, J., & Jordan, G. (2011). *InSideOut coaching: How sport can transform lives*. Simon & Schuster.

Ellis, C. (2004). *The ethnographic I: A methodological novel about autoethnography*. AltaMira Press.

Erdner, S. (2021). *Dear coach: What I wish I could have told you, letter from your athletes*. Morgan James Publishing.

Foucault, M. (2003). *Abnormal: Lectures at the Collège de France 1974–75*. Picador.

Freire, P. (2005). *Pedagogy of the oppressed* (pp. 89–90). The Continuum International Publishing Group, Inc.

hooks, b. (2000). A feminist revolution: Development through struggle. In *Feminist theory: From margin to center* (2nd ed.). Pluto Press.

hooks, b. (2004). *The will to change: Men, masculinity, and love*. Washington Square Press.

Kampoff, C. S., Armentrout, S. M., & Driska, A. (2010). The token female: Women's experiences as division I college head coaches of men's teams. *Journal of Intercollegiate Sport, 3*(2), 297–315.

Messner, M. A. (1988). Sports and male domination: The female athlete as contested ideological terrain. *Sociology of Sport Journal, 5*(3), 197–211.

Plank, L. (2019). *For the love of men: A new vision for mindful masculinity*. St. Martin's Press.

Real, T. (2002). *How can I get through to you? Reconnecting men and women*. Scribner.

Samuels, D. (2014). *The culturally inclusive educator: Preparing for a multicultural world*. Teacher College Press.

Sexton, J. Y. (2019). *The man they wanted me to be: Toxic masculinity and a crisis of our own making*. Counterpoint Press.

Stirling, A. E., & Kerr, G. A. (2008). Defining and categorizing emotional abuse in sport. *European Journal of Sport Science, 8*(4), 173–181.

Taylor, E. A., & Hardin, R. (2016). Female NCAA division I athletic directors: Experiences and challenges. *Women in Sport & Physical Activity Journal, 24*, 14–25.

10
EXPERIENCING SAME-GENDER AND TRANS VIOLENCE IN SPORT

Jordan Forrest Miller

Part 1: Playing a *Real* Sport

I was born at Cullman County Hospital in Alabama in November 1990 to a self-proclaimed dysfunctional working-class white nuclear family. Before I came along, it was Mama, Papa, my sister JB, 14 years older than I, and my brother JW, 10 years older than me. JB claimed me as hers since the day I was born, despite my mother's 36-hour labor and C-section. Upon arrival into this world and examination of my external genitalia, I was assigned female and raised *as a girl*, which had specific expectations from Mama, Papa, JB, JW, and not to mention, white Appalachian and US cultural norms. It is from this assignment of female that I have learned to perceive the world and my role within it. One institution in which I feel strict gender norms have caused me the most harm is within the realm of organized sport.

Papa was a formative influence on how I first felt the impact of strict gender expectations in relation to sport. Papa, now 71, I would describe as a white, Southern good ole' boy. Though I have distanced myself from him emotionally and physically, I find his demeanor comforting and much of his politics reasonable. We don't talk politics often, but when I am willing to have conversations, he is willing to listen and consider my perspective. Even still, I have many complaints about his stubbornness and sexism. We recently had a conversation where I updated him on my pronouns: they and them. He responded, "I hope it's okay that I don't understand. And I don't want to." He wanted me to know that my relationship to gender doesn't change how he feels about me, but he also made it clear he wasn't interested in understanding me as a person. As a kid, he would *poke fun* at my belly fat (and Mama's). He *wouldn't allow* me to do *boy's tasks* like mow the lawn or use a weed whacker. To this day, he refuses to call me by my chosen name, Jordan. Papa and Mama separated when I was 12 years old. I am still not sure the full story, but I do know Papa told Mama that she and I "needed to learn to be more independent." She passed away after a psychotic episode and mental health institutionalization at the age of 63 in November 2017. For a long time, I thought my life was *normal* prior to their separation, though a decade of therapy has taught me otherwise.

I distinctly remember asking Mama if I could join the local cheerleading squad in fifth grade. My main motivation being my best friend since kindergarten, Cookie, wanted me to join her. Her family was considered non-traditional in our majority white town in the sense that her mother was Black, in her early 40s, and dating a white man in his 70s. Mama told me to ask Papa about cheerleading. I cuddled up in his lap, and asked sweetly, "Papa, can I join cheerleading with Cookie??" He responded in a quick and stern tone, "If you're going to play a sport, you're going to play a *real* sport." I remember feeling upset that I couldn't spend more time with Cookie. Alternatively, my parents put me in gymnastics and dancing with some white friends in my Girl Scout troop, and I bawled my eyes out after the three practices I attended. I was nowhere near as talented as the others, and even the simple exercises were painful and scary for me. Feeling defeated and not fully understanding what was meant by a *real* sport, other than maybe it applied to basketball which he and my brother played growing up, I decided to join the middle school band with Cookie instead. My sister played the flute in middle and high school, too, and I had always admired her creativity and artistic abilities. Aunt Cool, Mama's older sister, moved from Alabama to New York when she was young to distance herself from the harms of family trauma. She told me once that the difference in her and my conspiracy-theorist uncle is that she left the South, and he didn't. It was always a treat when she sent books and clothing to my family. When I joined band, she generously gifted a brand-new Armstrong beginner's flute to me, paid for in installments for a year. Cookie was able to rent a clarinet, I assume with her father's cab driving money. Over the next few years, Cookie and I got very good at playing our chosen instruments; we even learned to transpose from treble clef to bass clef! Prior to Papa's denial of cheerleading for me, my resentment was building over his judgmental reaction to Cookie's mom *borrowing* the Girl Scout cookie money to cover her family's rent. The full story never came to light, but I remember Mama arguing with Papa about how unfair it was to forbid me to see my best friend because of her mother's choices. Though I was only 11, I also remember calling Cookie crying and complaining to her about my racist family. Though I didn't have a full comprehension of systemic racism, I knew better than to buy into my family's paradigm. Cookie and I started doing marathon *pamper me days* where we treated ourselves to feet-soaking, nail-painting, and gossiping in our respective homes while on the landline phone with each other all day.

Part 2: It's a Marathon, Not a Sprint

After my parents separated and I got on probation for joyriding with my neighbor, Mama decided to move us to another county where I would attend a much larger city school for sixth grade. We lived with Cookie and her mom for a while so that I would have in-county residence. After a few months of phone calls and paperwork, we finally got approved to live in a Section 8 house with my sister JB and her son, who was under a year old. Shortly upon moving to the city, I experienced numerous accounts of sexual misconduct from the boys and men in my life, much to the ignorance of the adults in my life who were nonetheless named *caretakers*.

Grown men, including both Mama and JB's boyfriends, made sexual advances toward me when they knew Mama and JB weren't paying attention, which was often. Mama's boyfriend, in his 50s, watched me give my boyfriend a blowjob through my bedroom door, and my sister's boyfriend, in his early 30s, slowly coerced me into having sex with him using alcohol and escalating manipulation tactics to decrease my self-confidence. Behind the church on the hill, a boy from school tried to force himself on me. As he pinned my arms down, my fight-or-flight instinct kicked in, and I bit his tongue hard, pushed him off me, and ran home quickly. I didn't tell anyone about the boy from school, partially because he was Black, and I was afraid of what my father would do and say to me. I never told Mama about her boyfriend being inappropriate with me, either; I didn't want to add to her trauma after he had physically assaulted her. It took me about six months to burst into anger at my sister about her boyfriend raping me. Once I did, the police came to our house, and the FBI showed up at school the next day and took me out of class to receive my testimony; I was 12 years old.

I don't know if I would have ever told my sister if I weren't so resentful that I was taking care of my nephew when she was out drinking. In fact, I hid her keys a lot. One time, she chased me around the house after getting home from the bar trying to get my nephew from me, screaming, "That's my baby!" as she tripped over the recliner in the living room. I locked my nephew in the bedroom and sang to him softly to block out her yelling through the door. I was so angry at her for being drunk and for not being able to be present with her son, or me. Her boyfriend fled police investigation, and I learned years later that he was shot and killed while trying to steal someone's guitar, a habit of which I was aware because he also stole Mama's wedding ring and necklace from Papa.

It was with this tumultuous past in tow that in eighth grade at the city school, I decided I would join the cross-country team to avoid being at home. And, wow, running those distances was demanding! Practice consisted of 5-mile runs and the cross-country girls were very skilled. They were nice enough and encouraging, but I was not a good long-distance runner. The male coach was surprisingly kind and didn't set off any alarms of sexual harassment, which was a relief. At my first cross-country meet the horn blew and I took off as fast as I could and fell over, heaving and throwing up after about 300 yards. I laid there for what felt like an eternity feeling like no one in the world cared about me, saw me, or believed in my potential. Sulking, I walked slowly back to the start line and waited for the race to be over. After that race, I decided I would get up early and go run at the high school track for extra practice. This was partially to leave the house early enough to get out of expectations of JB to care for my nephew. It also just felt good to be alone at 6 am out on the track. I didn't need to take off in a sprint. I could breathe.

My next cross-country meet, I finished second to last, but I was happy to have finished at all and to have my brother and his wife waiting at the finish line to see me. That was the only race I ever completed. Despite feeling proud of my accomplishment, I quit cross-country within a week—just before Mama's boyfriend physically assaulted her. After Mama's assault and me reporting the rape by JB's boyfriend, my brother asked if I would like to live with him and his wife until "things were more stable." I graciously accepted, hoping this would be my chance to learn what this concept *stability* could feel like.

Part 3: Cooter Punches

One day during eighth grade, I wore my cross-country shirt from my previous school. It depicted a girl running on the back with her hair in a ponytail and listed all her top-notch qualities, including strength, endurance, and speed. My new high school selected me as one of the *gifted* students which meant I took Algebra I Honors with Coach Trigger. On the basis of this shirt, she asked me, "Oh, you're a runner?" I smiled big, and said "Yes, I was on the cross-country team at my last school." She immediately invited me to practice with the girls' soccer team. As an eighth grader, I felt especially honored. I said, "Yes, of course!"

Like gymnastics and cross-county, I felt out of my wheelhouse in soccer, too, as my athletic skills were not on par with the girls on the team who had been playing since they were five. The senior girls were territorial and claimed their superiority loudly. As a person who never responded well to authority figures, I was not very liked by them. They were also *great* soccer players. They were so good that our team went to the state finals my freshman year. One day I ran past the senior girls at practice, making them so mad. Running fast for brief periods was one of my skillsets; so, I aimed to run as fast as I could in the last lap. The seniors participated in a hazing ritual of *cooter punching* teammates of freshmen status. This painful act consisted of a joke to distract you, followed by a hard underhanded punch to the groin area and then laughter from the group. After *cooter punching* me on the bus before a game, they asked me tauntingly, "Do you wipe from front to back or back to front?" In a panic, I responded, "Back to front," to which the seniors cackled and taught me lessons about UTIs. Even though I had broken my toe earlier in the day when I was kicking around the ball with Coach Trigger's nephew, I enthusiastically went in during the final minutes at the end of the senior's final game and ran as fast as I could possibly run, almost scoring. We won State, and the senior girls would soon be leaving!

Part 4: Sitting With Girls on the Bus

My first girlfriend in high school, Serena, and I went back and forth between dating each other and dating Coach Trigger's nephew who we were pretty sure was gay. When he and I were dating, he didn't make any sexual advances, bought me jewelry and dresses from the mall, and gave me rides home. Coach Trigger's husband started texting me dirty things at some point and whispering dirty comments to me when no one else could hear. I brushed them off as harmless at the time. I felt Coach Trigger was jealous of me because of the attention I received from many boys and men, including her nephew, her husband, and the young male soccer coach who would give me rides home after indoor soccer matches. Coach Trigger scowled at me for my promiscuity, rather than directing her anger at the men making sexual advances toward a teenager. I couldn't help enjoying the attention and car rides.

I liked the intensity and quick pace of indoor soccer, despite Coach Trigger admonishing me after I got a red flag saying, "Stop playing football!" I was actually talented at football and wished I could play in the mock football game, which the school deemed appropriate for girls, but Coach Trigger wouldn't allow soccer players to play. My cute boy neighbor taught me how to throw a football when I was about 7.

While I was away at Governor's School the summer of junior year, Serena, who was the soccer manager, told a fellow teammate that we were dating. Within a week, we were both outed as gay to the entire soccer team, and thus the school. After Coach Trigger found out about Serena and I dating she proceeded to gossip about us in the teacher's lounge.

Coach Trigger pulled me aside before a game my senior year and questioned me demanding, "Do I let boys sit with girls on the bus?" Confused, I responded, "No . . ." She continued, "Then, why do you think I should let you sit with Serena?" I mumbled that I sit right next to her, anyway. Coach Complicit, an assistant coach, stood in silence with sympathetic eyes. Later that semester, Serena told me that after that incident Coach Complicit read the nondiscrimination clause of the student handbook purposely looking her in the eyes, insinuating that Coach Trigger mistreated us and that Serena should report it.

Similar to the narratives offered by Tsang (2000), I remember a stage in high school when I deliberately choose to embody hegemonic femininity to appeal to gender expectations as a teenage girl. This specifically included shaving my legs, wearing makeup, straightening my hair, and wearing heels and dresses (when I wasn't in my soccer or band attire). Another key part of embodying this hyperfeminine ideal for me was to keep up the appearance of only dating cisgender straight men. Because of this fear of being ostracized at school and abandoned by loved ones, I wouldn't hold Serena's hand in public and kept my feelings about my gender and sexuality away from my family until I trusted I could be entirely financially independent from them.

Part 5: The Bathroom Problem

Surviving the high school experience in East Tennessee by adhering to my rules for safety and somehow excelling academically despite the toxic environment, I made my way to Knoxville for college. A full-ride income-based scholarship for families that make less than $23,000/year made this welcomed escape possible. I also had the remainder of the educational fund created by my Great Aunt in Arkansas who passed away ten years prior to my birth to use for books, technology, and other class supplies. I started out as a biochemistry and molecular biology major on the pre-med track in hopes of solving Mama's bipolar disorder through genome mapping (and to make my father proud). The second week of Organic Chemistry my third year, I decided to change my major to kinesiology (i.e., exercise science). This major did not require organic chemistry or a language beyond English I and II. This was an astute decision as I had barely made it through Latin I and the Chemistry I and Chemistry II series. Following the alcoholic trend of Mama and JB, I developed a drinking habit upon arrival at college, especially binge drinking. I also joined a sorority. My first night out with friends I took 23 shots of Jägermeister and got kicked out of a bar in the college's adjacent commercial district after throwing up in the bathroom and crying hysterically. Each binge drinking weekend out with my sorority induced PTSD flashbacks of the ways boys and men had violated my body and how the women in my life were shockingly unaware of my reality and trying desperately to hold themselves together. I wanted nothing more than to push my trauma out of my mind. As much as I tried, the memories flooded my brain space constantly. A reliable coping mechanism for me was to drink myself to the point of throwing up and lay in the bathtub in my dorm room (or a friend's) wallowing in my self-pity.

Once I switched majors, I saw myself in the material in a way I hadn't in the physical science domains. But, I found myself frustrated at the ways many professors presented the information as if the issues being discussed, like poverty and sexism, don't affect people who are in the class. My Introduction to Sport Psychology professor, who happened to invite me to contribute to this book chapter, saw me through my writing as a feminist. She didn't know my struggle in her classroom to breathe as I bound my chest with an ACE bandage for weeks, or my PTSD flashbacks as I struggled to face my emotions and memories of my past. She didn't know I was getting yelled at in the women's restroom for being perceived as a man because of my short hair, and that, as a response, I avoided campus restrooms unless they were one of a handful of single-stall or marked gender-neutral on campus. She didn't know of my internalized homophobia and fear of violence, but she actively encouraged me to identify myself in the material and express myself through writing and classroom discussion.

As the class discussed the harms of gender expectations in the realm of sport, I identified myself as someone with patterns of excessive exercise and bulimia, and empathized with the other coping mechanisms presented as sociostructural causes of health disparities. During this semester in her class, I learned more about LGBT+ identities and communities and found solace in the campus's Pride Center. There and in other dedicated spaces for LGBT+ people and our allies, I began to apply my organizational knowledge and skills to fostering LGBT+ resilience and increasing institutional access, finally finding a place for my rage that didn't include self-harm or harming others. I began to identify as transgender and embrace transgressing cultural norms around what it meant to be assigned female at birth within my cultural context.

Literature Review

Linking my personal narratives offered in these previous sections to academic literature—particularly as related to coach-athlete dynamics in high school—several aspects of sexual exploitation and the grooming process within youth sport contexts are evident (Brackenridge & Fasting, 2005; Dietz, 2018; Fasting et al., 2007; Lanning, 2018; Stirling & Kerr, 2009). These patterns of exploitation are embedded into social institutions, and are also preventable (Wurtele, 2012; Prewitt-White, 2019). My experiences also link to broader sport themes including sexism, biological essentialism, sex-testing, sex-segregated spaces, and lack of bodily autonomy. As explained by Brackenridge and Fasting (2005):

> Grooming is central to the abusive relationship and is a term taken from the social work and clinical sex offending literatures (Doyle, 1994; Morrison et al., 1994). It involves slowly gaining the trust of a potential victim before systematically breaking down interpersonal barriers prior to committing actual sexual abuse. This process may take weeks, months or years with the perpetrator usually moving steadily so that he [sic] is able to maintain secrecy and avoid exposure. Grooming is important because it brings about the appearance of co-operation from the athlete, making the act of abuse seem to be consensual. In other words, whereas harassment is *definitely unwanted*, abuse may *appear to be wanted* ([emphasis theirs]; or consented to) when the victim has been subjected to grooming.
>
> (p. 3)

Sexual exploitation and professional abuse of minors (under 18) within youth-serving organizations (YSOs) is well-documented, though no comprehensive study has been conducted to date (Wurtele, 2012). Media reports have highlighted sexual abuse of youths within YSOs including within school systems (Layton & Diskin, 2012; Irvine & Tanner, 2007), the Boy Scouts of America (Yardley, 2010), and other non-profits, mentor programs, and competitive sports (Adelson, 2011; Chuchmach & Patel, 2010; Fasting et al., 2007; Nack & Yaeger, 1999; O'Hagan & Willmsen, 2003; O'Keeffe, 2011; Volkwein et al., 1997; Wurtele, 2012; Zinser, 2011). Stirling and Kerr (2009) specifically discussed the role of power in coach-athlete dynamics and made recommendations for abuse prevention.

At the vital time of my parent's separation, I strongly desired to be *seen* by the adult figures in my life, including Papa, Mama, JB, JW, my teachers, and especially coaches once I decided to enter the world of formal sports in high school. My high school soccer coaches, in particular, held a lot of power in our coach–athlete dynamic; I wanted terribly to be a good player, to make Coach Trigger proud. Elements of the grooming process (Brackenridge & Fasting, 2005) are illustrated by Coach Trigger's abuse of power displayed after a soccer player outed me as being in a same-sex relationship. Though her and her husband's behavior, and that of the assistant coach who gave me rides home, did not escalate to a physical act of sexual abuse, their behaviors were emotionally and spiritually damaging and involved aspects of grooming (i.e., kindness, attention, material enticement, special privileges, and coercion; Dietz, 2018). While factors outside of the realm of sport influenced my risk factors for these abusive dynamics as a teenage athlete, the power dynamic between coaches and athletes is documented as a contributing risk factor in abuse within sport (Stirling & Kerr, 2009). Like many other athletes who have been sexually exploited and groomed in sport (Fasting et al., 2007), I chose to cope at the time indirectly and individually and did not report the behavior of my coaches to anyone. I have since found social support in therapy and from others with similar experiences.

Wurtele (2012) suggested aimed efforts to prevent sexual exploitation of minors in YSOs including within schools, sport teams, and faith centers. Changes suggested included strategies at national, state, and organizational levels (Wurtele, 2012). Prewitt-White (2019) offered additional resources for grooming prevention and boundary education programming.

Biological Essentialism

In addition to highlighting patterns of sexual exploitation and grooming, I see great overlap in my narratives and other systemic inequities within sport, including the history of sport cultures privileging biological essentialist claims to exclude minority populations from participation. The ancient Greek Olympic Games starting in the 8th century BC, for example, mandated athletes be "trained for at least ten months, of high moral character, not enslaved, and a male" (Elsas et al., 2000, p. 249). In addition, there was much pushback to the incorporation of women into the Olympics, including biological essentialist fears of women "enticing male voyeurs or harm[ing] female reproductive organs" (Pieper, 2016, p. 119). Sex and gender verification, *femininity tests*, and sex-testing, including visual examination and chromosomal tests, began not long after women entered formal sports along with fear-based claims of men (particularly from communist Eastern European countries) deceptively dressing as women and thus having an unfair advantage (Dickinson et al., 2002; Elsas et al., 2000; Flores et al., 2020; Pieper, 2016).

Originating from these Cold War anxieties, gender verification testing has since been used largely in women's sport to exclude women, trans people, and intersex people whose genetic and hormonal makeup does not fit into white Western criteria for appropriate female physical appearance, genetic composition, and hormonal range (Elsas et al., 2000; Flores et al., 2020; Pieper, 2016; see also Love, 2014; Reeser, 2005). "Non-feminine, non-Western, and non-white" women are especially impacted by these sex-testing policies (Dickinson et al., 2002; Flores et al., 2020; Pieper, 2016). For example, Caster Semenya, South African Olympic runner, is one athlete who has been marked *deviant* due to not fitting within white Western ideas of gender conformity. Having always understood herself as a woman, Caster ran and won the 800-meter 2009 World Track and Field Championships final in Berlin at 18 years, after having earlier received heavy scrutiny for her physicality and undergoing required gynecological testing (Cahn, 2011; Pieper, 2016). After her win, results revealed Caster had "higher than average [female] levels of androgens" (Pieper, 2016, p. 182) and officials withdrew her medals (Pieper, 2016). Following the receding of medals, Caster was required to take hormones to alter her testosterone levels, and her performance suffered—likely due both to the intense scrutiny and the impact of decreased testosterone on her strength training capacity. Without being informed of the purpose of the tests, Dutee Chand, Indian Olympic sprinter, was also forced to undergo medical testing during the 2014 Glasgow Commonwealth Games. Like Semenya, she had always understood herself to be a woman. To continue her career as an athlete, the Sports Authority of India (SAI) required her to have surgery or take hormones to reduce her androgen levels. Opposed to altering her body, Chand protested this mandate and ultimately gained the ability to compete due to the lack of scientific evidence regarding "the *degree* of the advantage that androgen-sensitive hyperandrogenic females enjoy over non-hyperandrogenic females" (Pieper, 2016, p. 184; Lennox, 1968). Renee Richards, American tennis player, was one of the first trans women in sport to receive national attention over winning the right to compete in the US Open which required athletes to compete in accordance with their chromosomal makeup (Birrell & Cole, 1990). Other athletes to win rights to compete have included Mianne Bagger, Michelle Dumaresq, Fallon Fox, and Laurel Hubbard.

Similar claims are rarely used against assigned-female-at-birth (AFAB) athletes who medically transition. Trans men are often included in men's sports leagues without contestation, though there is still pushback to full acceptance of trans boys and men in male-designated spaces. At the public high school level, the University Interscholastic League ruled that Mack Beggs, an American trans boy who was taking testosterone, must compete in the girls' wrestling division (Flores et al., 2020; Malagrinó, 2020). Despite having a desire to compete in the boys' wrestling division, Beggs received harsh criticism from fans and parents as he won the Texas Class 6A girls' state wrestling championship. Another strategy was adopted by California, where state law mandates that athletes compete in accordance with their gender identity, regardless of medical transition status (Cal. Educ. Code § 221.5). Finally, in North Carolina, House Bill 2 (HB2) mandates that transgender men like Beggs would be required to use women's restrooms and locker rooms according to his sex designation on his birth certificate (Flores et al., 2020).

Sadly, biological essentialist claims that are discriminatory against transgender people have a long history within racist institutions and are commonly employed today in anti-trans bills aiming to exclude trans people from curricula, healthcare, appropriate documentation, bathrooms, and sport. Furthermore, trans panic claims and those of *protecting females* fail to acknowledge the degree to which transgender women, particularly transgender women of color, are impacted by transmisogyny (Rosich, 2020). While fairness is certainly a factor to consider in regard to trans inclusion in sport, the degree to which androgens impact performance in sport is not entirely known, and much harm is caused by these medicalized and exclusionary policies.

The assumption undergirding the debate over transgender participation in sport is that assigned male at birth (AMAB) bodies are inherently stronger than those AFAB (Birrell & Cole, 1990; Pieper, 2016). Many athletes and scholars have argued that this belief denies the reality of trans lived experience and medical knowledge regarding transition (Flores et al., 2020; McKinnon, 2019). In other words, arguments calling for the separation of trans women and girls from women's sport are not justifiable based on the latest scientific evidence regarding the effects of hormone replacement therapy (HRT) on AMAB bodies; furthermore, the language in such bills does not acknowledge the socially constructed nature of sex and gender (Fausto-Sterling, 2000; Flores et al., 2020). Gender norms based on sex assignment are a social decision (Fausto-Sterling, 2000) and are heavily racialized (Currah, 2008; Martino et al., 2021). Binary divisions based on sex assignment are barely 100 years old; it has not always been this way. This decision maintains its power through markers on birth certificates, driver license's, passports, doctor's offices forms restrooms, binary sex-segregated sports teams, gyms, and more.

Though Olympic history has included a heavy reliance on biological essentialist claims, for instance in their previous exclusion of cisgender women from sport due to the assumption that sport was harmful to the female reproductive system (Pieper, 2016), current International Olympic Committee (IOC) standards allow trans women to compete, provided their hormonal levels fall within the "typical" range of cisgender women (World Athletics, 2019). Estrogen and progestins, as well as testosterone, have a tremendous impact on the body and its capacity including in building muscle mass and endurance; however, the latest research on the impacts of hormones on the body indicate trans women who have received HRT for one or more years are well within the typical cisgender woman's range (World Athletics, 2019). Though higher levels of testosterone do play a part in one's physicality and strength training, other factors are equally important to sport training (McKinnon, 2019). Furthermore, trans girls who have taken HRT in the form of puberty blockers have never undergone any bodily changes due to testosterone from first puberty, and, thereby, do not have the advantages that opponents of trans inclusion in sport argue gives trans girls and women an unfair advantage. In fact, *no* studies have documented long-term advantages for trans girls and women whose hormone levels are well within the range of girls and cisgender women.

Current IOC regulations require ongoing medical transition and testing to maintain eligibility (Pieper, 2016; World Athletics, 2019). Even with medical knowledge supporting sex differentiation (Birrell & Cole, 1990), many such as Malagrinó (2020) argue for transgender athletes' inclusion in sport based on gender identity alone regardless of sex characteristics.

Rachel McKinnon is a Canadian trans cyclist who has also experienced trans violence in sport. Her body, according to the officials of the IOC, is not a "woman's body." The claims used against McKinnon include that trans women have biological advantages over cisgender women. None of which are empirical-based claims (Flores et al., 2020; Pieper, 2016). As poignantly explained by McKinnon in her 2019 New York Times opinion piece:

> If you think I have an unfair competitive advantage, consider this: I lose most of my races. I won five out of 22 events in 2019; none of those I won were against strong international fields. The woman who took second place to me in the masters world championship sprint event, Dawn Orwick, beat me just days earlier in the 500-meter time trial. In the 12 times I've raced against Jennifer Wagner, who finished third to my first place in the sprint event in 2018, she beat me in seven. Wagner has beaten me more times than I've beaten her, head-to-head. How can I have an unfair advantage over her if she beats me most of the time? And why should my right to compete be contingent on not winning?

Recent sociological studies reveal several patterns in support and opposition for transgender athletes' participation in sport (Flores et al., 2020). In a representative survey of 1,020 men and women in the United States by Flores et al. (2020), support and opposition to transgender athletes' participation in sport were based on a Likert scale of strongly agree to strongly disagree, asking respondents about their comfort level with trans athletes' participation with others of their gender identity given the athlete had a *sex change*. Using this measure as an indicator of acceptance of trans athletes, four groups were more likely to oppose transgender athletes' participation in sport: (1) men, (2) those who hold traditional gender role beliefs, (3) those who embody greater gender identity conformity, and (4) sports fans. Alternatively, individuals with more contact with gay and trans people and stronger egalitarian views were more likely to support transgender athletes' participation in sport (Flores et al., 2020).

These findings have strong implications for current policy regarding the inclusion of trans athletes. Many factors beyond a *sex change* impact the abilities of the body; a more robust measure of support and opposition would need greater specificity to fully understand the nature of attitudes towards trans athletes' participation in sport. Nevertheless, these survey results reveal stronger opposition from individuals who more closely align with heteronormative US culture, which is very much embedded in sport cultures.

There is much to critique in reinforcing a world of sport that relies on biological essentialist categories of *male* or *female*—including its inherent exclusion of intersex, trans, and non-binary people who may or may not have the desire or access to medically transition. Beyond finding ways to include trans people in sport in equitable and just ways, predatory behavior in sport needs to be addressed, including abuses of power and non-consensual *gender verification* testing. With a sociological understanding of the intersectional nature of binary sex-segregated spaces and this social decision's embeddedness in white settler colonial logic, we must find a way forward that does not compromise the hard-earned rights women have organized for, does not exclude trans athletes from sport, and addresses the toxic environment that so many sports cultures embody.

Conclusion: Becoming My Queer and Trans Mentor

Years into therapy, I connected with my inner child and my inner parent and started to become the mentor I needed as a child. My queer adult self-accompanied me in my dreams to my 6-am runs before school. They started to time my laps. They were there during my first race, when I tried to run too quickly. They told me that I was strong, powerful, and loved, and that I didn't need to be perfect. They told me I was worthy and that my home environment was not my problem to solve. They told me I did not have to carry the responsibility of keeping my family together. They told me that it was okay to want to be seen. They told me that the harm that I experienced as a child was not my fault and that I could forgive myself for the harm I caused to those I loved in trying to keep myself safe. They encouraged self-compassion.

My therapist asked me, "What if a SWAT team could have been there to pick you up?" I was resistant and cried, "But I want my mother to be with me." She asked, "Could your mom come visit you in a safe place?" I envisioned a SWAT team picking me up from the alcoholic environment of my pre-teens and taking me to a dazzling park of giant mushrooms where I felt a sense of wonder and safety in my body.

While violence within sport has been a source of distress in my life, I have felt the potential of sport to be a place of healing and positive outcomes. During these not-so-isolated events of my childhood, I remember those who were there and may not have had the power to change our circumstances but witnessed and moved through those events with me. These allies and our ancestors protected me. While coaches and other adult figures mismanaged their power, I also experienced positive affirmation from coaches and mentors. Through sport, I have personally felt an "enhancement of autonomy, competence and relatedness" (Mageau & Vallerand, 2003; Stirling & Kerr, 2009, p. 227), which I find valuable to reclaim.

I dream of a Queer & Trans Swim Club and other spaces where I can creative positive memories of team sports. I want this for myself, as well as for queer and trans youth who, likewise, cannot find safety within binary, heteronormative sport cultures. Now, as a 30-year-old non-binary, transmasculine queer person and educator, I reclaim my power to love myself deeply, fully, and unconditionally. I continue to seek joy and share it with others. I continue to practice tennis and play my flute, move my body, and develop my voice. I continue to unlearn, deconstruct, and reimagine the systems into which I was born into. I do so alongside my comrades who likewise see a vision of a different kind of future. I hold space for our collective rage, as we continue to heal from wounds. I remember that it was never my fault and that it is my choice now.

Discussion Questions[1]

1. What is your working definition of power?
2. How does this definition shape how you experience being powerful or powerless?
3. Think back to a time when you felt powerful. What was the context? Who was present? What was the nature of the interaction? How, if at all, does this event influence your life today?
4. Think back to a time when you felt powerless. What was the context? Who was present? What was the nature of the interaction? How, if at all, does this event influence your life today?
5. What is your relationship to gender in sports? In what ways did this essay challenge you to think of gender in sports differently?

Note

1. The first four questions are derived from Jackson (2018).

References

Adelson, E. (2011). Why sports and sex abuse too often mix. *The Post Game*. www.thepostgame.com/features/201111/how-widespread-sex-abuse-sports

Birrell, S., & Cole, C. L. (1990). Double fault: Renee Richards and the construction and naturalization of difference. *Sociology of Sport Journal*, 7, 1–21.

Brackenridge, C., & Fasting, K. (2005). The grooming process in sport: Narratives of sexual harassment and abuse. *Autobiography Journal*, 13(1), 33–52. https://doi.org/10.11910967550705ab016oa

Cahn, S. (2011). Testing sex, attributing gender: What Caster Semenya means to women's sports. *Journal of Intercollegiate Sport*, 4(1), 38–48.

Chuchmach, M., & Patel, A. (2010). ABC news investigation: USA swimming coaches molested, secretly taped dozens of teen swimmers. *ABC News*. http://abcnews.go.com/Blotter/abc-news-investigation-usa-swimming-coachesraped-molested/story?id=10322469#.UAf9

Currah, P. (2008). Stepping back, looking outward: Situating transgender activism and transgender studies—Kris Hayashi, Matt Richardson, and Susan Stryker frame the movement. *Sexuality Research & Social Policy*, 5(1), 93–105. https://doi.org/10.1525/srsp.2008.5.1.93

Dickinson, B. D., Genel, M., Robinowitz, C. B., Turner, P. L., & Woods, G. L. (2002). Gender verification of female Olympic athletes. *Medicine & Science in Sports & Exercise, 34*(10), 1539–1542. https://doi.org/10.1097/00005768-200210000-0000

Dietz, P. (2018). Grooming and seduction. *Journal of Interpersonal Violence, 33*(1), 28–36. https://doi.org/10.1177/0886260517742060

Doyle, C. (1994). *Child sexual abuse: A guide for health professionals*. Chapman and Hall.

Ellis, C. (1997). Evocative autoethnography: Writing emotionally about our lives. In W. Tierney & Y. Lincoln (Eds.), *Representation and the text: Re-framing the narrative voice* (pp. 116–139). SUNY Press.

Ellis, C. (1999). He(art)ful autoethnography. *Qualitative Health Research, 9*(5), 669–683. https://doi.org/10.1177/104973299129122153

Ellis, C. (2007). Telling secrets, revealing lives: Relational ethics in research with intimate others. *Qualitative Inquiry, 13*(1), 3–29. https://doi.org/10.1177/1077800406294947

Elsas, L. J., Lungqvist, A., Ferguson-Smith, M. A., Simpson, J. L., Genel, M., Carlson, A. S., Ferris, E., de la Chapelle, A., & Ehrhardt, A. A. (2000). Gender verification of female athletes. *Genetics in Medicine, 2*(4), 249–254.

Fasting, K., Brackenridge, C., & Walseth, K. (2007). Women athletes' personal responses to sexual harassment in sport. *Journal of Applied Sport Psychology, 19*(4), 419–433. https://doi.org/10.1080/10413200701599165

Fausto-Sterling, A. (2000). *Sexing the body: Gender politics and the construction of sexuality*. Basic Books.

Flores, A. R., Haider-Markel, D. P., Lewis, D. C., Miller, P. R., Tadlock, B. L., & Taylor, J. K. (2020). Public attitudes about transgender participation in sports: The roles of gender, gender identity conformity, and sports fandom. *Sex Roles, 83*, 382–398.

Irvine, M., & Tanner, R. (2007). AP: Sexual misconduct plagues US schools. *Washington Post*. http://chwe.net/safety/marken/irvinetanner2007.pdf

Jackson, V. (2018). Power: A user's manual: A power literacy resource. *Healing Circles*.

Lanning, K. (2018). The evolution of grooming: Concept and term. *Journal of Interpersonal Violence, 33*(1), 5–16. https://doi.org/10.1177/0886260517742046

Layton, M. J., & Diskin, C. (2012). Sex abuse in schools: Prosecutors say manipulation often begins with a text or email. *NorthJersey*. www.northjersey.com/news/138307709_Sex_abuse_in_school_Rise_in_arrests_is_a_troubling_trend.html

Lennox, B. (1968). Some observations on the difficulties of determining sex. *Bulletin of the British Association of Sport Medicine, 3*(2), 80–85.

Love, A. (2014). Transgender exclusion and inclusion in sport. In J. Hargreaves & E. Anderson (Eds.), *Routledge handbook of sport, gender, and sexuality* (pp. 376–383). Routledge. https://doi.org/10.4324/9780203121375-52

Mageau, G. A., & Vallerand, R. (2003). The coach-athlete relationship: A motivational model. *Journal of Sports Sciences, 21*, 883–904.

Malagrinó, D. O. (2020). May they play: Soule v. Connecticut Association of Schools, Inc., Title IX, and a policy of inclusion for high school transgender athletes without prerequiring hormone therapy or puberty blockers. *Marquette Sports Law Review, 31*(1), 35–84.

Martino, W., Omercajic, K., & Cumming-Potvin, W. (2021). YouTube as a site of desubjugation for trans and nonbinary youth: Pedagogical potentialities and the limits of whiteness. *Pedagogy, Culture & Society*, 1–20.

McKinnon, R. (2019). I won a world championship: Some people are unhappy. *The New York Times*. www.nytimes.com/2019/12/05/opinion/i-won-a-world-championship-some-people-arent-happy.html

Morrison, T., Erooga, M., & Beckett, R. (Eds.). (1994). *Sexual offending against children: Assessment and treatment of male abusers*. Routledge.

Nack, W., & Yaeger, D. (1999). Every parent's nightmare. *Sport's Illustrated*.

O'Hagan, M., & Willmsen, C. (2003). Coaches who prey: The abuse of girls and the system that allows it. *The Seattle Times*. https://archive.seattletimes.com/archive/?date=20031214&slug=coaches14m

O'Keeffe, M. (2011). With sexual predators prowling the sidelines, parents can't trust anyone. *NY Daily News*. www.nydailynews.com/sports/i-team/sexual-predators-prowling-sidelines-parents-trust-article-1.110165

Pieper, L. P. (2016). *Sex testing: Gender policing in women's sports*. University of Illinois Press.

Prewitt-White, T. R. (2019). I was his litmus test: An autoethnographic account of being groomed in sport. *Journal of Clinical Sport Psychology*, *13*(2), 180–195.

Reeser, J. C. (2005). Gender identity and sport: Is the playing field level? *British Journal of Sports Medicine*, *39*, 695–699. https://doi.org/10.1136/bjsm.2005.018119

Rosich, G. R. (2020). Sexual citizenship theory and employment discrimination among transgender-identified people. *Societies*, *10*(17), 1–17.

Stirling, A., & Kerr, G. (2009). Abused athletes' perceptions of the coach-athlete relationship. *Sport in Society*, *12*(2), 227–239. https://doi.org/10.1080/17430430802591019

Tsang, T. (2000). Let me tell you a story. *Sociology of Sport Journal*, *17*(10), 44–59.

Volkwein, K. A. E., Schnell, F. I., Sherwood, D., & Livezey, A. (1997). Sexual harassment in sport: Perceptions and experiences of American female student athletes. *International Review for the Sociology of Sport*, *32*(3), 283–295.

World Athletics. (2019). *International federations discuss consensus on establishing rules for transgender athletes*. www.worldathletics.org/news/press-release/international-federations-rules-transgender-a

Wurtele, S. (2012). Preventing the sexual exploitation of minors in youth-serving organizations. *Children and Youth Services Review*, *34*(12), 2442–2453. https://doi.org/10.1016/j.childyouth.2012.09.009

Yardley, W. (2010). $18.5 million in liability for Scouts in abuse case. *New York Times*. www.nytimes.com/2010/04/24/us/24scouts.html?_r=1

Zinser, L. (2011). Coaching gives abusers opportunity and trust. *New York Times*. www.nytimes.com/2011/12/11/sports/culture-of-sports-works-against-children-especially-boys-reporting-abuse.html

11
I COULDN'T STAY QUIET

Shannon Mulcahy

Several years since this event occurred, I still do not have complete clarity on what truly happened. For this reason, I do not believe that the details of this story are mine to tell. With that said, the details do not change the impact that sexual assault has on the lives affected by it, including my own. Therefore, I will be sharing my lived experience and the impact it had on me from the perspective of a bystander, a perspective that is not often highlighted. While I do wish to clarify that my experience and trauma are minor compared to survivors of sexual assault, I hope to shed light on the impact that sexual misconduct can have on the coaches, teammates, and staff close to the situation.

To illustrate this story, I want to share a few of my early experiences with sexual misconduct and how it may have shaped the adult I have become. I was an adolescent the first time I became aware of inappropriate coaching behavior. I swam competitively on a local club swim team I joined when I was six years old and continued to swim for until I was a senior in high school. As a young child of six or seven years old, my coaches were supportive and pushed me to discover what both my mind and body were capable of accomplishing. I was motivated to break our team's records and dreamed of qualifying for nationals one day. Like so many other athletes, my sport was my life. The coaches I had in these first few years of my swimming career helped me cultivate my love for racing, and to this day, I am grateful for that.

However, when I was around ten years old, a teammate and close friend commented on how cute she thought our new coach was, the one we had for the summer. I remember her saying she wanted to look as sexy as she could whenever he was around. Thinking back on this story, I am heartbroken that I did not challenge her statements. Part of me wishes I had the wisdom at ten years old to know children are not meant to be "sexy," while the other part of me is appreciative that I did not pay much attention to what "sexy" even meant for us.

In nearly every stage of my life, I have been the youngest of the people around me. For example, the girls I regularly swam with growing up were typically a few years older than I was. When my friend said she wanted to look sexy for our coach, I was confused, shocked, and uncomfortable; but, I also figured she knew more than I did. I attributed my feelings to being too young to understand, and so I dismissed the comment altogether.

As the season continued, though, her comment lingered in the back of my mind. I began to wonder if we were supposed to look sexy. Was that the expectation our coaches had of us? I became more aware of my body and the bathing suits I wore to swim practice. Throughout one summer, I learned that how my body appeared mattered, particularly to men. It had never occurred to me that a coach might look or think about me sexually; but, it could not be undone once that realization arose. What started as a brief conversation about our new coach became a wake-up call for me. In many ways, it was also the end of my naivety about how girls and women are thought of and expected to be.

Over the next several years, instances like the one I previously recounted began to happen more frequently. I began to notice our male coaches looking at the bodies of the older girls on the team. It was even more apparent when the girls wore two-piece bathing suits to practice in the summer. I remember thinking it was gross and made me uncomfortable; but, it also never occurred to me that these glances could ever turn into a physical relationship or interaction. It is only now that I realize how naive and sheltered I was as a child.

Perhaps this was a blessing. For most of my time swimming competitively, I did not consider what I wore or how coaches looked at me. Instead, I focused on performance and swimming as fast as I could. Looking back, I often wonder if this naivety protected me. I did not feel pressure to dress or act in a certain way for the boys or the coaches on our team. If someone said or did something that made me uncomfortable, I would remove myself from that environment. Being younger than many of my teammates meant that when the conversation turned to sex, I was confused and embarrassed to show that I did not know what they were talking about. I figured out that staying quiet was a way to not stand out.

As a senior in high school, I switched swim teams due to a shoulder injury and an unsupportive coach. I knew numerous swimmers as well as several of the coaches on my new team. When I showed up the first day, I saw the head coach smack one of my friends on the butt with a kickboard, and it was as if with that one smack, my naivety shattered. Again, I felt uncomfortable and gross, but also again, confused. She was seemingly flirting back with him and not at all upset or bothered by what had happened. This was not the type of behavior I was used to experiencing at swim practice. The team I had left was serious to a fault. Flirting and goofing around was not a part of our practices.

It quickly became clear to me that this was not a one-time occurrence for this coach and the swimmer. I said something to a different friend about how strange their interaction was, and her response was, "that is just how he is." I was seemingly the only one who thought this was inappropriate, and by being the only one, I wondered if I was being too dramatic about the situation. If everyone thinks this is okay, it must be okay. I felt shame for not being fun enough or flirtatious enough to fit in.

Although tame by many accounts, these early experiences on swim teams influenced my behavior and thoughts about sexual misconduct as an adult bystander. Fresh out of graduate school, I took a job as an assistant swim coach at a small college. I had a friend on the team who had told me there was an opening; so, I applied. With no prior coaching experience, I was shocked to get an interview and to be given the job as soon as the interview started. I thought my friend must have put in a perfect world with the coach and was grateful he was willing to take a chance on me. However, I quickly came to see that my friend was getting special treatment from this coach. She would often say that the other girls on the team did not like her, so her only friend was the coach. She and the coach texted back and forth daily, even about whom she was dating. I remember one day over the summer before the season had even started, my friend came to me crying because the coach was so mad at her about her new boyfriend. The coach did not like him and wanted her to end the relationship. This was the first moment I started to sense something was not right. I might have been new to college coaching, but it felt wrong for a coach to be so involved in an athlete's dating life. When I said this to her, she justified it by saying that the coach is like a parent to her, so it was not a big deal.

As the season started, I focused on learning the ins and outs of coaching and getting to know the more than 40 athletes on the team. I saw brief bits of favoritism for my friend, like when a house party they were at got busted, and several swimmers got arrested but the coach covered for my friend so that she would not get in trouble.

It was not until I was at a sport psychology conference that autumn where I read a magazine article about sexual misconduct in swimming. As I read the article, it felt like I had been punched in the stomach. With each line, the story reminded me more and more of my friend's relationship with her coach, a person I now had to work alongside. I started to see that many of the things I initially thought were weird were grooming techniques. The more I read, the more horrified I became. By the time I came home from the conference, I was sure something was not right. However, I knew I needed to remain objective and not make any accusations until I had some form of proof. I did not want to ruin this coach's life or destroy my reputation by jumping to conclusions.

What resulted was copious note-taking on my part. I documented everything I could think of to get a clearer picture of what was going on. I started noticing small things that I either had missed previously or made excuses for to ease the dissonance. I ran into them at lunch together several times, and they were often having meetings in his office with the door closed. He would drive her to team functions but would not allow other athletes to ride with them.

After one particular swim meet where the coach was mad at this swimmer and refused to coach her, I decided to talk to Human Resources. I was unsure if I was making a career-ending mistake; but, I knew I could not stay quiet any longer. I decided that if something was going on between them and I stayed silent and let it happen, I would not forgive myself. I also knew that I could get over a wrong career choice as much as it could be challenging.

I remember telling the Title IX coordinator that I hoped I was incorrect and misinterpreting these behaviors. I wanted so badly to be wrong and to be misreading the situation. However, I knew from other collegiate scandals that often one person's account is not enough. So, I spoke up with the intent of creating a paper trail. If something more concrete surfaced or if any other swimmers stepped forward, I did not want them to be alone.

Over the next three months, three swimmers on the team accused the coach of inappropriate behavior. First, I was relieved that I was not the only one suspicious, and then I immediately felt guilty for feeling this way. Throughout those three months, I began to doubt myself and to question what was real or fake. Both the coach and the swimmer vehemently denied there was anything going on.

I believed I had been wrong, and although I was surprised, I was also relieved. I could handle being wrong if it meant my friend was safe. However, more accusations were made. The louder the accusations became, the more the coach and swimmer insisted everything was fine. It began to feel like emotional whiplash. The experience felt oddly like being gaslit, which I experienced during a relationship with my college boyfriend.

I then questioned everything. I wondered if I had made it up. But I have always been a person who trusts her gut. When my instincts told me there was something inappropriate between this coach and the swimmer, I listened, observed, and asked questions. Furthermore, seemingly, I was right. Now, I want to point out here that this is not about being right; it is about highlighting what can happen when a person starts to believe that their reality has been a lie or fabricated. I was repeatedly told that the accusations were false. I did not know what to believe. I thought if I was mistaken about this, what else was I wrong about? Why did I lead myself and others down a path that was not true? I started to think that maybe I should not trust my intuition.

At some point, I realized that no matter what the truth was, I was being made to believe that things I had seen had been innocuous. Maybe that time I ran into them at lunch off-campus was just a meeting about something swimming-related. I tried to convince myself to see how they were selling it, but I could not.

During one meeting with Human Resources, in fact, it was suggested to me by the Title IX coordinator that the only reason I had been hired in the first place was to keep their relationship a secret. This swimmer was my friend, and he was my superior. I was fresh out of graduate school. I would not dare speak up about what was going on. Alternatively, maybe they just thought I was dumb enough not to notice and that I would believe their lies. This implication furthered my spiral of self-doubt.

When I was hired to work with the team, I believed it was because I could do a good job. On paper, I was not the most qualified for the job—having minimal experience—but I knew I had the skills for it. When I was hired without an interview, I naively believed it was because my friend had convinced the coach that I was worth the risk. I was proud and happy to accept the position. And not even a full year later, it was being suggested that I was only hired to protect their relationship. I began to doubt my skills and competence. Maybe I am not as good as I thought I was.

To add another layer to this story, I had to keep my suspicions and beliefs quiet from the team. As the coach was asked to step down temporarily, I was asked to step in and step up. There were days when I would show up to practice a few minutes late because I was coming back from a two-hour meeting with Human Resources. There were days when I would lock myself in the bathroom between practices and cry because I did not know how to do this. I did not know how to carry on.

When the investigation wrapped up, I got a call from the Title IX coordinator while driving to lunch at the end of the season. She told me it was finally over after four months, and that the coach would not be returning. I pulled my car over and sobbed. I sobbed because it was over, and I could start to move forward. I sobbed because I would not have to work with or face this man anymore. I sobbed because I still did not know the truth about what happened. Without the truth, I could never be sure if my intuition was correct.

Moreover, for somebody like me who had experienced emotional abuse in the past, this situation was devastating. It became clear that I would have to rebuild my trust in myself without having all the answers. Maybe it was her intuition, but later that week, the Title IX coordinator reached out again to share with me that inappropriate coaching behavior was conducted regardless of what was or was not found in the investigation. Meeting an athlete off-campus for lunch does not mean they are in a romantic or sexual relationship, but it should not happen.

Reflecting on this experience now, I recognize mistakes I made several years later. There are things I would have done differently and assumptions I made about the situation that I would now change. I also recognize that I did the best I could in a rough and confusing time. I learned that my teacher's advice to trust my intuition is still the most crucial piece of advice I have ever been given.

I often wonder what would have happened had I not reached out to Human Resources. What would have happened if I had ignored my suspicions because I did not want to ruin someone's career? I also learned that I have my wounds and my biases that impacted my decisions in this scenario. I was in a relationship in college that was riddled with emotional abuse. It was through that experience that I knew that getting help is more complicated than it sounds. I understood that you could one day seemingly find yourself in a situation you never asked for and not know how to get out of it. I took this knowledge with me into how I handled what was going on with this swim team.

There were also so many questions that came up for me throughout this particular season. I had previously understood the concept of consent and that the legal age for sex was 18. In addition, I knew that having a relationship with a coach was unethical. However, I did not initially know that the NCAA considers a coach-athlete sexual relationship as inappropriate because the athlete cannot give consent; even if the athlete believes they are a consenting adult, the power imbalance/dynamics between the coach and themselves makes it impossible to consent in this situation.

I also wrestled with my anger toward my friend for not telling me. I was infuriated that she chose to be in a relationship with this coach, often forgetting that she was the victim. My biggest regret is that I did not show her more compassion. I was so hurt by being used and lied to that I put my personal feelings above hers. I prioritized what I believed was her well-being without really considering what she was going through. I was frustrated when she took his side and defended him repeatedly, ignoring the complexities in play that were influencing the entire situation. I could not look at what was going on objectively, and, truthfully, this still affects me.

Even though my story and experience could be considered mild or tame by many, it has affected my life significantly. I still wonder what happened. Even though I wish I did not, I want to know the truth. I still must work on trusting myself when something feels off or wrong. I still regret not handling many aspects of the situation better. I wish I had done more to provide resources and help for the other swimmers on the team. However, then I remember that we were all going through this in one way or another. At the time, I did the best I could with what I had and with what I knew. Many professions prohibit professionals from working with close friends or family members because they cannot remain objective. Psychologists see other psychologists. We cannot treat ourselves. I try to remember this when I feel guilty for not doing more or a better job.

Throughout this experience, I have also learned how much I care about protecting the athletes who experience sexual misconduct or mistreatment from coaches. I wish so badly I could say that this is the only encounter I have had, but it is not. I have seen teams with verbally abusive coaches, coaches stalking athletes, and coaches meeting up with players late at night to "talk." I have learned that my story is not unique.

I am not sharing my story because I think I am the only one who has experienced this kind of scenario. I share it because most accounts of sexual misconduct are from individuals who have experienced it themselves. The impact that these situations have on the rest of the team is considered secondary. And, I am in no way saying that my situation was more challenging than someone who has lived through misconduct themselves. It is not.

Nevertheless, that does not mean it has been easy for those of us around the sexual misconduct. When we can better take care of all of the people involved, we make sports a safer place for everyone, not just victims. That is the thing about being a bystander—you are affected in ways that other people may not consider.

Prologue

After that season was over, I took a new job and moved 400 miles away. I wanted a fresh start and to escape the stress I had previously experienced. Since then, I have had coaches and sport psychology professionals tell me I am hyper-focused on finding abusive coaches. I have been told I look for things that are not there. I have had male coaches tell me they are uncomfortable working with me because they are worried I will accuse them of inappropriate behavior. Initially, this bothered me. Now, I respond and say I will only accuse them if they act inappropriately.

The reality is that these cases happen more frequently than we know. They happen but are swept under the rug or are not talked about because it makes people uncomfortable. For example, if you are the athletic director who hired a coach who has an inappropriate relationship with an athlete, did you contribute to that happening? We do not like to feel guilty or complicit. It is far easier to cover something up than admit a mistake was made or that a wrongdoing occurred.

Recently I found out a local college swim coach was accused of sexual misconduct. It hit close to home, not just because it opened up the old wounds from my own experience but because this was a coach with whom I was acquainted. Hearing the news hit me hard. I wondered if I was being naive to think that sexual misconduct was not happening on every college campus. I wondered how many more times in my career will I be a bystander? I wondered if I could or even wanted to take on the stress of going through something like that again, potentially multiple times.

I have been told that I hate men and I have been asked by family members what happened in my life that made me hate men so much. It is hurtful, sad, and no longer surprising that speaking out about sexual misconduct by a male coach is equated to hating men. I am repeatedly reminded that we will be criticized more for negatively impacting a man's career. I distinctly remember being warned that speaking out would hurt this man's family, and being asked if I wanted that to happen to them. How are you supposed to make the "right" decision when facing these questions and pressures? Moreover, how could this be my fault? It felt like they preferred that I continue to pretend that misconduct does not happen; however, the reality is that it is happening whether or not it is reported. Sexual misconduct in sport, and in other industries, is happening and has been happening for centuries. It is not something new or political; but it is finally being brought to light.

Ten years after I quit competitive swimming, it is surreal for me to reflect on my experiences. Seemingly every time I do, I remember something else related to sexual misconduct that should not have been happening. I am reminded of the power imbalances that sport creates between athletes and coaches and how these imbalances create a perfect environment for misconduct.

As a club team swim coach now, I coach eight-year-olds to 18-year-olds. I take my experiences as a swimmer and as a coach and carry them with me. I let them guide the decisions

I make and the lessons I teach my athletes. I am constantly wondering how the words I use will impact those around me. Could the clothing I wear or ways I give feedback be misconstrued in any way?

In some ways, I hate that this has become such a substantial part of my thoughts. However, I see coaches I work with seemingly oblivious to these thoughts. Wouldn't it be so lovely to show up and coach without having to analyze everything I say and do? Nevertheless, then I think about the idea of impact versus intention. For so many children and adolescents, sports are one of the most memorable parts of their lives. I know that having one lousy coach can ruin an athlete's relationship with sport.

Thus, I continue to focus on the impact my work has on my athletes. I know that I will not change the world or change the entire sports culture or even swimming, but I know that I can change these kids' lives. I can model what healthy coaching looks like. I can teach them what inappropriate behavior is.

Discussion Questions

1. Do you have a plan for what you'll do if you suspect or identify sexual misconduct in your spaces? Consider who you would report to and what behaviors you would report.
2. What are some of the indications that a coach is grooming an athlete? What might this look like in your sport?
3. How would you identify the line between sexual misconduct and a close athlete-coach relationship?

12
EXPERIENCING SEXUAL MISCONDUCT AS A STUDENT-MANAGER IN INTERCOLLEGIATE ATHLETICS

Emily J. Tyler

As I begin to write this chapter, I am stumped by the question, "Will I get in trouble for sharing these stories?" One of the first things I was told when I started working in an intercollegiate athletics department was, "What happens here, stays here." The confidentiality agreement all employees of the athletic department must adhere to indicated that all employees have an "obligation to maintain the confidentiality of information obtained while employed."[1] Further,

> any misuse or unauthorized release of [private, confidential or sensitive information], either during employment or subsequent to the conclusion of employment, may be grounds for disciplinary action that may include termination, and/or the initiation of legal action.

The words: "private, confidential, or sensitive information" rummage through my head as I struggle to decide whether a lawsuit awaits me upon sharing my story. What does "private, confidential, or sensitive information" mean? Is knowing that a former student-athlete raped a former student-manager considered "sensitive information?" Is that information protected under the law, even if it happened to me?

It begs the question, how much do non-disclosure agreements and *what happens here, stays here* mentalities—that are fostered in collegiate athletics—silence survivors and tolerate the perpetration of sexual violence? No wonder why so many who have experienced sexual misconduct in sport do not come forward. Nonetheless, on the basis of my lived experiences and research, I have learned that there is a pervasive problem in athletics where rape culture and sexual violence are promoted; and, if sharing my experience can shed light on this problem, I believe it is my duty and privilege to do so.

In this chapter, I include three stories of sexual misconduct that I experienced during my tenure as a student-manager. The first two may seem *minor* or insignificant, the last more severe; nonetheless, these stories resonate and bother me most when I think about my four years working as a student-manager for an elite men's collegiate team. Non-identifying details and pseudonyms have been provided to maintain anonymity but the stories and harm

DOI: 10.4324/9781003125884-14

experienced are absolute. These are the stories I have lost sleep over and have shaped my identities as a woman, researcher, future counseling psychologist, and survivor. What I share is not simply *my story* or *my truth*; rather, it is *the truth* as I experienced it.

Duties of a Student-Manager

A student-manager of a team in intercollegiate athletics is more than a job or a hobby; it is a lifestyle and an opportunity that few college students experience. The selection process for the program in which I worked was highly competitive. During my tenure, about 70 undergraduate students applied for the student-manager program each year. Applicants who had obtained at least a 2.5 GPA in the previous semester were invited to participate in the hiring process, which consisted of working in the university's summer sports camps. The camps were essentially a two-week audition and an opportunity for the hiring committee (e.g., current student-managers, coaches, director of equipment services and student manager program) to work with the applicants and get to know them. The number of available student-manager positions per sport varied each year. On average, two students would be selected to work for each team. Each student-manager is assigned one team to work with for the year and until they graduate. The duties of the student-managers varied on the basis of the sport team or program to which they were assigned.

The men's sport program I worked for was considered elite and required more managerial involvement and responsibilities than other sport teams within the athletic department. Our student-manager team consisted of eight undergraduates, including one *head manager* who was typically the most experienced manager with strong leadership skills who served as the representative and direct liaison to the coaches, director of equipment services, and other athletic department personnel. Of the eight managers, one or two were women, and the rest were men. During the season, we worked about 30 hours each week and about 20 hours during the off-season. The general rule we followed was, "If you aren't in class or studying, you are working." The managers were at the bottom of the hierarchy on staff and considered the *behind-the-scenes team*. We rarely got credit or were acknowledged for our work due to our positionality, but we played a critical role in alleviating responsibilities from the players, coaches, and other staff, enabling them to focus on their primary responsibility, playing or coaching.

One of our main responsibilities involved equipment services. We tracked, organized, laundered, and distributed athletic apparel and equipment to the players, coaches, and staff daily. We attended every practice and game to ensure the success of the program. Typical duties during practices and games included: assisting coaches with drills, providing equipment, tracking statistics, and filming. Other duties I fulfilled involved performing a wide range of administrative tasks including developing travel itineraries, preparing scouting reports, recruiting materials, and practice plans, assisting coaches with coordinating on-campus recruiting activities, planning team meals, and managing the recruitment database.

Our program was a *players-and-coaches-first* program, meaning that whatever the coaches and players needed was a priority and whatever we could do to make their lives easier, we did. For example, we were responsible for ensuring that all players were in attendance for team meetings and practices which involved knocking on the players' hotel doors to wake them up while on road trips. It was also common for the managers to perform a *curfew check* on the nights before games to ensure the players were in their dorm or hotel rooms. Though the managers were undergraduate students like the players, we were members of the staff and allies to the coaches. We were expected to be respectful, maintain professionalism, *stay in the background*, and do whatever we could to ensure the program's success.

Sexual Harassment of Student-Manager by Member of Coaching Staff

As a student-manager, one of my duties was to serve as a departmental ambassador and assist the coaches with hosting top-rated recruits and their families during their recruiting visits on campus. From managing travel plans, creating itineraries, and ordering meals, my job was to ensure that the recruit and his family were well cared for and that they enjoyed the visit. Typically, the office staff, including other women student-assistants and student-managers, also provided tours of the athletic facilities and campus to the recruits and their families.

One day, a member of the coaching staff told me that there was a last-minute change of plans and the scheduled tour with student-assistant, Amy,[2] was being moved to a time when she was out of the office for her professional cheerleading practice. I assured him that I was available and would be happy to do the tour. However, he insisted that Amy do the tour. The following is a depiction of how our conversation went:

Jim: The recruit will not get to campus until later, so we will need to do the tour after practice.
Emily: Okay, I will let Amy know. I am available after practice so I can do the tour.
Jim: Oh. Well, is there any way that Amy can still do it?
Emily: I can ask, but she usually does not work at that time because she has cheer practice. It really is no problem for me, and I would be happy to do it!
Jim: That's not necessary. I would prefer Amy did it, cause . . . you know.
Emily: What do you mean?
Jim: Well, you know. She is uh . . . we typically want to sway our recruits to come here and having a girl like Amy, you know, a beautiful cheerleader, giving the tour usually helps quite a bit! [laughs]

Whether this was an insult to my appearance or an objectification of Amy, Jim's reluctance about me and his insistence on Amy providing the tour was clear. Even if Jim was joking, as is typical for most sexual harassment incidents, this was demeaning not only to me but also to Amy, who was not present.

Though Jim did not say these words aloud, what he implied appeared to be, "Emily, you are not beautiful, pretty, skinny, or worthy to give a high-level recruit and his family a tour of our facilities." Furthermore, "Emily, you are not good enough at your job or qualified to do this." As a woman and one of the only women on the staff, Jim's comments stung me because I was belittled for my looks, not the quality of my work or ability to do a job. Moreover, Jim's words implied that Amy's worth, relevancy, and competency in her role resides in her appearance and status as a cheerleader, not her performance, work ethic, or skills.

My identity as a student-manager and member of the team shifted after this. I started to doubt myself in this role and my ability to do my job. I felt self-conscious about my appearance. Was I supposed to always style my hair down and wear full makeup every day and while at practice? Did the coaches think less of me for not being as pretty or fit as Amy? These questions, and many others, circulated in my mind every day after that. Moreover, these comments bred and perpetuated harmful ideas about my need to compare myself to and compete with the women around me in order to earn respect from men in the program.

Aside from how this hurt me personally, let's look at this from a larger scope. The world of college athletics relies heavily on insignificant details that seemingly make a large difference for 17- to 18-year-old men and women deciding to commit to the university. For instance, recruits typically choose where they want to go to college based on the experience they had and how they felt being there. As silly as it sounds, even though he may have been half-joking, one of the recruits who ended up signing with our program said the biggest reason he wanted to commit to our program was because of the brownies that were served at dinner! No joke, he really said this. Understandably, coaches and staff want a recruiting visit to go perfectly when hosting a recruit and their family. Whether it is the dessert provided at dinner or tickets to and atmosphere at the Saturday football game, small details are important in swaying an athlete to commit to the athletic program.

This is the culture of collegiate athletics—we cannot turn away from this reality. Although the decision between tour guides may have seemed insignificant, the culture of athletics in higher education normalizes the integration of these trivial details into the decision-making processes of these coveted student-athletes. While they ruminate over which college had the prettiest tour guide, the women in the background are left with a harmful and demoralizing mindset about their positionality and worth. This was only the first of several demoralizing events I experienced as a student-manager.

Student-Athlete Demands Sex From Student-Manager on Road Trip

BAM . . . BAM . . . BAM . . . *"Hey! Give me some head!"* . . . BAM . . . BAM . . . BAM

It was two in the morning, and I was sound asleep in my room at the team hotel when John, one of the players, abruptly awoke me by banging on my door and demanding that I perform oral sex on him. He continued to knock and yell for what seemed like hours, even though it was only a few minutes. I did not answer the door.

Because I was one of the only women on staff, I was afforded my own hotel room on road trips. Unfortunately, when this happened, I was truly alone and did not know what to do. I was torn between my role as a manager and my role as a young woman. As a manager, I felt a responsibility to protect the team and its image and reputation. If anyone heard him being disruptive, that could negatively affect the team. I also felt a responsibility to the players, providing them what they needed to be successful and enforcing rules set by the coaches (e.g., show up on time). As I previously mentioned, one of my duties as a manager was to do curfew checks and wake-up calls for the players. If a player was not in his dorm or hotel room during curfew checks, we would report that to the coaches. Since John was not in his hotel room past curfew, it seemed like it was my responsibility to get him to his room (even though he was a 20-something-year-old young man and should be capable of doing that himself).

Aside from my role as a student-manager, as a young woman, I felt disrespected and objectified. I was stunned that a man would feel so compelled to demand oral sex from me; further, that he would feel entitled to me and my body. I was angry and disappointed that I was in this position. I felt like I could not react without making the situation worse. As a young woman, I wanted to yell at him, tell him, "Absolutely not!" and stand up for myself. I wanted to send a message that his behavior was not okay and would never be okay. I wanted him to know how extremely inappropriate and offensive his behavior was. However, I worried about my job and did not want to jeopardize my position or the team's reputation.

I was devastated. I felt powerless.

I wondered,

> If I answered and told him no, would he go away quietly? If he wakes up a hotel guest and gets in trouble for banging on my door, will I get in trouble? If someone saw him at my door, would they think I invited him to my room?

I did not have any answers to these questions and did not know what to do, so I ignored the knocks and tried my hardest to fall back to sleep, which did not happen for several hours. Ruminating thoughts and several crippling emotions kept me awake. My mind raced with questions like

> Why would he think that I would be willing to do that? What if he told his teammates that he was going over to my room to "get head" and then told them he did? What if the coaches overhear one of these lies and I get fired?

Even though he did eventually go back to his room, I felt like I had no control over the situation and worse, I felt like I was objectified and demoralized once again.

Coach always called road games *business trips* and enforced that while on the road, the players, coaches, and staff were there for business. I considered everything I did with the team as business and part of my job. Whether it was doing their laundry, ordering meals, wiping sweat from the floors, or handing out water, these duties were part of my job responsibilities and I considered them a privilege. When John demanded I perform oral sex on him in the middle of the night, I wondered, "Does he think *this* is part of my job description? *Is this* part of my duties as a student-manager?" Absolutely nothing about this was okay and it was truly hurtful.

The next day, after much internal conflict, tears, and deliberation, I reported the incident to my manager colleagues, including the head manager. Much to my surprise, I was dismissed and laughed at. The managers (three collegiate men) thought it was hilarious that one of the players would solicit sex from me in the middle of the night while on a road trip. Although they believed me, they told me not to tell anyone and act like it did not happen. *Of course*.

I was so bothered by what happened that a few days after the road trip I told one of the assistant coaches about the incident with John. Someone in authority needed to know to address the situation. I felt the need to clear my name and let the staff know that I refused and maintained my professionalism. I also did not want it to happen again to me or anyone else. Fortunately, I had a good working relationship with the coach and he graced me with understanding and *some* concern. He assured me that he would speak to John and that it would not happen again. However, nothing else happened after this. I do not know whether John was spoken to, if the head coach was briefed on the situation, or if a report was filed with the athletics department or Title IX. Because I was never asked about it, I assume little-to-nothing happened. The lack of follow-up and concern really bothered me. Not only did the coach or another staff member, including the managers, neglect to check in with me to see how I was doing, no one followed up to assure me that the player was talked to and would not violate my psychological or physical safety again.

This incident happened early in the season, so I had to navigate several road trips with him after that. Since I never got an apology from John or assurance that he was talked to, I feared every road trip thereafter. I worried that he would, again, show up at my door wanting sex, or worse, physically force himself on me. I feared being in situations when I could potentially be alone with him. While on the road, I avoided being the manager to knock on his hotel room door for wake-up calls, curfew checks, or to collect laundry. My fear motivated me to avoid him and being in his presence as much as possible throughout the season, which was a huge challenge since we regularly shared space at practices, games, and team meetings.

Although John was a member of our team, I struggled to support him and see him do well. Hearing his name announced or fans cheering for him hurt. I witnessed his public success and favorability while I privately and quietly processed my anger and devastation. Of course, I wanted our team to be successful and wanted him to play well, but it was hard to see him praised when he did something so hurtful to me. The additional stress and emotional labor took a toll on me and, at times, made me dislike my job, a previously high-coveted and meaningful job to me.

At the time, I did not know about the Office of Title IX or that there was an administrator within the athletics department that I could speak to. If I could do this part over again, I would. It is interesting to see now that student-managers like myself were never made aware of resources such as the Title IX coordinator or the administrator whose jobs were to help when sexual misconduct occurred. In fact, it was never talked about as a potential problem or concern. The only messaging I received as a student-manager was, "Don't sleep with the players!" as if it were my responsibility alone to maintain a safe and professional culture on our team. It seemed like it never occurred to anyone that the players would try to use their power to solicit sex from the managers.

Student-Manager Raped by Student-Athlete

One of my duties as a student-manager was to wipe up sweat off the floor during practice and games to keep the players from slipping and falling. As I approached many of my responsibilities, I took this task seriously and toiled to ensure the court was dry. One of the players, Jack, nicknamed me Scrub, because I *scrubbed* the floors. This so-called term of endearment irritated me, as it functioned to dehumanize and belittle me. After a while, some of the other players started to call me Scrub when we saw each other on and off campus. It was awkward trying to explain to my friends why they called me that. At the time, though it was embarrassing, I did not think it was anything more than a funny nickname or an underhanded term of endearment. Honestly, I was not that bothered by it. It was not until the day after Jack raped me that I began to wonder if there was a connection between how Jack groomed and sexually violated me and him seeing me as a *scrub*—an inanimate object meant to serve him. Though it may not be related to the nickname, I wonder about the connection and the unconscious ways Jack viewed me and then acted on these beliefs.

One night during the off-season, I met up with a few of my friends for dinner and drinks. As the night ended, I ran into Jack and his partner, Jill, as I left the bar. They kindly offered me a ride home and insisted that I get home safely. I knew Jill because we previously had classes together and she had been dating Jack for several years. I had planned to get an Uber home, but since they offered, I accepted, assuming I would get home safely with these acquaintances. I was not wrong in making this assumption. Jill, accompanied by Jack, drove me to my apartment, dropped me off, and I got home safely with no problem.

It was not until later in the night when a familiar, startling sound woke me from my comatose sleep.

BAM . . . BAM . . . BAM . . . BAM

When I went to the door, I was half-asleep and saw Jack. I thought something was wrong, so I opened the door and asked if everything was okay. He was by himself and holding a plastic bag.

I was stunned and frightened when he grabbed my shoulders and shuffled me out of the doorway and into my bedroom. He pushed me onto my bed and proceeded to take off his clothes. He turned the lights on and hovered over me, naked with his penis in my face, insisting I give him oral sex.

I was confused and terrified.

I refused to perform any sexual acts with him. However, he did not take my refusal, my repetitive no for an answer. My yells did nothing except make him more aggressive. He removed my clothes and began to penetrate my mouth with his penis.

I was frozen. This felt like forever.

After a while, he reached into the plastic bag he brought for a box of condoms. Other than the receipt, the condoms were the only thing in the bag. He purchased them only ten minutes before arriving at my apartment.

He calmly put on a condom and forcedly penetrated my vagina with his penis while on top of me for what seemed like hours. I remember thinking, "Please hurry up and finish so you can leave." I wanted him out; I wanted it to be over. I worried about what he would do if I continued to say no. Tears streamed down my face the entire encounter. It felt as if he was entitled to my body and had no respect for me or my rejections. He had every advantage over me: his size, his power, his position. I felt powerless, violated, helpless, and used. I had to survive it to return to some resemblance of safety. My body was completely dominated by him. My thoughts, emotions, attention, and overall well-being continued to be dominated by him even after the rape ended.

He abused his power and my trust. Worse, he saw me as an object he could use. When Jack saw that I needed a ride home, he likely offered that he and Jill take me so he could see where I lived and could come back later that night. He knew that I lived alone because he asked me that question during the car ride to my apartment. He saw an opportunity. I trusted him, but he used me. He groomed me, then used me.

It was like he knew that I would not be able to say anything to anyone about this. Unfortunately, he was right. I had a responsibility as a student-manager to cater to him and his teammates. He knew this and used it against me and for his advantage. Further, his well-known name and status in the town and campus would surely protect him. He and I both knew that no one would believe me if I reported this and would insist that I was making a false claim. Because of my connections to the program, I did not want this to get out and rupture my relationships with my employer, the coaching staff, or the athletics department. I feared if I took any action my name would get out, my reputation would be ruined, and I would not be believed. For these reasons and more, I kept quiet. It seemed like I had choices of reporting this incident, accessing support, or protecting myself. But in my position at the time, so deeply embedded in the dynamics of normalized rape culture and hierarchies of sexism, there was nothing I could do. I did eventually make a report to the police. With very little evidence, they did not go forward with an investigation.

The combination of victim-blaming and slut-shaming culture that surrounds college campuses and athletic departments reinforced my silence. I did not want to be blamed for accepting a ride home or opening my apartment door for him. Further, I did not want to be thought of as the stereotypical *slutty manager* who sleeps with the players, even if it was non-consensual. There is an abhorrent stereotype about student-managers sleeping with student-athletes, especially women who work for men's teams. When friends, acquaintances, or even colleagues would talk with me about my experience as a student-manager, I was always asked, "How many players have you slept with?" or "Which player has the largest penis?" Not only were these questions the norm, and something I still typically face, I often wonder when potential employers look at my resumé and see former student-manager if they ask themselves, "I wonder if she slept with the players" or worse, just assume I did.

After receiving multiple text messages from him asking what my weekend plans were in the weeks after the rape, I felt compelled to be straightforward and tell him that what happened was not consensual, and to leave me alone. I texted him and said that what he did to me was unwanted and harmful and that I did not want it to happen again to me and it should not happen to anyone else. I wanted him to know that what he did was wrong because clearly, he had no awareness or was indifferent. He responded with, "Really? Alright. No problem." No remorse, apology, or ownership.

Luckily, this happened after my last season as a manager ended and as I was wrapping my managerial duties and getting ready to start a new position within the athletics department. I did not have to interact with him after that; however, I regularly saw him and Jill for the two additional years I worked in the athletics department. Whenever I saw him or heard his voice, I felt a sense of painful panic. I avoided him as much as possible. Even after I told him that what he did was wrong, he acted like everything was okay. About a year later, he approached me at a reunion in front of hundreds of people and said, "Hey Scrub! It's been a while. How are you doing?" while hugging me. I felt repeatedly violated and used, even when he looked at me. Every time we were in a room together, I wondered, "Is he picturing me naked? Is he thinking about how he pleasured himself by forcing his penis inside of me? Does he even care how much hurt he has caused me?" My distress continued, event outside of his presence. If I heard his name or saw his name somewhere, intense anxiety and anger flooded me.

My healing from this experience is a journey. In addition to taking actions that felt safe for me at the time (e.g., making a police report, telling him to leave me alone), psychotherapy and researching sexual violence on college campuses and in athletic settings fostered my healing. Time certainly helped as well. It has been five years since I was raped, and I can confidently say that I have not allowed him or anyone else to destroy me. Despite the compromising of my comfort, dignity, and sanity, I possess enough fortitude, courage, and character to not let Jim, John, Jack, or anyone else destroy me, spoil my student-manager experience, or darken fond memories of a program and job that I loved.

Discussion Questions

1. How does sport generally and athletic departments and teams more specifically create an environment where some athletes feel entitled to others'—particularly female-identified—bodies?

2. What may be the reasons student-managers and other student-workers are not given a voice in athletic departments, research, and literature?
3. What stereotypes or biases do you hold about female-identified student-workers, including managers, office assistants, and volunteers working in an athletic department or program? Where do they come from?
4. How might you react if your co-worker were to tell you that someone you were subordinate to had sexually harassed or raped them?

Notes

1. Non-identifying details and pseudonyms have been provided to maintain anonymity. Contrary to traditional scholarship, I provide no direct references for any of the quotes from athletic department guidelines for fear of recrimination.
2. Pseudonyms are used to maintain anonymity.

SECTION III
Recommendations

13
ATHLETIC PROGRAMMATIC PREVENTION

No More, Not Here, Not Within These Walls

Tess M. Kilwein, Matt J. Gray, and Taylor A. Stuemky

The stories from survivors of sexual misconduct you have encountered in the book thus far cannot be erased. In fact, they point to the need for increased attention on how we move forward, do right by survivors, and prevent future incidences of violence. To create a more welcoming and equitable sport environment for athletes, we must ask ourselves how we both prevent future incidents of sexual misconduct in sport and mitigate harm that has already occurred. Throughout this chapter, we critically examine existing sexual misconduct prevention programs in sport and provide recommendations for enhancing these efforts. As authors of this chapter, we acknowledge that we are informed by working for an institution of higher education and collectively having experience with athletes, administration, trauma-informed therapy, survivor advocacy, sexual violence prevention research and programming, and, in one case, personal experience with sexual misconduct in sport. These experiences situate the content and critique in our writing.

Although evidence-based prevention programming is the most essential element in preventing sexual misconduct in sport, we emphasize that responding quickly and effectively when misconduct occurs is also crucially important. Sport institutions that have experienced recurring and unabated sexual misconduct often implement modest sanctions for misconduct, or worse, fail to take decisive action at all (Mangan, 2017). This disconnect communicates to athletes that adherence to sexual misconduct prevention policies is aspirational but not binding. While certain disciplinary actions without formal grievance processes are prohibited (e.g., updated Title IX regulations for intercollegiate athletes), there remain viable policies that sport administrators can institute. For example, they can enforce no-contact orders if both parties are from the same institution (e.g., athletic department, Olympic team) or temporarily suspend perpetrators from team practices, competitions, and activities until an investigation can be completed. At a minimum, a trauma-informed response warrants that survivors of sexual misconduct in sport are believed, supported, and connected with necessary resources (e.g., emergency medical care, mental health counseling, sexual violence advocacy) and that their input is considered throughout reporting/investigation processes.

DOI: 10.4324/9781003125884-16

Necessity of Prevention Programming in Sport

We encourage readers to remember that every statistic of sexual misconduct represents an already existing survivor. Ripped from the headlines, statistics represent a young boy molested by a powerful coach (Chappell, 2012), an Olympic gymnast sexually assaulted under the guise of medical treatment (Guardian News and Media, 2018), or a college student raped by a group of football players (Given, 2019). We acknowledge that trauma—an emotional response to deeply distressing experiences (American Psychological Association, n.d.)—is at the core of sexual misconduct and can have unique psychological, emotional, and physical effects on both survivors and their loves ones. Through a trauma-informed lens, we recognize that developing and implementing sexual misconduct prevention programming within sport institutions cannot be done without truly valuing and listening to the stories of survivors, as gruesome as they may be. While these stories remain crucial in examining what behavior we are willing to accept in the world of sport, we emphasize that through widespread institutional change and culture shifts, future sexual misconduct *can* be prevented.

While most athletes are *not* sexual perpetrators, research has consistently demonstrated that athletes are at higher risk to perpetrate sexually aggressive behavior in comparison to their non-athlete peers (McCray, 2015; Murnen & Kohlman, 2007). Factors that have been hypothesized to contribute to elevated incidents of sexual violence in sport include promotion of and adherence to traditional masculinity norms (Miller, 2008, 2009; Steinfeldt & Steinfeldt, 2012), greater acceptance of rape myths (Forbes et al., 2006), and pronounced hypermasculinity (Murnen & Kohlman, 2007). In addition, values of loyalty, betrayal, and team identification are often heightened on sports teams and can result in reluctance to intervene in problematic situations (Gable et al., 2017).

Equally important, however, is research highlighting factors unique to athletics that may bolster programmatic prevention efforts including: Leadership qualities (Dobosz & Beaty, 1999), influential coaches (Fraser-Thomas et al., 2005), and visibility/high-status positions that enable athletes to serve as effective role models (Moynihan et al., 2010). On college campuses in particular, student-athletes are visible members of the campus community with high levels of social capital (Clopton & Finch, 2010; Clopton, 2012). However, while student-athletes have the potential to function as influential opinion leaders in the prevention of sexual assault (Banyard et al., 2009), both coaches and sport administrators maintain the responsibility of communicating expectations surrounding prevention of sexual misconduct to athletes (Kroshus et al., 2018).

Programmatic Prevention for Sexual Misconduct

Public health prevention researchers have defined three levels of prevention for sexual misconduct: 1) *Primary prevention:* Approaches employed *before* sexual misconduct occurs to prevent initial perpetration/victimization; 2) *Secondary prevention:* Immediate response *after* sexual misconduct occurs that deals with short-term consequences of violence by reducing harm to victims and addressing perpetrators; and 3) *Tertiary prevention:* Long-term response *after* sexual misconduct occurs that addresses the lasting consequences of victimization and the treatment/management of perpetrators (Association for the Treatment of Abusers, 2020). In addition, prevention efforts have historically targeted individual, programmatic, and systemic levels. Bystander intervention programs, for example, are programmatic prevention efforts that equip members of a community to recognize and respond to problematic behaviors (e.g., misogynist language, sexist behavior) which contribute to sexual assault. While early researchers examining these programs focused solely on intentions, confidence, and self-efficacy, more recently, the results of large and well-controlled studies have demonstrated reductions in both sexual violence victimization and perpetration (Coker et al., 2016).

This is not to say, however, that all bystander intervention programs are always done well, nor do they always address individual or systemic levels of prevention that are also necessary for institutional change. First, bystander intervention approaches situate the problem—and, therefore, the solution—on others rather than on perpetrators and systems that promote sexual violence in the first place. Second, many bystander intervention programs are mandatory in nature, which has been known to diminish buy-in (DeGue et al., 2014). These programs stand to benefit from improved messaging around their mandatory nature and/or infusing optional programs like *Green Dot*[1] into existing programming. Third, many bystander intervention programs, particularly those delivered online, include information and language about bystander intervention behaviors yet do not provide experiential opportunities to practice these skills, identify personal barriers, or delineate different bystander strategies that may work best for each individual.

The "Me Too" era has resulted in heightened awareness around sexual violence and a reckoning with the reality of sexual misconduct in sport (Me Too, 2020). Programmatic prevention efforts for sexual misconduct in sport must focus on all layers (i.e., primary, secondary, tertiary) and levels (i.e., individual, programmatic, systemic), as well as incorporate a trauma-informed response. In addition, continued acknowledgment of the larger roles that systemic factors like misogyny, rape culture, and toxic masculinity play in sexual violence is warranted. As outlined by Fisher and Anders (2020), to disrupt systemic disempowerment of sexual violence survivors and cultures of sexual exploitation, we must recognize that sexual misconduct in sport spaces largely persists due to the privilege structures under which athletes train and complete.

Existing Sexual Misconduct Prevention Programming in Sport

While sexual misconduct prevention programming in sport has evolved over the past decade, most programs have been restricted to university settings and are approaches employed *before* sexual misconduct has occurred to prevent initial perpetration/victimization (i.e., primary prevention) rather than secondary or tertiary in nature. In addition, these programs typically address the programmatic level of prevention, rather than the individual or systemic levels. Throughout the next section, we offer an overview of programmatic prevention efforts among youth/adolescent, intercollegiate, and Olympic/professional athletes.

Youth/Adolescent Sports

To our knowledge, the only well-developed, evidence-based program targeting youth/adolescent athletes is *Coaching Boys into Men* (Miller et al., 2012). This is a primary prevention program aimed at reducing dating violence perpetration among adolescent male athletes via bystander intervention. Given the highly influential role of coaches on high school athletes, the program consists of coaches participating in a 60-minute violence prevention training before utilizing a *Coaches Kit* to engage athletes in weekly, 15-minute conversations about eliminating violence against girls/women. Coaches also have access to trained advocates throughout program delivery. An evaluation of the program demonstrated higher intentions to intervene, recognition of abusive behaviors, and prosocial bystander behavior in the short term (Miller et al., 2012), as well as reduced levels of dating violence perpetration and negative bystander behaviors (e.g., laughing and going along with abusive behaviors among peers) at the one-year post-intervention mark (Miller et al., 2013).

While *Coaching Boys into Men* utilizes an effective model (i.e., the influential position of coaches) and has demonstrated positive behavioral outcomes, it does little to address perpetrators of sexual violence directly and it remains unclear whether and to what extent a 60-minute training program provided to coaches—and brief conversations with athletes—provides a sufficient level of education for institutional changes to occur. In addition, the range of governing bodies over youth/adolescent sport (e.g., school districts, state athletic associations) make it nearly impossible to assess the extent of prevention programming at this level, particularly secondary or tertiary interventions. Specifically, questions around who should be responsible for providing prevention programming, to whom athletes should report, what resources are available to athletes, and who is responsible for institutional response are far from clear or standardized.

Intercollegiate Athletics

In 2017, the National Collegiate Athletic Association (NCAA) first adopted a Board of Governors Policy on Campus Sexual Violence, which requires athletic departments to provide yearly sexual violence prevention education for all student-athletes, coaches, and administrators (NCAA, 2017). However, athletic departments vary in their efforts to abide by these regulations and there is not currently a gold standard sexual assault prevention program at the collegiate level (Kroshus et al., 2018). Thus, many departments instead rely on one-time guest speakers (e.g., sexual assault survivor Brenda Tracy; Brenda Tracy, n.d.), online learning modules (EVERFI, 2021), and/or resources gleaned from the NCAA Sexual Violence Prevention Toolkit (NCAA, 2019). Due to the number of one-time, single university, and/or pilot programs that have been developed for college athletes (e.g., Exner-Cortens & Cummings, 2017; Holcomb et al., 2002; Moynihan & Banyard, 2008), this review cannot be exhaustive; instead, we focus on those programs which have been more widely evaluated by researchers and/or disseminated across college campuses.

Bystander intervention programs, which invite college students to become active bystanders to decrease sexual misconduct on college campuses, have been specifically modified to fit the student-athlete population. For example, a single, 4- to 5-hour session of *Bringing in the Bystander* (Banyard et al., 2007) delivered to intercollegiate athletes resulted in improvements in self-reported bystander confidence and intentions to engage in bystander behaviors (Moynihan et al., 2010). Similarly, *Step UP!* (Orsini et al., 2019) resulted in self-reported improvement in knowledge, attitudes, and self-efficacy to utilize bystander intervention behaviors among student-athletes. One bystander intervention-based prevention program, *Mentors in Violence* (*MVP;* Katz, 1994), leverages the influential role of coaches, athletics staff, and student-athletes themselves in combatting sexual misconduct. Cissner (2009) demonstrated that participation in *MVP* reduced self-reported sexist attitudes and improved self-efficacy to intervene among fraternity and sorority members, though did not assess student athletes. Similarly, while Eriksen (2015) demonstrated improved self-efficacy and willingness to engage in a range of bystander behaviors among student-athletes who participated in *MVP*, student-athletes were combined with other student leaders and the researchers did not assess actual bystander behaviors or rates of sexual violence.

Unfortunately, therefore, no prevention programs developed for or evaluated using student-athletes has demonstrated an impact on actual rates of sexual misconduct. In fact, the only bystander intervention program that is known to impact actual rates of victimization on college campuses is *Green Dot* (Coker et al., 2016), which, to our knowledge, has not been evaluated using the student-athlete population. While *MVP* emphasizes the importance of tailoring curriculums and trainings to specific groups (e.g., student-athletes vs. senior leadership), the typical frequency and duration of this program in college settings as well as its efficacy in reducing gender-based violence specifically among intercollegiate student-athletes are not readily available. Without an existing research base, the efficacy of *MVP* likely depends upon several factors, including frequency, duration, packing, implementation, and how intensive and distributed they are. Finally, existing programs in the collegiate setting rarely address the individual or systemic layers of sexual misconduct prevention, telling us little about their ability to create sustainable culture shifts in collegiate athletic settings. Secondary and tertiary prevention efforts also vary widely across athletic departments.

Olympic/Professional Sports

While certain policies (e.g., National Football League [NFL]'s Personal Conduct Policy [NFL, 2016], National Basketball Association/National Basketball Players Association [NBA/NBPA] Policy on Domestic Violence, Sexual Assault, and Child Abuse [NBA/NBPA, 2017]) may act to prevent instances of gender-based violence (Janusz, 2012), no researchers have examined the effectiveness of these policies in preventing sexual misconduct. For example, the International Olympic Committee (IOC) regularly updates its Consensus Statement on Sexual Harassment and Abuse in sport (Mountjoy et al., 2016) and in 2017 launched a toolkit to assist in the development and implementation of policies/procedures that safeguard athletes from harassment and abuse. Even more recently, The US Center for Safe Sport took on responsibility for responding to allegations of sexual misconduct among US Olympic/Paralympic athletes (Johnson et al., 2020) and secondary prevention measures (e.g., welfare officers, sexual violence counseling centers) have been implemented at recent Olympic Games (Ortiz, 2018). However, while existing primary prevention programs (e.g., *MVP*) have been extended to professional sports, we are not aware of any sexual misconduct prevention program designed specifically for and/or widely disseminated among professional athletes or Olympians.

The greatest limitation of sexual misconduct prevention programming in Olympic and professional sport is that it is reactive in nature. While secondary and tertiary levels of sexual misconduct prevention targeting these populations are becoming increasingly available and standardized, they hardly suffice when there is a sheer lack of primary prevention efforts in place. Similarly, while strong policies and procedures play an important role in preventing future incidents of sexual misconduct, without strong research, it is unclear to what extent these have an impact on actual rates of sexual misconduct. In fact, many of these policies and procedures as well as secondary and tertiary prevention efforts did not exist until high-profile incidents of sexual misconduct had already taken place (e.g., Larry Nassar's widespread sexual abuse of Olympic gymnasts).

Barriers to Prevention Programming in Sport

Given the lack of prevention programming identified in youth/adolescent and professional/Olympic sports, little remains known about who this responsibility does (or rather, should) fall on. In fact, when sports organizations are inundated with mandatory trainings and compliance meetings, sexual misconduct prevention efforts that are most likely to enact changes are often not selected due to practical and/or financial constraints. While prevention programming has evolved to fit the time constraints of college athletics specifically (e.g., annual 60–90-minute trainings), this results in student-athletes only receiving approximately five brief trainings related to sexual misconduct throughout the duration of their athletic career. It is no wonder, therefore, that these models have proven to be less effective in implementing widespread cultural change in university settings. An emphasis on the organizational time, money, and resources that could be saved on reduced incidence of sexual violence by way of effective prevention programming (Kellison, 2016; National Sexual Violence Resource Center, n.d.; The Industrial Relations School, 2018) is imperative for administrative buy-in.

In addition, the responsibility for sexual misconduct prevention/response in collegiate athletic settings often falls to one or two administrators (e.g., compliance officer, senior woman administrator [Wells et al., 2020]). We cannot help but wonder why the responsibility for preventing and responding to incidents of sexual misconduct would fall solely on administrators, professionals who spend more time on risk management than interacting with student-athletes themselves. Even more limiting is research highlighting that senior woman administrators are often left out of important oversight duties, including supervision of men's basketball and/or football and revenue discussions. Unfortunately, when the directive for programming comes from the administration, what often results is a lack of buy-in from sport-specific coaches and student-athletes, despite research demonstrating that collegiate football players are more likely to identify intentions to act as prosocial bystanders in sexual misconduct situations when their *coaches* effectively communicate expectations/consequences for off-field behavior (Kroshus, 2018). These findings suggest that coaches can play an integral role in encouraging prosocial bystander behaviors when administrators provide the necessary framework, expectations, and incentives for coaches to do their part in creating an athletic environment that does not tolerate sexual misconduct.

Finally, sexual misconduct prevention programming often relies on *real life* scenarios in trainings yet does little to account for the intersection of race, ethnicity, sexual orientation, gender identity, and disability with sexual violence. Research has consistently demonstrated that sexual violence disproportionately affects individuals with disabilities (Bowers Andrews & Veronen, 1993; Cantor et al., 2015), Black, Indigenous, and people of color (Department of Justice [DOJ], 2004), and those who identify as gay, lesbian, bisexual, transgender, genderqueer, or non-conforming (de Heer & Jones, 2017; Martin-Storey et al., 2018). Despite this knowledge, and recent advancements in prevention programming, these intersections are less frequently examined in the sexual violence prevention literature and are rarely represented in programmatic prevention materials (e.g., written or audio-visual scenarios) in athletic settings.

Prevention Programming Recommendations

The most compelling reason to implement substantive and effective sexual misconduct prevention programming in sport is humanitarian in nature: We have a duty to reduce the alarming rates of sexual violence and their profound psychological impacts on athletes. However, there are also practical and institutional reasons to do so. In the most severe and visible instances of sexual misconduct in sport (e.g., Baylor University football team's sexual assault scandal; Lavigne & Schlabanch, 2017), failure to meaningfully prevent and respond to sexual misconduct has resulted in the dismissal of athletic personnel, firing/resignation of administrators, NCAA sanctions, and multimillion dollar lawsuits. Despite increased media attention surrounding allegations of sexual misconduct against athletes, elevated rates of sexual assault among student-athlete populations (MacGregor, 2018; McCray, 2015), and the aforementioned personal and institutional impacts of sexual violence, there is little evidence that the rate of sexual misconduct in sport is experiencing a meaningful reduction (Beaver, 2019; Moorman & Osborne, 2015). Unfortunately, many sport organizations continue to implement mandatory, one-time annual trainings and occasional awareness events and speakers, which fall short of systematic and integrative approaches necessary to meaningfully shift the culture around sexual misconduct. Later, we offer specific recommendations for prevention programming gleaned from the larger sexual violence prevention literature (DeGue et al., 2014).

Ongoing Assessment of Sexual Misconduct via Climate Surveys

Sexual misconduct advocates and researchers have long recognized that formal crime statistics and/or Title IX complaints do not accurately capture the endemic of sexual misconduct (Tjaden & Thoennes, 2000). First, the vast majority of sexual assaults are not reported to formal authorities, and, thus, represent only a small subset of assaults that have ultimately taken place (DOJ, 2017). Second, enhanced sexual assault programming, awareness, and structural support for victims can result in an increase in sexual assault reports even if overall rates are declining; specifically, if survivors believe that they will not be blamed, that their complaint will be handled well, and that they will be supported, they may be more likely to make formal reports.

While there are several methods that may be utilized to assess factors surrounding sexual assault—such as qualitative one-on-one interviews or focus groups—the *only* way to thoroughly assess how prevalent rates of sexual misconduct are in a particular community is to utilize well-conducted climate surveys (DOJ, 2018). Such surveys are common on college campuses and generally converge on estimates of one-in-five to one-in-four students experiencing a sexual assault during college, with some communities (e.g., athletics, Greek-life) demonstrating higher rates (Muehlenhard et al., 2017). Without conducting institution-specific climate surveys, sport administrators could understandably misperceive that sexual misconduct was well-handled by virtue of providing (limited) programming and tallying formal reports of assault. Decreasing sexual violence will require accurate, local, and recurrent assessment of the problem within and across sport organizations.

Incentives of Distributed and Integrative Programming

A recent review of sexual violence prevention research affirmed that mandatory, one-time or annual, brief (i.e., 60–90 minutes) sexual assault awareness trainings are ineffective in reducing rates of sexual assault and promoting sustainable changes in attitudes and/or behavior even when more modest or indirect outcomes (e.g., rape supportive beliefs) are examined (DeGue et al., 2014). Instead, effective prevention programming is typically longer in duration and spread out over multiple occasions. As previously mentioned, despite the financial and practical barriers to employing substantive integration of sexual misconduct prevention programming in sport, there remains a humanitarian and community need to do so. In addition, the reputational and economic costs of sexual misconduct within sport institutions (e.g., media coverage, costs of investigations) also highlight a financial incentive. Specifically, what may be seen as too time-intensive or expensive a priori may ultimately prove to be time and resources well spent if a scandal and harm to others are prevented.

Target Attitudes and Beliefs: A Culture Shift Is Needed

Although enhanced tracking of sexual misconduct perpetration and behavioral outcomes is critical, it should *not* be concluded that attitudinal variables (e.g., rape myth acceptance, bystander efficacy, social norms) are unimportant or uninformative. It takes several months to years for prevention programs to impact actual rates of victimization, necessitating the examination of proximal indices that provide context about the impact of a program and help gauge the likelihood of sexual violence within a specific setting. With recognition that what is needed in sport is a dramatic change in *culture*[2] where sexual violence is concerned, those interested in sexual misconduct prevention should also concern themselves with support for survivors and cultivating a shared responsibility to challenge dialogue and ideations that give rise to sexual violence in the first place.

To demonstrate the importance of examining attitudes and beliefs, Thompson et al. (2013) found that the extent to which one's peer group accepts use of force against women in sexual situations predicted male perpetration of sexual assault over four years of college. Male athletes are especially influenced by social norms, as they may experience more pressure to engage in casual, impersonal sex and act in hyper-masculine manners to gain social acceptance (Murnen & Kohlman, 2007). In addition, research has demonstrated that perceived team norms surrounding the acceptability and prevention of sexual assault are predictive of an individual's own expected behaviors (Brown & Messman-Moore, 2010; Kroshus, 2019).

Fortunately, research in promoting behavior change suggests that those with high social capital within a given group can play an important role in maintaining or shaping norms through endorsement of prevention-oriented behaviors (Valente & Pumpuang, 2007). Thus, assessing social norms related to sexual assault prevention, rape-supportive beliefs, and perceptions of peer support for sexual aggression are important to: 1) ascertain whether there is a culture of sexual coercion in a specific setting; 2) identify targets for sexual misconduct prevention efforts; 3) identify the need for norm correction interventions; and 4) engage key individuals (e.g., coaches, team captains) in shaping prevention-oriented norms. While bystander intervention programs target perceived norms surrounding prosocial bystander behavior, directly targeting beliefs that are less visible and more culturally/systemically determined (e.g., adherence to rape myths, acceptability of sexual aggression) is equally important to promote sustainable culture shifts.

Bystander Intervention and Collective Responsibility

Perhaps the greatest development in sexual misconduct prevention programming in recent years is recognition of a shared, community obligation to promote safety from gender-based violence (DeGue, 2012). Given the specter of sanctions, loss of scholarships, dismissals from teams, and most importantly, the adverse impacts on survivors within sport, there are many salient justifications that could be better leveraged to promote genuine communal buy-in for a shared, community obligation to promote safety from gender-based violence. All too often though, sexual misconduct prevention programming is introduced to athletes as something that is *required*, which understandably conveys to recipients that it is an irritating, obligatory hurdle to be cleared rather than an effort that can enhance the collective well-being of one's community.

Historical prevention approaches that taught women "how not to be raped" or men not to rape were misguided and ineffective (DeGue et al., 2014). By recognizing that one need not be a victim or a prospective perpetrator to combat sexual violence and promote a safe campus community, bystander approaches stand to get more people involved in the fight against sexual misconduct. Framing prosocial bystander behaviors as consistent with currently endorsed values (e.g., being a good teammate) and providing opportunities for team members and coaches to demonstrate these values off-field may be particularly effective for the implementation of bystander-oriented programming in sport settings (Kroshus, 2019). However, most importantly, all members of an organization—from administrators to coaches to student-athletes themselves—must receive ongoing training, education, and accountability on sexual misconduct as well as opportunities to engage in meaningful dialogue around the systematic nature of sexual violence to truly promote a culture shift away from gender-based violence.

Zero Tolerance

Finally, we emphasize that sexual misconduct investigations should be efficient, and sanctions should be appropriately weighted. Should a formal investigation process be warranted and ultimately conclude that sexual misconduct likely occurred, formal sanctions may include: Suspensions ranging from a single game to an entire season, scholarship withdrawals or mandatory fines, and, in more extreme cases, dismissal from an organization/institution. For variants of misconduct that may not result in formal, institutional sanctions (e.g., sexual harassment), some form of response (e.g., discussion with coaches/administrators, educational interventions) is warranted to convey that such behavior is also deemed unacceptable and will be dealt with firmly. To create a hierarchy of sexual violence minimizes and dismisses the mental and physical toll that all variants of sexual misconduct play on survivors, particularly those who have experienced sexual harassment for years and/or from multiple perpetrators within the same institution. Ultimately, however, it is important to note that even efficient and appropriate sanctions taken against perpetrators do little to acknowledge and resolve the institutional culture under which the sexual misconduct was allowed to take place.

The NCAA (2020) now requires student-athletes to disclose incidents of sexual misconduct to both identify perpetrators before they are admitted to an institution (e.g., incoming freshmen, transfer student-athletes) and annually assess personal conduct of current student-athletes. One limitation to this policy is that the NCAA allows each institution to individually determine how to collect this information, which may result in inconsistencies and discrepancies between institutions. Little is known about similar efforts in high school, professional, and/or Olympic sports. Ultimately, as suggested by MacGregor

(2018), administrators who are made aware of sexual misconduct within their organizations and refrain from acting have violated contractual relationships by not taking reasonable efforts to create a safe environment for athletes, and, thus, should be held liable for negligence and resulting harms.

Conclusions

It is no longer enough to be moved by the resilience and testimonies of athletes who have experienced sexual misconduct in sport. It is time to live out the commitment of eradicating the pervasive culture of silence in sport so there are no more stories to be told. Sexual misconduct in sport will continue to exist without: 1) integrated and distributed prevention programming; 2) an emphasis on the safety and well-being of an entire sport community; and 3) increased recognition of the systemic nature of sexual misconduct in sport (Fisher & Anders, 2020). While several effective and promising prevention programs that are designed to be distributed over time and emphasize the safety of an entire community already exist, the question we pose to prevention experts and sport administrators is this: *Do these existing programs address the systemic nature of sexual misconduct in sport, and, if not, what will be done differently?* Until zero tolerance for sexual misconduct is woven throughout the infrastructure of all levels of sport, not only will we be ineffective in preventing future incidents of sexual misconduct but also we will be insufficient in our efforts to reconcile with the inherently traumatic acts of violence that have already been inflicted upon our athletes. The only way to do justice by our athletes is to not only say but truly live: No more, not here, not within these walls.

Discussion Questions

1. What are the shortcomings of brief, one-time or annual prevention programs in reducing sexual violence in athletics settings?
2. How do prevention experts best communicate the humanitarian and financial incentives of distributed and integrative sexual misconduct prevention programming?
3. How can highly influential personnel within athletics programs (e.g., head coaches) be encouraged to be more involved in sexual misconduct prevention programming efforts?
4. How can sport staff and coaches be better equipped with the tools to appropriately respond to an athlete that discloses experiencing sexual misconduct?
5. What would it look like for zero tolerance to move beyond individual *problem* athletes and truly be woven throughout the infrastructure sport?

Notes

1. Green Dot is a sexual violence prevention program that aims to prevent dating violence, sexual assault, and stalking on college campuses by empowering students, staff, administrators, and faculty to engage in bystander intervention behaviors (Alteristic, 2017).
2. *Culture* refers to institutionalized attitudes and beliefs toward gender-based violence, as well as the underlying power structures and dynamics that promote and maintain these attitudes and beliefs within systems.

References

Alteristic. (2017, September 6). *Green dot for college.* https://alteristic.org/services/green-dot/green-dot-colleges/

American Psychological Association. (n.d.). *Trauma and shock.* www.apa.org/topics/trauma/

Association for the Treatment of Abusers. (2020). *Sexual misconduct prevention* [Fact sheet]. www.atsa.com/sexual-violence-prevention-fact-sheet

Banyard, V. L., Moynihan, M. M., & Crossman, M. T. (2009). Reducing sexual violence on campus: The role of student leaders as empowered bystanders. *Journal of College Student Development, 50*(4), 446–457.

Banyard, V. L., Moynihan, M. M., & Plante, E. G. (2007). Sexual violence prevention through bystander education: An experimental evaluation. *Journal of Community Psychology, 35*(4), 463–481.

Beaver, W. (2019). College athletes and sexual assault. *Society, 56*(6), 620–624.

Bowers Andrews, A., & Veronen, L. J. (1993). Sexual assault and people with disabilities. *Journal of Social Work & Human Sexuality, 8*(2), 137–159.

Brenda Tracy. (n.d.). *Brenda Tracy.* www.brendatracy.com/

Brown, A. L., & Messman-Moore, T. L. (2010). Personal and perceived peer attitudes supporting sexual aggression as predictors of male college students' willingness to intervene against sexual aggression. *Journal of Interpersonal Violence, 25*(3), 503–517.

Cantor, D., Fisher, B., Chibnall, S. H., Townsend, R., Lee, H., Thomas, G., . . . Westat, Inc. (2015). *Report on the AAU campus climate survey on sexual assault and sexual misconduct.* Westat.

Chappell, B. (2012). Penn State abuse scandal: A guide and timeline. *National Public Radio.* Retrieved from: https://www.npr.org/2011/11/08/142111804/penn-state-abuse-scandal-a-guide-and-timeline.

Cissner, A. B. (2009). Evaluating the mentors in violence prevention program. *Center for Court Innovation,* 451–468.

Clopton, A. W. (2012). Social capital, gender, and the student athlete. *Group Dynamics: Theory, Research, and Practice, 16*(4), 272.

Clopton, A. W., & Finch, B. L. (2010). Are college students' bowling alone? Examining the contribution of team identification to the social capital of college students. *Journal of Sport Behavior, 33*(4), 377.

Coker, A. L., Bush, H. M., Fisher, B. S., Swan, S. C., Williams, C. M., Clear, E. R., & DeGue, S. (2016). Multi-college bystander intervention evaluation for violence prevention. *American Journal of Preventive Medicine, 50*(3), 295–302.

Coker, A. L., Fisher, B. S., Bush, H. M., Swan, S. C., Williams, C. M., Clear, E. R., & DeGue, S. (2015). Evaluation of the green dot bystander intervention to reduce interpersonal violence among college students across three campuses. *Violence Against Women, 21*(12), 1507–1527.

DeGue, S., Holt, M. K., Massetti, G. M., Matjasko, J. L., Tharp, A. T., & Valle, L. A. (2012). Looking ahead toward community-level strategies to prevent sexual violence. *Journal of Women's Health, 21*(1), 1–3.

DeGue, S., Valle, L. A., Holt, M. K., Massetti, G. M., Matjasko, J. L., & Tharp, A. T. (2014). A systematic review of primary prevention strategies for sexual violence perpetration. *Aggression and Violent Behavior, 19*(4), 346–362.

de Heer, B., & Jones, L. (2017). Measuring sexual violence on campus: Climate surveys and vulnerable groups. *Journal of School Violence, 16*(2), 207–221.

Department of Justice. (2004). *American Indians and crime, 1992–2002.* www.bjs.ojp.gov/content/pub/pdf/aic02.pdf

Department of Justice. (2017). *National crime victimization survey, 2010–2016.* www.bjs.gov/content/pub/pdf/cv16.pdf

Department of Justice. (2018, November 5). *Protecting students from sexual assault.* www.justice.gov/archives/ovw/protecting-students-sexual-assault

Dobosz, R. P., & Beaty, L. A. (1999). The relationship between athletic participation and high school students' leadership ability. *Adolescence, 34*(133), 215.

Eriksen, S. (2015). *Program evaluation of the mentors in violence prevention leadership training at California State University, Long Beach.* www.mvpstrat.com/wp-content/uploads/2016/03/executive-summary.pdf

EVERFI. (2021, January 20). *Sexual assault prevention training for student-athletes.* https://everfi.com/courses/colleges-universities/sexual-assault-prevention-student-athletes/

Exner-Cortens, D., & Cummings, N. (2017). Bystander-based sexual violence prevention with college athletes: A pilot randomized trial. *Journal of Interpersonal Violence*, 1–24.

Fisher, L. A., & Anders, A. D. (2020). Engaging with cultural sport psychology to explore systemic sexual exploitation in USA gymnastics: A call to commitments. *Journal of Applied Sport Psychology, 32*(2), 129–145.

Forbes, G. B., Adams-Curtis, L. E., Pakalka, A. H., & White, K. B. (2006). Dating aggression, sexual coercion, and aggression-supporting attitudes among college men as a function of participation in aggressive high school sports. *Violence Against Women, 12*(5), 441–455.

Fraser-Thomas, J. L., Côté, J., & Deakin, J. (2005). Youth sport programs: An avenue to foster positive youth development. *Physical Education & Sport Pedagogy, 10*(1), 19–40.

Gable, S. C., Lamb, S., Brodt, M., & Atwell, L. (2017). Intervening in a "sketchy situation": Exploring the moral motivations of college bystanders of sexual assault. *Journal of Interpersonal Violence, 36*(1–2), 311–334.

Given, K. (2019, January 25). *Brenda Tracy fights sexual violence, one locker room at a time.* www.wbur.org/onlyagame/2019/01/25/brenda-tracy-sexual-violence-athletes

Guardian News and Media. (2018, January 26). How was Larry Nassar able to abuse so many gymnasts for so long? *The Guardian.* www.theguardian.com/sport/2018/jan/26/larry-nassar-abuse-gymnasts-scandal-culture

Holcomb, D. R., Savage, M. P., Seehafer, R., & Waalkes, D. M. (2002). A mixed-gender date rape prevention intervention targeting freshmen college athletes. *College Student Journal, 36*(2), 165–180.

The Industrial Relations School. (2018, September 25). *Lifetime cost of assault.* www.ilr.cornell.edu/news/research/lifetime-cost-assault

Janusz, S. (2012). The NFL's strict enforcement of its personal conduct policy for crimes against women: A useful tool for combating violence or an attempt to punish morality. *Seton Hall Journal of Sports and Entertainment Law, 22,* 93.

Johnson, N., Hanna, K., Novak, J., & Giardino, A. P. (2020). US center for SafeSport: Preventing abuse in sports. *Women in Sport and Physical Activity Journal, 28*(1), 66–71.

Katz, J. (1994). *Mentors in violence prevention (MVP) trainer's guide.* Northeastern University's Center for the Study of Sport in Society.

Kellison, B. (2016, December 1). *How sexual assault may affect salaries post-graduation.* www.huffpost.com/entry/campus-sexual-assaults-are-economically-traumatic-for-victims-_b_8688698?ncid=twe etlnkushpmg00000056

Kroshus, E. (2019). College athletes, pluralistic ignorance and bystander behaviors to prevent sexual assault. *Journal of Clinical Sport Psychology, 13*(2), 330–344.

Kroshus, E., Paskus, T., & Bell, L. (2018). Coach expectations about off-field conduct and bystander intervention by U.S. college football players to prevent inappropriate sexual behavior. *Journal of Interpersonal Violence, 33*(2), 293–315.

Lavigne, P., & Schlabach, M. (2017). *Violated: Exposing rape at Baylor University amid college football's sexual assault crisis.* Center Street.

MacGregor, W. (2018). It's just a game until someone is sexually assaulted: Sport culture and the perpetuation of sexual violence by athletes. *Education & Law Journal, 28*(1), 43–73.

Mangan, K. (2017). At Baylor, a scandal's constant drip means a relentless spotlight. *Chronicle of Higher Education, 63,* A21–A22.

Martin-Storey, A., Paquette, G., Bergeron, M., Dion, J., Daigneault, I., Hébert, M., & Ricci, S. (2018). Sexual violence on campus: Differences across gender and sexual minority status. *Journal of Adolescent Health, 62*(6), 701–707.

McCray, K. L. (2015). Intercollegiate athletes and sexual violence: A review of literature and recommendations for future study. *Trauma, Violence, & Abuse, 16*(4), 438–443.

Me Too. (2020, July 16). *Get to know us: History & inception.* https://metoomvmt.org/get-to-know-us/history-inception/

Miller, E., Tancredi, D. J., McCauley, H. L., Decker, M. R., Virata, M. C. D., Anderson, H. A., O'Connor, B., & Silverman, J. G. (2013). One-year follow-up of a coach-delivered dating violence prevention program: A cluster randomized controlled trial. *American Journal of Preventive Medicine, 45*(1), 108–112.

Miller, E., Tancredi, D. J., McCauley, H. L., Decker, M. R., Virata, M. C. D., Anderson, H. A., Stetkevich, N., Brown, E. W., Moideen, F., & Silverman, J. G. (2012). "Coaching boys into men": A cluster-randomized controlled trial of a dating violence prevention program. *Journal of Adolescent Health, 51*(5), 431–438.

Miller, K. E. (2008). Wired: Energy drinks, jock identity, masculine norms, and risk taking. *Journal of American College Health, 56*(5), 481–490.

Miller, K. E. (2009). Sport-related identities and the "toxic jock". *Journal of Sport Behavior, 32*(1), 69.

Moorman, A. M., & Osborne, B. (2015). Are institutions of higher education failing to protect students: An analysis of Title IX's sexual violence protections and college athletics. *Marquette Sports Law Review, 26*, 545.

Mountjoy, M., Brackenridge, C., Arrington, M., Blauwet, C., Carska-Sheppard, A., Fasting, K., . . . Starr, K. (2016). International Olympic committee consensus statement: Harassment and abuse (non-accidental violence) in sport. *British Journal of Sports Medicine, 50*(17), 1019–1029.

Moynihan, M. M., & Banyard, V. L. (2008). Community responsibility for preventing sexual violence: A pilot study with campus Greeks and intercollegiate athletes. *Journal of Prevention & Intervention in the Community, 36*(1–2), 23–38.

Moynihan, M. M., Banyard, V. L., Arnold, J. S., Eckstein, R. P., & Stapleton, J. G. (2010). Engaging intercollegiate athletes in preventing and intervening in sexual and intimate partner violence. *Journal of American College Health, 59*(3), 197–204.

Muehlenhard, C. L., Peterson, Z. D., Humphreys, T. P., & Jozkowski, K. N. (2017). Evaluating the one-in-five statistic: Women's risk of sexual assault while in college. *The Journal of Sex Research, 54*(4–5), 549–576.

Murnen, S. K., & Kohlman, M. H. (2007). Athletic participation, fraternity membership, and sexual aggression among college men: A meta-analytic review. *Sex Roles, 57*(1–2), 145–157.

National Basketball Association/National Basketball Players Association. (2017, June 30). *Joint NBA/NBPA policy on domestic violence, sexual assault, and child abuse.* https://atlhawksfanatic.github.io/NBA-CBA/joint-nbanbpa-policy-on-domestic-violence-sexual-assault-and-child-abuse.html

National Collegiate Athletics Association. (2017). *NCAA board of governors policy on campus sexual violence.* https://ncaaorg.s3.amazonaws.com/ssi/violence/NCAA_CampusSexualViolencePolicy.pdf

National Collegiate Athletics Association. (2019). *Sexual violence prevention: An athletics tool kit for a healthy and safe culture* (2nd ed.). Sport Science Institute.

National Collegiate Athletics Association. (2020). *Board of governors expands sexual violence policy.* www.ncaa.org/about/resources/media-center/news/board-governors-expands-sexual-violence-policy

National Football League. (2016). *Personal conduct policy: League policies for players.* https://static.nfl.com/static/content/public/photo/2017/08/11/0ap3000000828506.pdf

National Sexual Violence Resource Center. (n.d.). *The cost of rape.* www.nsvrc.org/blogs/cost-rape

Orsini, M. M., Milroy, J. J., Bernick, J. B., Bruce, S., Gonzalez, J., Bell, B., & Wyrick, D. L. (2019). Bystander intervention training that goes beyond sexual violence prevention. *American Journal of Health Studies, 34*(2).

Ortiz, E. (2018). *In age of #metoo, Winter Olympics in South Korea opens centers to address sexual assault.* www.nbcnews.com/storyline/winter-olympics-2018/age-metoo-winter-olympics-south-korea-opens-centers-address-sexual-n846816

Steinfeldt, M., & Steinfeldt, J. A. (2012). Athletic identity and conformity to masculine norms among college football players. *Journal of Applied Sport Psychology, 24*(2), 115–128.

Thompson, M. P., Swartout, K. M., & Koss, M. P. (2013). Trajectories and predictors of sexually aggressive behaviors during emerging adulthood. *Psychology of Violence, 3*(3), 247.

Tjaden, P. G., & Thoennes, N. (2000). *Full report of the prevalence, incidence, and consequences of violence against women: Findings from the national violence against women survey.* US Department of Justice.

Valente, T. W., & Pumpuang, P. (2007). Identifying opinion leaders to promote behavior change. *Health Education & Behavior, 34*(6), 881–896.

Wells, J., Smith, A., Taylor, E., Walker, N. A., Sartore-Baldwin, M., Siegele, J., . . . Alwell, K. (2020, December 9). *The designation, stigmatization, and marginalization of SWAs.* https://athleticdirectoru.com/articles/designation-stigmatization-marginalisation-of-senior-woman-administrators/

14
TITLE IX AND SEXUAL HARASSMENT IN ATHLETICS

James H. Bemiller

Introduction

Over the last half century, Title IX has had a dramatic effect on the sport landscape of the United States (Masteralexis et al., 2012). Title IX is commonly understood to address gender discrimination in sport participation and the equitable experiences of those participating in school-sponsored sports. Unfortunately, the full scope and effect of Title IX is misunderstood by not only the public at large but also school and sport administrators. In this chapter, I focus on the other significant application of Title IX concerning sexual harassment in educational settings.

Brief Background

Definition

Title IX is a brief, 37-word federal statute enacted on June 23, 1972, and is focused on eliminating discrimination. It is part of the Educational Amendments of 1972 and was enacted during an era of social awareness and in the wake of the 1960's Civil Rights legislation. The text of Title IX states:

> No person in the United States shall, on the basis of sex, be excluded from participation in, be denied the benefits of, or be subjected to discrimination under any education program or activity receiving federal financial assistance.
>
> *(Title IX, 1972)*

The popular understanding of Title IX has informed its application related to student-athletes; for example, it has traditionally been applied to student-athlete participation opportunities, comparable facilities and experiences, as well as equitable scholarship assistance. More importantly we focus in this chapter on the use of Title IX to address instances of sexual harassment and assault.

DOI: 10.4324/9781003125884-17

Enforcement and Interpretation

Title IX enforcement and interpretation begin with the text of the law itself passed by the legislative branch. The *executive branch* is tasked with enforcement of the law and must flesh out the definitions, details, and exceptions of enforcement. The Department of Education (DOE), through its division of the Office of Civil Rights (OCR), is responsible for developing the details and enforcement of the regulations of Title IX. Once approved by Congress, the OCR Regulations have the force and effect of federal law which courts are required to recognize. *Policy interpretations* are further detailed explanations and examples of how the DOE gives guidance to how the regulations and policy interpretations should work together to implement Title IX in the lives of students in the United States educational system (Carpenter & Acosta, 2005).

The brief and powerful practicality of Title IX addresses gender discrimination in any educational program receiving federal funds. The broad stroke of the legislation applies to gender discrimination in both public and private institutions receiving federal funding such as student Pell grants or other federal funding or financial aid. In fact, the statute itself does not mention athletics, sports, sexual harassment, or assault. However, although there is no specific mention of sport participation or sexual harassment, these have become the most high-profile applications of Title IX over the past five decades.

These high-profile applications of Title IX enforcement reflect both the American sporting culture and the major risk of increasing incidents of sexual assault on high school and college campuses across the United States. For example, research demonstrates that women college students are three times more likely to experience sexual assault than women non-college students (RAINN, 2021). In addition, over the past two decades, numerous high-profile college athletic programs have litigated and settled multi-million-dollar sexual harassment cases involving student athlete perpetrators.

For example, in 2007, the University of Colorado at Boulder settled a case for more than $2.5 million. In 2014, the University of Connecticut settled a sexual assault claim by five student-athletes for $1.3 million. In 2016, Florida State University settled a Title IX sexual assault case involving Heisman trophy winning quarterback Jameis Winston for $950,000; in that same year, the University of Tennessee paid $2.48 million to settle sexual assault claims accusing student athletes. Another high-profile example of mishandling student athlete sexual assault occurred at Baylor University which settled for an undisclosed amount in 2018 and led to the President of the University being demoted, the resignation of the athletic director, and the firing of the head football coach Art Briles for both their inability to properly address these allegations and retaliating against a complainant (Strader & Williams-Cunningham, 2017).

However, perhaps the most abusive and high-profile example of collegiate sport sexual assault involved Michigan State University (MSU) and long-standing team physician and assistant professor Dr. Larry Nassar. Nassar worked as a sports physician at MSU from 1997 to 2016. He also served for 18 years as the team doctor for USA Gymnastics. During this time, he sexually assaulted hundreds of young women, including 31 MSU Students and elite gymnasts including gold medalists Simone Biles, Gabby Douglas, Aly Raisman, and McKayla Maroney (Kwiatkowski, 2021). Nassar was convicted and sentenced to a de facto life sentence for a combination of state and federal criminal sexual assault and pornography charges. In 2019 the US Department of Education fined MSU $4.5 million for its "systematic failure" to appropriately address and properly disclose reports of abuse by Nassar (Dwyer, 2019). In 2018 MSU also settled a federal lawsuit involving Nassar and 332 victims for $500 million. Public backlash forced the resignation of MSU President Lou Anna Simon (Levenson, 2018). More than 500 women have sued USA Gymnastics alleging abuse by Nassar and other USA Gymnastics personnel. The President and CEO, as well as the entire Board of Directors of USA Gymnastics, resigned and the governing body filed bankruptcy in 2018 citing pending lawsuits related to Nassar's abuse of athletes (Kwiatkowski, 2021). Settlement talks to resolve the USA Gymnastics litigation were ongoing as of the 2021 Tokyo Olympics (Armour, 2021).

As these incidents continue to arise and have long-lasting effects on victims of sexual abuse, the ongoing importance of Title IX as a tool to combat sexual harassment and assault in educational institutions is vital.

An exploration of the controlling case law, regulations, and policies that have been developed to address how Title IX has been used to combat sexual assault in the educational sport setting—particularly as it relates to student-athletes—is the focus of this chapter. The branch of Title IX which protects against sexual harassment is a natural outgrowth of the core concept of the 1972 one-sentence statutory mandate. Sexual harassment is a well-established form of gender discrimination; thus, even though the Title IX statute does not specifically refer to or define sexual harassment, the core principles of Title IX have been used to extend protection to students who have been assaulted or harassed, depriving them of an educational opportunity based on this form of gender discrimination. In 2021, OCR clarified that Title IX's coverage of discrimination includes discrimination on the basis of sex, including sexual orientation or gender identity (Enforcement of Title IX, 2021).[1]

However, the Civil Rights Act of 1964 preceded Title IX and is a comprehensive federal statute broadly prohibiting discrimination across multiple settings including education, employment, public facilities, housing, and federally funded programs (Civil Rights Act, 1964). Title VII of the Civil Rights Act addresses employment discrimination and has been used to protect employees from sex-based discrimination in the workplace (Title VII, 1964). It was not until guidelines were issued in 1980 that the Equal Employment Opportunity Commission (EEOC), the administrative agency which enforces Title VII, acknowledged sexual harassment as *discrimination because of sex*. The EEOC guidelines defined sexual harassment as:

> 1. Unwelcome sexual advances, requests for sexual favors, and other verbal or physical conduct of a sexual nature constitute sexual harassment when submission to such conduct is made either explicitly or implicitly a term of condition of an individual's employment; 2. Submission to or rejection of such conduct by an individual is used as the basis for employment decisions affecting such individual; or 3. Such conduct has the purpose or effect of unreasonably interfering with an individual's work performance or creating an intimidating, hostile or offensive working environment.
>
> *(Osborne, 2013, p. 559)*

The conditions listed in the EEOC guidelines set out the definitions for the two types of sexual harassment we know generally today. Quid pro quo harassment is described in the first condition referenced earlier; it is recognized as trading something such as a raise or better grade, playing time, or other status symbols in exchange for sexual favors. The second condition extends the concept of quid pro quo to all tangible employment actions which could equate to making the team or being dismissed. The last condition is well known as hostile environment gender discrimination which is pervasive but more difficult to prove. Further, crude and inappropriate remarks and sexist unprofessional behavior must be sufficiently pervasive to create an abusive working environment (EEOC, 1990).

Because of its longer history, courts have continued to borrow from Title VII and its explanation of sexual harassment and apply them to Title IX harassment cases. However, the Supreme Court has developed an independent line of reasoning dealing with institutional liability for sexual harassment under Title IX. Over the last 20 years, Title IX case precedent and evolving DOE policy statements have developed a clearer understanding of institutional responsibility to protect students from sexual harassment that diminishes educational opportunities (Enforcement of Title IX, 2021).

Significant Case Precedent Establishing Title IX Sexual Harassment Protections

Over the past 30 years, the courts have addressed sexual harassment through their application of Title IX and different relationship contexts such as adult/teacher/coach on student sexual harassment, and student peer-on-peer sexual harassment. The US Supreme Court established that Title IX authorizes private suits for damages under certain circumstances in *Franklin v. Gwinnett County Pub. Sch.*, 503 U.S. 60 (1992), and *Cannon v. Univ. of Chi.*, 441 U.S. 677 (1998).

Two landmark Supreme Court cases explained how the Court interpreted Title IX sexual harassment cases. In *Gebser v. Lago Vista Independent School District*, 524 U.S. 274 (1998), the case involved teacher on student sexual harassment. In *Davis ex rel. Lashonda D. v. Monroe County Board of Education*, 526 U.S. 629 (1999), the case involved student peer-on-peer sexual harassment.

Gebser v. Lago Vista Independent School District 524 U.S. 274 (1998)

In *Gebser*, an eighth-grade female student was seduced by her teacher and engaged in a sexual relationship, although no school officials were aware or on notice of the relationship. The student and her mother sued the school district under Title IX and the Supreme Court addressed two important questions. First, can an employer (the school district) be held liable for the sexual harassment by its employees? Second, must the employer have notice of the harassment by their employee to be liable under Title IX? The Supreme Court in a split 5–4 decision answered "Yes" to both questions (Gebser, 1998, p. 282). Title IX "conditions an offer of federal funding on a promise by the recipient not to discriminate, in what amounts essentially to a contract between the Government and the recipient of the funds" (Gebser, 1998, p. 286). The Court reasoned that a school funding recipient based on this contract relationship could be "liable in monetary damages for noncompliance" (Gebser, 1998, p. 287). The Supreme Court held that a student's claim for money damages based on sexual harassment by a teacher could arise under Title IX, but only if (1) "an official who *at a minimum has authority to address the alleged discrimination* and to institute corrective measures on the recipient's behalf has *actual knowledge* of discrimination in the recipient's program and *fails adequately to respond*," and (2) the inadequate response "must amount to *deliberate indifference* to discrimination" (Gebser, 1998, p. 290; emphasis added). Therefore, since the school district officials had no knowledge or notice of the teacher's sexual harassment of the student, the school district was not liable for damages under Title IX.

Davis v. Monroe County Board of Education, 526 U.S. 629 (1999)

Title IX requires that to be held liable, an institution[2] receiving federal funding must have actual notice and be deliberately indifferent to the reported harassing behavior. In *Davis v. Monroe County Board of Education* (1999), the Supreme Court addressed the standard required to impose liability and monetary damages in Title IX sexual harassment cases. Lashonda Davis, a fifth-grade female student endured prolonged sexual harassment from a male classmate. The male classmate made demeaning and vulgar statements and fondled her during class. The harassment continued for several months and escalated even though Davis and her mother repeatedly reported the harm Lashonda experienced to the teacher and the principal. After three months, Davis' desk was moved away from the harasser to a different side of the classroom but the harassment continued. The teacher and principal failed to intervene and Lashonda deteriorated physically and emotionally. Her grades dropped, she was fearful and reluctant to attend school, and contemplated suicide.

At the end of the school year, Davis' mother sought redress through the criminal court system and the student harasser pled guilty to sexual battery. The harassment continued and Davis sued the school board since the school officials had been informed of the harassment and criminal charges but failed to take any action to investigate or stop the harassing behavior. The Supreme Court agreed that Title IX entails a private right of action for student-on-student sexual harassment.

The Court addressed two components of the Title IX peer-on-peer claim. The first was the nature and extent of the injury or effects of the harassment on the student. The Supreme Court held that harassment by a student peer constitutes discrimination under Title IX if it is "so severe, pervasive, and objectively offensive, and . . . so undermines and detracts from the victim['s] educational experience, that the victim-student is effectively denied equal access to an institution's resources and opportunities" (Davis, 1999, p. 651). The second component the Supreme Court addressed in *Davis* was the responsibility of the school district, administration, and teaching staff:

> If a funding recipient does not engage in harassment directly, it may not be liable for damages unless its deliberate indifference subjects its student to harassment. That is, the deliberate indifference must, at a minimum, cause students to undergo harassment or make them liable or vulnerable to it.
>
> *(Davis, 1999, pp. 644–645)*

In other words, the Court found that institutional intent must show *deliberate indifference* to acts of which the institution has *actual knowledge*. Therefore, school officials with actual notice of student-on-student sexual harassment must promptly respond in an effective manner to avoid Title IX liability.

Williams v. Board of Regents of the University System of Georgia, 477 F.3d 1282 (2007)

Tiffany Williams was a female undergraduate student at the University of Georgia (UGA). She was raped by three male basketball players in a campus dorm room. University officials—including the athletics director and basketball coach—were aware that one of the attackers had a history of sexual assault; however, he was still recruited to play basketball and given special admission to the university. University officials took no steps to educate or supervise the repeat offender regarding institutional policies regarding sexual harassment. Ms. Williams left the University shortly after the incident fearing retaliation for reporting the rape. It took almost a year for the institution to hold disciplinary hearings and university officials decided not to sanction the players (Williams, 2007).

Williams brought Title IX claims of student-on-student sexual harassment and failure to supervise claims against the university. The United States Court of Appeals for the Eleventh Circuit upheld her Title IX claims against the university administration. The Court of Appeals held that UGA and the University of Georgia Athletic Association (UGAA) were sufficiently proven to be federal funding recipients for Title IX purposes. Secondly, appropriate persons—in particular the athletic director and basketball coaches of the institution—had actual knowledge of:

> (1) Cole's recruitment and admission despite his past misconduct at several other schools; (2) the January 14, 2002 rape involving Cole, Brandon Williams, and Thomas; and (3) the discrimination that Williams faced as a result of UGA's failure to respond adequately to her allegations against Cole, Williams, and Thomas. Additionally, the coach and athletic director had authority to take corrective measures for UGA and UGAA to end the alleged discrimination.
>
> *(Williams, 2007, pp. 1294–1295)*

The Appellate Court went on to explain the Supreme Court standard elicited in *Davis*—that the university exhibited deliberate indifference to the harassment which was clearly unreasonable considering the known circumstances. Recruiting and giving special admission to a student athlete with a history of sexual assault put university officials on notice of the need to educate and supervise athletes regarding the sexual harassment policies of the university. Moreover, UGA failed to adequately supervise or monitor this threat which subjected Ms. Williams to further discrimination.[3]

The University of Georgia was also deliberately indifferent to the harassment by its slow and inadequate response in addressing the matter through its disciplinary process, which took almost a year to conclude. Further evidence of the deliberate indifference of university officials toward Ms. Williams harassment was evident in their lack of action and support for the victim which led to her withdrawal from the university (Williams, 2007). The heinous nature of the rape led by the student-athletes and their telephone calls to the victim afterward was discrimination so "severe, pervasive, and objectively offensive" to satisfy gender discrimination under Title IX (Williams, 2007, p. 1298). Because the violent sexual assault and the cycle of discrimination and deliberate indifference to her attack lasted almost a year, the 11th Circuit reasoned that it ultimately resulted in Ms. Williams' withdrawal and decision not to return to UGA; this effectively barred her from access to an educational opportunity or benefit (Williams, 2007).

Simpson v. Univ. of Colorado Boulder, 500 F.3d 1170 (2007)

Similar to the *Williams* case, the Tenth Circuit Court of Appeals held that the University of Colorado (CU) administration and coaches had prior notice of on-campus sexual assaults by football players and recruits but showed a continued indifference to the problem. Lisa Simpson and Anne Gilmore were sexually assaulted by Colorado football players and high school recruits during a recruiting weekend in early December of 2001. They brought suit against the institution under Title IX.

In its review of the case, the Appellate Court noted the high-level success of the football program over the previous decade. In particular, they highlighted their national championship in 1990 and multiple conference championships including during the 2001 season. Along with the success of the football program, Colorado was also earning a reputation as a hotbed for sexual assaults committed by its football players. A 1989 *Sports Illustrated* article documented the unlawful conduct of CU football players and reported on several cases of sexual assault by members of the football team (Simpson, 2007). In fact, the Boulder District attorney met with university officials regarding community concern about student hostesses[4] being made available to recruits for sex and emphasizing that changes needed to be made to the supervision and protocols for football recruits. Additionally, there was evidence of internal communications between the Chancellor and Athletic Director regarding sexual assaults by football players and the need for clear rules and expectations for recruiting visits (Simpson, 2007).

For example, in September, 2001, a female student athletic trainer was raped by a CU football player. The head coach Gary Barnett met with the victim himself and told the victim that if she pursued the criminal case, her "life would change," and that he was a players' coach and he would support the player (Simpson, 2007, p. 1183). The female student trainer did not press criminal charges and the player faced no significant punishment. These are but a few examples of the atmosphere surrounding the CU football program at that time.

The lead plaintiff in the case, Lisa Simpson, was intoxicated and asleep in her own bed when she was sexually assaulted in her apartment by CU football recruits and players. At the same time in the same room, Ms. Gilmore was sexually assaulted by a player or recruit and she testified she was too intoxicated to consent. Another female student had nonconsensual sex with two players after leaving the apartment and three others were sexually harassed by football players. Ms. Simpson later withdrew from the university, and Ms. Gilmore left the university for a year (Simpson, 2007, p. 1180).

The main question the 10th Circuit Court of Appeals addressed was whether the risk of sexual assault during CU recruiting visits was obvious to the institution such that Title IX liability should be imposed. Based on the institutional officials' knowledge of the risks of sexual assault on campus in general, and the specific history of occurrences on CU's campus specifically involving CU's football recruiting program combined with the inadequate response by university officials and the football coaching staff to the threat to women on campus, it could reasonably be concluded that the institution had actual and prior knowledge of the issue, and that their actions constituted deliberate indifference (Simpson, 2007, pp. 1184–1185). Specifically, the Appellate Court reasoned:

> In sum . . . (1) Coach Barnett, whose rank in the CU Hierarchy was comparable to that of a police chief in a municipal government, had general knowledge of the serious risk of sexual harassment and assault during college-football recruiting efforts; (2) Barnett knew that such assaults had indeed occurred during CU recruiting visits; (3) Barnett nevertheless maintained an unsupervised player-host program to show high-school recruits "a good time"; and (4) Barnett knew, both of the incidents reported to him and because of his own unsupportive attitude, that there had been no change in atmosphere since 1997 (when the prior assault occurred) that would make such misconduct less likely in 2001. A jury could infer that the need for more or different training of player-hosts was so obvious, and the inadequacy so likely to result in Title IX violations, that Coach Barnet could reasonably be said to have been deliberately indifferent to the need.
>
> *(Simpson, 2007, pp. 1184–1185)*

The Court of Appeals remanded the case to be set for trial and in short order the university settled the case prior to trial, agreeing to pay the lead plaintiff Lisa Simpson $2.5 million and $350,000 to Anne Gilmore. The Simpson case gave notice that institutions and athletic departments which create or condone hostile environments may be held liable under Title IX.

As we can see from these examples, in a series of cases, the Supreme Court and US Court of Appeals established that sexual harassment and assault violated Title IX because it denied equal access to educational opportunities under the premise that Title IX promises an educational environment free from discrimination based on sex, sexual orientation, and gender identity. In such cases (i.e., in a school setting), the victim of sexual harassment must prove that:

> (a) she [he or they] is [are] a member of a protected group based on her sex; (b) she [he or they] was [were] subjected to unwelcome conduct of a sexual nature; (c) the conduct was so severe, pervasive, and objectively offensive that it denied equal access to the school's educational opportunities or benefits; (4) a school official with authority to take corrective action had actual knowledge or notice of the behavior; and (5) the school official was deliberately indifferent to the conduct and failed to reasonably respond.
>
> *(Osborne, 2013, p. 563)*

Policy Development Influencing Title IX Sexual Harassment Enforcement

As previously stated, the one-sentence law that is Title IX and the case law discussed earlier have the full force and effect of law. Explaining the details, nuances, and priorities as to how the law is implemented and enforced is the responsibility of the executive branch and its agencies. The Office of Civil Rights (OCR), part of the Department of Education, is charged with developing and enforcing the regulations that govern the working procedural policies of the statute (Carpenter & Acosta, 2005). Federal Regulations are published by executive branch agencies and have the force of law, which entail more specific details and directives to enforce legislation. Regulations are the product of hearings, public comment, and debate prior to being assembled by federal agencies such as OCR and must be approved by Congress to carry the force of law.

On July 21, 1975, Congress approved comprehensive regulations governing Title IX for the first time to guide institutions in implementing the law. From that time forward, the OCR also published policy statements or Dear Colleague Letters (DCL) to further clarify the agencies' stance on interpreting and implementing the existing laws and regulations (related to Title IX, in this case). The policy statements are recommendations that are influenced by the political administration in office and their political appointees.

The first Title IX Policy Interpretations were issued in 1979 by the OCR (OCR, 1979). The original Title IX regulations and policy interpretations focused on participation opportunities, facilities, equipment, financial aid, and developed the three-prong test for compliance. Because of the US political process and election cycles, leadership of federal agencies such as OCR shifts over time, reflecting national election outcomes. Because of this relatively frequent change in leadership, policy interpretations evolve, which makes a summary of current policy most likely outdated by the time of publication. Therefore, I use a recent well-known example of Title IX policy to illustrate the power and effect of policy implementation in the following section.

The 2011 OCR Dear Colleague Letter from the Obama Administration is the most well-known and effective policy example directed at sexual harassment in our nation's public schools (Wilson, 2017). Spearheaded by the then Vice President Joe Biden, the policy was issued by the OCR on April 4, 2011 and entitled, "Dear Colleague Letter: Sexual Violence" and was designated as a *significant guidance document* for funding recipients to meet their obligations under the law (Dear Colleague, 2011). In 2017, the Trump administration rescinded the 2011 guidance letter; however, in March of 2021, President Biden signed an Executive Order to review Title IX policy regulations by June 16, 2021 (Executive Order, 2021). President Biden has promised to restore the Obama Title IX policy guidance, including the 2011 Dear Colleague Letter (The Biden Plan, 2020). A discussion of the 2011 policy letter can serve as illustrative of the impact of such policy tools and in all likelihood, this letter will continue to influence Title IX policy in the near future.

The 2011 Policy Letter had an immediate and significant impact on raising concern surrounding the issue of sexual assault on campus. Although the Supreme Court had determined sexual harassment and assault violated Title IX, school administrators at the scholastic and college level were either reluctant or ignorant of the pervasiveness of the problem. The 2011 Dear Colleague Letter stated bluntly:

> Acts of sexual violence are vastly under-reported. Yet, data show that our nations' young students suffer from acts of sexual violence early and the likelihood that they will be assaulted by the time they graduate is significant . . . When young women get to college, nearly 20% of them will be victims of attempted or actual sexual assault, as will about 6% of undergraduate men.
> *(Dear Colleague Letter, Summary: Sexual Violence, Background, Summary & Fast Facts, 2011, p. 1)*

The purpose of the 2011 DCL was to remind schools of their affirmative responsibility to respond to sexual harassment under Title IX. The 2011 DCL defined sexual violence as:

> Physical sexual acts perpetrated against a person's will or where a person is incapable of giving consent. A number of acts fall into the category of sexual violence, including rape, sexual assault, sexual battery, and sexual coercion.
>
> *(Dear Colleague Letter, 2011, p. 1)*

These alarmingly high rates of (reported) sexual assault on high school and college campuses had been a long-standing concern of then Vice President Biden, and the various institutions nationwide had differing procedures to deal with sexual assaults on their campuses. Institutions could take months to respond and investigate students' reports and complaints; schools differed as to which burden of proof was used to determine responsibility in sexual assault cases, with many opting for a much more difficult *beyond a reasonable doubt* criminal liability type standard. The 2011 DCL provided a clear procedural path to schools creating a framework of consistent standards to respond to sexual assault on campus. OCR published a summary letter to the 2011 DCL which states:

"What Did the 2011 Dear Colleague Letter Do?"

- Provide guidance on the unique concerns that arise in sexual violence cases, such as the role of criminal investigations and a school's independent responsibility to investigate and address sexual violence.
- Provide guidance and examples about key Title IX requirements and how they relate to sexual violence, such as the requirements to publish a policy against sex discrimination, designate a Title IX coordinator, and adopt and publish grievance procedures.
- Discusses proactive efforts schools can take to prevent sexual violence.
- Discusses the interplay between Title IX, FERPA, and the Clery Act relating to the complainant's rights and sanctions facing the perpetrator.

What Are the Institutions/Schools Obligations Regarding Sexual Violence Under Title IX?

- Once a school knows or reasonably should know of possible sexual violence, it must take immediate and appropriate action to investigate or otherwise determine what occurred.
- If sexual violence has occurred, a school must take prompt and effective steps to end the sexual violence, prevent its recurrence, and address its effects, whether or not the sexual violence is the subject of a criminal investigation.
- A school must take steps to protect the complainant as necessary, including interim steps taken prior to the final outcome of the investigation.
- A school must provide a grievance procedure for students to file complaints of sex discrimination, including complaints of sexual violence. These procedures must include an equal opportunity for both parties to present witnesses and other evidence and have the same appeal rights.

- A school's grievance procedures must use the preponderance of the evidence standard to resolve complaints of sex discrimination.
- A school must notify both parties of the outcome of the complaint (Dear Colleague Letter, Summary: Sexual Violence, Background, Summary & Fast Facts, 2011, p. 2).

Conclusions

The 2011 Dear Colleague Letter (DCL) had a profound effect on how institutions addressed sexual assault issues on campuses across the US and gave national attention to the issue with the full attention of the executive branch. It became clear that many schools and universities lacked effective grievance procedures; thus, schools across the country were put on notice to revamp policies or retool their Title IX compliance by hiring and training new staff and rewriting outdated procedures.

The 2011 DCL was effective on many levels. First, it brought national attention to the issue of sexual harassment in our schools when administrators were ignorant or inconsistent in dealing with the issue. Second, it created a national standard which clearly spelled out that institutions needed to resolve complaints promptly and fairly. Third, the 2011 DCL also unified the expected burden of proof in sexual assault cases as a preponderance of the evidence standard which required institutions to find responsibility if the evidence is 50.1 % likely to show that an assault occurred. Fourth, the policy also strongly discouraged schools from permitting parties to directly question or cross-examine each other during a hearing to alleviate potential continuing trauma to victims (Dear Colleague Letter, 2011).

The Trump administration received significant criticism and court challenges for its rollback of the 2011 DCL and regulations perceived to favor respondents by tightening the definition of sexual assault on campus and allowing direct cross-examination of the victim in live hearings. In 2020, a coalition of 18 state attorneys general filed lawsuits challenging the Trump Title IX regulations. California and Massachusetts passed state laws in response to the Trump regulations imposing additional obligations on schools to address sexual misconduct (Anderson, 2020).

Political power shifts over time and subsequent administrations will continue to revise policy through regulation and policy development. Educational institutions and their administrators must continually be vigilant to policy change and manage accordingly. The 2011 Dear Colleague Letter is a prime example of executive policy which had a lasting effect on the process to effectively address the national issue of sexual assault in our nation's schools. It was a mandate for schools to update their staff, training, and procedures to more promptly and fairly respond to this important issue. The 2011 DCL will continue to be an important policy example in the years to come.

Discussion Questions

1. Explain the three major elements of the original Title IX Statute.
2. What is the rationale linking sexual assault to Title IX?
3. Sport is not mentioned in the original statute; why has Title IX become commonly associated with sport?

4. Explain the "deliberate indifference" standard and its application to educational institutions.
5. Explain the significance of administrative guidelines and policies on Title IX enforcement.

Notes

1. As of June 16, 2021, Title IX was expanded by the DOE to include discrimination based on sexual orientation and gender identity, based on the SCOTUS 2020 decision expanding the federal civil rights law to include LGBTQ Americans as a protected class. So, the status has been clarified since the draft was written.
2. Title IX and other Civil Rights-based legislation are grounded is eliminating government discrimination, or state/institution-based discrimination. So, the focus is on institutional liability—what did the institution know and how did they respond—and not as focused on the perpetrator.
3. In terms of policy recommendations for collegiate athletic departments related to transfer athletes, it would behoove them to do background checks or ask/inquire about athletes' previous criminal history or disciplinary actions. Although some recruits may not want to respond honestly, or previous schools may not want to divulge this information over privacy concerns, at least the new school could say they were not deliberately indifferent.
4. This included not only sport hostesses but also other female student workers in places like a student-athlete academic center.

References

Anderson, G. (2020). Attorneys General Sue DeVos, education department over Title IX rule. *Inside Higher Education*. www.insidehighered.com/quicktakes/2020/06/05/attorneys-general-sue-devos-education-department-over-title-ix-rule

Armour, N. (2021). USA gymnastics hoping to settle with survivors, emerge from bankruptcy by this summer. *USA Today*. htpps://www.usatoday.com/story/Oympics/2021/02/26/usa gymnastics-summer settlement-survivors-larry-nassar/6835734002

The Biden Plan to End Violence Against Women. (2020). https://joebiden.com/vawa/

Cannon v. Univ. of Chi., 441 U.S. 677, 717, 99 S. Ct. 1946, 60 L. Ed. 2d 277 (1998).

Carpenter, L. J., & Acosta, R. V. (2005). *Title IX*. Human Kinetics.

Civil Rights Act of 1964, Pub. L. 88–352, 78 Stat. 241 (1964).

Davis ex rel. Lashonda D. v. Monroe County Board of Education, 526 U.S. 629, 119 S. Ct. 1661, 143 L. Ed. 2d 839 (1999).

Dear Colleague Letter: Sexual Violence. (2011, April 4). https://www2.ed.gov/about/offices/list/ocr/letters/colleague-201104.html

Dear Colleague Letter Summary: Sexual Violence, Background, Summary, and Fast Facts. (2011, April 4). https://www2.ed.gov/about/offices/list/ocr/docs/dcl-factsheet-201104.html

Dwyer, C. (2019). Michigan state university to pay $4.5 million fine over Larry Nassar Scandal. *NPR*. www.npr.org/2019/09/05/757909245/michigan-stateuniversity-to-pay-4-5-million-fine-over-larry-nassar-scandal

EEOC Notice 915.050. (1990, March 19). *Policy guidance on current issues of sexual harassment*. https://www.eeoc.gov/laws/guidance/policy-guidance-current-issues-sexual-harassment

Enforcement of Title IX of the Education Amendments of 1972 With Respect to Discrimination Based on Sexual Orientation and Gender Identity in Light of Bostock v. Clayton County 2021, 86 Fed. Reg. 117 (2021, June 22) (to be codified at 34 C.F.R. pts. 32637–32640).

Executive Order on Guaranteeing an Educational Environment Free from Discrimination on the Basis of Sex, Including Sexual Orientation or Gender Identity (2021, March 8). www.whitehouse.gov/briefing-room/presidential-actions/2021/03/08/executive-order-on-guaranteeing-an-educational-environment-free-from-discrimination-on-the-basis-of-sex-including-sexual-orientation-or-gender-identity/

Franklin v. Gwinnett County Pub. Sch., 503 U.S. 60, 76, 112 S. Ct. 1028, 117 L. Ed. 2d 208. (1992).
Gebser v. Lago Vista Independent School District, 524 U.S. 274, 118 S. Ct. 1989. (1998).
Kwiatkowski, M. (2021). Larry Nassar's abuse of gymnasts, including Simone Biles went back decades: Why it still matters in Tokyo. *USA Today*. www.usatoday.com/story/sports/olympics/2021/07/27/usa-gymnastics-larrynasser-abuse-scandal-looms-over-tokyo-olympics/5375279001/
Levenson, E. (2018). Michigan state university reaches $500 million settlement with Larry Nassar victims. *CNN*. www.cnn.com/2018/05/16/us/larry-nassarmichigan-state-settlement/index.html
Masteralexis, L. P., Barr, C. A., & Hums, M. A. (2012). *Principles and practice of sport management*. Jones and Bartlett.
Office of Civil Rights, A Policy Interpretation: Title IX and Intercollegiate Athletics. (1979, November 12). *Federal register* (Vol. 44, No. 239). https://www2.ed.gov/about/offices/list/ocr/docs/t9interp.html
Osborne, B. (2013). Sexual harassment. In D. J. Cotton & J. T. Wolohan (Eds.), *Law for recreation and sport managers* (pp. 559–571). Kendall Hunt.
Rape, Abuse, & Incest National Network (RAINN). (2021). *Campus sexual violence: Statistics*. www.rainn.org/statistics/campus-sexual-violence
Simpson v. Univ. of Colo. Boulder, 500 F.3d 1170, 2007 U.S. Appl LEXIS 21478. (2007).
Strader, D. L., & Williams-Cunningham, J. L. (2017). Campus sexual assault, institutional betrayal, and Title IX. *The Clearinghouse*, *90*(5–6), 198–202.
Title VII of the Civil Rights Act of 1964 sect. 7, 42, U.S.C. 2000e et seq. (1964).
Title IX of the Education Amendments of 1972, 20 U.S.C. 1681 et seq. (1972).
Williams v. Bd. of Regents, 477 F.3d 1282, 2007 U.S. App. LEXIS 2945, 20 Fla. L. Weekly Fed. C 318 (United States Court of Appeals for the Eleventh Circuit. (2007, February 9).
Wilson, R. (2017). How a 20-page letter changed the way higher education handles sexual assault. *Inside Higher Education*. www.chronicle.com/article/how-a-20-page-letter-changed-the-way-higher-education-handles-sexual-assault/

15
SUPPORTING SURVIVORS OF SEXUAL VIOLENCE

Heather Imrie

Introduction

A message to the survivors reading this chapter: I worked with survivors of sexual violence for 15 years, and I can tell you without hesitation that it is not your fault. If you are struggling with self-doubt and self-blame, know you are not alone. It is common for survivors to grapple with self-blame (Frazier, 1990; Sigurvinsdottir & Ullman, 2015). Self-blame is due to a complex set of factors discussed in this chapter but suffice it to say you are not to blame.

The only person to blame is the person who chose to hurt you. The only one to blame is the person who prioritized their wants over your right to autonomy and choice. You deserve to be heard, supported, and believed. You deserve to live in a world without harm. There are people on the other end of a text or phone call at RAINN.org who will listen, believe you, and can help you find support services near you.

My clients found this quote by Maya Angelou comforting, and I hope it helps you, too. "You may not control all the events that happen to you, but you can decide not to be reduced by them" (Angelou, 2009, p. IX). You are deserving of support, and this chapter is about how people can better support you. This chapter is different than the others in this book as I provide actionable things individuals can do to respond positively to survivors and create a culture of support.

Definitions and General Information About Sexual Violence

Scope of the Problem

In this section, I outline the scope and effect of sexual violence and key ideas and definitions that will be used later in the chapter. Throughout this chapter, I use both *victim* and *survivor* to describe people who were sexually assaulted. In general, *victim* is used to describe someone immediately after the rape or assault, and *survivor* is used to describe someone further into their recovery (Rape, Abuse, & Incest National Network, 2021). Either term is acceptable to use when discussing sexual violence.

Chances are you know a survivor of sexual violence. Statistically, every 68 seconds, someone in the United States is sexually assaulted (Morgan & Truman, 2020). Most sexual violence is committed by someone the victim knows (Sinozich & Langton, 2014; Fisher et al., 2000; Morgan & Truman, 2018). One in five women and one in 14 men will survive attempted or completed rape in their lifetime (Smith et al., 2018). Of the 4.4 million incidents of maltreatment reported to Child Protective Services in 2019, almost ten percent were accounts of sexual abuse (Child Welfare Information Gateway, 2021).

In addition, sexual violence is prevalent across the lifespan. One in 53 boys and one in nine girls under 18 are sexually abused or assaulted (Finkelhor et al., 2014; Rape, Abuse, & Incest National Network, 2021). Between the ages of 11 and 18, those numbers drop to one in three girls and one in four boys (Smith et al., 2018). Twenty-three percent of undergraduate women and 5.4% of undergraduate males are victims of sexual violence (Cantor et al., 2015). Further, transgender, genderqueer, and gender non-conforming college students are more likely than their cisgender peers to be sexually assaulted (Cantor et al., 2015). Survivors might be our friends, family, partners, neighbors, colleagues, mentors, teachers, coworkers, classmates, athletes, coaches, or teammates. People who have survived sexual violence cross all genders, races, sexualities, abilities, classes, religions, ethnicities, ages, and other identities and belief systems.[1]

The Effects of Sexual Violence on Survivors

The physical, psychological, and social injuries from sexual violence are life-altering. Physical harms survivors can experience include injuries, sleep disturbances, migraines, and sexually transmitted diseases (RAINN, 2021). Some survivors self-injure, self-medicate with alcohol or drugs, have eating disorders, or commit suicide (RAINN, 2021). Adult survivors of childhood sexual violence are four times more likely to experience depression, PTSD, and self-medicate with drugs and alcohol (RAINN, 2021; Zinzow et al., 2011). Seventy-five percent of survivors experience moderate to severe socio-emotional challenges (Langton & Truman, 2014).

The adverse psychological effects of sexual assault include anxiety, guilt, anger, sadness, distrust, and vulnerability (Chivers-Wilson, 2006). Survivors also experience symptoms of post-traumatic stress disorder, have difficulty concentrating, and anxiety, and depression. Additionally, the social and career impacts can be many; over 65% of victims experience some negative effect on work or school life, increasing to almost 85% if they had a relationship with the person who harmed them (Langton & Truman, 2014). Survivors report loss of friendships and other support groups (Borja et al., 2006; Ellis et al., 1981; Jordan et al., 2014; Langton & Truman, 2014; Schumm et al., 2006). Some of the adverse impacts of sexual violence are the result of or exacerbated by experiencing victim blaming and self-blame.

Victim Blaming, Hindsight Bias, Just World Hypothesis, Rape Myths Self-Blame

Victim blaming is a common but harmful response to stories of sexual violence (Bieneck & Krahé, 2011; Gravelin et al., 2018). Victim-blaming language is where we hold survivors partially or wholly responsible for an assault (Ryan, 1971). Some of the reasons people blame victims are hindsight bias, just world hypothesis, to avoid getting hurt themselves or use it as a cautionary tale to help protect against it happening again to the victim or others (Walster, 1966). Victim blaming sounds and looks different depending on the situation and target of harm (Gravelin et al., 2018).

Hindsight bias, also called "Monday Morning Quarterbacking," can contribute to victim blaming. Hindsight bias makes past events seem more predictable than they would have been at the time (American Psychological Association, 2020). Because we know the outcome, we look for what we assume were the clues as to why something did or did not happen, which can lead to judgment and blame. Hindsight bias is common in cases of rape or sexual assault. Janoff-Bulman et al. (1985) found that hindsight bias increased the likelihood of victim blaming.

Just world hypothesis is the belief in an orderly world where good things happen to good people and bad things happen to bad people (Hafer & Sutton, 2016; Lerner, 1980). This hypothesis helps give people a sense of control and predictability in an unpredictable world. The more one believes that there is a "just world," the more likely one is to blame the victim (Hafer & Sutton, 2016; Lerner, 1980).

Rape myths are beliefs and misinformation about sexual violence that hold survivors responsible for the crime. Bohner et al. (2009) classify four rape myth types. The first type of rape myth is victim blaming. An example of a victim-blaming rape myth is the belief that the way a woman dresses attracts sexual violence. The second type is the belief that most victims lie about sexual violence, or that the majority of reports made to police are false. The third type of rape myth is when someone diminishes the perpetrators' responsibility. An example of this is the saying "boys being boys" to excuse boys and men when they sexually harass or commit sexually violent behavior. The last type of rape myth is the belief that only certain *types* of women are assaulted. This includes sexist, racist, heterosexist, ableist, classist, cis-sexist, and other identity stereotypes that define *good victims* versus *bad victims*. Rape myth acceptance is correlated with victim blaming (Blumberg & Lester, 1991; Cowley, 2014).

Self-blame is when we attribute the harm we experienced to ourselves, our behaviors, and choices rather than to situational factors or others and is common among survivors of sexual violence (Janoff-Bulman, 1979; Saunders et al., 2016). Self-blame is due to a complex set of factors. Some self-blame is due to a long history of victim blaming, and the propagation of rape myths often learned through media, legal institutions, and even friends and family (Baugher et al., 2010; Ullman & Peter-Hagene, 2014).

Moving forward, if we want to create a community of care, belonging, inclusion, and empowerment, we must support survivors of sexual violence. Supporting survivors can happen in several ways. We can support survivors by listening and providing emotional support. We can make sure survivors know what their resources are and help them connect to them. Calling out victim-blaming and debunking rape myths when we hear them also helps. Implementing systemic change by applying consent models and clear and actionable policies is also essential. Finding different ways to support survivors and change the culture to reduce these crimes is critical. By supporting survivors, we can help them feel empowered and provide them access to helping resources. By changing the culture, we can reduce future harm.

Supporting Survivors

While all of this may feel overwhelming to read, know that a positive response from the survivor's community, access to healing resources, and support from friends, family, coaches, and others can help (Campbell, 2006; Campbell et al., 2001; Filipas & Ullman, 2001; Orchowski et al., 2013; Patterson & Tringali, 2014; Relyea & Ullman, 2015; Ullman, 1996). Survivors who perceived positive reactions to their disclosure had better psychological recovery than those who encountered negative ones (Campbell et al., 2001; Frazier et al., 2004; Littleton & Breitkopf, 2006; Steel et al., 2004).

Believe Them

One of the most important things you can say to a survivor of interpersonal violence is that it is not their fault (RAINN, 2021). Reinforce that what happened was not deserved and not something they brought on themselves. Survivors are also not at fault for not anticipating that someone was going to hurt them. Survivors spend a lot of time rehashing what happened; it is not helpful to add to their anxiety by reviewing what happened with them.

Most survivors do not report the crime to anyone in the criminal legal system (Morgan & Truman, 2020). Many survivors fear they will be blamed, not believed, or accused of making a false report (Kilpatrick et al., 2007); however, Lonsway's (2010) meta-analysis found between 2% and 8% of reports of sexual violence to the police are false. Therefore, it is unlikely that the person coming to you for help is lying. If someone tells you they were raped or assaulted, you can believe they are telling you the truth.

If a survivor decides to confide in you, they are likely doing so because they trust you and believe you will support them. Survivors are more likely to report to informal resources like friends, family, and others close to them (Ahrens et al., 2007). A coach, trainer, athletic director, or sport psychology professional may be perceived as both an informal and formal resource in the sport context. As one of these professionals, your response could be essential to the survivor's healing process on multiple levels. Also, to parents, friends, and family, know that your response can be more critical to healing than formal resources (Campbell et al., 2001; Littleton & Breitkopf, 2006).

In addition, negative reactions to disclosure are related to more adverse psychological symptoms (Campbell et al., 1999; Littleton & Breitkopf, 2006; Ullman, 1996). A reaction that is perceived as unsupportive can be more harmful than no reaction at all (Campbell et al., 2001; Littleton & Breitkopf, 2006). On the other hand, positive responses to disclosure have shown improved outcomes for survivors like reduced PTSD symptoms (Filipas & Ullman, 2001). Survivors who are told "I believe you" and are encouraged to talk about what happened have fewer physical and psychological symptoms than those who do not receive such positive responses (Campbell et al., 2001; Littleton et al., 2009). Starting with an affirmation like "I believe you" is a seemingly simple but powerful thing you can say that makes a real difference in a survivor's recovery.

Talk Less and Listen More

Listening to someone seems like an easy thing to do although it can prove to be more complicated than we realize. Often, what we call "listening" is us waiting for our turn to share what we want to say (Osten, 2016). Everyone has done this before. Imagine the last time you argued about politics with someone of the opposite belief as yourself. Reflect and be honest in your assessment: Were you more interested in listening or giving your opinion? When a survivor or anyone looking to you for help asks for your advice, use active listening skills.

Practice Active Listening

The central theme in active listening is to pay attention and concentrate on what the speaker is saying (Alessandra & Hunsaker, 2008; Weger et al., 2010). Do not worry about what you should say or how you can fix it. You cannot fix this, but you can show you care. Concentrate on both what is said and the body language. Look for signs of anxiety. If they seem anxious, ask if they need a break or if they need something to drink. A glass of water or a hot non-caffeinated beverage can help center them and give them a moment to breathe.

Use verbal and non-verbal encouragers to let the person know you are following what they say (Decker, 1989). Non-verbal encouragers are things like nodding your head, leaning forward, and reacting facially to what you are hearing. Verbal encouragers are "yes," "uh-huh," "mmmm," and other small sounds that say to the other person you are engaging in what they are saying. Summarize what you hear to clarify you understood what was said (Skills You Need, 2021). Summarization will also show you are tracking the conversation and give the survivor the chance to make clarifications if you misunderstood (Skills You Need, 2021).

When it is your turn to talk, do not ask the "why" questions (Johnson, 2021). Why questions might include:

> "Why were you there?"
> "Why were you drinking?"
> "Why did you dress that way?"
> "Why were you with that person?"
> "Why were you out that late?"
> "Why didn't you fight back?"
> "Why did you fall asleep?"
> "Why did you go to that party?"
> "Why were you walking alone?"

These are all questions that center the blame on the victim rather than the person who chose to force someone to have sex. Remember that everyone has a right to live a life without threat or assault.

Do ask questions about what survivors need and how you can help. Ask if they need medical attention. Ask if they want you to come with them to see the doctor, make a report, or talk to an advocate. An advocate is someone with training on how to support sexual violence survivors.

Sexual assault advocates support survivors in multiple ways. In the medical realm, advocates explain medical procedures, coordinate clothing for the survivor to wear home, rides home, and provide emotional support and referrals. In the legal realm, advocates explain victims' rights, the criminal and civil legal processes, referrals to lawyers, and provide emotional support during police interviews and court hearings. Advocates can also supply comfort and support to family members though their primary goal is to support the survivor. Advocates have confidentiality, meaning what the survivor tells them is confidential between the survivor and the advocate unless the survivor explicitly gives written permission to speak with other professionals, usually to coordinate legal services or helping resources.

Follow Their Lead and Remember Healing Takes Time

You cannot rush healing which can feel frustrating for survivors and those who care for them. Be patient and remember you cannot force the survivor to *heal faster*. What will help is continuing to be present in the survivor's life. Remember that they are more than what someone did to them. Hyper-focusing on the trauma when the survivor is not making that their focus is not helpful (Kvarnstom, 2018; Substance Abuse and Mental Health Service Administration, 2014).

Rape is a crime where someone takes away someone else's autonomy and control. One way to help survivors take back control is to let them dictate the terms of their recovery. When survivors feel they have control over their healing, they recover faster (Frazier et al., 2005). Also, let the survivor choose what to tell you and when regarding the trauma. Forcing someone to talk about sexual violence can be triggering and is creating another situation where they may feel their choice is being taken away (Kvarnstom, 2018; Substance Abuse and Mental Health Service Administration, 2014). In my practice, survivors often did not want to talk about the assault but did want to talk about the negative impacts the assault had on their life. I have also worked with survivors for whom the assault was ancillary to other matters in their life like housing, employment concerns, the racist response of helpers, and fears of retaliation. We do not choose to define the crisis in their life—they do.

Do not force a victim to do something they do not feel safe doing. To the parents reading this chapter, this won't be easy. I have watched parents force their children to drop out of school because they thought that was best for their child. Several clients told me that they feared telling their parents because they would make them move back home. School and athletics can be part of their recovery process. Engaging with their friends, teammates, and classmates can positively impact survivors' recovery (Frazier et al., 2005). Universities and other higher education institutions typically provide access to counseling and medical resources.

Remember we all respond differently to trauma. Even if it is well-meaning advice, do not tell a survivor how they should feel about what happened, or how they should react. Everyone reacts differently to trauma based on their own history, and even good intentioned advice on how we believe someone should act or feel can be harmful (Substance Abuse and Mental Health Service Administration, 2014).

Talk with the survivor about what feels best for them and then support their choice. As long as survivors are not indicating they will hurt themselves or others, they should have a say in what happens in their lives. This stuff is hard, remember to be patient with yourself, also, as this is also a difficult position to be in. Remember you and those close to the survivor will also need, and deserve, care and support.

Create a Culture of Belonging

A culture of belonging is an equitable and inclusive one where people feel seen and appreciated. Language choice is one aspect of a culture of belonging. Inclusive language is often maligned as *politically correct (P.C.)*. The term P.C. undermines the importance of inclusive language which focuses on respect, inclusion, and dignity. Barcena et al. (2020) describe inclusive language as being "free from words, phrases or tones that reflect discriminatory views" (p. 39) regarding marginalized groups of people. Inclusive language does not support stereotypes, bias, or prejudice (Barcena et al., 2020). Using inclusive language and inclusive examples in your training invites your entire team into the conversation. Use the language the survivor feels comfortable with; for example, while you may define what happened to them as "rape," they may not want to use that word. Regardless of what we call it, taking away someone's autonomy to decide what happens to their body is wrong. When talking about sexual violence, it is critical that everyone feels included in the conversation.

Inclusive language is rooted in resiliency and is a strengths-based approach to communication. The strengths-based approach focuses on people, assets, and personal power (Pattoni, 2012). Using person-first language, such as saying "people with disabilities" rather than "disabled people," enables helpers to focus on the person rather than a diagnosis (Centers for Disease Control, 2020). The term *survivor* is an example of focusing on the strength of rape victims. Inclusive and strengths-based language sends a clear message to community members that they are respected and belong.

Another way to create belonging is by interrupting victim blaming. Be on the lookout for common victim-blaming phrases such as: "What did you expect would happen?"; "You should know better than to . . ."; "If you had been home, this never would have happened." Other phrases that diminish the perpetrator's responsibility are: "This sounds like a miscommunication issue,"; "I'm surprised, they are such a great person,"; "Do you want to ruin their life over mistakes you both made?" When you hear folks asking these questions, take the time to educate them on why these statements or questions are harmful.

Sexist, racist, heterosexist, ableist, classist, cis-sexist, and other identity stereotypes and tropes contribute to victim blaming and create a dangerous narrative about who is believed and who is not. For example, victim blaming specific to people with disabilities is often related to the ableist stereotype and myth that people with disabilities are not sexual and hence could not be the target of sexual violence (Brown, 2017). The rape myth this corresponds with is that rape is a crime of sex rather than one that uses sex as a weapon. Women who are not considered conventionally attractive also hear this when they report rape. Transgender and non-binary folks are often both desexualized and hyper-sexualized, blamed for what happened, and simultaneously denied that someone would hurt them that way. Black girls face adultification which is the imbuing of adult traits to black children; results from Epstein, Blake and González's (2017) study on the adultification of black girls demonstrated that they are seen as less innocent than their white counterparts.

Bias is a component of many rape myths and victim-blaming statements. Taking an anti-sexual violence stance means simultaneously taking a stance against objectification and prejudice in all forms. Creating a culture of support means actively correcting bias speech, victim blaming, and rape myths when you hear them and also eliminating them from your language. Doing so creates an environment where survivors will more likely feel safe coming forward.

Take Every Report Seriously

Remember that with great power comes great responsibility. As a leader in an educational or professional athletic community, it is your responsibility to take all reports seriously and respond appropriately. As a parent, teammate, or friend, your support throughout the reporting process is essential.

Leaders must know the policies and protocols and most importantly follow them. You are not responsible for investigating, but you are responsible for supporting the survivor and making sure they know what will happen next in the system. Regularly update your group about the policies and procedures concerning sexual violence. Know and provide education about your organization's policies regarding retaliation, bullying, gossip, discrimination, and harassment. If there are not clear existing policies regarding these topics in your organization, be proactive and reach out to stakeholders to create them.

Tell Them Their Options

Tell survivors, "I believe you, it is not your fault, and you have options." Victims of crime often feel powerless. They can feel overwhelmed and not able to see options. You can help.

If you know the survivor in a professional capacity, be sure that you and your entire leadership staff have a list of resources. Do not offer the police as the only option or helping resource. The history between rape survivors and the criminal legal system is complicated; the majority of survivors do not report for fear of not being believed or being retaliated against (Department of Justice, 2013). Additionally, we need to consider that not all communities will feel safe working with law enforcement.

The resource list should have information on medical services, advocacy, and counseling services. Be aware that not all services are created equal. Make sure your list is inclusive and offers culturally appropriate resources. An inclusive list means you have organizations listed that understand the unique needs of survivors across myriad cultures, identities, and experiences. If survivors do not feel welcome or understood, the resource will not be a helpful one.

Contextual Issues and Barriers

People often imagine sexual violence as a random act committed in isolation. We reduce it to one person's choice to harm another. But sexual violence is more complicated than one person's choice. Sexual violence is an interplay of societal conventions, personal beliefs, and community response. Setting community norms that will increase respect and decrease harm is important. Survivors know they can count on those leaders and loved ones who they see working for change.

Get Educated and Provide Education on Sexual Violence

It is highly recommended that you and your leadership work with a local rape crisis center to get training in rape crisis advocacy. You are not an advocate, but the course will give you training in everything outlined in this chapter.

Invite educators to come in and hold regular training on consent, rape, healthy relationships, unconscious bias, and bystander intervention. Parents and friends reading this can also attend classes on rape victim advocacy. Look for courses on unconscious bias and on power, privilege, and oppression.

Unequal access to helping resources is rooted in systemic bias. If you do not know where to find educational providers in your area, but you have access to a computer, look online. If you do not have access to a computer, you can call the National Sexual Violence Hotline 1-800-656-4673 for referrals or you can call your state anti-sexual violence coalition. Both the National Sexual Violence Hotline and your state anti-violence coalition can direct you to resources that serve your area. You can learn online through national service providers such as: RAINN; the National Sexual Violence Resource Center; National Coalition of

Anti-Violence Programs; Black Women's Blueprint; Know Your IX; For Ourselves: Reworking Gender Expression (FORGE); National Organization of Asians and Pacific Islanders Ending Sexual Violence; 1 in 6 support for Male Survivors of Sexual Violence; End Abuse of Persons With Disabilities; Strong Hearts Native Helpline; National Indigenous Women's Resource Center; The National Latin@ Network; LGBT National Hotline; National Council of Jewish Women; Asian Pacific Institute on Gender Based Violence; Pennsylvania Coalition Against Rape Faith Based Services Guide; Huddle-Up; and your state and local rape crisis centers and coalitions. Another incredible resource is Raliance, a national collaboration of service providers, researchers, and educators committed to ending sexual violence in one generation. Raliance has a database of sports specific resources for ending domestic and sexual violence. This list is a starting point and not all-inclusive. A list of the websites associated with these groups can be found after the References section.

Barriers to Accessing Resources for Marginalized and Other Underserved Populations

Historically, survivors from marginalized communities have faced systemic bias and other barriers to getting support (Campbell et al., 2001; Flowers et al., 2018). Marginalized populations are groups with less access to resources at the systems level and they experience social, economic, educational, and/or cultural exclusion and discrimination on interpersonal, group, and systems levels (National Collaborating Centre for Determinants of Health, 2021). For example, Black women have not always found counselors or advocates who understand the intersectionality of racism and sexism. Black, Indigenous, and other survivors of color face systemic racism and unequal distribution of healing resources in their communities as compared to primarily white communities. Immigrant and undocumented survivors face fears of deportation and language barriers. LGBTQIA survivors report facing ignorance about their bodies, homophobia, and transphobia from healthcare workers, counselors, and advocates. Folks for whom English is a second language may not find that every healthcare center, counselor, or advocacy organization has staff who can speak their language. Indigenous, Inuit, and Native people do not always have access to advocacy or health care resources and may have to travel hours to access these resources (RAINN, 2019). Additionally, Indigenous, Inuit, and Native sexual violence survivors are statistically assaulted by people from outside their community but often do not feel welcome reporting to resources outside their community (RAINN, 2019). Persons with disabilities face barriers of inaccessible spaces or no services to accommodate persons with visual or hearing impairment. Folks from devout religious backgrounds may only want support from within their faith organizations. Underserved communities are those who have had less access to healthcare services than other groups (U.S. Department of Health and Human Services, 2020). While not part of a marginalized community, male-identified survivors are often underserved by rape crisis services and may fear coming forward due to hegemonic ideas about masculinity and sex (Riccardi, 2010). Again, remember the intersection of identities differently impacts survivors. For example, black male survivors are negatively impacted by both hegemonic masculinity and racist tropes about black men being hypersexual and predatory—making black male survivors virtually invisible (Allen et al., 2020; Livingston, 2021)

If survivors do not feel comfortable utilizing the resources you provide, they will not use them. These barriers, and more, can keep survivors from gaining access to resources that provide support, medical assistance, lessen the impact of PTSD, or give them a place to process what comes next for them in their journey (American Civil Liberties Union, 2015; Office for Victims of Crime, 2002, 2011).

This list may feel like an overwhelming task for you to put together. As mentioned earlier, I recommend always working with experts from local rape crisis centers. They can help you create an inclusive list of resources and help train your staff in everything outlined in this chapter. Education and training will increase both your and your staff's confidence in supporting survivors in your athletic programs, departments, and communities.

Mandated Reporters and Confidentiality

Some of you reading this are mandated reporters who may work with survivors 18 years of age or older in higher education. Mandated reporters are people who students could reasonably believe have authority to address sexual misconduct on campus (White House Task Force to Protect Students from Sexual Assault, 2014). Examples of mandatory reporters in this setting are professors, graduate assistants, coaches, athletic trainers, student advisors, and housing staff. In general, a mandated reporter in higher education must let campus Title IX directors know when a survivor tells them a crime occurred on campus. There are also mandated reporting laws for people working with minors. Mandated reporting laws are different from state to state and RAINN.org has a comprehensive list of rules per state (RAINN, n.d.a). Generally, mandated reporters working with minors are required to call state authorities (RAINN, 2020). Confidentiality when supporting a survivor is critical whether you are a mandated reporter or not.

If you are a mandated reporter on a college campus, let those you are responsible for (i.e., collegiate student-athlete) know up front that you must report what they're telling you to local authorities. Mandated reporters must only tell who they are compelled to inform. The best practice is to consistently let your team or group know that you are required to report and can help connect them to support services.

Trying to inform someone of this responsibility while they are telling you what happened to them is complex. You want to respond with empathy and be supportive. Use your active listening skills and allow yourself to show compassion and concern. Your role is to listen, not judge. You want to help them by providing resources and making sure their immediate health and safety needs are met. Lastly, you need to let them know that while you will not share the information with the team or other staff, you must report it to campus Title IX authorities. Here is an example of how you can protect their rights and still be supportive in this situation:

> Before we go any further, for your protection, I want to remind you that I am a mandated reporter. That means I must report crimes like sexual violence to the Title IX office. I am honored you would trust me with this information and promise that I will not discuss this with anyone other than those I am mandated to tell. I also want you to know I will be here for you. After we talk, I will outline what happens next and, if you want, I can connect you to other support services. Do you have any questions?

Non-Mandated Reporters

For those of you who are not mandated reporters (i.e., parents, friends, and other associates whom the survivor may tell), you, too, should keep this information confidential. However, you may feel the need to process with others. Safe spaces for you to process are confidential sources like a counselor or advocate. Your local rape crisis center can provide you with resources like short-term counseling if you need it. You can also look into Employee Assistance Programs (EAPs) at your worksite for temporary counseling support. The National Sexual Violence Hotline 1-800-656-4673 is also a confidential place you can ask questions and be connected to resources.

Other Things to Consider

Physical Touching or Hugging as Support

An instinct many of us have is to hug or touch someone to comfort them. But, after an assault, this can be a triggering action rather than a comforting one. Always ask before you touch someone, even if hugging or kissing is part of your usual way of greeting each other. Asking for consent may seem awkward at first, but the survivor having autonomy over their body is crucial for recovery. Ask for their consent, and respect the answer, in every situation.

Coaches, mentors, and teachers, rethink your physical interactions with your athletes or students. Survivors of sexual violence often suffer from hyper-sensitivity, hypervigilance, and an increased startle response which makes unanticipated touch very alarming for them (Dunleavy & Slowik, 2012). Hyper-vigilance is a state of heightened awareness where the survivor is constantly scanning their surroundings for signs of threats to their safety (Richards et al., 2014). A startle response is an exaggerated physical fear response to an unexpected stimulus like a loud noise or unexpected touch (Birbaumer & Flor, 2009). Touch without warning or consent can trigger panic, anxiety, or even a flashback in a survivor (Matsakis, 1998). Because of the negative impacts of unanticipated touch, it is recommended you do not tap people on the shoulder or arm or adjust a physical position or stance without their knowledge or permission. This is especially critical for athletic coaches to be aware of as coaching often entails physically assisting athletes with mechanics and movements. The American College of Sports Medicine (ACSM) provides a sample of *Exercise Is Medicine*'s (2021) informed consent for participation in a health and fitness training program form that includes information on touching while being trained. The language used in the consent to participate in training is as follows:

> I also understand that during the performance of my personal fitness training program physical touching and positioning of my body may be necessary to assess my muscular and bodily reactions to specific exercises, as well as to ensure that I am using proper technique and body alignment. I expressly consent to the physical contact for the stated reasons above.
>
> *(Exercise Is Medicine, 2021)*

The National Strength and Sports Conditioning Association (2009) also cites getting informed consent as a best practice in their NSCA Strength and Conditioning Professional Standards and Guidelines paper. The consent to touch form can be problematic if it is approached as the only solution. A signed consent to touch form approaches the concept of consent singularly as a legal, rather than an ethical, practice. Consent is a practice grounded in equitable relations where people have autonomy over their own bodies. It is, of course a legal issue, but more importantly, it is an ethical one. Second, and arguably the more important issue, is that consent to touch can be withdrawn at any time, making the document as the only practice more policy theater than actual protection.

Understandably, asking before every adjustment will make training for some sports almost impossible. Following advocacy models and my own practice with clients, I believe that a multi-pronged approach—where folks are getting information in different ways and in different stages—makes sense. Start by providing a thorough explanation of the athlete-trainer or coach relationship. That can be first in a form as described earlier; however, remember that those forms are not the only piece and consent can be rescinded at any time. Second, describe the kinds of touches that will be necessary to the client, student, or athlete beforehand. Describing what will happen in the session will alert the survivor a touch will be coming and give them the opportunity to agree or limit the areas they are comfortable being touched. Third, you should not assume blanket consent; each time you work with athletes, you should have this discussion. Four, respect the answer means that when an athlete, client, or patient says no, stop, I need a moment or other stop messages we end the behavior. Finally, implement this change at the start of all your training and coaching sessions with all athletes and clients, not just with people you know are survivors.

Some may ask: *Why change the group training dynamic if we have only one report?* First, they may not be the only survivor in your group; statistically, they are likely not the only survivor in the program. Second, establishing consent as the model is a best practice for all aspects of your professional life. Asking for consent to touch and adjust in the start of every program also allows for participants to set boundaries and normalizes consent to touch as a normal activity. Setting a consent model will also help illuminate those who do not follow that standard. Third and finally, it keeps cover for the current survivor and does not shine a light on them as the only one getting new and different treatment. Setting this as a universal policy also helps to negate uncomfortable feelings for the students or athletes.

Ask advocates from local sexual violence advocacy centers to help establish protocols and provide education on consent to your staff. They can also be part of your team; you can contract with them to provide a place for your group members to report incidents or get support. They can also help you brainstorm ways to change your practice habits while still getting the results you need both skill-wise and safety-wise.

Access Support for Yourself, Your Team, or Your Family

I am ending this chapter with a personal note about access support services for yourself. Some of you reading this will be survivors who are now able to help others navigate their trauma. Listening to stories about sexual violence may trigger you. Supporting others can cause a resurgence of some post-traumatic stress symptoms. Your health and welfare are also important. There are resources available for you through RAINN and the other resources listed earlier and in the References section. Even if you are not a survivor, supporting someone through the trauma of sexual violence is hard and you can experience vicarious trauma. Taking care of yourself is important—you matter too.

Make self-care a standard practice for yourself, your team, and your family. Self-care is not one day of massage or taking a day off, although those can be part of your self-care plan. Self-care is a holistic wellness plan which includes taking care of yourself mentally, physically, emotionally, spiritually, and socially (Stoewen, 2017; Substance Abuse and Mental Health Service Administration, 2016). Everyone's self-care plan will be different; however, including physical, mental, social, or spiritual well-being ideas and actions should be in everyone's plan (Stoewen, 2017; Substance Abuse and Mental Health Service Administration, 2016).

Though often portrayed as a reaction to a stressful day, self-care is a plan that should be implemented daily. As leaders, you can implement self-care in your organization in different ways. You can encourage staff to use their personal time off, offer fair compensation, provide access to a variety of snacks and beverages, model and provide education on healthy boundary setting, and more. Remember that you, too, should take time off, deserve fair compensation, and access to other support resources.

Honor boundaries when people set them and implement your own. The cliché of putting on your oxygen mask before helping others is good advice in life; you cannot show up for others if you are not showing up for yourself first. As leaders in your field, modeling these positive behaviors sets a tone that lets your staff know self-care is encouraged. Modeling self-care also helps establish this as a regular practice in your own life. The Substance Abuse and Mental Health Service Administration has a helpful guide to get you and your team started on your self-care journey (Substance Abuse and Mental Health Service Administration, 2016).

Summary

Thank you for taking the time to read this chapter. Your commitment to making the world a more equitable and supportive place for survivors is what is needed to move the dial and mitigate sexual violence. Remember to believe first, remind folks that it is not their fault, and be sure to let them know their options. Be cognizant of barriers to reporting and work to make sure you are creating access for all survivors. If you are a mandated reporter, make sure you are transparent about your responsibilities and let survivors know of your responsibility to report. Keep all reports confidential—do not share information with others. Utilize inclusive and person-first language. Create a safe environment by quashing rumors, victim blaming, and bias speech when you hear it. Practice consent-based models for all interactions in your personal, coaching, and work spaces. Avoid "why" questions and instead ask, "What can I do to help?" Take all reports seriously and respond to them appropriately. Make sure policy and protocols are clear and everyone is trained on how to implement them. Get educated about sexual violence and how you can support survivors. Emphasize self-care both for the survivors and also you, your team, family, and everyone impacted. Finally, reach out to local advocates and educators to help support you on your way. Individual and collective healing is possible—with time.

Discussion Questions

1. What are three things you can say to someone who tells you they were sexually assaulted? How can you support survivors of sexual violence?
2. What barriers to accessing resources do marginalized persons face? How can you help negotiate or eliminate those barriers for your athletes, students, clients, or patients? Further, what is inclusive language and why is it important to creating belonging? How can you create belonging for all survivors in your program? What resources can you utilize to help train staff on inclusivity and belonging for your athletes, students, clients, or patients?
3. Why is self-care important and what would be in your self-care plan?

4. What is victim blaming? What are rape myths and how are they tied to bias? How does Hindsight Bias and Just World Hypothesis contribute to victim blaming?
5. Why is it important to ask before you touch in training and conditioning?

Note

1. Most of this chapter focuses on the experiences of survivors 18 years of age and older. Information about sexual violence victims under 18 will be included but will be limited.

References

Ahrens, C. E., Campbell, R., Ternier-Thames, N., Wasco, S. M., & Sefl, T. (2007). Deciding whom to tell: Expectations and outcomes of rape survivors' first disclosures. *Psychology of Women Quarterly*, *31*(1), 38–49. https://doi.org/10.1111/j.1471-6402.2007.00329.x

Alessandra, T., & Hunsaker, P. L. (2008). *The new art of managing people, updated and revised: Person-to-person skills, guidelines, and techniques every manager needs to guide, direct, and motivate the team* (Revised, Updated ed.). Free Press.

Allen, Q., Metcalf, H. S., & Chunnu, W. N. (2020). Up to no good: The intersections of race, gender, and fear of black men in U.S. society. In T. D. Boyce (Ed.), *Historicizing fear: Ignorance, vilification, and othering* (pp. 19–34). University Press of Colorado.

American Civil Liberties Union. (2015). *Responses from the field sexual assault, domestic violence, and policing (10 25 2015 Report)* [Report]. ACLU.

American Psychological Association. (2020). Hindsight bias. In *APA dictionary of psychology*. American Psychological Association. https://dictionary.apa.org/

Angelou, M. (2009). *Letter to my daughter*. Virago Press Ltd.

Barcena, E., Read, T., & Sedano, B. (2020). An approximation to inclusive language in lmoocs based on appraisal theory. *Open Linguistics*, *6*(1), 38–67. https://doi.org/10.1515/opli-2020-0003

Baugher, S. N., Elhai, J. D., Monroe, J. R., & Gray, M. J. (2010). Rape myth acceptance, sexual trauma history, and post-traumatic stress disorder. *Journal of Interpersonal Violence*, *25*(11), 2036–2053. https://doi.org/10.1177/0886260509354506

Bieneck, S., & Krahé, B. (2011). Blaming the victim and exonerating the perpetrator in cases of rape and robbery: Is there a double standard? *Journal of Interpersonal Violence*, *26*(9), 1785–1797. https://doi.org/10.1177/0886260510372945

Birbaumer, N., & Flor, H. (2009). Psychobiology. In *Comprehensive clinical psychology* (pp. 115–172). Elsevier. https://doi.org/10.1016/b0080-4270(73)00218-2

Blumberg, M. L., & Lester, D. (1991). High school and college students' attitudes toward rape. *Adolescence*, *26*(103), 727–729.

Bohner, G., Eyssel, F., Pina, A., Siebler, F., & Viki, G. T. (2009). Rape myth acceptance: Cognitive, affective, and behavioural effects of beliefs that blame the victim and exonerate the perpetrator. In M. A. H. Horvath & J. M. Brown (Eds.), *Rape: Challenging contemporary thinking* (pp. 17–45). Willan.

Borja, S. E., Callahan, J. L., & Long, P. J. (2006). Positive and negative adjustment and social support of sexual assault survivors. *Journal of Traumatic Stress*, *19*(6), 905–914. https://doi.org/10.1002/jts.20169

Brown, L. Z. (2017). Ableist shame and disruptive bodies: Survivorship at the intersection of queer, trans, and disabled existence. In *Religion, disability, and interpersonal violence* (pp. 163–178). Springer International Publishing. https://doi.org/10.1007/978-3-319-56901-7_10

Campbell, R. (2006). Rape survivors' experiences with the legal and medical systems. *Violence Against Women*, *12*(1), 30–45. https://doi.org/10.1177/1077801205277539

Campbell, R., Ahrens, C. E., Sefl, T., Wasco, S. M., & Barnes, H. E. (2001). Social reactions to rape victims: Healing and hurtful effects on psychological and physical health outcomes. *Violence and Victims*, *16*(3), 287–302. https://doi.org/10.1891/0886-6708.16.3.287

Campbell, R., Sefl, T., Barnes, H. E., Ahrens, C. E., Wasco, S. M., & Zaragoza-Diesfeld, Y. (1999). Community services for rape survivors: Enhancing psychological well-being or increasing trauma? *Journal of Consulting and Clinical Psychology, 67*(6), 847–858. https://doi.org/10.1037/0022-006x.67.6.847

Cantor, D., Fisher, B., Chibnall, S., Townsend, R., Lee, H., Bruce, C., & Thomas, G. (2015). *Report on the AAU campus climate survey on sexual assault and sexual misconduct* (Association of American Universities) [Report]. Westat. www.aau.edu/sites/default/files/%40%20Files/Climate%20Survey/AAU_Campus_Climate_Survey_12_14_15.pdf

Center for Disease Control and Prevention. (2020, September 16). *Communicating with and about people with disabilities*. Disability and Health Promotion, Communicating with and about People with Disabilities | CDC.

Child Welfare Information Gateway. (2021). *Child maltreatment 2019: Summary of key findings* [Report Summary]. U.S. Department of Health and Human Services, Administration for Children and Families, Children's Bureau. www.childwelfare.gov/pubs/factsheets/canstats/

Chivers-Wilson, K. A. (2006). Sexual assault and post-traumatic stress disorder: A review of the biological, psychological and sociological factors and treatments. *McGill Journal of Medicine, 9*(2). https://doi.org/10.26443/mjm.v9i2.663

Cowley, A. D. (2014). Let's get drunk and have sex. *Journal of Interpersonal Violence, 29*(7), 1258–1278. https://doi.org/10.1177/0886260513506289

Decker, B. (1989). *How to communicate effectively*. Kogan Page.

Department of Justice, Office of Justice Programs, Bureau of Justice Statistics, Female Victims of Sexual Violence, 1994–2010. (2013). https://bjs.ojp.gov/content/pub/pdf/fvsv9410.pdf

Dunleavy, K., & Kubo Slowik, A. (2012). Emergence of delayed post-traumatic stress disorder symptoms related to sexual trauma: Patient-centered and trauma-cognizant management by physical therapists. *Physical Therapy, 92*(2), 339–351. https://doi.org/10.2522/ptj.20100344

Ellis, E. M., Atkeson, B. M., & Calhoun, K. S. (1981). An assessment of long-term reaction to rape. *Journal of Abnormal Psychology, 90*(3), 263–266. https://doi.org/10.1037/0021-843x.90.3.263

Epstein, R., Blake, J., & González, T. (2017). Girlhood interrupted: The erasure of black girls childhood. *SSRN Electronic Journal*. https://doi.org/10.2139/ssrn.3000695

Exercise Is Medicine. (2021). *Informed consent for participation in a health and fitness training program* [Form]. American College of Sports Medicine. Retrieved July 10, 2021, from www.exerciseismedicine.org/wp-content/uploads/2021/04/EIM-informed-consent.pdf

Filipas, H. H., & Ullman, S. E. (2001). Social reactions to sexual assault victims from various support sources. *Violence and Victims, 16*(6), 673–692.

Finkelhor, D., Shattuck, A., Turner, H. A., & Hamby, S. L. (2014). The lifetime prevalence of child sexual abuse and sexual assault assessed in late adolescence. *Journal of Adolescent Health, 55*(3), 329–333. https://doi.org/10.1016/j.jadohealth.2013.12.026

Fisher, B. S., Cullen, F. T., & Turner, M. G. (2000). *The sexual victimization of college women: Research report (NCJ-182369)* [Report]. Department of Justice, National Institute of Justice; Bureau of Justice Statistics. https://files.eric.ed.gov/fulltext/ED449712.pdf

Flowers, Z., Lovelace, T., Holmes, C., Jacobs, L., Sussman, E., Wee, S., & Muro, M. (2018). *Showing up: How we see, speak, and disrupt racial inequity facing survivors of domestic and sexual violence* (A Report on From Margins to Center Listening Sessions, An Initiative of The Racial & Economic Equity For Survivors Project Grant No. 2015-TA-AX-K016 awarded by the Office on Violence Against Women) [Report]. Center for Survivor Agency & Justice. https://csaj.org/document-library/REEP_Report_Showing_Up_FINAL.pdf

Frazier, P. A. (1990). Victim attributions and post-rape trauma. *Journal of Personality and Social Psychology, 59*(2), 298–304. https://doi.org/10.1037/0022-3514.59.2.298

Frazier, P. A., Mortensen, H., & Steward, J. (2005). Coping strategies as mediators of the relations among perceived control and distress in sexual assault survivors. *Journal of Counseling Psychology, 52*(3), 267–278. https://doi.org/10.1037/0022-0167.52.3.267

Frazier, P. A., Tashiro, T., Berman, M., Steger, M., & Long, J. (2004). Correlates of levels and patterns of positive life changes following sexual assault. *Journal of Consulting and Clinical Psychology, 72*(1), 19–30. https://doi.org/10.1037/0022-006x.72.1.19

Gravelin, C. R., Biernat, M., & Bucher, C. E. (2019). Blaming the victim of acquaintance rape: Individual, situational, and sociocultural factors. *Frontiers in Psychology, 9*. https://doi.org/10.3389/fpsyg.2018.02422

Hafer, C. L., & Sutton, R. (2016). Belief in a just world. In *Handbook of social justice theory and research* (pp. 145–160). Springer. https://doi.org/10.1007/978-1-4939-3216-0_8

Janoff-Bulman, R. (1979). Characterological versus behavioral self-blame: Inquiries into depression and rape. *Journal of Personality and Social Psychology, 37*(10), 1798–1809. https://doi.org/10.1037/0022-3514.37.10.1798

Janoff-Bulman, R., Timko, C., & Carli, L. L. (1985). Cognitive biases in blaming the victim. *Journal of Experimental Social Psychology, 21*(2), 161–177. https://doi.org/10.1016/0022-1031(85)90013-7

Johnson, E., R. N., & Sane-A, C. (2021). *How to support someone who has been sexually assaulted*. HealthPartners. Retrieved July 19, 2021, from www.healthpartners.com/blog/how-to-support-survivors-of-sexual-assault/

Jordan, C. E., Combs, J. L., & Smith, G. T. (2014). An exploration of sexual victimization and academic performance among college women. *Trauma, Violence, & Abuse, 15*(3), 191–200. https://doi.org/10.1177/1524838014520637

Kilpatrick, D. G., Resnick, H. S., Ruggiero, K. J., Conoscenti, L. M., & McCauley, J. (2007). *Drug-facilitated, incapacitated, and forcible rape: A national study*. Bibliogov.

Kvarnstom, E. (2018). *How to avoid retraumatization when talking to your loved one with PTSD*. BrightQuest Treatment Centers [Online article]. www.brightquest.com/blog/avoid-retraumatization-talking-loved-one-ptsd/

Langton, L., & Truman, J. (2014). *Socio-emotional impact of violent crime*. Bureau of Justice Statistics.

Lerner, M. (1980). *The belief in a just world: A fundamental delusion (critical issues in social justice)* (1980th ed.). Springer.

Linvingston, J. (2021). *Predator or prey: The analysis of gender and race on the perception of black men as sexual assault victims* (Undergraduate Journal). Caravel Undergraduate Research Journal Spring 2021. https://sc.edu/about/offices_and_divisions/research/news_and_pubs/caravel/archive/2021_spring/2021_predator_prey.php

Littleton, H., Axsom, D., & Grills-Taquechel, A. (2009). Sexual assault victims' acknowledgment status and revictimization risk. *Psychology of Women Quarterly, 33*(1), 34–42. https://doi.org/10.1111/j.1471-6402.2008.01472.x

Littleton, H., & Breitkopf, C. (2006). Coping with the experience of rape. *Psychology of Women Quarterly, 30*(1), 106–116. https://doi.org/10.1111/j.1471-6402.2006.00267.x

Lonsway, K. A. (2010). Trying to move the elephant in the living room: Responding to the challenge of false rape reports. *Violence Against Women, 16*(12), 1356–1371. https://doi.org/10.1177/1077801210387750

Matsakis, A. T. (1998). *Trust after trauma: A guide to relationships for survivors and those who love them* (1st ed.). New Harbinger Publications.

Morgan, R. E., & Truman, J. J. (2018). *Criminal victimization, 2017* [Bulletin]. Department of Justice, Office of Justice Programs, Bureau of Justice Statistics. ojp.gov

Morgan, R. E., & Truman, J. J. (2020). *Criminal victimization, 2019* [Bulletin]. Department of Justice, Office of Justice Programs, Bureau of Justice Statistics. ojp.gov

National Collaborating Centre for Determinants of Health. (2021). *Glossary marginalized populations* [Glossary]. Retrieved July 23, 2021, from https://nccdh.ca/glossary/entry/marginalized-populations

The National Strength and Sports Conditioning Association. (2009). NSCA strength and conditioning professional standards and guidelines. *Strength & Conditioning Journal, 39*(6), 1–24. https://doi.org/10.1519/ssc.0000000000000348

Office for Victims of Crime. (2002). *Chapter 8 respecting diversity: Responding to underserved victims of crime* [Archived webpage]. www.ncjrs.gov/ovc_archives/nvaa2002/chapter8.html

Office for Victims of Crime. (2011). *Put the focus on victims: Consider culture and diversity* [SART ToolKit resources for sexual assault response teams]. OVC. www.ncjrs.gov/ovc_archives/sartkit/focus/culture-print.html

Orchowski, L. M., Untied, A. S., & Gidycz, C. A. (2013). Social reactions to disclosure of sexual victimization and adjustment among survivors of sexual assault. *Journal of Interpersonal Violence, 28*(10), 2005–2023. https://doi.org/10.1177/0886260512471085

Osten, C. (2016, October 5). Are you really listening, or just waiting to talk? *Psychology Today*. Retrieved July 15, 2021, from www.psychologytoday.com/us/blog/the-right-balance/201610/are-you-really-listening-or-just-waiting-talk

Patterson, D., & Tringali, B. (2014). Understanding how advocates can affect sexual assault victim engagement in the criminal justice process. *Journal of Interpersonal Violence, 30*(12), 1987–1997. https://doi.org/10.1177/0886260514552273

Pattoni, L. (2012, May 12). Strengths-based approaches for working with individuals insight 16. *Iriss*. Retrieved July 14, 2021, from www.iriss.org.uk/resources/insights/strengths-based-approaches-working-individuals

Rape, Assault, & Incest National Network. (2019). *Barriers to reporting in indigenous communities*. The Rape, Assault, Incest National Network, Barriers to Reporting in Indigenous Communities | RAINN. Retrieved August 1, 2021.

Rape, Assault, & Incest National Network. (2020). *Mandatory reporting requirements: Children*. The Rape, Assault, Incest National Network. Retrieved June 21, 2021.https://apps.rainn.org/policy/compare/children.cfm

Rape, Assault, & Incest National Network. (2021). *Effects of sexual violence*. The Rape, Assault, Incest National Network. Retrieved June 29, 2021, from www.rainn.org/effects-sexual-violence

Rape, Assault, & Incest National Network. (n.d.a). *State law database*. The Rape, Assault, Incest National Network, RAINN | Rape, Abuse and Incest National Network. Retrieved June 21, 2021.

Relyea, M., & Ullman, S. (2015). Unsupported or turned against: Understanding how two types of negative social reactions to sexual assault relate to post-assault outcomes. *Psychology of Women Quarterly, 39*(1), 37–52. https://doi.org/10.1177/0361684313512610

Riccardi, P. (2010). Male rape: The silent victim and the gender of the listener. *Primary Care Companion to the Journal of Clinical Psychiatry, 12*(6), PCC.10l00993. https://doi.org/10.4088/PCC.10l00993whi

Richards, H. J., Benson, V., Donnelly, N., & Hadwin, J. A. (2014). Exploring the function of selective attention and hypervigilance for threat in anxiety. *Clinical Psychology Review, 34*(1), 1–13. Retrieved July 1, 2021, from https://doi.org/10.1016/j.cpr.2013.10.006

Ryan, W. (1971). *Blaming the victim* (1st ed.). Orbach & Chambers.

Saunders, B. A., Scaturro, C., Guarino, C., & Kelly, E. (2016). Contending with catcalling: The role of system-justifying beliefs and ambivalent sexism in predicting women's coping experiences with (and men's attributions for) stranger harassment. *Current Psychology, 36*(2), 324–338. https://doi.org/10.1007/s12144-016-9421-7

Schumm, J. A., Briggs-Phillips, M., & Hobfoll, S. E. (2006). Cumulative interpersonal traumas and social support as risk and resiliency factors in predicting PTSD and depression among inner-city women. *Journal of Traumatic Stress, 19*(6), 825–836. https://doi.org/10.1002/jts.20159

Sigurvinsdottir, R., & Ullman, S. E. (2015). Social reactions, self-blame, and problem drinking in adult sexual assault survivors. *Psychology of Violence, 5*(2), 192–198. https://doi.org/10.1037/a0036316

Sinozich, S., & Langton, L. (2014). *Rape and sexual assault victimization among college-age females, 1995–2013 (NCJ 248471)* [Special Report]. Department of Justice, Office of Justice Programs, Bureau of Justice Statistics. Rape and Sexual Assault Victimization Among College-Age Females, 1995–2013. ojp.gov

Skills You Need. (2021). *Active listening*. Retrieved July 21, 2021, from www.skillsyouneed.com/ips/active-listening.html

Smith, S. G., Zhang, X., Basile, K. C., Merrick, M. T., Wang, J., Kresnow, M., & Chen, J. (2018). *The national intimate partner and sexual violence survey: 2015 data brief—updated release*. Centers for Disease Control and Prevention.

Steel, J., Sanna, L., Hammond, B., Whipple, J., & Cross, H. (2004). Psychological sequelae of childhood sexual abuse: Abuse-related characteristics, coping strategies, and attributional style. *Child Abuse & Neglect*, 28(7), 785–801. https://doi.org/10.1016/j.chiabu.2003.12.004

Stoewen, D. L. (2017). Dimensions of wellness: Change your habits, change your life. *The Canadian Veterinary Journal = La Revue Veterinaire Canadienne*, 58(8), 861–862.

Substance Abuse and Mental Health Service Administration. (2014). *A treatment improvement protocol: Trauma-informed care in behavioral health services tip 57* [Guide]. U.S. Department of Health and Human Services Publication No. (SMA) 13-4801. TIP 57 Trauma-Informed Care in Behavioral Health Services (samhsa.gov)

Substance Abuse and Mental Health Service Administration. (2016). *Creating a healthier life: A step-by-step guide to wellness* [Guide]. https://store.samhsa.gov/sites/default/files/d7/priv/sma16-4958.pdf

Ullman, S. E. (1996). Social reactions, coping strategies, and self-blame attributions in adjustment to sexual assault. *Psychology of Women Quarterly*, 20(4), 505–526. https://doi.org/10.1111/j.1471-6402.1996.tb00319.x

Ullman, S. E., & Peter-Hagene, L. (2014). Social reactions to sexual assault disclosure, coping, perceived control, and ptsd symptoms in sexual assault victims. *Journal of Community Psychology*, 42(4), 495–508. https://doi.org/10.1002/jcop.21624

U.S. Dept. of Health & Human Services. (2020). *Serving vulnerable and underserved populations* [Online training guide]. www.hhs.gov/guidance/sites/default/files/hhs-guidance-documents/006_Serving_Vulnerable_and_Underserved_Populations.pdf

Walster, E. (1966). Assignment of responsibility for an accident. *Journal of Personality and Social Psychology*, 3(1), 73–79. https://doi.org/10.1037/h0022733

Weger, H., Castle, G. R., & Emmett, M. C. (2010). Active listening in peer interviews: The influence of message paraphrasing on perceptions of listening skill. *International Journal of Listening*, 24(1), 34–49. https://doi.org/10.1080/10904010903466311

White House Task Force to Protect Students from Sexual Assault. (2014, April). *Intersection of Title IX and the Clery Act* [Press release]. White House Task Force.

Zinzow, H. M., Resnick, H. S., McCauley, J. L., Amstadter, A. B., Ruggiero, K. J., & Kilpatrick, D. G. (2011). Prevalence and risk of psychiatric disorders as a function of variant rape histories: Results from a national survey of women. *Social Psychiatry and Psychiatric Epidemiology*, 47(6), 893–902. https://doi.org/10.1007/s00127-011-0397-1

Websites

1 in 6 Support for Male Survivors of Sexual Violence (https://1in6.org/)
Asian Pacific Institute on Gender Based Violence (www.api-gbv.org/)
Black Women's Blueprint (www.blackwomensblueprint.org/)
End Abuse of Persons With Disabilities (www.endabusepwd.org/)
For Ourselves: Reworking Gender Expression (FORGE) (https://forge-forward.org/)
Huddle-Up to End Gender Violence (https://powerofthehuddle.com/)
Know Your IX (www.knowyourix.org/)
LGBT National Hotline (www.glbthotline.org/national-hotline.html)
National Coalition of Anti-Violence Programs (https://avp.org/ncavp/)
National Council of Jewish Women (www.ncjw.org/)
National Indigenous Women's Resource Center (www.niwrc.org)
The National Latin@ Network (www.nationallatinonetwork.org/)

National Organization of Asians and Pacific Islanders Ending Sexual Violence (https://napiesv.org/)
The National Sexual Violence Resource Center (www.nsvrc.org/)
Pennsylvania Coalition Against Rape Faith Based Services Guide (https://pcar.org/)
RAINN (www.rainn.org/)
Raliance www.raliance.org/
Strong Hearts Native Helpline (https://strongheartshelpline.org/)

16
THE "SEX TALK" IS A CONTINUAL CONVERSATION

Tanya Prewitt-White, Lauren Spirov, and Sarah Malone

Myths Surrounding Sexual Misconduct

Let's start with the heavy reality that there is a lot of false information that circulates about sexual misconduct and the survivors affected by it. For example, a few myths include the following: (a) sexual assault is believed to be an act of lust and passion that can't be tamed; however, we know sexual assault is about power and control and is not motivated by sexual gratification (Groth et al., 1977); (b) survivors lie about sexual misconduct when the fact is that only 2–5% of sexual misconduct cases are falsely reported, the same percentage as for other felonies (Lonsway et al., 2009); (c) sexual assaults and misconduct do not happen *that* often when statistics suggest there are an average of 293,066 survivors of sexual assault ages 12 years and older each year in the United States (US). This means that one sexual assault happens every 107 seconds in the US (Department of Justice, 2013); and, (d) the majority of sexual assaults occur by individuals unknown to the victim when in reality the majority of sexual assaults are often between people who know one another or exist in the same space (e.g., teammates, both student-athletes at an institution, classmates, colleagues, relatives, friends of friends or family friends; Department of Justice, 2017). Further, of child and teen victims of sexual violence, 93% know the perpetrator (Department of Justice, 2000).

Like many issues that feel overwhelming, readers may be thinking, "The problem feels insurmountable; there's little I can do about it." In actuality, if all of us did our part, we would have the power to mitigate sexual misconduct in sport and society. Like many issues, what we can control and the actions we can take start at the personal level. Noble and Vermillion (2014) found that coaches and administrators believed sexual abuse is a serious problem, though they did not view it as an issue at their respective institutions or organizations. Denial and avoidance do nothing to ameliorate sexual misconduct in sport, in communities or in families.

Start by Breaking the Silence

To begin, we can recognize that sexual misconduct happens everywhere and that student-athletes, coaches, athletic staff, and administrators in our departments and programs are

DOI: 10.4324/9781003125884-19

affected by sexual misconduct. Yes, looking oneself in the mirror and getting comfortable talking about sex with our own children, with the children or young adults we coach and/or influence as well as among ourselves as professionals, colleagues, and adults is our first step in mitigating sexual misconduct. Owning there are likely both survivors and those who have caused harm in our presence is important. We know it is uncomfortable. Yet, like many things in life, it does get easier to talk about sex and sexual misconduct prevention with practice; if it does not, we need to be open with being uncomfortable because our ability to co-create transformational spaces of care and healing depend on it.

Most all of us have been in a situation that felt awkward when talking about sex. Many families and societies do not normalize sex and sexuality, let alone talking about it because doing so is often considered taboo. The second author, Lauren reflected on her role as nanny to a Norwegian family in her early twenties. The children were between ages two and four years old and at bedtime, asked to read an illustrated children's book about bodies and sex, specifically. Growing up in an environment where talking about sex was uncommon, Lauren immediately clammed up at this request. Ultimately, Lauren read the story, and the children were open, receptive, and interested in having these conversations. Later, when recounting the evening with the children's mother, their mom confidently stated that sexual education at an early age was in fact very common in Norway.

Findings from Wilson et al.'s (2010) US study focused on understanding parents' perspectives in talking to their pre-teenage children about sex align with Lauren's experience; results suggested that parents believed it is important to talk to their children about sex, that doing so can be effective, but many had not done so. Primary barriers were parents' perception that their children were too young in addition to not knowing how to talk to their children about the subject (Wilson et al., 2010). You may be one of these parents or adults in a child's life.

As the reader, this chapter may be uncomfortable for you. As authors, we are asking you to be open to the discomfort in these conversations. When people are open, feel heard, and accepted as their authentic selves, the change happens. Further, when children and emerging adults recognize sex and sexual curiosity is not to be accompanied by shame, we have the possibility to mold safer communities, organizations, families, and intimate relationships. Certainly, we all have different values or comfort levels when talking about sex; yet, one truth cannot be ignored—kids are interested in sex and at an early age at that. Breuner and Mattson (2016) who serve on the Committee of Psychosocial Aspects of Child and Family Health for the American Academy of Pediatrics share that it is normal for children as young as two years to explore sexual behavior such as masturbation or show interest in genitalia. Sex and sexuality are a normal part of human life and have been since the beginning of human existence and yet so many of us learn(ed) to silence the questions we have and feel shame for sexual attraction and/or urges we might experience.

Ignoring or denying children and emerging adults' sexuality serves to make it unfamiliar and makes harm more likely when sex inevitably happens. Further, shielding youth and emerging adults from sex will not prevent them from having sex or protect them from harmful sexual experiences. Abstinence education has repeatedly been shown to be ineffective. Stanger-Hall (2011) sought to evaluate the sex education approach in the US and to identify the most effective educational approach for reducing the high US teen pregnancy rates. Based on a national analysis of all available state data, results indicated that abstinence-only education did not reduce and likely increased teenage pregnancy rates (Stanger-Hall, 2011). Silence around sex only breeds harm because if children and student-athletes do not learn about sex from reputable sources, then they will learn about it from the Internet, and namely, from pornography. While pornography is not inherently bad, it lacks the disclaimers children and young people would need to understand that many of the depictions are merely fantasies. Moreover, sexual consent occurs off camera (if it happens at all).

When sex is openly and accurately discussed, it reduces harm because it can prevent or mitigate sexual assault via discussions of what harm looks like, what to expect during sex, and how to successfully implement boundaries. The harm resulting from sexual assault is immensely detrimental to the lives of those affected and is often the impetus of mental health challenges such as PTSD, anxiety, depression, and/or substance use disorders (Kilpatrick et al., 2003) that result in reduced academic and athletic performance (Bennett et al., 2021; Brewer & Thomas, 2019; Stirling & Kerr, 2013). Thus, it is imperative for adults, coaches, and sport stakeholders to do their part in preventing or, at minimum, mitigating this harm. When we look at it this way, our discomfort around discussions of sex with youth may become less sustainable. If our goal is to prevent sexual violence, we would be prudent to begin openly discussing sex with our youth and empowering them to have autonomy over their bodies.

Safe Sex: Conversations on Consent

As the reader, you may be thinking, "How do we empower youth to have autonomy over their bodies?" Simply put, we, as parents and guardians, should teach them consent and make consent an ongoing conversation in all we do. We typically think safe sex is talking about condoms and forms of birth control; this is part of the conversation yet consent needs to come first and is very much related to safety. It is the determining factor between what is assault and what is not; therefore, youth should have a strong understanding of what this means, how to give it, and when it is being received or not. Violating a person's consent is harmful—period.

Consent means agreeing to something (Freitas, 2018). It is important for us to recognize we should not violate consent because it harms people instead of thinking we should not do it because we will get into (social/legal) trouble. We need to talk about not only how to give and receive consent but also the why to—we cannot be stuck in a "yes means yes" mentality because technical consent is not enough (Freitas, 2018). Consent means actively agreeing to take part in a sexual activity with a partner(s). It is "an explicitly, communicated, reversible, mutual agreement made when all parties are capable of making that decision. Consent may or may not be verbal, but it has to be unambiguous and voluntary" (Rotman, 2020, p. 13). This might be touching, kissing, oral, vaginal, or anal sex.

We should also strive for enthusiastic consent and sex should be enjoyable and pleasurable for sexually intimate partners. It is about saying "yes" to what you want, not just saying no to what you do not want to do. You can use both words and body language to say or show what you want and don't want. Getting and giving consent before taking part in any sexual activity with a partner means you can both be sure that the sexual activity is wanted and agreed to; and, if you're not sure if your partner(s) consent(s) to something, you do not have consent (Rape, Assault, & Incest National Network, 2021a). Always ask because doing something sexual to someone without their consent is sexual assault (Beres, 2014; Gilbert, 2018). Consider for example, the act of removing a condom without consent which is called *stealthing*;

in the winter of 2021, California lawmakers attempted to pass a bill making it illegal when it occurs without verbal consent (Fiorzi, 2021).

Now is a good time to debunk the myth that wearing revealing clothing, behaving provocatively, or being under the influence of conscious-altering substances means the victim was "asking for it." This type of victim blaming is harmful and simply untrue. In fact, perpetrators select and often groom victims (see Chapter 4 of this text); the victim's behavior or clothing choices do not mean that they are consenting to sexual activity (National Child Traumatic Stress Network, 2010).

A Deeper Dive Into Consent

First, we strongly advise athletic departments and organizations to consider offering educational sessions and workshops with vested professionals who are skilled in facilitating conversations for stakeholders, coaches, and athletes to better understand consent. Offering stakeholder/coach and athlete sessions separately may allow for greater openness and discussion while also ensuring all parties receive the same information. Skilled professionals can also guide athletic departments in further discussions and walk alongside organizations and stakeholders invested in the conversations and experiences necessary to mitigate sexual misconduct.

Now, let's get a little more detailed so readers have a solid understanding of consent. If we are going to be the adults who guide and inform young people, we must be educated and comfortable to share what we know. First, consent is not a *given*; just because someone consented to an act in the past, it does not mean they have consented to it forever. Second, consent is not a free pass. Saying "yes" to one act does not mean you have to consent to other acts. Each requires its own consent. For example, saying "yes" to oral sex does not automatically mean that someone is saying "yes" to intercourse or other forms of sexual activity. Third, consent can be revoked at any time; even if individuals are in the middle of sexual activity, if someone begins to feel uncomfortable, they always have the right to stop. Fourth, it's not consent if someone is afraid to say "no" and it's not consent if you're being manipulated, pressured, or threatened to say "yes." Fifth, it's also not consent if you or a partner is unable to legitimately give consent which includes being asleep, unconscious, under the influence of conscious-altering substances, or not able to understand what you're saying "yes" to in the moment (Beres, 2014). Finally, depending on the state or country one is in, the age of consent varies; thus, it is incredibly important that parents, coaches, and administrators educate children and emerging adults about the age of sexual consent (e.g., statutory rape laws) in their location.

If you had not recognized it before, and you are still reading this chapter, you are most likely beginning to understand there is nuance to consent. In a healthy relationship, giving and receiving consent is an ongoing process, and establishing boundaries by discussing what sexual acts partners are comfortable with prior to engaging in sexual activity is crucial. As a rule of thumb, always ask first and be clear and direct with your partner(s) about what you are comfortable and uncomfortable with doing. Individuals should not feel embarrassed to refuse sexual activity, to be honest, and/or to speak their truth and feelings. If the other person is not listening to you, you have every right to leave the situation. Consent is about respecting each other; but, when that respect is absent, youth and all people should feel free to act in a way that restores their sense of safety.

There are numerous ways to give and withhold consent. For example, you can express what you want and do not want through your words, body language, hand gestures, or facial expressions. Thus, consent is about being in tune with your sexual partner, concerned with their pleasure and comfort.

True consent requires the capacity to read and hear the verbal and nonverbal cues of your partner, but it also presumes that both partners enter a sexual situation with the capacity to value and regard each other as people worthy of care, concern and attention that consent requires (Freitas, 2018, p. 17).

Below are some examples of verbal and non-verbal consent:

Verbal and Non-Verbal Consent Examples

Examples Verbal Consent	*Examples Non-verbal Consent*
An enthusiastic moan	Direct eye contact
"I want you/it/that"	Pulling closer
"That feels good" or "Don't stop"	Nodding yes
"I still want to . . ."	Smiling
"I'm sure" or "I want you"	Touching and caressing
"Yes!" or "More!"	Loose/open arms and legs
"I'm ready" or "I want this"	Comfortable naked

Lack of consent or non-consent looks and feels much different from consent. Again, it is important to remember someone cannot provide consent to sexual activity when incapacitated by conscious-altering substances and if they are not of the legal age in your state or country to provide consent. Below are some examples of verbal and non-verbal non-consent:

Verbal and Non-Verbal Non-Consent Examples

Examples Verbal Non-Consent	*Examples Non-verbal Non-Consent*
"No" or "Maybe" or "I want to but . . ."	Avoiding eye contact
"Please don't."	Pushing you away
"Please stop" or "Stop"	Avoiding touch
"I can't" or "I'm not ready"	Crying; looking sad, or fearful
"This feels wrong"	Tense, stiff or closed arms and/or legs
"I want to but not right now"	Turning away
"I don't want to do this anymore"	Silent

In summary, when thinking about consent, remember it can be withdrawn at any time and everyone has the right to change their mind. Even if someone has consented to a sexual activity previously, it does not mean they have consented to every following sexual activity. Also, if a partner withdraws consent, or says they do not want to carry on, respect their choice and stop immediately. We can think about consent in some of the following ways:

- Did you and your partner(s) both/all agree to sex?
- Did you both/all agree to every sexual activity you did?

- Did you feel you could say "no" to anything you did not want to do?
- Could the person(s) you were with openly say "no" to you without feeling pressure?
- Is it what you wanted to do?
- Is this what the person you were with wanted to do?

If the answer is "no" to any of these questions, it is not consent and may have been sexual assault or sexual coercion.

Sexual Coercion Is Not Consent

Sexual coercion is the act of using pressure, alcohol or drugs, or force to have sexual contact with someone against his, her, or their will and includes persistent attempts to have sexual contact with someone who has already refused (RAINN, 2021b). In a relationship where sexual coercion is occurring, there is a lack of consent, and the coercive partner does not respect the boundaries or wishes of the other. Sexual coercion generally involves constant begging to make someone feel obligated to do something they do not want to do. It's not consent if a partner is or partners are being manipulated, pressured, or threatened to say "yes."

We can think of sexual coercion as a spectrum or range. It can vary from someone verbally egging a partner on to someone forcing another to have sexual contact with them. It can be verbal, physical, and emotional, in the form of statements or actions that make a person feel pressure, guilt, humiliation or shame (RAINN, 2021b). Sexual coercion could also be present when an athlete is being groomed in sport. As an example, a college athlete may feel obligated to perform sexual acts with a coach (who has power over them) for playing time, keeping a scholarship, and/or to remain on the team (see Chapter 4). An individual can also be made to feel forced through more subtle actions. For example, a partner might make their significant other feel like they owe them sex because they are in a relationship or because they have had sex before, or because they spent money on them or took them on a trip or bought them a gift. It might also be assumed that because someone went home with them that they are entitled to have sex. They certainly are not.

Additional forms of coercion may include giving compliments that sound extreme or insincere as an attempt to get someone to agree to something they do not want to do. Or, they may offer drugs and alcohol to reduce someone's inhibitions. We often may not think of buying someone multiple drinks as sexual coercion but if we take a more critical stance, we can see more clearly it is.

Further, a partner may say, "sex is the way to prove your love for me" or "if I don't get sex from you, I'll get it somewhere else." Pressuring someone to feel obligated to sexual activity is coercion. The person may continue to pressure the individual after they say "no" by trying to normalize their sexual expectations. For example, an individual may say, "I need it, I'm a sexual being." In all the earlier situations, know that these are coercive acts and are not consent.

As parents/caregivers, coaches, and stakeholders in the sport, and individuals invested in the healthy development of children and young people, we can start early in teaching children they have power over and choices regarding their bodies. We can teach and instill in children that others, even family members, parents, and athletic coaches, can only hug them or touch their bodies when they have been given permission to do so (see Chapters 4 and 15). In the first author, Tanya's family, they teach their children "my body, my choice" sending the message to not only the children but also the adults in their sphere of influence that no one, not even their parents, can touch their bodies without the children's consent. The conversation can begin here, and it needs to continue as children grow and gain greater access to digital devices, the Internet and become more sexually curious.

Safe Sex in the Virtual Age

Children cannot unsee what has been seen and this makes it imperative for adults to commit to having healthy and sex-positive conversations with children before children are exposed to sex via media, the Internet, their friend groups, or even their own experience(s). The average age for children's first exposure to Internet pornography is 13 years (Bischmann & Richardson, 2017). No matter readers' individual viewpoints on pornography, we might all agree that pornography exposed to children misconstrues what sex is and how to have a healthy sexual, consensual relationship. Pornography is not intended to educate children on sex; however, it may be many children's educational source. Currently, the top pornography site, Pornhub, is the third biggest bandwidth consuming company behind Google and Netflix, having more daily visits than Netflix, Amazon, and Twitter combined. Further, studies indicate 90% of teens have viewed porn online and this is partly due to increased smartphone usage among children and adolescents (Hartford Healthcare, 2021).

As adults, we must recognize that accessing pornography content has become incredibly easy for young people and in a way, pornography has become the source of sex education for them. Most children, if not intentionally accessing pornography, are only a few clicks away from accidentally accessing it on the Internet and if children have not had affirming and healthy conversations about sex prior to viewing pornography, children may be left with guilt, shame, false realities, and uncertainty around sexual relationships. Moreover, pornography exposure over time can lead to an increase in sexual dysfunction or decrease in relationship satisfaction; though, parental and adult discussions about pornography, consent, and safe sex can mitigate risks with pornography consumption.

Further, while sexual activity and the prevalence of having sexual intercourse are decreasing among high school-aged children (American College of Obstetricians and Gynecologists, 2016) sexting has become a more common form of sexual exploration. Sexting is defined as "the sending or receiving of sexually explicit or sexually suggestive images (photos or video) usually via mobile devices" (Patchin & Hinduja, 2020, p. 1). Sexting can also be a form of coercion used to see what boundaries can be pushed or how far one will go in sexually explicit conversation and/or in sharing nude photos.

Murphy and Spencer (2021) conducted research with women and men from the ages of 18 to 22 who reflected on their accounts of sexting experiences as adolescents. From their research, Murphy and Spencer learned sexting is part of the coming-of-age culture today and is central to normal adolescent sexual growth and development (2021). As more communication and human "connection" occurs over digital devices, we should not find it alarming that sexual exploration in youth is following suit with the trend. Thus, as adults we might better serve young people by acknowledging sexting as a normal part of sexual growth and development to help young people traverse the risks of sexting and establish healthy ways to navigate *safe* sexting behavior (Murphy & Spencer, 2021).

Unfortunately, some children who have found themselves sexting have faced significant reputational, educational, and legal trouble. Minors found participating in sexting can be charged criminally depending on interpretations of child pornography statutes (Patchin &

Hinduja, 2020). For example, in 2010, when Phillip Alpert, 18 years old at the time, was upset with his 16-year-old girlfriend he shared explicit images she had shared with him to her contact list. He had forgotten he had even done so and was later arrested for charges on child pornography and is now registered as a child sex offender (Mabrey & Perozzi, 2010). We also know that children as young as 14 years have been charged as felons for distributing child pornography when sharing explicit images of themselves, even when the image was shared without their consent (Patchin & Hinduja, 2020).

This provides even more reason to talk with young people and emerging adults about the possible consequences of sexting while equipping them with the knowledge necessary to reduce harm that might result. It is not about encouraging sexting behaviors, but recognizing young people are sexually curious, and some may explore behaviors with or without informed counsel from trusted adults. Patchin and Hinduja (2020, p. 141), academic researchers in political science and criminology, provide ten lessons on safe sexting we can share with adolescents and young adults who are developmentally ready for the conversation while protecting themselves and others:

1. If someone sends you a sext, do not send it to—or show—anyone else. This could be considered non-consensual sharing of pornography, and there are laws prohibiting it and which outline serious penalties (especially if the image portrays a minor).
2. If you send someone a sext, make sure you know and fully trust them. "Catfishing" is where someone sets up a fictitious profile or pretends to be someone else to lure you into a fraudulent romantic relationship (and, often, to send sexts). It happens more often than you think. You can, of course, never really know if they will share it with others or post it online but do not send photos or videos to people you do not know well.
3. Do not send images to someone who you are not certain would like to see it (make sure you receive textual consent that they are interested). Sending unsolicited explicit images to others could also lead to criminal charges.
4. Consider boudoir pictures. Boudoir is a genre of photography that involves suggestion rather than explicitness. Instead of nudes, send photos that strategically cover the most private of private parts. They can still be intimate and flirty but lack the obvious nudity that could get you in trouble.
5. Never include your face. Of course this is so that images are not immediately identifiable as yours but also because certain social media sites have sophisticated facial recognition algorithms that automatically tag you in any pictures you would want to stay private.
6. Make sure the images do not include tattoos, birthmarks, scars, or other features that could connect them to you. In addition, remove all jewelry before sharing. Also consider your surroundings. Bedroom pictures could, for example, include wall art or furniture that others recognize.
7. Turn your device's location services off for all your social media apps, make sure your photos are not automatically tagged with your location or username, and delete any metadata digitally attached to the image.
8. If you are being pressured or threatened to send nude photos, collect evidence when possible. Having digital evidence (such as screenshots of text messages) of any maliciousness or threats of sextortion will help law enforcement in their investigation and prosecution (if necessary) and social media sites in their flagging and deletion of accounts.

9. Use apps that provide the capability for sent images to be automatically and securely deleted after a certain amount of time. You can never guarantee that a screenshot was neither taken, nor that another device was not used to capture the image without you being notified but using specialized apps can decrease the chance of distribution.
10. Be sure to promptly delete any explicit photos or videos from your device. This applies to images you take of yourself, and images received from someone else. Having images stored on your device increases the likelihood that someone's parent, the police, or a hacker will find them. Possessing nude images of minors may have criminal implications. In 2015, for example, a North Carolina teen was charged with possessing child pornography, although the image on his phone was of himself.

Remember, we do not have to have all the answers, but we can create a safe space for young adults and athletes to talk about sex with us. It can be as simple as sharing these ten lessons and asking an intermixed group of young people and adults (e.g., athletes and coaching staff on your team and/or your family) what surprises them from the list or what they did not already know. Encourage everyone to be honest and non-judgmental. As authors, we trust you will be surprised by the open conversation and learning that ensues.

The *Sex Talk* Is Not a Single Talk but an Ongoing Conversation

If you are still reading you may be feeling overwhelmed and asking yourself, "can I even do this—it feels too daunting?" or "what can I do today?" The answer: begin talking about sex and sexual relationships long before children are interested and/or exposed to sexting, pornography, and/or engaging in sexual relationships. Talk about sex before there is a sexual misconduct case or allegation on your team, athletic department, campus, or in your own family.

But, most importantly, the *sex talk* is not just one talk but a culmination of conversations that should begin long before children are contemplating having sex and/or in romantic relationships. Talking about sex is one topic families find difficult to do well, often leaving parents/caregivers tongue tied and filling the room with awkward and pregnant pauses (Feiler, 2013). As adults, we may have been socialized to not talk about sex with our elders let alone our own or other people's children. Though, we would be wise to start talking about sex before children are even verbal (Silverberg, 2015).

Talking About Sex With Young Children

It is never too early to start talking about sex. The American Academy of Pediatrics (2016) recommends speaking to children as young as 18 months about sexuality. When children are babies, we can properly name and identify body parts. Also, giving names (e.g., your wee wee, dinkey, or rosebud) for body parts might give the idea to children that there is something wrong or bad with the proper name (American Academy of Pediatrics, 2016). We should never shame children about their curiosity by laughing or giggling, even when we find their questions comical. It is best to keep our responses brief and ask children if they want or need to know more (Feiler, 2013). These conversations are more normalized in some cultures and families and may feel uncomfortable, unorthodox, and/or premature; but, on all accounts materialize as being beneficial in the healthy development of sexual relationships and experiences in children's and future adults' lives.

Tanya, the first author, is a parent of two young children and empathizes with how society quiets and discourages such practices. When her eldest son was two and a half years old, he began asking many questions on how his younger sibling was going to "get out of momma's belly." It was a moment of reckoning as a parent. Was she going to avoid or divert the conversation or was she going to say, "I go to the hospital and the doctor brings out the baby?" Or was she going to say, "magic" or give them "the story of the stork?" While not attempting to minimize any of the choices others might have decided to make, she opted with scientific truth. She shared that when the baby was being born that she might be in some pain as she was planning to stay home as long as possible during labor before having the care and guidance of her midwife at the hospital. She also did not want her son to be scared or feel that it was unnatural for her to moan or appear to be in pain during contractions. She assured her son she was strong and when his younger sibling was ready that she would push hard, and the baby would ultimately leave her body through her vagina. Yes, she said "vagina." At the time, her son seemed happy with that and neglected to ask any more follow-up questions. Admittedly, Tanya felt a bit of relief.

Though, the very next day when picking her son up from daycare the daycare provider met her with eyes wide open stating:

> Your son told me all about how your baby will be born and I did not know what to say or how to respond?! He said you would push the baby out of your vagina!

Tanya still laughs when she thinks about this as if to imply she told her child a lie. Culturally, we have undermined the awesomeness of humanity to continue from generation to generation and the strength and power of the human body to be a portal for new life.

As you can imagine, the conversations have continued and the fascination and perplexity of how babies are created and brought into this world has only led to more questions. Over the course of the last two years, Tanya and her partner continue to use scientific terms so that their children do not have to unlearn any more in this life than will already be brought on by society. Not only does this (hopefully) encourage trust between a parent and child, but it also provides a foundation for conversations about sex in the future.

If we are looking for books to read with young children to open up conversations, we could start with Silverberg's trilogy (2012, 2015, 2016). The first book, *What Makes a Baby: A Book for Every Kind of Family and Every Kind of Kid* (2012) is an inclusive children's book for preschoolers to age eight that reflects all children and families so most will be able to educate their children without having to erase their own experience. The second book, *Sex Is A Funny Word: A Book About Bodies, Feelings And You* (2015) is a comic book for children between the ages of eight to ten that includes children and families of all makeups, orientations, and gender identities. Finally, the third book, *You Know, Sex: About Bodies, Gender, Puberty and Other Things* (2016) grounds sex education for pre-teens in social justice and addresses modern day conversations including, but not limited to, body autonomy, safety in our media-saturated world, pornography, masturbation, power, and pleasure and being a decent human being. If we do nothing else, reading these books with children and being open to the conversations and questions that ensue is a great place to start.

Talking About Sex With Adolescents

Pre-teen and teenage years are a time of development and transition, and we know young people are more likely to begin having sex each year they grow older (Witwer et al., 2018). Moreover, in 2017, 57% of 12th graders had sexual intercourse, while one-fifth of ninth graders had and one of every 10 students reported experiencing sexual violence in the past year (Witwer et al., 2018). The challenge is that most caregivers, adults, and organizations begin talking about sex with children after it is too late. As a rule of thumb, the best time to talk about sex is before children are interested in having it.

When children reach the point of sexual intercourse, 40% do so without first talking with their parents about birth control or sexually transmitted diseases (The American College of Obstetricians and Gynecologists, 2016). Further, adolescents who discuss sexuality and contraception with a parent or guardian are more likely to use contraception consistently and are less likely to become pregnant (Amialchuk & Gerhardinger, 2015). In national surveys conducted by The National Campaign to Prevent Teen and Unplanned Pregnancy, teens report that their parents have the greatest influence over their decisions about sex. Most teens also say they share their parents' values about sex and making decisions about delaying sex would be easier if they could talk openly and honestly with their parents (Albert, 2012).

So, we know children want to talk with parents/caregivers about sex but if parents are not doing so, we might ask ourselves, "where are children learning about sex then?" The answer could include friends, television, social media, and/or pornography. Here, as authors, we want to address the reader who feels it is not their place to talk about sex with athletes or youth within their sphere of influence. First, we want to remind you of your responsibility to care for the well-being of young people and that educating children and emerging adults about sex is not encouraging them to have sex; and second, that you are hands down a better resource than television or pornography. We encourage you not to doubt your ability and potential positive impact.

Further, if we do not think talking about sex matters, we should consider that in Europe, where research conveys that sex is more openly discussed within families and public education, teenagers have sex an average of two years later, and the rate of teen pregnancy is eight times lower than in the US (Feiler, 2013). For those of us fumbling for where to start Feiler (2013) also provides four rules for the sex talk:

> (1) *Blow jobs are sex, too*. ("You can't imagine how many girls [and children] think oral sex doesn't count."); (2) *always use a condom*. ("I usually give a quick demonstration on my finger. The school nurse is not allowed to."); (3) *if you're not mature enough to buy a condom yourself, you're not mature enough to have sex*. "(I tell the kids, until your brain catches up with your bodies you really should hold off."); and (4) *only have sex when you have nothing left to share*. ("If you can pick your nose in front of them, if you can share any thought with them, if you can tell them "no," then you're beginning to understand").
>
> *(p. 130)*

Most importantly, when talking with adolescents about sex be open, withhold judgment and relax. Look for unique opportunities to have conversations (i.e., after a relevant television show, after a storyline on the news, or following up conversations from their health class earlier in the day). Having conversations early and often over time makes more of a difference than a single conversation. Building a healthy dialogue about sexuality also minimizes feelings of shame, guilt, or other negative feelings that may emerge when a child/emerging adult is curious about sex and/or interested in having it. Also, recognize that if a child/emerging adult comes to you with questions about sex that they trust you and feel comfortable enough to do so. This in and of itself is an honor; be sure to treat it as such. Lastly, this is worth reading again. Know that talking about sex in healthy ways does not mean you are encouraging them to have it; however, you are better educating young people for when the time comes in their lives when they choose to engage in sexual intercourse.

Talking About Sex With Young Adults

We may make assumptions that we are the last people young and emerging adults want to discuss sex with. We have found this to be far from the truth. Co-creating space for both university students and student-athletes to talk about sex has made us aware that young people are craving open and honest conversations in a non-judgmental environment full of communal care and curiosity. Many share they have never talked about sex with a trusted adult and others acknowledge they have many questions but do not know who to ask or who might feel comfortable having the conversation.

Yes, some of us may feel that it is not our role or that we do not want to overstep boundaries or feel unprepared or anxious. If these are some of your thoughts, we charge readers to grapple with the thought that both our individual and collective refusal to address sexual misconduct in our spheres of influence plays a role in co-creating systemic and pervasive harm affecting young children and emerging adults in our care. We all have a role to play.

When we create an environment where the genuine needs and concerns of young people are expressed, we learn they desire to talk about their views on being sex positive, the positives and negatives of waiting until marriage, the pressures they feel to have sex as well as their curiosity about sex, their qualms on hookup culture, their struggles with social media as it relates to their body image, and romantic relationships among other topics. As professionals and adults, we can choose to provide this space if we equip ourselves and if we do not feel comfortable doing so, we can, at minimum, call on others trained and able to do so effectively.

Before creating space for a conversation on sex with young adults, we would be wise to be aware of the unique challenges youth coming of age today have as it pertains to sex. First, we cannot discredit the impact social media and cell phones have on young people's ability for in-person intimacy and relationship building. Think of this for a moment: more and more young people have full "conversations" and/or most of their relationships, both romantic and platonic, built via SnapChat and text messages. Thus, we have a generation of young people with fewer experiences having intimate, in-person conversations with one another and yet they have sexual urges and curiosities just as every generation before them.

Now, add to this the hookup culture prevalent in society today. The sexual contract of a hookup involves: (1) some form of sexual intimacy; (2) the sexual interaction being brief; and/or (3) neither party getting emotionally attached (Freitas, 2018). The hookup conveys sexual ambivalence—not having feelings for one's partner. However, if you recall from earlier in the chapter, expressing you do not care about someone is counter to consent. We must facilitate conversations on sex and consent amid hookup culture rather than disregarding or shunning the culture. We can endorse sex positivity and recognize that hookup culture "disregards sexual agency, desire and communication" (Freitas, 2018, p. 15). We should be open to reckoning with and asking student-athletes and young people their thoughts on hookup culture. By doing so, we can better understand the challenges emerging adults face when navigating their personal and sexual lives. Trust us when we say, if you ask, young people are eager to share.

Keep in mind that, though, we may not have the same experiences, but we can empathize with the challenges emerging adults face. We can walk alongside them as they decide how to have conversations with their sexual partners. For example, we can help young people explore the importance of having conversations like *"is it just sex"* or "do we/I have romantic feelings and hope for developing a relationship?" We can create space to discuss how the hookup culture comes with accompanying gender norms or stereotypes and we/they can disrupt them. We can share with young people that the responsibility to have a condom falls on all parties who intend to have sex with someone with a penis (not just on males to have them). We can encourage them to seek out professionals who can walk them through birth control options and where and which birth control is right for them. We can be open about pornography and not vilify young people if/when they admit they consume it and remind them pornography is fantasy and performance, not (necessarily) what they should expect or strive for in intimate or sexual relationships.

Further, when we are aware that 15- to 24-year-olds account for almost half of all new sexually transmitted disease (STD) infections, we can ensure young people are educated on how STDS are spread, how to be safe and have conversations that minimize shame and stigmas surrounding STDs (CDC, 2021). We can normalize and uplift queer sex and sexuality and not place our values on those in our midst by being open to conversations on asexuality, demisexuality, and polyamory. Most importantly, we can do our part in ensuring emerging adults are informed and equipped with the knowledge they need to make informed decisions in their sex lives, so they and their sexual partners are safe.

Conclusion

We would be wise to make conversations on sex more than a one-time educational event that teaches technicalities and induces shame. We must start grappling with conversations on power, connection, autonomy, and care because to get to a place where consensual and safe sexual intimacy is cultural, we all, not just a few of us, must be invested in talking about sex to change the culture. Navigating conversations of sex and/or sexual violence only when it creates problems is reactive in a world where proactive action is required. Sport claims to be a powerful force of good for young people and it is time we live up to our claim as stakeholders.

To begin, we can ask ourselves what fears or concerns we have talking about sex and/or sexual misconduct? Then, we can talk through our thoughts and feelings with trusted colleagues and adults so we are aware of what might surface for us and/or an area of ignorance we may have that requires us to further educate ourselves. We would be wise to remind ourselves it is a courageous and necessary responsibility to create space for youth and emerging adults to feel brave and open when talking about sex with us. Most importantly, it is best we begin today rather than wait until we will feel (more) comfortable talking about sex with young people. Just like sport skills, our skill and comfort of talking about sex improves with practice. Let's be open to being and remaining uncomfortable and improve one conversation at a time.

Discussion Questions

1. How do you envision normalizing conversations on safe sex and consent in your family, athletic department, and your sphere of influence?
2. What fears or concerns do you have talking about sex with your child athlete, athletes you coach, or student-athletes you work with in your organization?
3. What do you need to further learn to feel (more) comfortable talking about sex with youths and emerging adults?
4. What, in sport and culture, makes talking about sex feel taboo?

References

Albert, B. (2012). *With one voice: America's adults and teens sound off about teen pregnancy*. The National Campaign to Prevent Teen and Unplanned Pregnancy. Retrieved March 15, 2021, from http://thenationalcampaign.org/ resource/one-voice-2012

American Academy of Pediatrics. (2016). *Sexual behaviors in young children: What's normal, what's not?* Retrieved August 3, 2021, from www.healthychildren.org/English/ages-stages/preschool/Pages/Sexual-Behaviors-Young-Children.aspx

American College of Obstetricians and Gynecologists. (2016). Comprehensive sexuality education, Committee Opinion No. 678, *Obstetrics & Gynecology*, *128*, e227–e230, Retrieved July 17, 2021, from www.acog.org/Clinical-Guidance-and-Publications/Committee-Opinions/ Committee-on-Adolescent-Health-Care/Comprehensive-Sexuality-Education

Amialchuk, A., & Gerhardinger, L. (2015). Contraceptive use and pregnancies in adolescents' romantic relationships: Role of relationship activities and parental attitudes and communication. *Journal of Development and Behavioral Pediatrics*, *36*, 86–97.

Bennett, E. R., Snyder, S., Cusano, J., McMahon, S., Zijdel, M., Camerer, K., & Howley, C. (2021). Supporting survivors of campus dating and sexual violence during COVID-19: A social work perspective. *Social Work in Health Care*, *60*(1), 106–116. https://doi-org.proxy.cc.uic.edu/10.1080/00981389.2021.1885566

Beres, M. A. (2014). Rethinking the concept of consent for anti-sexual violence activism and education. *Feminism & Psychology*, *24*(3), 373–389. https://doi-org.proxy.cc.uic.edu/10.1177/0959353514539652

Bischmann, A., & Richardson, C. (2017). *Age and experience of first exposure to pornography: Relations to masculine norms*. Poster Session, American Psychology Association Convention.

Breuner, C., & Mattson, G. (2016). Sexuality education for children and adults. *Pediatrics*, *138*(2), e20161348. https://doi.org/10.1542/peds.2016-1348

Brewer, N. Q., & Thomas, K. A. (2019). Intimate partner violence and academic performance: The role of physical, mental, behavioral, and financial health. *Social Work in Health Care*, *58*(9), 854–869. https://doi-org.proxy.cc.uic.edu/10.1080/00981389.2019.1659905

Center for Disease Control and Prevention. (2017, September 21). *STDs in adolescents and young adults, 2016 sexually transmitted diseases surveillance*. Retrieved July 16, 2021, from www.cdc.gov/std/stats16/CDC_2016_STDS_Report-for508WebSep21_2017_1644.pdf

Department of Justice, Office of Justice Programs, Bureau of Justice Statistics. (2000). *Sexual assault of young children as reported to law enforcement*. Department of Justice.

Department of Justice, Office of Justice Programs, Bureau of Justice Statistics. (2013). *Female victims of sexual violence, 1994–2010*. Department of Justice.

Department of Justice, Office of Justice Programs, Bureau of Justice Statistics. (2017). *National crime victimization survey, 2015–2019*. Department of Justice.

Feiler, B. (2013). *The secrets of happy families: Improving your mornings, rethink family dinner, fight smarter, go out and play and much more*. Harper Collins Publisher.

Fiorzi, P. (2021, February 10). California could become the first state to make it illegal to remove a condom without consent. *The Washington Post: Social Issues*. www.washingtonpost.com/nation/2021/02/10/condom-removal-bill/

Freitas, D. (2018). *Consent on campus: A manifesto*. Oxford University Press.

Gilbert, J. (2018). Contesting consent in sex education. *Sex Education, 18*(3), 268–279. https://doi-org.proxy.cc.uic.edu/10.1080/14681811.2017.1393407

Groth, A., Burgess, W., & Holmstrom, L. (1977). Rape: Power, anger, and sexuality. *American Journal of Psychiatry, 134*(11), 1239–1243. Pubmed.gov.

Hartford Healthcare. (2021). *Dealing with today's teen issues*. Retrieved July 21, 2021, from https://hartfordhealthcare.org/health-wellness/health-resources/health-library/detail?id=te7273

Kilpatrick, D., Ruggiero, K., Acierno, R., Saunders, B., Resnick, H., & Best, C. (2003). Violence and risk of PTSD, major depression, substance abuse/dependence, and comorbidity: Results from the national survey of adolescents. *Journal of Consulting and Clinical Psychology, 71*(4), 692–700.

Lonsway, K., Archambault, J., & Lisak, D. (2009). False reports: Moving beyond the issue to successfully investigate and prosecute non-stranger sexual assault. *The Voice, 3*(1).

Mabrey, V., & Perozzi, D. (2010). *"Sexting": Should child pornography laws apply?* Retrieved July 26, 2021, from https://abcnews.go.com/Nightline/phillip-alpert-sexting-teen-child-porn/story?id1-410252790

Murphy, D., & Spencer, B. (2021). Teens' experiences with sexting: A grounded theory study. *Journal of Pediatric Healthcare, 35*(4), 387–400. https://doi-org.proxy.cc.uic.edu/10.1016/j.pedhc.2020.11.010

National Child Traumatic Stress Network. (2010). *It's never your fault: The truth about sexual abuse*. National Center for Child Traumatic Stress.

Noble, J., & Vermillion, M. (2014). Youth sport administrators' perceptions and knowledge of organizational policies on child maltreatment. *Children and Youth Services Review, 38*, 52–57. https://doi.org/10.1016/j.childyouth.2014.01.011

Patchin, J. W., & Hinduja, S. (2020). It is time to teach safe sexting. *Journal of Adolescent Health, 66*(2), 140–143. https://doi-org.proxy.cc.uic.edu/10.1016/j.jadohealth.2019.10.010

Rape, Assault, & Incest National Network. (2021a). *What consent looks like*. The Rape, Assault & Incest National Network. Retrieved July 31, 2021, from www.rainn.org/articles/what-is-consent

Rape, Assault, & Incest National Network. (2021b). *Statistics*. The Rape, Assault & Incest National Network. Retrieved July 31, 2021, from www.rainn.org/statistics

Rotman, I. (2020). *A quick and easy guide to consent*. Limerence Press.

Silverberg, C. (2012). *What makes a baby: A book for every kind of family and every kind of kid*. Seven Stories Press.

Silverberg, C. (2015). *Sex is a funny word: A book about bodies, feelings and you*. Seven Stories Press.

Silverberg, C. (2016). *You know, sex: About bodies, gender, puberty and other things*. Seven Stories Press.

Stanger-Hall, K., & Hall, D. (2011). Abstinence-only education and teen pregnancy rates: Why we need comprehensive sex education in the U.S. *PLoS One, 6*(10), e24658. https://doi.org/10.1371/journal.pone.0024658

Stirling, A. E., & Kerr, G. (2013). The perceived effects of elite athletes' experiences of emotional abuse in the coach-athlete relationship. *International Journal of Sport and Exercise Psychology, 11*(1), 87–100.

Wilson, E. K., Dalberth, B. T., Koo, H. P., & Gard, J. C. (2010). Parents' perspectives on talking to preteenage children about sex. *Perspectives on Sexual and Reproductive Health, 42*(1), 56–63. https://doi.org/10.1363/4205610

Witwer, E., Jones, R., & Lindberg, L. (2018). *Sexual behavior and contraceptive and condom use among U.S. high school students, 2013–2017*. Guttmacher Institute. https://doi.org/10.1363/2018.29941

17

MOVING FORWARD

No More Sweeping Sexual Misconduct Under the Rug

Tanya Prewitt-White

We Must Step Up and Not Only Do Something But Do More

As Tarana Burke, the founder of the #MeToo movement, a Black woman who deserves credit for what she started, quoted, "Get up. Stand up. Speak up. Do something" (Variety, 2018). Let's be clear—many sport entities and stakeholders have utterly failed to address sexual violence, many doing nothing until their program's reputation and bottom line were being compromised. Our response to sexual misconduct has demonstrated that our systems are broken (Kasarek, 2018). Until institutions (who are comprised of people) are most invested in protecting their constituents and changing the culture of sexual misconduct in sport and society, little sustainable change will be accomplished. Reading this book alone or alongside colleagues, having an invited speaker come to talk with your athletes and coaches, and/or sitting through workshops on trauma-informed coaching is a first step but it is not enough. There is no quick or easy fix. We must find a way past lip service and performative public statements that do little or nothing to initiate change. The question we all must ask ourselves is this: Are we committed to mitigating acts of sexual violence and building more accountability, more reconciliation, and healing responses to sexual injustice, in and out of sport? If not, and if sport leaders continue to be most concerned with covering up potential scandals, protecting the image and reputations of their programs, and the financial bottom line continues to supersede care, nothing will shift.

Stakeholders—from athletic directors, chancellors, principals, board members, coaches, educators, administrative staff, sport psychology professionals, parents, and athletes—all must be involved in a collective revolution. We cannot change the past, but we can reimagine and toil for a future where we *believe* survivors of sexual misconduct when they tell us what they need.

What they are telling us is that the status quo is suffocating and harmful. And, all too often, survivors are required to move forward without as much as an apology. In addition, we might consider the ways we are collectively instructed to place both the onus and responsibility on survivors; often the inclination is to victim-blame (e.g., asking "why were you at that party?" or "were you drinking?") while many perpetrators go without any or a little form of accountability or retribution (Prewitt-White, 2021). When we contemplate the statistic from

DOI: 10.4324/9781003125884-20

the Rape, Abuse & Incest National Network (RAINN, 2021) that out of every 1,000 sexual assaults 995 will walk free, we might pause to acknowledge the severity of the structural and societal harm we cause survivors (Prewitt-White, 2021). Let's remember that "ultimately victims are assaulted because someone chose to attack them" (Kendall, 2020, p. 54).

We need to continue the difficult conversations on topics such as consent, abuse of power, and coercion. Bluntly, we need to "teach people not to rape" and "how not to be a rapist" (Kendall, 2020, p. 55). A yearly Everfi online sexual harassment compliance training or similar programs publicly funded institutions require is scraping the bare minimum. Compliance is not enough; zero harm should be the goal for every sport entity.

Who Is Sexual Misconduct Harming the Most?

Sexual misconduct prevention is a social justice issue. Like all issues, sexual violence harms communities and people disproportionately. I will not be the white, educated, cishetero, able-bodied woman (see my writings in *Applied Feminist Sport Psychology* Chapters 3 and 18 for more detail) that does not "name a thing a thing." So, let's be real and reiterate what women of color have been shouting for generations—while all genders and people are impacted by sexual misconduct, we know that "girls [and women] of color in a patriarchal system have experienced more abuse, violence, adversity, and deprivation than protection" (Kendall, 2020, p. 52). All of us need to be concerned, and, further, we need to be in the fight of protecting those society and intuitions ignore. Black women, women of color, trans women, members of the LGBTQIA, and disabled communities are at greater risk than all other communities, with transwomen of color being the least protected (Carter, 2020; Kendall, 2020; Love, 2020; Oluo, 2018). Racism, heteronormativity, homonegativity/homophobia, and transphobia, as we have read, play an active role in sport and society, and impact who is not only believed when reporting sexual violence but also who is found guilty of sexual misconduct (Kendall, 2020).

The fetishization, adultification, and exoticization of Black girls and women as well as girls and women of color place women and girls living in dark skinned bodies at heightened risk, in and outside of sport, for sexual violence (Kendall, 2020; Love, 2019). The dehumanization of Black women, women of color, trans women—particularly trans women of color—LGBTQIA, and disabled persons also affects white cisheteropatriarchal perceptions of credibility, determinations of fault, and feelings of empathy in institutional fact-finding processes related to sexual misconduct (Cyphert, 2018). We must do better.

For these reasons and more, culturally humble and responsive coaches, sport administrators, counselors, sport psychology consultants, and educators (just to name a few) are direly needed to create environments of care and liberation. But that is not enough—we also need diverse representation and leadership to co-create cultures where all athletes and sport constituents can bring their full selves, feeling safe and deeply cared for by those not only co-creating but curating the culture. Further, all sport stakeholders need to be equipped to report without doing further harm, even though at the current moment, the care and sensitivity required are lacking for survivors and most notably for trans women, LGBTQIA persons, and women of color (Kendall, 2020). As Kendall (2020) noted:

> [Y]et we tell people that reporting assault will stop it. Yet, if those who commit the assaults, statistically speaking white men are most likely to assault, are insulated from

accountability and consequences, then what help is the punitive system for women, but especially for Black women, women of color and trans women?

(Breathe this in. p. 58)

Statistically speaking, white men commit sexual violence more than any other group (Kendall, 2020; RAINN, 2021). If you feel uneasy reading this, please pause and reflect on what is making you feel unsettled or defensive. However, I want to remind readers that not every man or white man is a perpetrator; there are systems and cultural norms at play (e.g., power, control, racism, sexism, toxic masculinity, to name a few) that create an environment where white males might feel entitled to power, experiences, and bodies that they are most certainly not entitled to have.

An example of white male entitlement in sport is the very public case of the former Stanford scholarship swimmer Brock Turner who, in 2015, raped an unconscious woman of color, Chanel Miller. If it were not for two male graduate students who witnessed the assault in the alley as they were biking and chased Brock down as well as kept him from escaping until police arrived, there may have been no form of accountability (Miller, 2019). Turner was convicted for the assault yet Judge Aaron Persky only sentenced Turner to six months in jail (Flynn, 2018; Miller, 2019). Turner was later released after three months for good behavior (Flynn, 2018). We cannot ignore the influence race and white privilege or (as my colleague, Dr. Robert E. Owens taught me) white entitlement has in cases such as this. Further, for girls and women of color, there is often little to no presumption of innocence by institutions and people outside their communities; thus, "unpunished sexual violence remains a constant threat" (Kendall, 2020, p. 52).

In addition, as Cyphert (2018) points out, survivors are often "forced to prosecute their case through a system designed to disbelieve them," while at the same time, "the very process of doing so may be hostile and traumatizing. As a result, many survivors may be unable or unwilling to do so" (p. 72). This stands for all survivors, and I hope we can agree that every survivor deserves better. Black and brown communities and survivors, who may be reticent to report sexual violence to any punitive system because of their distrust of institutions and officers who criminalize their family members, friends, and even themselves, deserve better. Additionally, Indigenous survivors who are often not allowed to press criminal charges against non-Native perpetrators in their tribal courts, who are demanding for alternatives outside of the colonizing and dehumanizing criminal justice responses in the United States, also deserve better (Kasarek, 2018).

Further, 44% of lesbians, 61% of bisexual women, 26% of gay men, and 37% of bisexual men experience rape, physical violence, or stalking by an intimate partner (Human Rights Campaign, 2021). The 2015 US Transgender Survey found that 47% of the transgender/non-binary community are sexually assaulted at some point in their lives (James, Herman, Rankin, Keisling, Mottet, & Anafi, 2016). Among trans/non-binary Black Indigenous People of Color (BIPOC) who completed the survey, Indigenous people (65%), multiracial (59%), Middle Eastern (58%), and Black (53%) were most likely to have been sexually assaulted (Human Rights Campaign, 2021; James et al., 2016). The LGBTQIA community and survivors deserve better, too.

Punitive Justice Is Not Working

At this point, I am thinking that most of us still reading this chapter recognize that moving forward with the status quo is choosing to be complicit to the harm we co-create by not intervening, speaking up, and resisting the oppression inherent in sport and society. We have turned away from harm for far too long. We recognize our existence survives in an environment where victims fear reporting due to the victim blaming and ostracizing they may likely endure. We have also given thought to the adversarial policies of most institutions' grievance processes that create arduous burdens for sexual violence survivors. As Sophie Kasarek, a sexual assault survivor and activist wrote in the New York Times:

> Sexual injustices exist in many forms, from casual sexism and harassment to sexual assault and rape. But people harmed by them have, by and large, only two options: They can try to have the perpetrator formally punished, or they can do nothing. The process of reporting formally is important to many survivors and must be protected; we know, however, that a vast majority of people will not choose this path. And all survivors—regardless of whether a report is filed or a harm-doer is exposed—deserve justice, healing and trust.
>
> *(Kasarek, 2018, p. 7)*

Most advocates have become disillusioned with an emphasis on punitive justice (e.g., terminations, expulsions, probations and in some cases, prison sentences). Reconciliation and restorative practices decenter criminal justice responses (i.e., an offender broke the law of the state or the rules of conduct at an institution) to communal care and reparation (i.e., the harm caused to the victim and community deserves healing and a restored sense of safety and connection; Jones, 2017; Olson & Dzur, 2003). Reconciliation and restorative practices often provide a more empowering and survivor-oriented approach than the Westernized traditional criminal justice system (Brenner, 2013). We have seen firsthand how punitive justice rarely works in survivors' best interest or healing because its measures are not designed to provide full support, acknowledgment, or resolution, and cannot and do not guarantee that those who harmed will not do so again (Kasarek, 2018).

Restorative Practices and Its Origins

Alternative forms of justice are present and have been for generations. Healing and reconciliatory responses are available; but are we listening? Restorative justice practices that are becoming popularized (dare I say co-opted?) as Western responses to justice reform have "deep roots in Indigenous peacemaking" (Marsh, 2018, para. 1) and are derived "from Indigenous cultures from thousands of years ago" (Jones, 2017, p. 23). It is important to note that:

> Restorative justice in the Westernized sense often indicates the implementation of tools used to resolve conflict, but indigenous peacemaking is inseparable from the restorative healing practices that are lived every day in connection with oneself, one's community, and nature according to tribal traditions and lifeways.
>
> *(Marsh, 2019, para. 4)*

Restorative and reconciliatory customs continue to be found in culturally responsive practices that address injustices of historically and intentionally ignored groups, including the Truth and Reconciliation Commission in South Africa (Truth and Reconciliation Commission, 2003), family group conferences practiced by the Maori people of New Zealand (Pranis, 2005), and circle sentencing practices used by some First Nations' members in Canada (Ellis, 2009). These are just some examples for those interested in reading more.

More recently, Black Women's Blueprint, an organization that advocates for black women who are survivors of sexual violence, convened a Truth and Reconciliation Commission conceived by its members (Black Women's Blueprint, 2016). Survivors were provided space to share their stories and be affirmed by the community. Space was also created for harmdoers or those who enabled them, to take responsibility (Black Women's Blueprint, 2016). Some males in attendance admitted to sexually harming women and offered apologies while taking the burden off survivors to initiate reconciliation (Kasarek, 2018). Because the roots of reconciliation and restorative practices are in providing culturally sensitive redress to historically marginalized groups and on emphasizing the addressing of power dynamics in communities (Karp, 2013; Karp & Schachter, 2018), such practices are a promising way of addressing the issue of racial bias in punitive justice hearings that are influenced by institutional, structural, personal, and interpersonal racism (Alexander, 2011; Anderson, 2016; Kendi, 2019; Rothstein, 2017). To be sure, there are alternative responses like reconciliation and restorative justice practices, and they deserve serious consideration.

Why Restorative Justice?

Those who practice restorative justice methods resist simple description and application of them, because no single definition or example of restorative justice exists (Cyphert, 2018). In fact, theorists and practitioners urge against developing fixed definitions of restorative justice or establishing guidelines for its practice, for fear of closing off creative solutions or responsiveness to the needs of those affected (Jones, 2017). Rather, restorative justice is an inclusive term that incorporates a variety of practices, from facilitated conferences between the parties, to community circles, accountability, truth telling, governance, and reparations; each of these practices carry potential for rebuilding and repairing community where all parties affected are invited to weigh in on how to address and ameliorate the collective harm caused (Cyphert, 2018; Jones, 2017; Oola, 2015).

At its essence, those who practice restorative justice hold the conviction that harm has been done and someone is responsible for repairing it (Cyphert, 2018; Jones, 2017). Further, they acknowledge that when a person does harm, they affect the person(s) they hurt, their community, as well as themselves (Jones, 2017).

Those who utilize a restorative justice approach seek to answer three key questions: (1) Who has been harmed?; (2) What are their needs?; and (3) Whose obligation is it to meet those needs? (Zehr, 2002). Additional questions a restorative justice facilitator might ask include:

- What happened? What were you thinking at the time?
- How have you been affected?
- Who do you think has been affected by what happened? In what way?
- What has been the hardest thing for you?

- What do you need to make things right?
- How can we make sure this doesn't happen again? (Jones, 2017, pp. 59–61)

Conceptually, restorative justice brings together perpetrators, victims, and communal leaders to promote healing and reconciliation in response to the harm caused (Jones, 2017). Thus, restorative justice theory is predicated upon both an "expanded understanding of who is harmed by wrongdoing [and also] an expanded understanding of who is responsible for causing and repairing harm" (Coker, 2017 p. 188). It is an alternative approach to seeking healing and rebuilding relationships as whole as possible (Jones, 2017).

Restorative justice is not mediation. For example, restorative justice requires—as a pre-condition to participation—that the responsible person accepts responsibility whereas mediation does not (Cyphert, 2018). Further, Campbell (2015) suggests if forgiveness and reconciliation are not included in responses to all modes of trauma—in particular sexual violence—long-term transformation and stability may be unlikely.

Academics, too, have been assembling a case that more and better options, including restorative justice, is necessary and viable for social healing. Dr. Mary Koss, a white feminist academic at the University of Arizona, has done trailblazing research and work on campus rape; she implements restorative justice practices in sexual assault cases on college campuses (see, e.g., Hopkins et al., 2004; Hopkins & Koss, 2005; Koss, 1988, 1989, 1991, 1992a, 1992b, 1993, 2000, 2003, 2006a, 2006b, 2006c; Koss & Achilles, 2008; Koss et al., 2003; Koss & Cleveland, 1996; Koss & Cook, 1998; Koss & Gidycz, 1991; Koss & Harvey, 1987, 1991; Koss & Leonard, 1984; Koss et al., 2011). In particular, the program Restore consensually brings together the person harmed, the responsible party, and friends and/or family members to share in a structured and professionally facilitated consultation (Koss, 2014; Koss et al., 2014). Facilitated conversations allow every party involved to be heard, and the survivor/victim to describe the impact of the harm. The meetings (which may take place over several sessions) conclude with a formal plan, created in collaboration with all participants, to best repair the acknowledged harm (Koss & Chisholm, 2020). Facilitators have training in both sexual violence issues and restorative-justice practices; they also have a general protocol to follow to ensure that the gatherings are not only safe but also healing and productive (Koss & Chisholm, 2020).

Admittedly, restorative justice may not be the answer for every case of sexual misconduct or for every survivor. Some survivors may prefer a punitive model; however, institutions can frame restorative justice as one of several options that a survivor may choose in moving forward (Cyphert, 2018). Adding a restorative justice option to potential responses to sexual misconduct does not prohibit a victim from pursuing conventional action either; it simply adds options to address and repair harm.

Perhaps given additional alternatives that do not pit survivor and the one who has harmed against each other in an adversarial and harmful environment, more survivors might come forward? Also, if sexual misconduct could be adequately faced rather than swept under the rug, we might start making progress towards mitigating it (Koss & Chisholm, 2020). Survivors often feel stripped of power and control, and conventional punitive responses can create more trauma for survivors. Survivors who choose to participate in restorative justice practices and feel and believe it is vital to their healing process can speak face-to-face with the person who caused them harm and reclaim their power (Koss & Chisholm, 2020). For some survivors, this can be a vital part of their healing process and for others this may be further traumatizing or triggering; though, survivors deserve to have a choice.

Beyond healing more deeply by using restorative justice practices in comparison to current punitive justice practices, there are additional reasons survivors may prefer restorative justice. Research supports the notion that survivors have unique needs that may well be met by restorative justice practices, including the need to tell their own stories (in their time and way), the desire to observe offender remorse for the harm caused, and wanting to have choice and agency in co-developing the path of the resolution (Cyphert, 2018; Karp, 2013; Karp & Schachter, 2018). Because restorative justice is predicated on an acknowledgment of responsibility from the offending party, it may also satisfy survivors' yearning to be believed and vindicated (Karp & Schachter, 2018). For these reasons, many support offering restorative justice programs in response to sexual violence. The same could be true in the sport context if only we begin to explore these practices as an alternative.

Again, as those advocating for restorative justice also point out, restorative justice should not be the only option available. Survivors should always be counseled about all their options before beginning a restorative justice process (Cyphert, 2018). If the survivor prefers to pursue restorative justice, the accused is invited to participate, but may only participate if they are willing to admit responsibility (Cyphert, 2018, Karp, 2013). Certainly, the accused needs to be provided counsel on the potential ramifications of participating (e.g., legal consequences) and all parties should be made aware they have the right to withdraw their consent at any time. Lastly, institutions and organizations must have quality trained facilitators who have progressed with support and supervision specific to the field of sexual assault restorative justice (Cyphert, 2018).

Further, restorative justice does not remove punishment as an option (e.g., an institution could still decide to terminate a coach or suspend an athlete from a team) and restorative justice processes do not absolve institutions from their responsibility to address sexual misconduct seriously (Brodsky, 2016). Rather, it provides another option for restoration, healing, and moving forward. Even when restorative practices result in gentler repercussions than the criminal justice or punitive model of resolving sexual misconduct and Title IX claims, this is not a bad thing; not every survivor may want his, her, or their assailant expelled, terminated, suspended, or imprisoned (Cyphert, 2018). Of course, institutions have a responsibility to protect sport community members beyond the wishes of survivors as recidivism is a genuine concern. Practices that include a stakeholder in restorative justice conferences to represent the institutional and community safety can help address this concern. Restorative justice may also provide space for perpetrators' needs for rehabilitation and healing. As Sophie Karasek, a survivor and sexual assault prevention advocate wrote, "putting him in prison seemed almost laughably ill-suited to what I needed. What I wanted was for him to change his behavior. He needed an intervention, not prison. He got neither" (Kasarek, 2018, para. 6).

We haven't yet given name to the recidivism of perpetrators. Recidivism has been found to be lower when restorative justice processes are facilitated and practiced by institutions (Sherman & Strang, 2007; Strang & Sherman, 2003). Thus, stakeholders might consider ways to infuse elements of restorative justice into their current processes. In sum, reconciliation and restorative practices hold promise to promote reflection, empathy, and accountability among all involved in sport communities. In addition to restorative justice, providing trauma informed coaching and response training can enhance all our ability to be better humans to one another.

The Need for Trauma Informed Coaching and Responses

Trauma is any deeply distressing or disturbing experience. Sometimes denial for both survivors and those supporting survivors may feel safe. Though, ignoring our feelings and emotions does not mean they are not present. Trauma lives in all our bodies, our DNA and becomes part of our hardwiring (Menakem, 2017; van der Kolk, 2015). For our individual and collective healing, it is important sport stakeholders are knowledgeable about trauma informed responses and sensitive to how trauma affects human souls and bodies, especially those who have experienced sexual harm.

We are most compassionate when we hold people with care and understand trauma changes us and yet, each of us is more than any pain we carry. Further, recognizing who we are prior to and after experiencing trauma evolves is essential to provide patience, grace, and love to survivors of trauma. Thus, we can also shift from asking ourselves, "what is wrong with the athlete/person?" to asking ourselves "what happened to them?" (Perry & Winfrey, 2021). This in and of itself humanizes individuals. Experiencing sexual misconduct is traumatic whether it be stalking, sexual harassment, sexual assault, rape or abuse, cyber harassment or sexual exploitation, or degrading sexual imagery. We should all educate ourselves on trauma informed responses to create a culture of care in and outside of sport and seek those trained to educate and support us when necessary.

A Reminder and Call to the Sport Community

As we continue to examine sexual misconduct in sport more critically and intentionally, we may find that not only the individual who caused harm is responsible, but that sport stakeholders are also negligent or complicit in co-creating an environment of toxicity, avoidance, and/or acceptance of misconduct. This is what we must all reckon with: How each one of us has the potential to co-create a culture of misconduct. Behavior rarely occurs in a social vacuum. Misconduct harms not only the victim but also affects the entire community (e.g., coaches, teammates, friends, partners and parents of both victims and responsible persons, as well as athletic programs and institutions). We must remember that members of institutions may also feel a lack of safety and less vital to a community when they perceive high levels of misconduct and little to no response or authentic care from stakeholders.

Thus, all sport stakeholders have a role to play in ameliorating harm. Often, the end goal in sport is for athletes to take direct responsibility for their performance and actions while developing a stronger sense of community and team culture. It is time for us, as sport stakeholders, to walk the talk and lead by example in terms of ameliorating sexual misconduct in sport. It will take some reckoning, it will not be easy, but it will most definitely be worth it. We, as individual stakeholders, may not only need to accept responsibility but also forgive ourselves for our failures or missteps (Kymenlaasko, 2012). Forgiveness, especially self-forgiveness, is required as we choose to charter new ways forward for our children who participate in sport.

An organizational culture that does not take responsibility and does not promote individual and collective forgiveness will likely engage in destructive politics. Sport constituents will be afraid to share their true feelings and avoid speaking out. Thus, when leaders display dishonesty, organizational power politics, and manipulative command and control measures, a toxic organizational climate is created that damages not only internal relationships but also damages culture and rapport (Ferch, 2012; Kymenlaasko, 2012). In essence, developing a comprehensive leadership program that strengthens individual attributes and competencies such as empathy, emotional intelligence, accountability, humility, and compassion is critical for current and future sport leaders who intend to co-create an organizational environment that is physically, psychologically, and emotionally safe for all its members.

Recognize Survivors and Perpetrators Are Always in Our Midst

When we say all our members, it is important that we humanize the problem of sexual misconduct. Often, we might find ourselves simultaneously dehumanizing people who committed sexual assault for years by calling them *monsters* and then learn that the people who commit these crimes are our coaches, teammates, co-workers, and family members (Kasarek, 2018; Prewitt-White, 2021). It is important we remind ourselves that like survivors, "perpetrators are in every space we find ourselves, too" (Prewitt-White, 2021, para. 1). We would be wise to pause, sit with this realization, and breathe it in—this is not the narrative most of us consume (Prewitt-White, 2021). It has the potential to shift our approach to sexual misconduct prevention because this truth makes it more visceral and real when we face our denial.

Sexual misconduct is not an issue that happens outside our community—it happens *in* our communities. Thus, we might more fully recognize we have a role to play when we stop perceiving those who harm as only *sick*, *demon-like*, or *monsters*. This is not to say that their behavior is not deplorable, and survivors deserve justice. We are not condoning their behavior but humanizing the crisis we face; sexual violence is a human problem. Once we realize the accused/perpetrators are our student-athletes, colleagues, teammates, friends, partners, and neighbors, we humanize the problem. If we have the courage to humanize both survivors and those who harm as human souls needing support, care, rehabilitation, transformation (as hard as it can be to do so), we can begin to make a difference and transform our systems and culture.

We may often feel we must do the impossible to change the culture. However, culture changes in both big and small shifts. Moving forward, we can start by:

> recognizing that to support survivors also means disrupting the sexist, patriarchal, homonegative, transphobic, white supremacist narratives we are taught to develop, prioritize, believe and protect. Once we understand both survivors and perpetrators of sexual misconduct are always in our midst, we must take brave moments, no matter how small, to disrupt cultural norms that condone sexual violence.
> *(Prewitt-White, 2021, para. 3)*

For example, when we are having a drink with colleagues or teammates, and someone insinuates that a female should not be at the bar alone, we could respond by making them aware that 8 out of 10 sexual assaults are committed by someone known to the survivor (National Sexual Violence Resource Center, 2015), that 55% of sexual assaults occur at or near the survivor's home, and another 12% happen near or at the home of a friend or relative (Planty et al., 2013). When an athlete or teammate in the locker room names their sexual encounters as "body counts" or "kills," we can take a moment to explain how dehumanizing it is to depict a sexual partner (even if only a hook-up) as physically dead. This also may be the moment when we can enter in and explain the importance of care and consent in sexual relationships (see Chapter 16).

At a personal level, we can ask ourselves: Are we interrogating our thoughts and challenging harmful biases or stereotypes we hold? Are we examining the ways society and sports media hypersexualize, exoticize, and colonize dark bodies for (white) capitalist patriarchy? Do we realize that sexual misconduct affects every community no matter the socioeconomic class, religion, race, gender, sexuality, nationality, education level, and so on?

Closing Thoughts

Moving forward, when we think of supporting survivors, let's remind ourselves that perpetrators are everywhere we are, too (Prewitt-White, 2021). Let's choose to not be silent when harmful conversations and viewpoints are shared in our presence. This can be one small tangible action each of us can take to do our part in addressing a societal problem and social justice issue.

I believe we must also center survivor voices. When they tell us what they need, we must believe them. And, to every survivor, I stand with you. Feel all the things you feel; no one is entitled to your story – tell (or don't tell it) on your timeline; there is no wrong way to heal. Please also know you are worthy of healing, love, and care. I wrote this meditation for all of us who are survivors in a moment of my own healing journey:

> *Dear survivor, I know you did nothing to deserve the harm done to you and that you are more than the pain and experience you carry. Yes, feel your pain and process your experience. Though, choose also to heal every opportunity the universe provides rather than harden with shame and anger. Live with your face towards the sun and shine bright in your truth. We did not have control over what happened to us, but we can write our very own beautiful ending.*

To all of us, please continue having the difficult conversations, reimagining your organizations, leadership, and processes to be both restorative and transformative in nature, believe survivors, and most of all, seek for ways to collectively heal. We all deserve this. Yet, we cannot heal until we face the harm we have experienced or co-created. It will be arduous; but, the safety and well-being of all athletes, sport stakeholders, and our children are worth it. A first step of many is refusing to push sexual misconduct in sport under the rug.

Discussion Questions

1. What questions or concerns do you have when incorporating restorative justice and restorative practices to cases of sexual misconduct?
2. What feelings or thoughts arise for you when you reflect on the reality that both survivors and perpetrators of sexual misconduct are in your midst?
3. In what ways are you committed to mitigating sexual misconduct moving forward?
4. Craft a tangible action plan to implement your commitment to mitigating sexual misconduct. What have you included? What challenges will you face? How might you overcome the said challenges?

References

Alexander, M. (2011). *The new Jim Crow: Mass incarceration in the age of colorblindness.* The New Press.

Anderson, C. (2016). *White rage: The unspoken truth of our racial divide.* Bloomsbury.

Black Women's Blueprint. (2016). When truth is justice and not enough: Executive summary to the black women's truth and reconciliation commission report. A Publication of Black Women's Blueprint. https://d6474d13-2b53-4643-b862-e78077ee7880.filesusr.com/ugd/f0223e_59bbcc47c9084087be7966b2b92c3bfe.pdf

Brenner, A. (2013). Resisting simple dichotomies: Critiquing narratives of victims, perpetrators, and harm in feminist theories of rape. *Harvard Journal of Law & Gender, 36*(2), 503–568.

Brodsky, S. (2016, June). Is discipline reform really helping decrease school violence? *The Atlantic.* Retrieved from https://www.theatlantic.com/education/archive/2016/06/school-violence-restorative-justice/488945/

Campbell, A. (2015). Forgiveness and reconciliation as an organizational leadership Competency within restorative transitional justice instruments. *The International Journal of Servant-Leadership, 11*(1), 139–186.

Carter, L. (2020). *Feminist applied sport psychology: From theory to practice.* Routledge.

Coker, D. (2017). Crime logic, campus sexual assault, and restorative justice. *Texas Tech Law Review, 49*(1), 147–159.

Cyphert, A. (2018). The devil is in the details: Exploring restorative justice as an option for campus sexual assault responses under Title IX. *Denver Law Review, 96*(1), 50–85.

Ellis, J. (2009). First nations justice initiatives in Canada. *TOTEM: The U.W.O. Journal of Anthropology, 17*, 37–42.

Ferch, S. R. (2012). *Forgiveness and power in the age of atrocity.* Lexington Books.

Flynn, M. (2018, June 16). Voters remove judge who sentenced Brock Turner to six months in Stanford sexual assault case. *Washington Post.* www.washingtonpost.com/news/morning-mix/wp/2018/06/06/voters-remove-judge-who-sentenced-brock-turner-to-six-months-in-stanford-rape-case/

Hopkins, C. Q., & Koss, M. P. (2005). Incorporating feminist theory and insights into a restorative justice response to sex offenses. *Violence Against Women, 11*, 693–723.

Hopkins, C. Q., Koss, M. P., & Bachar, K. J. (2004). Applying restorative justice to ongoing intimate violence: Problems and possibilities. *St. Louis University Public Law Review, 20*, 289–312.

Human Rights Campaign. (2021). *Sexual assault and the LGBTQ community.* www.hrc.org/resources/sexual-assault-and-the-lgbt-community

James, S., Herman, J., Rankin, S., Keisling, M., Mottet, L., & Anafi, M. (2016). *The report of the 2015 U.S. transgender survey.* National Center for Transgender Equality. www.transequality.org/sites/default/files/doc s/USTS-Full-Report-FINAL.PDF

Jones, S. (2017). *Restorative justice and restorative practice: Training manual.* Shaniqua Jones Publishing, LLC.

Karp, D. (2013). *The little book of restorative justice for colleges and universities: Repairing harm and rebuilding trust in response to student misconduct.* Good Books.

Karp, D., & Schachter, M. (2018). Restorative justice in universities: Case studies of what works with restorative responses to student misconduct. In T. Gavrielides (Ed.), *The Routledge international handbook of restorative justice.* Routledge.

Kasarek, S. (2018, February 22). I'm a campus sexual assault activist. It's time to reimagine how we punish sex crimes. *New York Times.* www.nytimes.com/2018/02/22/opinion/campus-sexual-assault-punitive-justive.html

Kendall, M. (2020). *Hood feminism: Notes from the women that a movement forgot.* Viking.

Kendi, I. (2019). *How to be an antiracist.* One World.

Koss, M. P. (1988). Hidden rape: Incidence, prevalence, and descriptive characteristics of sexual aggression reported by a national sample of postsecondary students. In A. W. Burgess (Ed.), *Rape and sexual assault* (Vol. 2, pp. 3–25). Garland Publishing Co.

Koss, M. P. (1989). Sexual aggression and victimization in a national sample of students in higher education. In M. A. Pirog-Good & J. E. Stets (Eds.), *Violence in dating relationships: Emerging social issues* (pp. 145–168). Praeger.

Koss, M. P. (1991). Changed lives: The psychological impact of sexual harassment. In M. A. Paludi (Ed.), *Ivory power: Sex and gender harassment in the academy* (pp. 73–92). SUNY Press.

Koss, M. P. (1992a). Rape on campus: Facts and measures. *Planning for Higher Education, 20*, 21–28.

Koss, M. P. (1992b). The underdetection of rape: Methodological choices that influence incidence estimates. *Journal of Social Issues, 48*, 61–75.

Koss, M. P. (1993, August 3). The wrong response to rape. *The Wall Street Journal*.

Koss, M. P. (2000). Shame, blame, and community: Justice responses to violence against women. *American Psychologist, 55*, 1332–1343.

Koss, M. P. (2003). Evolutionary models of why men rape: Acknowledging the complexities. In C. Travis (Ed.), *Evolution, gender, and rape* (pp. 191–205). MIT Press.

Koss, M. P. (2006a). Restorative justice for sex crimes outside the context of intimate partner violence. *Sexual Assault Report: Law, Prevention, Protection, Enforcement, Treatment, & Health, 10*, 1–10.

Koss, M. P. (2006b). Restoring rape survivors: Justice, advocacy, and a call to action. In F. Denmark, H. Krauss, E. Halpern, & J. Sechzer (Eds.), *Violence and exploitation against women and girls*. New York University Press.

Koss, M. P. (2006c). Restoring rape survivors: Justice, advocacy, and a call to action. *Annals of the New York Academy of Sciences, 1087*, 206–234.

Koss, M. P. (2014). The RESTORE program of restorative justice for sex crimes: Vision, process, and outcomes. *Journal of Interpersonal Violence, 29*(9), 1623–1660.

Koss, M. P., & Achilles, M. (2008). *Restorative justice for sexual assault*. Peer Reviewed Online Publication. www.VAWnet.org

Koss, M. P., Bachar, K. J., & Hopkins, C. Q. (2003). Restorative justice for sexual violence: Repairing victims, building community, and holding offenders accountable. In R. Prentky & A. W. Burgess (Eds.), *Understanding and managing sexual coercion: Annals of the New York academy of sciences* (Vol. 989, pp. 384–396). https://journals.sagepub.com/doi/abs/10.1177/15248380211029408

Koss, M. P., & Chisholm, K. (2020, February 16). The time is now: Restorative justice for sexual misconduct. *The Chronicle of Higher Education*. www.chronicle.com/article/the-time-is-now-restorative-justice-for-sexual-misconduct/?cid2=gen_login_refresh&cid=gen_sign_in

Koss, M. P., & Cleveland, H. O. (1996). Fraternities and athletics as predictors of date rape: Self-selection or different causal processes? *Violence Against Women, 2*, 180–190.

Koss, M. P., & Cook, S. L. (1998). Facing the facts: Date and acquaintance rape are significant problems for women. In R. K. Bergen (Ed.) *Issues in intimate violence* (pp. 147–156). Sage Publications.

Koss, M. P., & Gidycz, C. J. (1991). The impact of sexual assault. In A. Parrot (Ed.), *Acquaintance rape* (pp. 270–284). John Wiley and Sons.

Koss, M. P., & Harvey, M. R. (1987). *Rape: Clinical and community approaches to treatment*. Stephen Greene Press.

Koss, M. P., & Harvey, M. R. (1991). *The rape victim: Clinical and community interventions* (2nd ed.). Sage Publications.

Koss, M. P., & Leonard, K. E. (1984). Sexually aggressive men: Empirical findings and theoretical implications. In N. Malamuth & E. Donnerstein (Eds.), *Pornography and sexual aggression* (pp. 213–232). Academic Press.

Koss, M. P., White, J., & Kazdin, A. (2011). *Violence against women and girls: Volume II: Navigating the solutions*. American Psychological Association. https://doi.org/10.1037/12308-000

Koss, M. P., Wilgus, J., & Williamsen, K. M. (2014). Campus sexual misconduct: Restorative justice approaches to enhance compliance with Title IX guidance. *Trauma, Violence, & Abuse, 15*, 242–258. https://doi.org/10.1177/1524838014521500

Kymenlaasko, I. V. (2012). Forgiveness as a leadership tool. *Global Conference on Business and Finance Proceedings, 7*(1), 432–445. www.forgivenessandhealth.com

Love, B. (2019). *We want to do more than survive: Abolitionist teaching and the pursuit of educational freedom.* Beacon Press.

Marsh, C. (2018). Honoring the global indigenous roots of restorative justice: Potential restorative approaches for child welfare. *Center for the Study of Social Policy: Ideas into Action.* https://cssp.org/2019/11/honoring-the-global-indigenous-roots-of-restorative-justice/

Menakem, R. (2017). *My grandmother's hands: Racialized trauma and the pathway to mending our hearts and bodies.* Central Recovery Press.

Miller, C. (2019). *Know my name: A memoir.* Viking.

National Sexual Violence Resource Center. (2015). *Info and stats for journalists: Statistics about sexual violence.* www.nsvrc.org/sites/default/files/publications_nsvrc_factsheet_media-packet_statistics-about-sexual-violence_0.pdf

Olson, S., & Dzur, A. (2003). Reconstructing professional roles in restorative justice programs. *Utah Law Review, 1,* 57–89.

Oluo, I. (2018). *So you wanna talk about race.* Seal Press.

Oola, S. (2015). *Forgiveness: Unveioing an asset in peacebuilding* [Special issue]. Refugee Law Center. http://refugeelawproject.org/files/others/Forgiveness_research_report.pdf

Perry, B., & Winfrey, O. (2021). *What happened to you? Conversations on trauma, resilience, and healing.* Flatiron Books, An Oprah Book.

Planty, M., Langton, L., Krebs, C., Berzofsky, M., & Smiley-McDonald, H. (2013). *Female victims of sexual violence, 1994–2010.* Bureau of Justice Statistics.

Pranis, K. (2005). *Circle processes.* Good Books.

Prewitt-White, T. (2021). Perpetrators are everywhere we find ourselves, too. *Medium.* https://drtanyaraquel.medium.com/perpetrators-are-everywhere-we-find-ourselves-too-c753e7ea164b

Rape, Assault, & Incest National Network. (2021). *The criminal justice system: Statistics.* The Rape, Assault, Incest National Network. Retrieved July 17, 2021, from www.rainn.org/statistics/criminal-justice-system

Rothstein, R. (2017). *The color of law: A forgotten history of how our government segregated America.* Liveright Publishing Corporation.

Sherman, L., & Strang, H. (2007). *Restorative justice: The evidence.* Smith Institute.

Strang, H., & Sherman, L. (2003). Repairing the harm: Victims and restorative justice. *Utah Law Review, 1,* 15–43.

Truth and Reconciliation Commission. (2003). *Promotion of national unity and reconciliation act 34 of 1995.* https://ihl-databases.icrc.org/applic/ihl/ihl-nat.nsf/0/AF494D2C3E5803FEC1256AF400524BE5

Van der Kolk, B. (2015). *The body keeps the score: Brain, mind, and body in the healing of trauma.* Penguin Publishing Group.

Variety on Twitter [Variety]. (2018, April 11). *#MeToo founder Tarana Burke on how to get involved* [Twitter moment]. https://twitter.com/variety/status/984165665626980352?lang=en

Zehr, H. (2002). *The little book of restorative justice.* Skyhorse Publishing Company.

INDEX

Note: Page numbers in **bold** indicate a table on the corresponding page.

#MeToo 18, 44, 52, 71, 202

1 in 6 support for Male Survivors of Sexual Violence 176
10th Circuit Court of Appeals 161
11th Circuit Court of Appeals 160

Abramson, K. 54
abuse: anti-LGBTQIA+ 27–29, 34; athlete 37; child 8; childhood 57; child sexual 38–39, 58; emotional 3, 41, 104, 125, 126; institutional betrayal and 61–62; interpersonal 59; of males 66; sexual 3, 6, 10, 12, 15–22, 42–47, 169, 187; sport 4, 5, 42; sport-related 11, 40; statistics 169; targeted 27; of transgender athletes 31; verbal 55, 126; warning signs 82; *see also* grooming; RAINN; survivor
abuse of power 115, 118, 135, 203
abuse prevention 61, 114
abuser: dependency on 60; difficulty of confronting 21; fear of 43; techniques used by 39; trusted confidant as 29; *see* Nassar, Larry; Sandusky, Jerry; Strauss, Richard E.; Trigger (Coach)
acquiescence 39, 56
ACSM *see* American College of Sports Medicine (ACSM)
adultification 174, 203
Ahern, K. 58, 62
amateur athletes 22; *see also* Olympics
Amateur Athletic Union 79
American College of Sports Medicine (ACSM) 178

amnesia *see* traumatic amnesia
androgens 116
androgen-sensitive hyperandrogenic females 116
Angelou, Maya 168
Applied Feminist Sport Psychology (Prewitt-White) 203
Asbury University 30
asexuality 26, 199
Asian Pacific Institute on Gender Based Violence 176
assigned-female-at-birth (AFAB) 109, 114, 116
assigned-male-at-birth (AMAB) 116
Athlete Ally 27–28
athletic administrators 80–81
athletic directors 6, 8, 11, 127, 171
Athletic Equality Index (AEI) 27–28
athletic malfeasance 60
athletic personnel 147
athletic programmatic prevention of sexual misconduct 141–150; barriers to 146; bystander intervention programs 142–143; *Green Dot* 143, 145; recommendations 146–150; sexual misconduct 142–145
athletics: amateur 22; intercollegiate 129–137
athletic scholarship 69
athletics, sexual harassment in *see* Title IX and sexual harassment
athletic trainers 9, 29, 177

Bagger, Mianne 116
Barnett, Gary 161–162
bathroom problem, the 113–114

bathrooms, legislation regarding use by transgender individuals 30, 116
Baylor University 29–30, 147, 156
Beggs, Mack 116
believe survivors *see* survivors
Bennett, N. 39
betrayal 55, 142; *see also* institutional betrayal
betrayal blindness 59, 61
betrayal trauma 63
beyond reasonable doubt liability standard 164
Biden, Joe 163, 164
Big Ten 18
Big Ten Conference 22
Biles, Simone 12, 21, 156
biological essentialism 114, 115–118
black bodies 17
black girls, adultification of 174
Black, Indigenous, and People of Color (BIPOC) 146, 204
black male survivors of sexual assault 176
Black women 12, 21, 202, 203
Black Women's Blueprint 176, 206
blind obedience 104
Boy Scouts of America 21, 114
Brackenridge, Celia: four-stage model of grooming 40, 42–43, **45–46**
Brenda Tracy 144
Breuner, C. 188
Bringing in the Bystander 144
Bronfenbrenner's Ecological Systems Theory 4
Burke, Tarana 202
bystander effect 20
bystander 5, 6, 9, 127; adult 123; community of 23; meaning of 15–16; novice 78; prosocial 146, 149
bystander behaviour 144–145; prosocial 149
bystander intervention 175
bystander intervention programs 142–145, 148–150; *Bringing in the Bystander* 144; *see also* Green Dot
bystanderism 19, 20–21

California 116, 165, 190
Callisto 62
Calvin University 26
Campbell, A. 207
Cannon v. Univ. of Chi. 158
Casarez, J. 57
Celenza, A. 80
Chand, Dutee 116
child pornography 7, 194, 195
circle sentencing practices (First Nations) 206
cisheteronormativity 26, 27, 29, 30, 32
cisheteropatriarchy 5, 7, 12, 203

cisheterosexism 26–33; policies 29–32; in sports 27–29
Cissner, A. 144
Civil Rights Act of 1964 155, 157
civil rights law (US) 166n1
Clarendon, Layshia 26, 29
CNN 18
Coaches Kit 143–144
Coaching Boys into Men 143–144
Coakley, J. 17
"coerced collaboration in genital acts" 78
coerced silence 56
coercion 38–39, 203; gaslighting and 54; memories of (Forrest Miller) 110, 115; memories of (Prewitt-White) 70, 78; sexting as form of 193; sexual 43, 148, 164, 192–193
coercion or exploitation of power 39, 69
Coleman, Mark 19
common knowledge 15; theorizing 16–18; troubling 19–23
common sense 16
conditioning (grooming) 38
condoms 135, 189, 197, 199
confidentiality 177
consent 189–192; power dynamics and 4; *see also* non-verbal consent; sexual consent; verbal consent
Conte, J. 38
Correa, C. 55, 57
credibility in the grooming process 43, 44
credibility deficits and excesses 53, 61–62
credibility economy (testimonial) 52–54, 57, 61–62
Crenshaw, Kimberlé 12
Cunningham, G. 28
Cunningham, Janice (Judge)18
Curl, Rick 79
Cyphert, A. 204
Cyrus, K. 31

Dantzscher, Jamie 55
Davis, A. Y, 11
Davis ex rel. Lashonda D. v. Monroe County Board of Education 158–159
Davis, H. 30
Dear Coach: What I Wish I Could Have Told You, Letters from Your Athletes (Erdner) 106
Dear Colleague Letters (DCL) 163–165
demisexuality 199
Denhollander, Rachel 7, 16, 18
Dietz, P. 39
disability, disabilities 42, 43; credibility and 53; people with 174; sexual violence and 146

disconnection 104
discursive power 17
Dodd, Robert 79
dominant and *subordinate* 17
Don't Ask, Don't Tell policy 19
Douglas, Gabby 18, 156
Dumaresq, Michelle 116
Dzikus, Lars 59

Ellis, C. 71
End Abuse of Persons With Disabilities 176
environmental grooming 40
epistemic injustice 51–63; policies 63; recommendations 60–63; *see also* gaslighting; institutional denial; silencing
epistemic secondary harm 54
Epstein, D. 61–62
Epstein, Jeffrey 15
Epstein, R. 174
Equal Employment Opportunity Commission (EEOC) 157
Eriksen, S. 144
essential human condition 16
estrogen 117
Exercise is Medicine 178
exoticization 203

family group conferences (Maori)
Fasting, K. 37, 39
Feiler, B. 197
fetishization 203
Fierce Five women's gymnastics team 18
First Nations (Canada) 206
For Ourselves: Reworking Gender Expression (FORGE) 176
Foucault, Michel 16–17, 102
Fox, Fallon 21, 116
Franklin v. Gwinnett County Pub. Sch. 158
Freire, P. 105–106
Freyd, J. J. 59, 62

gaslighting 54–56; betrayal as distinct harm from 55; direct 54–55; indirect 55
gatekeepers 22, 61
gay athletes 27, 29, 31; personal story (Bequette) 87; personal story (Forrest Miller) 112; sexual assaults of 86; sexual violence against 146, 204
gay, lesbian, bisexual, transgender, gender-queer, or non-conforming 146; *see also* LGBTQ+
Gebser v. Lago Vista Independent School District 158–159
Geddert, John 18, 20

gender-based violence 145, 148–149
gender discrimination 19, 21, 155–158, 160; *see also* Title IX
gender expectations 114
gender identity 30, 42, 47, 81, 118; *see also* cisgender; same-gender violence; transgender
gender minority 32
gender-nonconforming 12, 81, 82, 146, 169
gender norms *see* norms
gender orthodoxies 16
gender/power hierarchies 41
gender queer (genderqueer) 146, 169
gender roles 28
gender verification 31, 115
Genovese, Kitty 20
Gentile, K. 19–21
Gill, D. L. 26
Gillespie, A. 39, 46
Gilmore, Anne 161–162
gold medalists (Olympics) 44, 156
Goodall, H. 71
Green Dot 143, 145, 150n1
grooming and sport 37–47; Brackenridge model 40, 42–43, **45–46**; concept and definition of 38, 39, 40, 46; Leberg's three categories of 39, 70; Mulcahy's memories of 124; Prewitt-White's account of 53, 69–82; Sinnamon's model 43–45, **45–46**; Tyler's account of 134–135; *see also* credibility in the grooming process 43, 44
grooming prevention 81–82
grooming process 38–39; youth sports contexts 114–115
grooming techniques 124
Groth, A. 38
Guinier, L. 11
Guice, Derrius 58

Hanne's story 37, 39
Hartill, M. 42
Hasenbush, A. 30
Herek, G. 29
heteronormative discourse 21
heteronormativity 26, 42, 118–119, 203; *see also* cisheteronormativity
hindsight bias 169, 170
homonegativism, homonegativity 23, 26, 27, 203, 210
homophobia 42; Bequette's account of 84–89; ignorance regarding 176; internalized 28, 113
homophobic language 32
homophobic scripts of sports 42

homosexuals 21; *see also* LGBTQ+
hooks, bell 6, 12, 104, 105
hormone replacement therapy (HRT) 116–117
hormones 31, 116–117
Hubbard, Laurel 116
Huddle-Up 176
human rights 32
hyperandrogenic females 116o
hyperfemininity 113
hypermasculinity 15, 41, 142, 148
hypersensitivity 178
hypersexualization 174, 176, 211
hypervigilance 178

institutional accountability 20
institutional betrayal 19, 21–22, 57–60, 61; three case studies 58–60
institutional courage 62–63
institutional denial 5, 7, 57, 59
institutional intent 159
institutional racism 206
institutional responsibility 20, 23, 58, 158, 159
International Olympic Committee (IOC) 8; Consensus Statement on Sexual Harassment and Abuse in sport 145; position on trans women 117
intersex people 12, 26, 115, 118

Jantzi, Sarah 16
JDoe 62
Jones, K. 54
Jordan, Jim 19
justice *see* punitive justice; restorative justice
just world hypothesis 169–170

Karasek, Sophie 208
Karolyi, Marta and Bela 18, 20
Karolyi Ranch Olympic training facility 18
Kasarek, Sophie 205
Kaufman, Zachary 15
Kerr, G. 41
Koss, Mary 207

Lanning, K. 38, 40
Leahy, T. 4
Leberg, E. 39, 70
Lefevor, G. 31
Level, B. 30
Levy, D.L. 30
LGBT+ identities 114
LGBT National Hotline 176
LGBTQ rights 19; as protected class 166n1

LGBTQIA+ : harassment and abuse of 26–33; risk of grooming 42; risk of targeted violence 203
LGBTQIA+ role models 26
Lonsway, K. 171
Louisiana State University 58

MacGregor, W. 149–150
Malagrinó, D. 117
male rape 18; *see also* rape; rapists
Maori people 206
Maroney, McKayla 18, 156
Marsh, C. 205
masculine ideal 17
masculinist discourse 41
masculinity: aggressive 41–42; hegemonic 176; sport and 102–105; toxic 23, 143, 204; traditional 104; *see also* hypermasculinity
masculinity norms 28, 142
masculinity values 5, 7
Matsuda, M. 11
Mentors in Violence [Prevention] (MVP) 144–145
Me Too 143
McKinnon, Rachel 52, 117
Melton, N. 27
Michigan State University (MSU) 18, 51–53, 156–157
Miller, Chanel 204
Miller, L. 63
mixed martial arts (MMA) 19
Moore, E. 54
Murphy, D. 193

Nassar, Larry 5–7, 12; as microcosm of society 15; at Michigan State University 18, 51–53, 156–157
National Basketball Association/National Basketball Players Association (NBA/ NBPA) Policy on Domestic Violence, Sexual Assault, and Child Abuse 145
National Collegiate Athletic Association (NCAA) 8; Board of Governors Policy on Campus Sexual Violence 144; coach-athlete relationship, position on 126; Nasser allegations, response to 7, 21; professed priorities of 60; sanctions issued by 147; Sexual Violence Prevention Toolkit 144; Strauss allegations, response to 21; student-athlete disclosure requirements 149
National Council of Jewish Women 176
National Football League (NFL) 30; Personal Conduct Policy 145
National Indigenous Women's Resource Center 176

National Latin@ Network 176
National Organization of Asians and Pacific Islanders Ending Sexual Violence 176
National Strength and Sports Conditioning Association 178
NCAA *see* National Collegiate Athletic Association (NCAA)
neoliberalism 16–17
neoliberal ideologies 22–23
Nery, M. 3–10
New Zealand 206
Nichols, Maggie 16, 18, 20, 22
Noble, J. 80, 187
non-affirming organizations 30
non-binary people 26, 118–119, 174; sexual assault rates among 204; *see also* Clarendon, Layshia
non-conforming (gender) 12, 81, 82, 146, 169
non-consensual acts 136, 194
non-disclosure agreements 129
non-discrimination policies 30, 112
"non-feminine, non-Western, and non-white" women 115
non-heterosexual relationships 29
non-judgmental behavior 195, 198
non-mandated reporters 177–178
non-traditional family 110
non-verbal consent **191**
non-verbal encouragement 172
"normal traumatization" of boys 104
norms 6; community 175; cultural 17, 23, 32, 204, 210; descriptive 9; established cultural 15; gender 26–28, 109, 114, 117, 199; injunctive 9; masculinity 28, 142; peer group 7, 8; social 20, 21, 148; sports 57, 101, 109; taken-for-granted 12; traditional masculinity 142; US cultural 109
nude photos 193–195
nude pic *culture* 23

Oath Keepers 15
Obama Administration 163
Office of Civil Rights (OCR) 156, 162
Ohio State University (OSU): revenues grossed by 22; Richard Strauss case 18–19, 52–53, 59, 62–63
Ohio Republican State Representatives 30
Olympic athletes see Biles, Simone; Chand, Dutee; Fierce Five; Maroney, McKayla; Semenya, Caster
Olympic Games: ancient Greek 115; London 2012 18; Tokyo 2020 12; women, inclusion and exclusion of 115, 117; *see also* International Olympic Committee (IOC)
Olympic gymnasts, molestation of 6, 7, 12, 55, 142, 145
Olympic medalists *see* gold medalists; Olympic gymnasts; Sofia's story
Olympics/professional sports 21; reactive nature of prevention programming in 145, 146; *see also* USA Gymnastics
Olympics sport industry 21
Olympic team, competing for spot on 56
Olympism 21
open secret 16, 18
Orwick, Dawn 117
Osborne, B. 157, 162
O'Shea, A. 62
Owens, Robert E. 204

Patchin, J. 194
patriarchal narratives 103, 105, 210
patriarchal norms 101
patriarchal system 203
patriarchal thinking 104
patriarchy 11; cisheteropatriarchy 5, 7, 12, 203; white capitalist 211
Pennsylvania Coalition Against Rape Faith Based Services Guide 176
Penn State 51, 58, 79
Penny, Steve 20, 22
performance enhancing drugs (PEDs) 19
Persky, Aaron 204
Petherick, W. 43
polyamory 199
pornography: children and 189, 193–199; Nassar and 7, 156; online 23; *see also* child pornography
Pornhub 193
Prewitt-White, Tanya 53, 115
priming the target (grooming) 27, 38, 43, 44, **45**
punitive justice 205–206, 207, 208
punitive system 204

quid pro quo harassment 157–158
quiescence 56

racism 4, 5, 7; biological essentialism and 116; interpersonal 206; systemic 110, 176; white male entitlement and 204; women of color versus men of color, experiences of 12
racism in sports 16, 203
racist stereotypes and victim blaming 170, 174, 176
RAINN, RAINN.org 168, 175, 177, 179

Raisman, Aly 18, 156
Raliance 176
rape: campus 207; crime of 173; male 18; sexual violence and 164; statistics 169; statutory 190; *victim* and *survivor* of 168; *see also Simpson v. Univ. of Colorado Boulder; Williams v. Board of Regents of the University System of Georgia*
rape crisis centers 177, 178
rape culture 129, 135, 143
rape myth acceptance 148
rape myths 170, 174
rape, personal stories: Arbetman 90–96; Forrest Miller 111; Sofia **46**; Tyler 134–136
rape prevention advice, misguided 149
rape supportive beliefs 147, 148
rape survivors 175
rape survivor advocacy organizations 81
rapists 86, 93; *see also* Turner, Brock
Real, T. 104
recidivism 208
recipients of federal funding *see* Title IX
reciprocation, expectation of 74
regimes of truth 16
reluctant acquiescence 56
restorative justice 16, 19, 22–23, 205–209
restorative practices 205–207, 211
Richards, Renee 116
Roman Catholic Church 21
Rosenthal, M. 60
Ross, Kyla 18

safe sex 189–190
same-gender violence in sports 109–119
Sand, T. 37, 39
Sandusky, Jerry 51, 54, 58, 79
Satore, M. L. 28
secrecy 27; Breckinridge's model regarding 42–44; maintaining 69, 114; securing 42–44, **45**
secret *see* open secret
seduced children 38
seducing 38; *Gebser v. Lago Vista Independent School District* 158; grooming and 69; priming girls for 37–39
Seeberg, Elizabeth (Lizzy) 58–59
self-care 179–180
self-blame 170
self-silencing 56
Semenya, Caster 115–116
sex change 118
sexism 4, 5, 6, 114; casual 205; hierarchies of 136; sexual misconduct and 7; silence and 105; women of color and 12, 176; *see also* cisheterosexism
sexist attitudes 144
sexist behavior 143, 158
sexist narratives 103, 210
sexist obstacles, overcoming 102
sexist stereotypes 170, 174
sex talk 187–200; talking with adolescents 197–198; talking with children 195–196; talking with young adults 198–199; *see also* coercion; consent
sexting 23, 193–195
sex trafficking 16
sexual abuse *see* abuse; Nassar, Larry; Strauss, Richard E.
sexual consent: as distinct from coercion 192–193
sexual coercion 43, 148, 164, 192–193
sexual harassment in sports *see* Title IX
sexual misconduct complaints, mishandling of : LSU 58; Penn State 58; see also Jordan, Jim; Nassar, Larry; Sandusky, Jerry; Strauss, Richard E.
sexual misconduct in sport 15–23; accountability and restorative justice for 202–211; cisheterosexism and 26–33; epistemic injustice and 51–63; experience of (personal account, Tyler) 129–136; myths surrounding 187
sexual misconduct prevention 203–204
sexual violence: accessing support for self 179–180; barriers to resources for marginalized populations 176–177; confidentiality related to 177; educating self and others regarding 175–176; effects of 169–170; as interplay of social conventions and community response 175; scope of problem 168–169; survivors of 168–180
silence around sex, harmfulness of 188–189
silence, silenced 17, 29, 41, 42; breaking the 47, 187–189; culture of 150; non-disclosure agreements and 129; Prewitt-White account of 72, 77, 78, 82; victim-blaming and 136
silencing 56–57; *acquiescence* 56; *coerced silence* 56; *quiescence* 56; *reluctant acquiescence* 56; *self-silencing* 56; *testimonial smothering* 56–57
Silverberg, C. 196
Simon, Lou Anna 157
Simpson, Lisa 161–162
Sinnamon, G. 39; seven-stage model 43–46
slut-shaming 136
Smidt, A. 62

Smith, C. P. 57, 58, 59, 61
Snyder-Hill, Steve 19
social capital 8
social norms 21
Sofia's story 44, **45–46**
special privilege 38
sport and exercise psychology professionals (SEPPs) 4, 7, 9–12
Sports Authority of India (SAI) 116
sports stakeholders 6, 9, 202–203; as advocates for athlete 32; anti-racist 16; education regarding consent 190; developing direct policies related to violent behaviours 8, 63; grooming as concern for 41, 47; mitigating harm as responsibility of 189; reflection questions for 97, 106
stalking 92, 126, 204, 209
Stanger-Hall, K. 188
Starr, K. 47
St. Clair, S. 59
Stephens, Greg 52
Step UP! 144
Stewart, H. 52, 61
Stirling, A. 4, 41
Strauss, Richard 15, 17–19, 21–22, 52, 59, 62, 63
Strong Hearts Native Helpline 176
Sweet, P.L. 55
Super Bowl 16
survivors: apps for reporting 62; attacks on 55; believing 171; caring for 8; case studies of institutional denial of 58–60; creating a culture of belonging for 173–174; disbelief confronting 52, 53; harms experienced by 51; leaders' responsibilities to take reports seriously 174–175; LGBTQIA+ 32; listening to 171–173; supporting 168–180; treatment-related policies for 63; voices of 61; women and men as 4; women and workplace 62; *see also* gaslighting; institutional betrayal silencing; sexual violence; testimonial smothering
survivor impact statements: Nassar 7, 16, 18
survivor insights 29; Starr 47
survivor stories 5–6; Arbetman 90–96; Bequette 84–89; Erdner 97–107; Forrest Miller 109–119; Mulcahy 122–128; Prewitt-White 69–82; Tyler 129–136

Tanner, J. 40
Taylor (Temple University professor) 58
testimonial injustice 52–54

testimonial smothering 56–57
testosterone 116, 117
Texas 18, 29, 116
Thomashow, Amanda 53
Thompson, M. 148
Title VII, Civil Rights Act 157–158
Title IX personal stories: Arbetman 92–96; Mulcahy 124–125; Thomashow 57; Tyler 133–134
Title IX regulations and sexual harassment 155–166; case precedents 158–162; enforcement and interpretation of 156–158, 162–165; intercollegiate athletes 141; mandated reporting under 177; restorative justice and 208; recipients of funding for 158–160, 163; schools' obligations regarding 164–165; statistics regarding 147
Toftegaard Nielsen, J. 80
toxic masculinity 23, 143, 204
training (grooming) 38
transgender athletes 31, 118
transgender girls and women 26–27, 203–204; gender verification and 31; HRT and puberty blockers 117
transgender individuals 28, 30; risk of sexual violence 169, 174, 204
transgression 76, 80, 114
transmasculine 119
transnegative bills (legislative) 28
trans panic 116
transparency (institutional) 61, 62
transphobia 28, 176, 203
transphobic language 32
trans violence in sports 109–119
trans women athletes of color 21
traumatic amnesia 60, 61, 63
Trigger (Coach) 111–112, 115
triggering, triggering experiences 5, 78–79, 173, 178, 179
Trombino, C. 62
Trump administration 15, 163, 165
Truth and Reconciliation Commission in South Africa 206
"truth tellers" 63
Tsang, T. 113
Turner, Brock 95, 204
Twistars Gymnastics Club 6, 7, 18

United States Court of Appeals for the Eleventh Circuit 160
United States Women's National Soccer Team (USWNT) 27

University of Colorado Boulder 161–162
University of Georgia (UGA) 160–161
University of Georgia Athletic Association (UGAA) 160
US Army 19
USA Gymnastics (USAG): Larry Nasser 6, 7, 12, 16, 18, 22, 27, 53, 79, 156; lawsuits filed against 157; team doctors 53
USA Swimming 79
USA Wrestling 19
US Center for Safe Sport 145
US Olympic/Paralympic athletes 145
US Transgender Survey 204

verbal abuse *see* abuse
verbal coercion 192
verbal consent 189, 190, 191, **191**
verbal encouragers in proactive listening 172
verbal harassment 29, 157
victim and perpetrator dynamic 39, 80, 169, 187
victim-blaming 16–17, 20, 55, 136; hindsight bias and 170; techniques to interrupt or quash 174, 180
victimization 142; children 70; rates of 148; sexual 38, 145
victimization and perpetration dynamic 143
victims: adult 43, 44; Arbetman's refusal of identification as 95; child 38; *controlling the victim* 44, **46**; conveying options to 175; *creating the victim* 44, **45**; isolation of 40; male 42; "male-perpetrator-female-victim" paradigm 42; *selecting the victim* 43, **45**; of sexual abuse 157; targeted 40, 43, **45**; terminology 168

victim's rights 172
victims/survivors 61
victim-student 159, 160; burden of proof 162; intimidation of 161; rate of assault 163; trauma of 165
Vriesema, Jonathan 26, 29

Wagner, Jennifer 118
Wang, Y. 56
Weinstein, Harvey 15
Wertheim, J. 59
whistleblowers 62–63
white male entitlement 204
white men 8, 11; as masculine ideal 17; heteronormative discourses centering 21; networks of knowledge and 19; sport and 103
whiteness 11
white settler colonial logic 118
white women 12
Wieber, Jordyn 18
Wiesemann, C. 31
Williams, Brandon 160
Williams, Tiffany 160–161
Williams v. Board of Regents of the University System of Georgia 160–161
Wilson, E. 188
WNBA 26
women of color 8, 12, 203–204
wrestlers: sexual abuse of 19, 21; transgender competitor 116
Wurtele, S. 115

zero harm 203
zero tolerance 81, 149–150

For Product Safety Concerns and Information please contact our EU
representative GPSR@taylorandfrancis.com
Taylor & Francis Verlag GmbH, Kaufingerstraße 24, 80331 München, Germany

www.ingramcontent.com/pod-product-compliance
Lightning Source LLC
Chambersburg PA
CBHW081551300426
44116CB00015B/2836